THE VICE OF
LUXURY

THE MORAL TRADITIONS SERIES
Founding Editor: James F. Keenan, SJ
Series Editors: David Cloutier, Kristin Heyer, Andrea Vicini, SJ

THE VICE OF
LUXURY

ECONOMIC EXCESS IN A
CONSUMER AGE

DAVID CLOUTIER

Georgetown University Press / Washington, DC

Library of Congress Cataloging-in-Publication Data

Cloutier, David M., 1972– author.
   The vice of luxury : economic excess in a consumer age / David Cloutier.
      pages cm – (The moral traditions series)
   Summary: The problem of luxury has been neglected in contemporary Christian theology and philosophy, as well as in the broader social debate about the morality of our common economic life. And according to moral theologian David Cloutier this neglect of luxury has had harmful consequences: Greco-Roman and Judeo-Christian traditions are filled with critiques of luxury as a vice that is destructive both to individual persons and to society. Current and recent studies of economic ethics focus on the structural problems of poverty, of international trade, of workers' rights–but rarely if ever do such studies speak directly to the excesses of the wealthy, including the middle classes of advanced economies. What happened? Why has the unquenchable pursuit of a luxury lifestyle gotten a free pass? In interpreting luxury as a moral problem, Cloutier proposes a new approach to economic ethics that moves beyond pro-market v. anti-market creeds and focuses attention on our everyday economic choices. In Part 1 he surveys the history of Christian attitudes toward luxury and greed and provides a primer on economics; in Part 2 he examines the meaning of luxury and how to develop a prudential ethic of consumption that is compatible with Christian morality.
   Includes bibliographical references and index.
   ISBN 978-1-62616-270-9 (hc : alk. paper) — ISBN 978-1-62616-256-3 (pb : alk. paper)—ISBN 978-1-62616-257-0 (eb)
   1. Luxury—Moral and ethical aspects.   2. Wealth–Moral and ethical aspects. 3. Wealth—Religious aspects—Christianity.   4. Consumption (Economics)—Moral and ethical aspects.   I. Title.   II. Series: Moral traditions series.
   BJ1535.L9C58   2015
   241'.68—dc23
                              2015007450

16 15   9 8 7 6 5 4 3 2 First printing

Printed in the United States of America

Cover design by Anne C. Kerns, Anne Likes Red, Inc. Cover photo by Rashch/iStock/ Thinkstock by Getty Images.

The seed sown among thorns is the one who hears the word, but then worldly anxiety and the lure of riches choke the word and it bears no fruit.
— Matthew 13:22, New American Bible

According to the common-sense ideal, the economic beatitude lies in an unrestrained consumption of goods, without work; whereas the perfect economic affliction is unremunerated labor. . . . If such an aversion to useful effort is an integral part of human nature, then the trail of the Edenic serpent should be plain to all men, for this is a unique distinction of the human species. A consistent aversion to whatever activity goes to maintain the life of the species is assuredly found in no other species of animal.
— Thorstein Veblen, "The Instinct of Workmanship and the Irksomeness of Labor"

The culture of prosperity deadens us; we are thrilled if the market offers us something new to purchase. In the meantime, all those lives stunted for lack of opportunity seem a mere spectacle; they fail to move us.
— Pope Francis, *Evangelii Gaudium*, no. 54

Contents

Acknowledgments

Books take a long time to finish. I first had the idea to write about the limits of our economic lives as I taught Mount St. Mary's undergraduates Catholic teaching on property. I realized almost all of them had difficulty conceiving the teachings about property having any other destiny than fulfilling their own preferences. Teaching this material in the context of virtue ethics I saw that this inability to perceive a moral problem was what the category of "vice" really meant. But what was its name? I soon discovered a complex history of the term "luxury" that I couldn't have imagined at the start of the project. A paper on the concept of luxury was very well received and provoked much discussion at the Society of Christian Ethics, and I began to see the vocabulary of luxury as something which, if recovered, could help us see things about virtue ethics, sacramentality, and modern economics that were otherwise overlooked. I also felt (every day) that it hit us where we live. Amid the policy-level discussions of economic turbulence, the problem of luxury is one encountered every day. There has been plenty of challenge; but there has also been the empowering hope that one could actually make changes that didn't have to make it through Congress!

I have a substantial list of thank yous to offer. First and foremost I thank Mount St. Mary's University for a sabbatical semester, which was augmented by a further semester sabbatical made possible by a generous grant from the Louisville Institute. The generosity from both enabled a full year of research, without which I could never have pulled this all together. I thank my colleagues for pulling together in my absence, too—in a small academic department there are always many things to do. Much of this book was written in the very hospitable spaces of the Hood College library, within walking distance of my house. I am extremely grateful for the generosity of the librarians there, who helped this outsider, and for their well-selected browseable book collection, which rarely failed to yield some excellent resource I hadn't expected to find. I am also grateful to the National Endowment for the Humanities, for a grant sponsoring my participation in a three-week interdisciplinary seminar on the history of economic thought. As a novice at economics, it was an incredible privilege to participate in these discussions, hosted by the Center for the History of Political Economy at Duke University. It was even better to learn in the company of my fellow "econ campers," who taught me a great deal in a short time. Special thanks to Christina McRorie, Jen Cohen, Scott Scheall, Solomon Stein, Joshua Foster, and the director of the seminar, Bruce Caldwell. While I'm sure the economics chapter remains the work of an amateur, I'm getting there.

I also benefited greatly from the opportunity to present parts of this project in the lecture series on Catholic Social Thought at Loyola University in Baltimore. Graham McAleer was a fantastic host, and the discussions never failed to make me think more deeply about the project. I thank Matt Boudway at *Commonweal*, who solicited an article on Pope Francis and luxury and provided great editorial feedback. I have received wonderful support from Richard Brown, the director at Georgetown University Press, who has shepherded this manuscript through several reviews that have improved it substantially; and from James F. Keenan, who encouraged me to submit my work for the Moral Traditions series. Jim's advice has been particularly helpful in moving the book from some scattered insights to a tighter whole. I also want to thank my colleague at the Mount, Jessy Jordan, who read and commented in detail on chapter 4 and who has been so interested in the project. Tom Shannon also provided wonderful comments on the entire manuscript.

Life goes on around such a project, and often contributes to it. I have three special debts of gratitude to acknowledge. First, I always benefit from the conversations and personal witness of Nicole Adams Blume on my soul-replenishing visits to Minneapolis. Nicole is a living reminder that the Christian life is not about getting fancy possessions but sharing in material joys that mediate larger, spiritual joy. Nicole, you will find your quote in the text, I'm sure. Second, during this time I have been privileged to serve on the board of directors of the Common Market, the consumer food cooperative in Frederick, Maryland. Being on the "inside" of such a great place and working with such good colleagues on the board and staff have been my constant reminder of what an economy of "reciprocity rooted in gift" might look like. Finally, I can't begin to count the number of great conversations on this topic that I've had with my choir friends at St. Thomas Apostle parish in Washington, DC. In particular, thanks to Bob Sullivan, Karen Clement, Tom Hutcheson, Barbara Hazelett, and Anthony Ahrens for more lengthy dialogues. I also want to thank my good friends Jeff McCurry, Amanda Beal, Kari-Shane Davis Zimmerman, and Bill Mattison for their support and conversations, peppered with references to this topic, both serious and humorous. My parents, too, are my friends, and I thank them in particular for raising me in a set of household circumstances where I could develop some immunity to the vice of luxury. They taught me the lessons about what is important that really anchor this book.

Finally, I owe a special debt of gratitude to Daniel Finn, for many reasons, but most especially for the astonishingly detailed comments he made throughout the final draft of this manuscript. Dan's graciousness has been a model to me for more than a decade, and the more I learn about theology and economics, the more I am appreciative of his outstanding work.

Despite all this help, I am sure there is plenty to argue with and quibble over in this text. The errors are all mine. I've always thought of this project as a conversation-starter, not as a final set of answers. Often enough, there is no conversation about this problem at all. Perhaps this is because judgments will necessarily be tentative, personal, and circumstantial. But that doesn't mean we can evade them.

Introduction

Why Luxury?

On July 15, 1979, President Jimmy Carter delivered a speech that has been called "the most sustained attack any American president had ever made on consumer culture."[1] In the midst of gasoline shortages and price spikes of 50 percent, Carter canceled a planned energy speech and holed up at Camp David for a week to bring in an unexpected array of visitors (from ordinary citizens to philosophically minded academics). Suspense built. "In the whole history of American politics," said a *Time* reporter, "there had never been anything quite like it."[2] The speech that resulted was hard hitting and severe in tone: "In a nation that was proud of hard work, strong families, close-knit communities, and our faith in God, too many of us now tend to worship self-indulgence and consumption. Human identity is no longer defined by what one does, but by what one owns. But we've discovered that owning things and consuming things does not satisfy our longing of [*sic*] meaning. We've learned that piling up material goods cannot fill the emptiness of lives which have no confidence or purpose."[3] Carter went on to lament the country's drop in productivity, the erosion of savings, and the loss of confidence in major institutions. He exhorted his listeners to accept energy conservation and urged them to "take no unnecessary trips," to "obey the speed limit," and even to "set your thermostats to save fuel," calling all of these acts of patriotism.[4] Carter framed the speech as a recognition that he needed to take on the "energy problem," but that "the true problems of our nation are much deeper."[5] He warned of a turning point and two paths to choose: "One is a path I've warned about tonight, the path that leads to fragmentation and self-interest. Down that road lies a mistaken idea of freedom, the right to grasp for ourselves some advantage over others. That path would be one of constant conflict between narrow interests ending in chaos and immobility. It is a certain route to failure."[6]

1

The speech was "an extraordinary rhetorical gamble. No modern president had ever attacked his countrymen's love of 'self-indulgence and consumption,' criticized their obsession with 'owning' and 'consuming,' or told them that 'piling up material goods' was not a route to happiness."[7] Yet it was not uncharacteristic of Carter's personal tendencies toward a strong Baptist moralism; it was almost as if he was calling sinners to conversion. Initially well received (a post-speech poll showed an 11-point rise in his approval rating), the address became known as the "malaise" speech, largely because its tone forcefully contrasted speeches made by Carter's 1980 election rival, Ronald Reagan.[8] Reagan eschewed somber and critical tones in favor of a sunny optimism. On the eve of the election, Reagan gave a characteristically soaring speech, saying pointedly: "I find no national malaise. I find nothing wrong with the American people."[9]

Americans chose Reagan's path. Through a painful period of high interest rates, the "inflation monster" was killed and the US economy embarked on a period now called The Great Moderation, during which steady economic growth was paired with minimal inflation over a twenty-year span.[10] However, that economy was fueled by a rapid increase in all kinds of debt and was coupled with speculative bubbles, first in technology and then in housing, eventually culminating in the financial crisis of 2008.[11] The period also saw the advent of globalization, financial crises around the globe, and a slow but sustained increase in economic inequality.[12] Bubbles and borrowing masked the growing problem, but the fact remained that workers in the bottom half of the economy found it increasingly difficult to maintain a living wage or even steady employment.

Living wages and secure employment for the middle class were surely the proudest achievement of Americans during the cold war era. This "mass affluence" or "affluent society" came to be taken for granted. Increasingly we have come to see how unusual the years between World War II and the early 1970s were. Productivity increases were regularly passed along to workers in the form of higher wages.[13] Unionization was strong throughout the economy.[14] Economic rivals were few, with part of the world behind an "iron curtain" and other parts in ruin. Energy was cheap. Trust in government was high.[15] Steeply progressive tax rates both discouraged excessive compensation for the top earners and redistributed wealth through generous government spending and benefits. Banking and finance were sleepy and steady, following the three-six-three model: take savings at 3 percent, loan it out at 6 percent, and be on the first tee by 3:00 p.m. The world economy was steadied most by the postwar arrangements worked out at Bretton Woods, which strongly controlled both the erratic flow of capital and the possibility of international shocks to economies.[16]

However exceptional they may have been, these years defined "the American Dream," and still do. Of course, some of this achievement was illusory—and relied on insulation from economic rivals, unsustainable access to cheap energy, and better living through chemistry. Moreover, mass affluence was not quite so "mass" as it had seemed: the suburban dreams of the 1950s left out "the other America."[17] The vision also rested on a "military-industrial complex" whose job-making abilities spilled over into its war-making follies.[18] What President Carter hoped to do, perhaps, was shift the country to a more sustainable, less materialistic vision of this dream.

In the wake of our present economic situation, Carter's message is needed more than ever. Yet Christian ethics—and ethical discourse in general—lacks a vocabulary for naming this "excess" that, if cleared away, might provide the direction toward a sustainable economic future. Brad Gregory rightly states that, "Westerners now live in societies without an acquisitive ceiling. . . . In the United States, 'excess' has now lost any socially significant meaning."[19] Lacking a useful language for this excess, our economic discourse has become mired in an impasse in which both sides trade on images of "the 1 percent" versus "the lazy, dependent poor"—both being caricatured demon-images that reflect the lack of imagination about our economic situation as a whole. Indeed, they manifest exactly the specter of conflict Carter foresaw. Our discussions of serious practical economic problems rest on such images matched with abstractions about markets and about government, rather than resting on what would appear to be the most incontestable fact of all: we have the materials and the productive capacity to sustain secure standards of life for centuries yet no one ever seems to have "enough." Maybe this is because we simply want way too much. We all could live solid lives but we want to live better than that. We want luxury.

The aim of this book is to revive and revise the ancient moral critique of luxury in a way that is informed by the history of this critique and sensitive to the significant changes in economics and culture that make our current context significantly different from that of the ancient moralists. The critique is particularly important in a consumer society. The concept of luxury assumes a moral understanding of our agency as consumers and in terms of virtue and vice. Personal consumption expenditures account for fully 70 percent of our economy—so when we talk about economic ethics we should expose those hundreds of millions of choices to proper scrutiny.[20]

The language of luxury fills a gaping hole in our economic debate. Without a critique of luxury, economic ethics cannot name limits. Michael Sandel notes that "market triumphalism" has meant "the expansion of markets, and of market values, into spheres of life where they don't belong," transforming us from "having a market economy to being a market society."[21] Sandel's *limiting* of markets is a laudable project, but it depends on being able to compartmentalize our lives into different logics that are constantly bumping against one another. What we really need are the limits and ethical lines *within* economic activity itself. If we agree that food should be produced and distributed primarily via market systems, does this mean that we can shop without concern for farmworkers or the environment? If we agree that family ties should be exempt from harsh economic realities, how do we understand the relationship between economic hardship and family breakdown that seems more and more prevalent in our society?[22] Simply permitting market forces into some parts of life and prohibiting them in others isn't enough.

Instead of compartmentalizing, I want to argue that all action is moral action, including economic choices.[23] What is needed is an ethics of virtue and vice that can form us as virtuous and charitable economic actors—so that we are whole persons acting with integrity in all areas of our lives. As Pope Benedict XVI writes, "authentically human social relationships of friendship, solidarity, and reciprocity can also be conducted within economic activity, and not only outside it or 'after' it. . . . [P]recisely because [economic activity] is human, it must be structured and governed in an ethical manner."[24] Such an account has to start with boundaries and limits that mark off what counts as excessive. The ancients used the term "luxury" to indicate when these limits had been violated. Without such a limit, we simply assume that more is better.

Positioning the Project: Beyond Three Dichotomies

This project is positioned within the debates over the economy and ethics, both secular and theological. Three particular ways of framing such moral debates present entrenched dichotomies that offer limiting and unsatisfactory analyses of our problems. Each conversation could be enriched and improved were the problem of luxury engaged directly. Too often, however, the conversations lead to incomplete solutions that either ignore the virtues and vices of individual consumption or instead offer such a "total" critique of them (as though every shopping trip is corrupt) as to lead most of us to despair. Rather than these all-or-nothing approaches to the moral problems of our economic system, we need to identify moral limits on consumption.

Markets versus State

The first and most common dichotomy to be transcended is the endless structural debate over markets and government action, or what Pope Benedict calls "the market-state binary."[25] When this debate gets tense, slogans like "the 1 percent" and "the 47 percent" appear. ("The 47 percent" was an infamous derogatory reference made by 2012 Republican presidential candidate Mitt Romney in reference to the portion of the population that doesn't pay income taxes.) A market-versus-state dichotomy starts looking like a proxy for the age-old conflict of rich and poor.[26] In Christian circles such debates often lead to widely varying "translations" of Christian economic teaching into competing and even contradictory policies.

In this frame of reference, both positions have compelling things to say. By focusing on *structural* questions, the debate also tends to leave things out only to arrive at an impasse. Significant differences in behavior *within* the categories of "rich" and "poor" go unnoticed. To put it bluntly, the conversations trade on stereotypes of both groups, whether positive or negative, and resort to anecdotal stories to reinforce a preferred stereotype. The rich are either rapaciously greedy or noble job creators; the poor are either struggling victims in need of compassion or lazy, dependent freeloaders in need of personal discipline and a sense of responsibility. But surely "the rich" and "the poor" are misleading abstractions and neither group is in fact homogenous. Such constructs often try to explain complex economic problems by scapegoating this or that subgroup: "Wall Street" or "welfare queens" or "government regulators" or "insurance company executives." Sadly, this passes for reasoned public debate.

Stereotyping and scapegoating do serve an important political function, however, which is a further consequence of the market-state binary: by focusing on groups of great wealth or severe poverty, the discussion tends to exempt the people in the middle. The problems are assigned to either the top or the bottom, excusing the vast arrays of activities of those who are neither poor nor rich. The target is always somewhere else. However, the large fortunes held by oil companies or the Walton family—and the meager pay of the gas station attendant or superstore clerk—are all set in motion through the support of millions of "us" every day. Woe to the politician (such as President Carter) who might suggest that solving the economic problems of society could begin by removing the "log" from the middle class's eye.

This critique of luxury does not map onto the market-state binary. A focus on the problem of luxury is *not* to make a claim about the relevance or irrelevance of state structures and regulations and is, indeed, quite the contrary. As will be seen, economists have shown how various economic structures encourage or discourage luxury. But, as Daniel Finn explains, a proper understanding of the "moral ecology" of an economy requires not only attention to how markets are constructed and to the related necessary redistributive functions; it must also attend to "the morality of individuals and groups" and to "the presence of a vibrant civil society."[27] The classical concern about luxury addresses these two latter areas, which are easily lost when government policy imperatives (or their alleged failings) monopolize the discussion.

On the other hand, a consideration of the problem of luxury isn't just an opportunity to go on an anti-market screed, either. One might wonder: Isn't a critique of luxury just a new version of the attack on the very wealthy? By no means. Attention to the problem of luxury will not touch on the "excesses" of the rich alone; it will touch on the excesses of all classes. As Jan De Vries notes, the first "scientific" study of poverty in 1797 tried to figure out if the phenomenon of new industrial poverty was due to "improvident spending" or "inadequate earnings."[28] This is a tricky subject, for sometimes accusations about the profligacy of the poor are merely a distraction from the much-more-excessive prodigality of the rich. Nevertheless, disciplined spending and budgeting make a huge difference in alleviating poverty but are often difficult to cultivate.[29] Simply ignoring the problem of spending—casting the poor entirely as victims—is both unrealistic and ultimately ineffective. It would be wrong to use such observations as a blanket condemnation of the poor or as a suggestion that present wage levels are adequate. The question of inadequate wage levels versus "improvident spending" should be a both-and, not an either-or.

A more important reason to critique luxury is to remove the distorting middle-class "exemption." Clive Crook is correct in saying that so-called populist outrage from the middle-class over welfare for either the poorest or the wealthiest fails, as a matter of arithmetic, to help the middle class; in either direction, "there are too few designated losers."[30] Instead, we must name the problem of luxury for the 83 percent of Americans who fall between the poverty line and $250,000 on the annual income scale—the supposed middle class.[31] Middle-class spending drives the economy as a whole, and middle-class aspirations tend to shape the strivings of those lower on the income ladder who want to show that they are "making it." Moreover, most middle-class families have more than enough; they have genuine discretionary income and their spending choices display this discretion.[32] The pressing question is: What are the right and wrong things to do with that discretionary income? We must address rather than avoid that question for two reasons: for the ultimate happiness of each middle-class person and for the common good. Because the middle class directs an enormous amount of resources with its spending choices, both middle-class frugality and middle-class overindulgence exercise a strong influence over everything else.

Small choices can have significant personal and social ramifications, even though we rarely think of them as "moral" questions. For example, Americans eat out at much higher levels than they did a few decades ago. Christian debt guru Dave Ramsey notes that when he counsels families about their debt problems and asks, "What can you cut? What don't you really need?" the first thing many identify is eating out frequently.[33] Frequent eating out is not only a spending problem: as former Surgeon General David Kessler outlines, casual restaurant chains continually "enhance" the food they serve, either by the magic of food chemistry or simply by loading in fats and sugars.[34] "It just doesn't taste that way at home" is a truism. But the way to get this taste contributes to our obesity crisis. Meals out have altered the character of the table of the home: as meals out have increased in frequency, regular family meals and meals hosted by neighbors have decreased. Theologian Julie Hanlon Rubio notes the significance of family meals by saying that, "[a]round a table, a family becomes more of who it is" and urges families toward an inclusive hospitality "oriented to love and justice."[35]

Given these associated problems, why would we eat out? Notice how hard it is to avoid the answer of "luxury" here. Eating out means not cooking, being served, and not cleaning up. It means having an array of choices that can be chosen simply at will—a characteristic of what Christopher Franks calls the "proprietary self," where "an exuberant sense of my entitlement" denies my "ontological poverty," that is, my dependence on God and others.[36] Ease, convenience, choice, no mess: the ugly parts of your meal—the food chemistry, the cattle on the industrial feedlot, even the kitchen staff (in most cases)—are carefully hidden from you. As we shall see, this is how the ancients described the luxury self. As Peter Brown notes of ancient villa life, the experience of "innocent abundance" was the goal.[37] At any Olive Garden Restaurant you will get innocent abundance reproduced for the masses, right down to the unlimited salad and breadsticks. Insofar as this mimicry pervades goods and services offered to those with discretionary income, the lure of luxury permeates the ordinary spending and experiences of middle-class American life and underlies larger structural problems that get more attention (obesity, poor wages for kitchen workers, consumer debt, animal welfare, unsustainable land use, to name just a few).

Pro-Consumerism versus Anti-Consumerism

A second frame for debates over the economy also falls short: defenses and critiques of "consumer society."[38] These debates are relatively recent arrivals on the theological scene, but such morally charged discussions have been going on in the United States since the late nineteenth century and even since the contrasting visions of founders Alexander Hamilton and Thomas Jefferson.[39]

Such debates often contrast a more traditional "producerist" ethic versus a new "consumerist" ethic. Like discussing market and state structures, this debate brings to light important points about economic context. And like the earlier-mentioned debate, each side has something going for it. Producerists, like their Luddite ancestors, tend to resist changes in production that disrupt their formerly settled way of life. They worry that the radical split between production and consumption ends up harming everyone. They often argue for the economic virtue of the "small"— small farms, small artisan studios, small shops—both because it encourages the arrival of more producers and because it makes consumption embedded within a thicker culture of relationships. They lament both big government and big business. They argue that supposed progress is really just a way of enriching the few. Eloquent recent defenders of producerism include Christopher Lasch and Wendell Berry.[40] A more theological version of this discussion can be found in the work of Catholic distributists like G. K. Chesterton and John Medaille.[41]

On the other hand, opponents of the producerists appeal to the extraordinary economic growth of the past century via what I call the hockey stick graph. The graph shows a stagnant economy for most of human history until about two hundred years ago, when the advent of industrial methods and more extensive free markets created a massive growth of wealth and enabled hundreds of millions of people to live secure lives.[42] These critics regard producerism as, at best, a noble fantasy that ignores the real productivity gains of the modern system. For them, economic improvement means extending benefits to everyone in the world, since despite the hockey stick, a billion people continue to live on less than a dollar a day. In response, producerists often wonder: Does the end of the hockey stick just go up forever?[43] Don't we ever get to the point of what has been called "a steady-state economy"? From where will future cheap, exploited labor and continuing natural resources, available throughout the "rapid growth" period, come?

Like the market-state debate, differences quickly polarize and often slip toward stereotype. Most especially, producerists get tagged as provincial advocates of prejudice—which has undeniably been present in strains of economic localism and nationalism—and of blindness to the actual vices of the "old" local and national structures for which they pine.[44] Furthermore, the supposed celebration of the small farmer and the artisan is criticized as "boutique" or as "the modern equivalent of French courtiers playing at milkmaids" that is only possible as a hobby for those in a society with significant excess wealth.[45] At the same time, a recourse to such ad hominem arguments against producerists lends support to the idea that their critics hold an unstated faith in secular progress that simply cannot be stopped. Such "Enlightenment optimism" about perpetual progress seems scarcely defensible in the wake of the twentieth century. Indeed, theologically Benedict XVI's encyclical *Spe Salvi* is a deep critique of this notion of progress as a deceptive substitute for Christian hope, an argument he supports by reference to many secular critics such as the Frankfurt School. Yet this assumption of the inevitability and benevolence of economic progress never seems to die.

My own sympathy for the producerist critique, and in particular its challenge to absentee and concentrated ownership, is limited by a recognition of the obvious benefits associated with division of labor and economies of scale, both of which are not necessarily accompanied by all the baneful effects noted by producerists.[46] There are evidently good and bad large companies, just as there are good and bad small ones. (Once again, notice how big and small—like rich and poor—tell us *something* but also abstract from significant *differences* within the categories.) Worse, the producerist critique can become a kind of nostalgia when not accompanied by actual practice. The vast majority of us are not going to become full-on producers—and I am more persuaded that genuine support for good producers will happen only when consumers adopt disciplined spending and consumption habits. In short, I am not against specialization, because such division of labor means that most of us will rely on others for meeting many daily needs.

Does that mean that consumers who take seriously the producerist critique in their shopping habits *are* just "playing at milkmaids"? Surely not.

Among the most ardent defenders of "good work" and not just fair pay is Pope John Paul II, who, in *Laborem Exercens*, insisted on the priority of the "subjective sense" of labor. In the Pope's language, consumers are important "indirect employers" when they are attentive to the moral terms of their consumption choices.[47] With consumer sovereignty comes consumer responsibility. Early critiques of the rise of consumer society claimed that "consumption thus becomes a substitute for compelling moral commitments, engaged political activity, or genuine selfhood."[48] But this way of putting matters simply invites the common pro-consumerist response: people are in fact exercising a kind of selfhood and expressing commitments through their consumption choices.[49] Consumption is in fact political, too, but the question ought to be: *whose* consumption? To *which* ends? The problem is that consumers tend to adopt models of choice that favor ease, low cost, quantity, novelty, and the like, instead of adopting models that limit their consumption and direct it toward fewer things and fewer services (but things and services actually made by "good work," as producerists rightly note). These problematic bases for consumer choice are both encouraged by and encourage structures in the market that produce just such bads that producerists worry about. Government regulations that try to manage these problems by "going around" consumer choices can have unwanted, even contradictory effects.[50] Consumers have to *want* to make choices in accord with the goods producerists promote. Sadly, many consumers choose on other grounds—grounds that have a lot to do with attachment to luxury.

Detachment versus Radical Renunciation

The third and longest-standing frame for Christian economic ethics has been "the Francis [of Assisi] problem": the evident radical challenge to wealth and riches that appears prominently in the gospels combined with the "community of goods" ideal portrayed as an eschatological result of the descent of the Holy Spirit in Acts 2 and 4 as well as the obvious fact that, for most of Christian history, most Christians have not adopted these ideals. The Francis problem presents us with a different kind of dichotomy that is an all-or-nothing temptation: radical renunciation or living not much differently from everyone else.

From very early on, Christians were forced to grapple with what these gospel stories meant in practical terms—and they did not all deduce the same answer. Their debates are instructive to us today. Peter Brown's enormous study of wealth in early Christianity depicts in detail the tension between two particular approaches: an approach that took with absolute seriousness the need for immediate renunciation of goods and the more measured approach stressing gradual dispossession of wealth, especially through almsgiving and support of religious initiatives (e.g., churches and monasteries). Brown's book provides the now-definitive portrait of the genesis of what might be called "the two-level ethic" for wealth in the Christian tradition: the outcome of this era was a dual focus on radical renunciation by a few versus pious acts for the rest. Summarizing the resolution of these debates in the work of John Cassian, Brown writes, "Wealth no longer needed to be a source of widespread, ill-defined anxiety. The wealthy were now offered a clear-cut choice of roles. Either one remained rich and became a pillar of the church as a donor and almsgiver, or one betook oneself to a monastery."[51] Yet, as is evident throughout the tradition from Francis of Assisi to the Radical Reformers to Dorothy Day, the persistence of the radical renunciation model outside the monastery has been amazing.

In the wake of Vatican II and Pope John Paul II's *Veritatis Splendor*, Catholics have begun to move beyond the two-level "solution" toward what *Lumen Gentium* identifies as "the universal call to holiness."[52] But how is such holiness to be exemplified in our mundane economic lives? The revival of a critique of luxury directly addresses the chronic tendency to "spiritualize to death" the biblical discourse about the dangers of wealth.[53] It avoids simply murmuring nice words about "detachment" that have little impact on our amassing stuff, but it also avoids a perfectionist ethic that idealizes but does not imitate "the Francis option" nor denies most Christians throughout history a share in the Kingdom. A critique of luxury offers a legitimate holiness ethic for Christians "in the world" that is neither the founding of Catholic Worker houses nor a merely *token* resistance to the dominant economy. The choice between radical renunciation or token almsgiving fails to attend to the actual use of most of the wealth for the vast majority of Christians. Theologically, what is needed is attention to the disciplined use of wealth in the world as an aspect of the universal call to holiness. Such a disciplined use of wealth is rooted first and foremost in identifying and avoiding the vice of luxury in favor of other uses of surplus wealth that can be called "sacramental."

In all three of these framings, then, overly stark dichotomies trade on stereotypes and extremes and often end in either a total challenge to our current way of life ("the Francis problem," producerism, or critiques of "the market" or capitalism *in toto*) or point to a virtual acceptance of it as morally unproblematic (that is, give some to charity, spread factories everywhere to help the poor, but leave the market alone). There is truth to be found in all these perspectives; however, all of these debates neglect the important questions: What is too much? What is excessive? Why? More important, why not emphasize morally disciplined spending as a way to approach problems and effect change?

These questions can sound problematic, even offensive, and easily devolve into what historian David Horovitz calls "moralism," whether the more traditional, hard-nosed Puritan kind of self-control or "modern moralism" that condemns "a nation of conforming, indulgent, and passive people."[54] His language of "moralistic accusation" can be taken to mean a kind of emotivist expression of disapproval for certain consumption choices that lacks clear grounding in either economic or moral reasoning. Horowitz worries that these critiques simply reflect a person's own "ethnic and class perspectives."

Yet these questions do not simply *trouble* people; they also seem to *fascinate* people—and they lead to an extremely wide array of answers. In practice, even if not in theory, most people do have some kind of "acquisitive ceiling"—albeit one that usually refers to egregious examples of celebrity extravagance. But how far should we go in defining and specifying this ceiling? Ancient and medieval and even early modern writers could not have imagined the kind of widespread wealth and lifestyle habits that many take for granted today. The ancient moralist Seneca counsels, "Avoid luxury. . . . If a man has always been protected from the wind by glass windows, if his feet have been kept warm by constant relays of poultices, if the temperature of his dining room has been maintained by hot air circulating under the floor and through the walls, he will be dangerously susceptible to the slightest breeze."[55] So, is central heating a luxury? Without more precision, a critique of luxury either slides into and eventually encompasses virtually *everything,* or it diminishes into a tirade against the actions of famous celebrities and billionaires.[56] There is a need for categories of everyday discernment to guide prudence; a need for a casuistry of how to identify luxury when we see it.

Barriers: Engaging the Challenges of Modern Philosophy, Theology, and Economics

Developing a casuistry of identifying what counts as luxury is the goal of the second half of this book; with the chapter on the historical evolution of the term, it could be read independently by the less theoretically inclined reader. However, for those interested, the recovery of the term *as a vice* requires significant spadework on three levels: philosophical (that is, accounts of moral psychology and virtue); theological; and economic. Recovering an account of luxury faces systematic methodological developments that exclude consideration of choices about right and wrong spending. Thus, one must clear a path for a contemporary casuistry of luxury.

This path-clearing is the work of chapters 2 through 4. First, the discussion engages issues in modern philosophical ethics and tries to understand why we have stopped asking normative questions about excessive material consumption. Even within the revival of virtue ethics, too little attention has been given to questions of economics, and the attention that is there often gets focused on the question of justice. Justice should rightly be a characteristic of our economic exchanges, but it is necessary for virtue ethics to go further in recognizing how economic injustices can often be traced back to outsized desires. After all, the disappearance of virtue and the disappearance of the luxury critique appear to be historically intertwined. As Jennifer Herdt shows in her history of the loss of virtue, seventeenth- and eighteenth-century defenses of luxury in particular mark a key shift in the movement to detach social ethics from traditional theological virtue: insofar as luxury is cast as a "socially beneficial" vice, it need no longer be concealed.[57] That is, today what is new is not that there is a problem with material self-indulgence, it is that it is not even seen as a problem. Some modern defenders of moral virtue may think nothing of indulging in the finest economic goods on offer in our economy; they disagree with David Hume philosophically but accept his conclusions as the great defender of luxury. But one cannot condemn Hume and Nietzsche for subjectivism in the sexual sphere and then turn around and let their ideas be allowed in the economic sphere.

Unfortunately, classical critiques of luxury often turned on one of two images: luxury makes a society "soft" and therefore weakens its ability to raise up soldiers to counter invasion; or luxury makes the poorer classes indulgent in ways that are socially threatening to their "betters," i.e., the stable aristocracy. In place of such militarism and snobbery we must revive the critique using Thorstein Veblen in order to redescribe the moral problem of luxury in terms of "workmanship." In his famous critiques of leisured consumption, Veblen is a striking foil for Hume; more often overlooked, however, is Veblen's constructive account of workmanship as the proper counter-response to the human temptation to "pecuniary consumption." Yet, work is something more than simply hours at a job. Instead, excellent human activity is described in terms of Alasdair MacIntyre's understanding of a practice. If we understand human activity as oriented toward goods of genuine excellence we will be able to recognize both why "following the passions" is inadequate and why the pursuit of luxury goods undermines the achievement of excellence.

Chapter 3 turns to an assessment of how theological ethics also neglect the problem of luxury. While in principle standard sources such as the Catholic Catechism teach clearly that private property should be oriented toward "the universal destination of goods" and toward the ordering of "this world's goods to God and to fraternal charity," wealthy Christians (and even some priests) think nothing of possessing and consuming expensive goods with their excess income.[58] It has not always been so: in the early twentieth century, Catholic social ethicist John A. Ryan could write the following as a natural complement to his analysis of social policy:

> The well-to-do and the rich could put away that false conception of life and values which permeates all classes of contemporary society, and which holds that right life consists in the indefinite expansion and satisfaction of material wants. They could spend very much less money for food, clothing, shelter, amusements, and "social" activities, and very much more for the cultivation of their hearts and minds. . . . The importance and necessity of this kind of individual action can scarcely be exaggerated.[59]

Ryan boldly goes on later to state in detail what is extravagant and what is moderate (an inquiry for later chapters). Ryan took for granted that superfluous wealth should be used for acts of benevolence, large and small, but as Christine Firer Hinze notes, in our culture of indefinite expansion of material wants, "the category of 'surplus' or of 'superfluous goods,' which one is obliged to distribute to the needy neighbor, effectively drops out."[60]

Yet, historically, Christian theology has often focused on the problems of excess wealth. It was a central issue for many Church Fathers in the first expansion of Christianity amid the Roman Empire, and reappeared over and over again. It is inescapable for two reasons: one, because scripture—in particular the gospels—has an intense but also rather disturbing preoccupation with the problem of riches; and two, because this problem hinges on a deeper question of the necessary relationship between materialism and transcendence. The issue is of particular import today since our material world has become so full of a seemingly endless stream of objects and aspirations, many of which promise not simply a functional purpose but an "experience" of emotionally satisfying goods and services.[61] These luxury goods peddle a kind of magic and function as pseudo-sacraments that are more easily accepted by Christians insofar as Christianity becomes interiorized and spiritualized.

By contrast, many early Christian writers avoided spiritualizing concerns over wealth; instead, they sacramentalized them. That is, they made the use of wealth an effective sign of the transformation inaugurated in Christ. This is especially true in their commitment to contrasting the vice of private luxury spending with the sacramental use of wealth in service to the poor. But the shift to the acceptance of luxury was complemented by open disdain for the poor. Key eighteenth-century writers not only praised luxury but also viewed the poor with scorn. The enclosures of common lands and the shift to factory production created substantial displacement in England during the early modern era, and many early classical economists saw the ultimate dismantling of ancient "poor laws"—in which the community was obligated to provide support for all its members—as a key move in creating a flexible, receptive labor market for growing capital-intensive production. In this view, luxury consumer demand is laudable because it spurs on the otherwise-indolent poor, whereas charity is economically wasteful and disincentivizes work. The eventual overthrow of the poor laws in the early 1800s opened the way for the massive degradation of the poor in England's industrialized slums, made famous by mid-nineteenth-century Victorian writers and theorized by Marx.

Thus a contemporary theological critique of luxury is rooted in two (related) theological projects. One is the recovery of a genuinely sacramental worldview in which the spiritual is participated in via the material.[62] Secular luxury consumption needs to be seen as a kind of rival liturgy, and in particular a rival to the centrality of using excess wealth to care for the poor. The second is the move away from "the two-level ethic" toward "the universal call to holiness."[63] This call to holiness in worldly activity has borne particular fruit in various theologies of sexuality, but an analogous challenge still awaits in the economic sphere. This is a challenge recently described well by Pope Benedict XVI in seeking an economy where *caritas* can be present *within* economic activity, not just subsequent to it:

> The Church's social doctrine holds that authentically human social relationships of friendship, solidarity and reciprocity can also be conducted within economic activity, and not only outside it or "after" it. The economic sphere is neither ethically neutral, nor inherently inhuman and opposed to society. It is part and parcel of human activity and precisely because it is human, it must be structured and governed in an ethical manner. The great challenge before us . . . is to demonstrate,

in thinking and behaviour, not only that traditional principles of social ethics like transparency, honesty and responsibility cannot be ignored or attenuated, but also that in *commercial relationships* the *principle of gratuitousness* and the logic of gift as an expression of fraternity can and must *find their place within normal economic activity* (italics in original).[64]

Such holiness means recognizing that even in our market activity as consumers, even with (or especially with) our "discretionary" income, we must handle holy things in a holy way—and means something different from the pursuit of luxury. Something perhaps *very* different.

Finally, a philosophical and theological critique of luxury must engage modern economics, which axiomatically takes individual consumer preferences as given and not subject to reasonable adjudication. It further bases its entire economic picture on the idea that these wants are, in principle, unlimited. As John Galbraith quipped, "Nothing in economics so quickly marks an individual as incompetently trained as a disposition to remark on the legitimacy of the desire for more food and the frivolity of the desire for a more elaborate car."[65] Paul Samuelson, at the beginning of his classic textbook, notes that the "absolute musts" of life today "far surpass the minimum physiological needs for food, clothing, and shelter," and "economists must reckon with consumer wants and needs whether they are genuine or contrived." Wants cannot be compared interpersonally and are entirely subjective and unlimited. Despite our wealth, "if you add up all the wants, you quickly find that there are simply not enough goods and services to satisfy a small fraction of everyone's consumption desires."[66] This vision of economics is not entirely supported in the work of many classical economists (such as Adam Smith) nor by actual consumer behavior, which varies in all sorts of dramatic ways from the "rationality" assumed by mainstream economics.

Beyond the image of the insatiable consumer lies a more subversive notion that economics presents for a critique of luxury: the idea that spending—including luxury spending—is actually economically beneficially for all. A critique of luxury seems to create for Christians what ethicist James Nash calls a "damning drawback."[67] We attack rich BMW drivers for not helping the poor . . . except that the production and maintenance of their cars employs people (or so the objection goes). Further, John Maynard Keynes's famous "paradox of thrift" is commonly taken to mean that our attempts to be virtuous and thrifty (especially in economic downturns) actually further depress the economy.[68] This is an up-to-date version of Bernard Mandeville's infamous "fable of the bees," where a productive hive pursuing self-interested excesses suddenly "gets virtue," becomes austere . . . and productivity collapses. It is a primary task of chapter 4 to show that this objection fails, or at least that it need not succeed, given that resources devoted to luxury consumption need not otherwise remain idle but can be allocated for other purposes. This will be an attempt to address the economic defense of luxury on the terms of the economic discipline itself.

Why do all this work? What I hope to show ultimately is that a full ethics of economic action *must* recover an understanding and critique of luxury in order to pursue economic good. Insofar as economic activity is genuinely free and not "automatic," it involves choice; that choice needs to be subjected to moral scrutiny. If this free choice is assumed to rest on entirely innocent subjective desires, it will be falsely shielded from proper scrutiny. Insofar as these free choices are not considered to be related to our hope for salvation, it detaches a whole realm of life from Christian holiness. Recovering a critique of luxury to our vision of economic activity, therefore, is integral to economic ethics, not merely an add-on. With these chapters of theoretical spadework done, I then turn to the casuistry.

Luxury and Economic Ethics: Moral Theology as the Task of Developing Language

What, then, is luxury? In a certain sense, of course, exact answers will not be forthcoming. The moral problem of luxury is analogous to that of "technology." As Albert Borgmann notes, the term "technology" is useful insofar as it "gathers intuitions and experiences" rather than proposes an exact "object of inquiry"; it is "finally a matter of proposing concrete observations and suggestions about the decisive pattern of our lives."[69] Like technology, luxury constitutes this kind of decisive pattern of our lives even if it is one that requires complex discernment particularly attentive to concrete circumstances.

Identifying patterns of practice requires language. It is difficult to cultivate virtue without having a coherent way of talking about what exemplifies virtue. The focus on the term "luxury" is a matter of consciously recovering and using a specific piece of language that is peculiarly missing and has peculiar potency for our economic lives. Herbert McCabe, in his classic study of Christian ethics, suggests that ethics is "the study of human behavior in so far as it is a piece of communication" and insofar as it is "meaningful"; the purpose of ethics is "to enable us to enjoy life more by responding to it more sensitively, by entering into the significance of human action."[70] An ethic of precise codification (legalism) and an ethic of loving intention (in McCabe's context, situation ethics) both leave things out. A concern about luxury is one of those omitted things: it cannot be precisely codified and it *seems* like no one gets hurt. But a focus on luxury alerts us to deeper lacunae in our standard economic language, in our language of the virtues, and in our language that connects our material and spiritual lives.

Christian ethics is more than a language; it is a person, One who speaks. Jesus's speaking has a great deal to do with our economic lives, but it is disorienting. It juxtaposes images of feasting and celebration with the example of a life of significant austerity. It seems to criticize almost any kind of accumulation of wealth for security, and yet it is a life lived not in a desert retreat but among the people, in the world. The Word must be interpreted, of course.[71] Jesus does not use the language of luxury. Just as the great Christian thinkers of the fourth century sought to discern what wealth meant for their situation of affluence, so, too, must we take up the same responsibility.

Thus, a focus on luxury is also a broader attempt to enrich how Christian ethics engages economics and what it means for Christians to be "faithful" in relation to their wealth. The tradition has often placed its moral focus elsewhere, in particular on issues of sex. It is true that questions about sexuality and marriage have, like those of wealth, been contested throughout history. But some of the faithful seem to take comfort in a supposed "clarity" that can be maintained in the sexual sphere. Any view of Christian economic ethics is forced to recognize the plurality of views, even in this patristic age. Daniel Finn's history of the Christian views of economics emphasizes the need for a hermeneutics of living tradition in which we must "discern carefully what those ancient texts mean for our life now."[72] Peter Brown's history confronts the reader with an extraordinarily messy array of views among early Christian leaders; these views are made even more complicated for us by an adequate recognition of how different "the economy" looked during the late Roman Empire. Nevertheless, that history is also a testimony to how seriously even the early Christians took the problems of wealth. So, too, should we. While this text focuses on a particular aspect of wealth, it will provide a template for the kind of work necessary for understanding other aspects of Christian economic responsibility, such as questions of investment and social welfare systems. Many of these other questions end up unresolvable without viewing luxury as a vice and turning away from a path of excess. If we avoid such excess we will find that resources are available to better confront many other problems.

There are hopeful stories. The ecumenical Boston Faith and Justice Network has propagated a small-group parish curriculum called Lazarus at the Gate, whereby the "intimate sharing" that is typical of small groups also extends to "talking about how much [one] earns and where it all goes." Participants share their family budgets and ways of thinking about money and are introduced to various socioeconomic problems, eventually being able to come to commitments about how much more giving they will do together.[73]

Perhaps this is too hopeful. Not everyone would find Lazarus at the Gate an attractive option at their church. Perhaps our economic system as it exists now is not sustainable over the long haul, and the empire we in the West have enjoyed for the last couple centuries is coming to an end. Yet, for Christians, history is not cyclical; we are not doomed to repeat mistakes of the past. Advisors of Franklin Roosevelt imagined something like this when they spoke of transitioning to a steady-state economy.[74] Karl Polanyi's still-landmark history of the rise of our current world economy portrays the entire process of the rise of the market as a utopian project to disembed the economy from traditional social relationships. He maintains that such utopianism always ends up provoking crises, which in turn lead to new attempts to impose social limits on the economy.[75] John Maynard Keynes imagined a future for his grandchildren where material wants were limited, capital was abundant, and there were no more rentiers.[76]

So, even while his direction for American society was rejected at the time, President Carter's starkly posed choice—to confront our excesses rather than deny them—remains available to us. On the whole it is likely not the actual desire of most persons, even in America, to make "the goods life" our ultimate goal, allowing them to overrun other human goods. Most people probably do not want to sacrifice their children, their social ties, or their souls to the consumption of unnecessary luxuries. One might therefore hope that the time is ripe to resurrect language about the vice of luxury that will illuminate and help us act on these deeper desires. In so doing we have nothing to lose except our 600-thread-count sheets.

Notes

1. Horowitz, *Anxieties of Affluence*, 239.
2. "Carter at the Crossroads," 20.
3. Carter, "Energy and the National Goals," 81.
4. Ibid., 85–86.
5. Ibid., 77.

6. Ibid., 83.

7. Sandbrook, *Mad as Hell*, 304.

8. "Carter's Great Purge," 12–13.

9. Sandbrook, *Mad as Hell*, quoting Reagan, 394.

10. Bernanke, "The Federal Reserve and the Financial Crisis."

11. On the growth of debt see Phillips, *Bad Debt*. On consumer credit see Hyman, *Borrow*, and Manning, *Credit Card Nation*.

12. On the overall phenomenon of post-1980 globalization see the work of its champion, Thomas Friedman, *The World Is Flat*; and the more skeptical Greider, *One World Ready or Not*. Key factors include free-trade agreements, the elimination of protectionist barriers and capital controls, and the advent of communication and transportation technologies that make global commerce more efficient. A quick summary is found in "Globalization," in Conway, *Fifty Economic Ideas*, 162–65. On inequality in the United States, see de Graaf and Batker, *What's the Economy For*, 118–19. In 1980 the top 1 percent earned less than 10 percent of national income; in 2008 the same group earned over 20 percent. The US Gini coefficient has increased from 0.388 to 0.45. The concentration of wealth in the top 20 percent has increased from thirty times the bottom 20 percent in 1960 to seventy-five times today, due to a combination of stagnant wages at the median and soaring wages at the top.

13. This wage-productivity link, enforced by relatively widespread unionization, is commonly understood to be the key shift in the post-1970s economic picture: since the 1980s, median wages have stagnated (when adjusted for inflation) even as productivity rose. See Medaille, "Equity and Equilibrium," 263; Graeber, *Debt*, 373–75; and Galbraith, *New Industrial State*, 870–71.

14. Union membership peaked at 35 percent of the workforce in 1954, and has dropped to around 11 percent today. See http://en.wikipedia.org/wiki/Labor_unions_in_the_United_States.

15. The gasoline CPI rose by an 8.55 times increase from 1970 to 2010, versus a 5.48 times increase for food and a mere 2 times increase for clothing (Bureau of Labor Statistics data in *World Almanac*, 2013, 79). On trust in government: data on pre-Watergate America showed a majority of citizens trusting in government, but now the percentage is in the teens and low twenties. See http://politicalticker.blogs.cnn.com/2011/09/28/cnn-poll-trust-in-government-at-all-time-low/. Sandbrook, *Mad as Hell*, 11, points out that the erosion in trust predates Watergate, with the significant crumbling of confidence taking place between 1966 and 1975.

16. On Bretton Woods see Berman, *Dark Ages America*, 49–66.

17. See Harrington, *Other America*, as a classic example. These studies were instrumental in energizing Lyndon Johnson's "war on poverty."

18. Thanks to YouTube, viewers can watch Dwight Eisenhower's famous warning about this in his 1961 farewell address: https://www.youtube.com/watch?v=8y06NSBBRtY.

19. Gregory, "Unintended Reformation," 17.

20. In 2011 the exact number was 70.898 percent. See http://www.bea.gov/newsreleases/national/gdp/2012/pdf/gdp3q12_2nd.pdf The numbers from the 1950s to 1960s period are in the low 60 percent range.

21. Sandel, *What Money Can't Buy*, 7–10.

22. See Cherlin, *Marriage-Go-Round.*
23. Keenan, *Virtues for Ordinary Christians*, 12.
24. Benedict XVI, *Caritas in Veritate*, no. 36.
25. Ibid., no. 39.
26. In 2012, presidential candidate Mitt Romney was caught on hidden camera telling wealthy donors that he wouldn't get the votes of the 47 percent of Americans who pay no net income taxes. https://www.youtube.com/watch?v=M2gvY2wqI7M.
27. Finn, *Moral Ecology of Markets*, 126–44.
28. De Vries, *Industrious Revolution*, 177.
29. Robert Frank notes that status purchases can sometimes be even more attractive to the poor, because the "gain" in esteem is so large, relatively speaking. There is "a larger advance in the rankings." See *Choosing the Right Pond*, 144. On social workers see Shipler, *Working Poor*, where the poor's top lament (in the early 2000s) was cable television.
30. Crook, "The Phantom Menace."
31. Thorngate, "Defining the Middle," 30–32.
32. As we will see in chapter 6, data suggests that 20 to 40 percent of households bring in significantly more income than they spend.
33. Ramsey, *Total Money Makeover.* I am not endorsing Ramsey; indeed, what is needed to *confront* Ramsey is a project that insists on *both* personal and structural economic issues, not just one or the other.
34. Kessler, *End of Overeating.*
35. Rubio, *Family Ethics*, 129. Rubio quotes Robert Putnam, noting that since the 1970s the percentage of families who say they usually eat together dropped by a third, and the amount of times families hosted friends for dinner dropped by 45 percent (130).
36. Franks, *He Became Poor*, 3, 8, 20.
37. Brown, *Through the Eye of a Needle.*
38. For a definitive history of consumer society critics in America, see Horowitz, *Morality of Spending* and *Anxieties of Affluence.* Concerns about commercial society go back even further: see Rasmussen, *Problems and Promise of Commercial Society*, and Muller, *Mind and the Market.*
39. For an overview of the debate since the nineteenth century, see Holt and Schor, "Introduction: Do Americans Consume Too Much?" For more on the founders see Lind, *Land of Promise.*
40. Lasch, *True and Only Heaven*; Berry, *Sex, Economy, Freedom, and Community.*
41. Medaille, *Vocation of Business* and *Toward a Truly Free Market.*
42. See, for example, Sachs, *End of Poverty.*
43. Daly and Farley, in *Ecological Economics*, note that the economy as a whole lacks a "when to stop" rule.
44. See Henwood, *After the New Economy*, 159–86, and Livingston, *Against Thrift*, 21–24. Such tomes frequently remind the reader of the Southern (read: racist) exemplars of American producerist populism.
45. Skidelsky and Skidelsky, *How Much Is Enough?*, 176, also calls them "middle-class baubles." Livingston, *Against Thrift*, 166–72, criticizes the bestselling *Shop Class as Soulcraft* as exemplifying exactly this kind of "hobby-esque" pursuit of "work as leisure."

46. See Cloutier, "Working with the Grammar of Creation."
47. John Paul II, *Laborem Exercens*, nos. 6 and 17.
48. Horowitz, *Morality of Spending*, xxvii.
49. See Twitchell, *Living It Up*.
50. See Salatin, *Everything I Want to Do Is Illegal*.
51. Brown, *Through the Eye of a Needle*, 419.
52. *Lumen Gentium*, nos. 39–42, in Abbott, *Documents of Vatican II*, 65–72; John Paul II, *Veritatis Splendor*, no. 18.
53. Stassen and Gushee, *Kingdom Ethics*.
54. Horowitz, *Morality of Spending*, xviii–xix, identifies the evolution from the first to the second in American history.
55. Seneca, "On Providence," 89.
56. The former approach is rare today, though Powers, *Twelve by Twelve*, is a narrative that shows how far some people can go; the latter is much more common, such as Frank, *Richistan*.
57. Herdt, *Putting on Virtue*, 271–72.
58. *Catechism of the Catholic Church*, no. 2401.
59. Ryan, *Church and Socialism*, 36–37.
60. Hinze, "What Is Enough?," 169.
61. Michman and Magee, *Affluent Consumer*.
62. For examples of a sacramental worldview or imaginary that penetrates all aspects of Christian life, see Eggemeier, *Sacramental-Prophetic Imagination*, and Smith, *Imagining the Kingdom*.
63. *Lumen Gentium*, nos. 39–42, in Abbott, *Documents of Vatican II*, 65–72.
64. Benedict XVI, *Caritas in Veritate*, no. 36.
65. Galbraith, *Affluent Society*, quoted in Skidelsky, *How Much Is Enough?*, 88.
66. Samuelson and Nordhaus, *Economics*, 26.
67. See Nash, "Toward the Revival," one of the rare recent articles connecting virtue and economic restraint.
68. As will be shown in chapter 4, Keynes's actual articulation (*General Theory of Employment*, 84, 111–12) emphasizes that the problem is not thrift per se, but rather saving under conditions that don't actually lead to investment.
69. Borgmann, *Power Failure*, 14.
70. McCabe, *What Ethics Is All About*, 92, 95.
71. *Dei Verbum*, no. 12, in Abbott, *Documents of Vatican II*, 120–21.
72. Finn, *Christian Economic Ethics*, 29.
73. MacDonald, "Christians Shatter Taboos," 17.
74. Kennedy, *Freedom from Fear*, 118–24.
75. Polanyi, *Great Transformation*.
76. See chap. 4.

Part I

CHAPTER 1

Luxury in History

A Brief Survey

What is luxury? Father James Martin tells the story of an old Jesuit, a "living rule," whose room he would visit for confession. His room is spartan, the bed "a single . . . nothing but a box spring and a mattress perched atop a rickety metal frame. But what caught my eye was the yellow bedspread. An inexpensive polyester spread barely covering the mattress, it looked ancient, thin nearly to the point of transparency, faded in color; it was the most meager bedspread I could imagine. 'Father,' I said, 'I think it's time for a new bedspread.' 'Mister,' he said with a laugh, 'that *is* the new bedspread.'"[1] Martin himself had asked for a new bedspread the week before, and here realized he had not really needed it.

Was this new bedspread a luxury? As Martin notes, American Jesuits may live simply compared to some "affluent Americans," but he admits they live less simply than countless poor around the world.[2] The category of luxury is a challenging and difficult one. This book seeks to answer the question of what luxury is. The concept must be defined inductively during the course of the discussion. The first task is to examine how writers in the Western tradition put flesh on the bones of this notion—but not all in the same way. History leads us into the crucial eighteenth century, where developments in philosophy, theology, and economics (subjects not yet fully distinguished from one another) interrupted the traditional critique in significant and problematic ways. However, even before that time the notion of *truphe/tryphe* or *luxuria* had an odd history. It appears as central, gets lost or overlooked in the moral discourse, and then later returns but often in a different way.

Luxury in the Ancient Traditions

In his narrative of the "eventful history" of the idea, Christopher Berry notes that luxury's "contemporary usage in the rhetoric of advertising is far removed from the opprobrium to which it was subjected by Cato the Elder."[3] Ancient usage is uniform in its moral condemnation of luxury. The related Greek terms, built on the root *truphe/tryphe*, all have strongly negative connotations. Yet their rendering in English is imprecise: a Greek-English lexicon offers a cluster of terms, including daintiness, fastidiousness, voluptuousness, licentiousness, extravagance, wantonness, and effeminacy.[4] This imprecision bespeaks an attempt to characterize some problem that is evident yet difficult to identify.

Berry points out that the basic moral assumption undergirding all classical criticisms of luxury was that "needs have fixed limits" and that exceeding these limits is ultimately destructive of both the person and the *polis*.[5] Criticisms of luxury rested on two sorts of limits. First, ancient writers assumed a definite teleology—a vision of the truly good life for humans. Luxury names some sort of excess beyond the limits set by the nature of the person. Second, within this teleology there is an assumed priority of common life over private life, such that one's resources should be directed toward the good of the civic order instead of for personal ease. Luxury names a "fastidious" and excessive attention to private goods that detrimentally diverts attention and resources from the city. This ideal of the priority of the common good reflects the general sense that civic life is a noble calling of the propertied class; the wealthy elite should not turn inward toward the luxury of a private life.[6] To lack the discipline of these limitations is to suffer from the vice of luxury.

Plato's criticism of the "luxurious city" in *The Republic* exemplifies the elements of classical critiques.[7] The city, in Socrates's description, is necessary for human life because "no human being is self-sufficient" (369b) and it is better "if each does the work nature has equipped him to do" (370c), thus dividing labor among different jobs. Socrates attempts to describe the different things needed in the city, but Glaucon breaks in on his description by saying Socrates is describing a "city of pigs" that lacks comfortable furniture and tasty food. Socrates retorts that Glaucon's vision would be "a city in a state of fever," but he accepts that "many will not be content with simple fare and simple ways" (372d). He then describes all the new professions that will be needed to satisfy this "fevered" city, a city that constantly demands to "be extended and filled up with superfluities" (373b). There is reference to the need for a surplus of doctors to treat all the diseases of the

luxurious city on account of the diet and the lack of exercise! Most especially, the city will need more land to satisfy all its wants and thus will need
to go to war because of its covetousness. It cannot live within its means.
The luxurious city is beset by conflict, both within and without, in contrast
to the harmony engendered by properly limited desire that characterizes
the ideal person and the ideal city.

Socrates's initial description of the ideal nonluxurious city is not one
of abject poverty. It has "bread, wine, clothes, shoes, and houses" (372b),
food is served on "mats of reeds" with desserts of "figs, chickpeas, and
beans," and all is enjoyed while wearing "garlands, and singing hymns to
the gods and enjoying one another's company . . . all the while drinking
in moderation" (372c). The ideal is not poverty, which leads to "meanness
and incompetence," but neither is it wealth, which "spawns luxury and
indolence" (422a). The problem is the desire for *fancy* food, *ornamental*
clothing, and *finely decorated* houses.

This critique of luxury is not peripheral but central to Plato's entire
argument. It appears and reappears throughout the dialogue. As Glaucon
exclaims in the discussion of appropriate music for the ideal city, "there
is something we have done without even noticing it. We have been purg-
ing away those things we discussed earlier that transformed our city into a
city of luxury" (399e). Appropriate music turns out to require only simple
instruments. In Plato, the city reflects the human soul in its tripartite division. Luxury in the city reflects a base dominance of the body over the
mind and the spirit—it is harmful both to the contemplative life and to
the next-best warrior life. Like the disordered soul, the disordered city is
eventually not headed to triumph but ruin. Ultimately, "unbalanced" cities do not deserve to be called cities at all; they are merely "aggregations of
factions" (422e). And what is faction's source? That source is none other
than "money-making and the acquisition of land and houses and gold and
silver," causing the originally virtuous guardians and rulers to fatally compromise and leading to the loss of independence for small proprietors, and
finally their subsequent coercion into work and (more important) warfare
(547b–c). Note well: a compromise with luxury is the first step in Socrates's
book-length description of the gradual decline of the city into tyranny.

This line of criticism of luxury as fundamentally disruptive for both
individual and social flourishing can be found throughout ancient literature, both Greco-Roman and Jewish. Aristotle carefully distinguishes
the art of economics from "chrematistics," with the latter indicating an
unlimited desire for material goods as *ends* rather than as a *means* to living
well.[8] While he refers to luxury only in passing in the *Nicomachean Ethics*

(1150b), Aristotle's account of prodigality and vulgarity as excesses in relation to the virtues of liberality and magnificence suggests many similar themes. (He also mentions luxury in a list of vices in the *Eudemian Ethics*.[9]) The discussion of these virtues comes immediately after a lengthy discussion of temperance, where the self-indulgent person is said to "delight either in the wrong things, or more than most people do, or in the wrong way" (1118b23–24), and thus "is led by his appetite to choose [pleasant things] at the cost of everything else" (1119a2). He then goes on to note that we call "prodigal" those "who are incontinent and spend money on self-indulgence." Aristotle explains that prodigals are usually "self-indulgent, for they spend lightly and waste money on their indulgences, and incline toward pleasures because they do not live with a view to what is noble." Prodigality turns out to be complex. The mean or miserly person simply cares too much for wealth (1119b29); the prodigal is careless in his giving and is neglectful of "taking" (1121a8–15). This, of course, leads to the problem that one cannot be prodigal for long, so prodigality then turns to "taking recklessly and from any source" (1121b2).[10] Prodigality leads eventually to social conflict.

Aristotle's assessment of magnificence, however, may seem to lie in some tension with Plato's criticisms. The magnificent man primarily spends on public splendor, so that even on "private occasions" (for example, a wedding), he "spends not on himself but on public objects" (1123a4–5). Yet Aristotle also considers one's house "a sort of public ornament" and so he licenses spending on lasting, beautiful, and becoming things. Still, at least the magnanimous man is not vulgar, which entails overspending the circumstances and displaying a "tasteless showiness" that is "not for the sake of the noble, but to show off his wealth, and because he thinks he is admired for such things" (1123a20–26). Aristotle, in line with his tendency to show less scorn for external goods than Plato, in essence expands the limits on material goods here. But he nevertheless retains such limits in describing what is excessive.

Stoic thinkers manifest a complex relation to Plato and Aristotle by shifting toward a less polis-centered view of life and a more nuanced position on external goods.[11] Given their belief that external goods are ultimately "indifferents," one might imagine them weakening the argument against luxury. In many cases, however, their more rigorous suspicion of "unnatural" individual desire strengthens the critique. More influentially, many cite the pursuit of luxury as the mark of the decline of the Republic, and their critiques remained accepted (if not always heeded) well into the eighteenth century.[12] The roots of this Roman critique lie in later Greek historians of the second and early first century BCE, such as Polybius and Posidonius, who cultivated a longstanding tradition of the "devastating consequences of *tryphe*" on cities, especially identified with the fall of Sybaris.[13] This theme is so dominant in the literature of ancient Rome that even contemporary economist Lester Thurow can quote Cicero on the Roman ideal: "The Roman people hate private luxury, they love public magnificence."[14] Augustine happily plays this same tune, remarking that the supposed Roman desire for peace and prosperity masks the "desire to enjoy your luxurious license unrestrained" and "thus to generate from your prosperity a moral pestilence which will prove a thousandfold more disastrous than the fiercest enemies."[15] Cicero organizes this critique clearly, suggesting that the basic duties of "mutual love and good nature among mankind" (that is, justice and beneficence) are natural but undermined by the "irregular and exorbitant appetite" rooted in love of riches.[16] Here, too, we find a consistent emphasis on exceeding natural limits, which is tied to "the use of wealth for personal or private advantage, not public well-being."[17] In short, ancient writers are unanimous that the "thinking about wealth was governed by the idea of limits. The exact location of these limits was disputed, but their existence was never in doubt."[18]

Israel's scriptures largely accord with these criticisms, although the point of accent is different.[19] In the prophets and even in Wisdom literature, the concern with luxurious living is focused on how it leads to disobedience of God's law, a disobedience that is not compensated for by empty ritual practices.[20] In this way, gold and silver are constantly put forward as idols, which God will (sometimes terrifyingly) sweep away. Ezekiel warns, "Their silver and gold cannot save them on the day of the Lord's wrath. They shall not be allowed to satisfy their craving or fill their bellies, for this has been the occasion of their sin. In the beauty of their ornaments they put their pride; they made of them their idols. For this reason I make them refuse" (Ezek. 7:19–20). Note that idolatry need not mean a literal "golden calf," but, rather, any pursuit of and trust in what is not God.

The biblical authors do add a crucial dimension to the Greco-Roman view, since this disobedience and idolatry is most acutely seen in the neglect of God's commands of generosity toward the poor.[21] Amos compares the women of Samaria to the fattened "cows of Bashan" (Am. 4:1) and criticizes those who "recline beside any altar" in "garments taken in pledge" from the poor (Am. 2:8). Even the relatively gentler Wisdom literature indicates that many are "ensnared by gold," they labor "to pile up wealth," and they rest only in "wanton pleasure" (Sir. 31: 2, 6) instead of freely lending to those in need or storing up "almsgiving in your treasure house" to "save you from every evil" (Sir. 29:12). The New Testament carries over nearly all these themes about wealth and possessions, except for "one conspicuous omission: never is material wealth promised as a guaranteed reward for either spiritual obedience or simple hard work."[22] A preoccupation with food and clothing, and wealth in general, is the most obvious form of distraction from "seeking first" the reign of God (cf. Matt. 6:25–37).[23] The lure of riches is identified with the thorns that choke off the seeds of the Gospel (Matt. 13:22). As in the Greco-Roman literature, the Bible depicts the luxury life as a dishonorable and sinful alternative to living out justice, although the Kingdom's justice is more radical and shows more attention to the needs of the poor.

The Church Fathers, without hesitation, applied these teachings, even in their much-more-wealthy urban contexts. Even the title of Clement of Alexandria's work is indicative: "Who is the rich man who can be saved?" Helen Rhee summarizes: "Christian self-definition includes unequivocal denunciation of avarice and luxury as irrational desires and displays of wealth."[24] While the teaching against wealth softened slightly over time — from an earlier "eschatological great reversal" of rich and poor to a later insistence on "redemptive almsgiving" as the binding together of rich and poor in one people before God — the Church Fathers uniformly mock the material indulgences of the wealthy in the strongest terms.[25] Rhee writes that Clement of Alexandria criticized avarice as a disease and derided "outrageous and even comical displays of luxury among the refined elites, from clothing, food, vessels, crowns, shoes, to jewelries and ornaments."[26] Like other Fathers, Clement was influenced by Stoicism, as seen in his recommending detachment and in the multiplying of possessions as "unnatural." But Clement goes beyond Stoicism in his insistence that luxury is a way of living that neglects the command to love the neighbor.[27] Hengel concludes that luxury was criticized based on the need for generosity and the ideal of common use that is leavened by a sense of personal ascetic detachment.

The late fourth-century writer Prudentius exemplifies the marriage of classical and biblical thought on luxury and dramatizes the struggle between virtue and vice as a series of battles in which a particular vice is described and then is conquered by a particular virtue. "Luxuria" takes the field "languidly belching after a night-long feast," living "only for pleasure," making "her spirit soft and nerveless," which serves "to enfeeble and undo her understanding."[28] She wins over the forces of virtue not by using "arrows and lances" but "by scattering baskets of flowers over her adversaries"; they are "struck dumb" and willingly submit to her enslavement, dazzled by her golden-plated chariot and reins.[29] The response comes from "Sobrietas," who (quite sacramentally) reminds his fighters of the counter-celebrations of God's providence, the manna in the desert, and the Eucharist. Sobrietas has no weapon except the cross. This frightens Luxuria's horses, which she cannot control in her softened state.[30] Interestingly, only in the wake of Luxuria's death does Avaritia (greed) take the field to gather her remnants and provoke conflict over these now-scarce prizes. Greed is defeated when Ratio (reason) takes the field, telling the fighters to "inflexibly scorn money."[31] Yet the battle is not quite complete, for then the vice of Frugi (thrift) takes the field and confuses the warriors, who must finally be driven off by "good works." "Good works" finally removes "the weight of money . . . by taking pity on the needy, whom she had cared for with kindly generosity."[32]

On Luxury and Avarice: What's the Difference?

Prudentius's story of the vices indicates that the ancient literature considers greed and luxury different vices, and luxury may in fact be the root of greed. Our language, both secular and Christian, retains a critique of greed despite losing that sense of luxury. As John Sekora notes, in the ancient discourse luxury is understood as a "fundamental vice . . . from which other subordinate vices would ensue."[33] Few Americans love money *per se*; if they did, they would not so often mismanage their funds. But many Americans love all the things money can buy. Thus greed functions as a parasite on a deeper problem: *luxuria*. If Prudentius is right, greed and the overt social conflict that goes with it is ultimately a product of scarcity. However, what produces greed occurs not in times of scarcity but in times of relative plenty, when we fall under the much lovelier spell of luxury and are captured by comfort and delight in material things. Critiques of both injustice and greed *follow from* the more fundamental preoccupation with luxury.

A differentiation between avarice and luxury is commonly found throughout Roman literature. In a speech defending a country man against city elites, Cicero concurs in Prudentius's ordering of vices: "The city creates luxury [*luxurie*], from which avarice [*avaritia*] inevitably springs, while from avarice audacity breaks forth, the source of all crimes and misdeeds."[34] Livy reproduces a speech from Cato, "lamenting that the state is suffering from those two opposing [*diversisque duobus*] evils, avarice and luxury [*avaritia et luxuria*], which have been the destruction of every great empire."[35] The example goes on to chronicle the consequent greed of rich women (and "often men") for goods if their prior penchant for luxury is not preemptively restrained by laws that limit extravagance in dress.

Interestingly, the Roman historian Sallust offers the reverse ordering in distinguishing avarice from luxury. In Sallust's description the successes of a nation lead to an increased availability of both riches and honors and result in a tendency toward two vices: *avaritia* and *ambitio*. He suggests that the former ends up being a more serious problem in the long run because wealth then becomes the norm and a frugal, simple life is seen as disgraceful. A consequence is that "the next generation becomes prey to *luxuria*."[36] In this description, over time the initial drive toward accumulation (avarice) leads to a preoccupation with ease, comforts, and the like (luxury).[37]

In either case, the chosen images suggest that avarice and luxury are distinct vices. The characterization of economic vice solely in terms of greed impoverishes our moral language and thus our understanding of what is wrong. It is worth taking a bit more space here to make the case for distinguishing them, since a critique of greed continues to be relevant in medieval thought but luxury (as material excess) drops out.

Aristotle offers a host of virtue and vice terms in relation to possessions, though attention is sometimes centered on the vice of *pleonexia*. MacIntyre explains that Aristotle's *pleonexia* "is no more and no less than simple acquisitiveness, [or] acting so as to have more as such."[38] He criticizes the naming of this vice by the English "greed," since greed appears to indicate one of many possible motives for engaging in acquisitive activities, whereas Aristotle is targeting "the tendency to engage in such activities *for their own sake*."[39] MacIntyre also criticizes the interpretation of *pleonexia* as "taking more than one's share." Understanding *pleonexia* using the broader term "graspingness" (Barnes's translation) is helpful.

But consider Aristotle's description within the larger conceptual scheme developed over several books of the *Nichomachean Ethics*. *Pleonexia* is introduced in Book V, *within the discussion of the virtue of justice* but following the books that deal with self-indulgence (III) and magnanimity (IV). While *pleonexia* is a vice related to justice in particular ways, other economic vices may appear in relation to the virtues of temperance and magnanimity.

Within Aristotle's complex discussion of justice, two further points are relevant to understanding what is meant by *pleonexia* and how it is related to other virtues and vices. One, injustice involves some kind of violation of either law or equity (also called proportionality). Law or equity violations are not the same, "for all that is unequal is unlawful but not all that is unlawful is unequal" (1130b12–13). Claims of injustice focus on a particular moral problem: the "grasping" involved is a matter of excess related to law and equity.[40] Two, Aristotle offers examples of cases that today we might broadly call injustice but which are not encompassed by justice in this focused sense. He discusses the cowardly act of abandoning fellows in battle but also the failure to assist a friend through meanness (1130a19). These are wicked acts but are not a matter of "grasping." They involve other vices. Similarly, a person who seeks money through adultery may be grasping "but not self-indulgent," whereas a person who commits adultery out of "the bidding of appetite" may be doing something unjust but is not proceeding out of "grasping." These examples suggest the need for a richer vocabulary beyond "greed" in order to understand the vicious dispositions related to material possessions.

How might these distinctions appear in contemporary form? Stanley Hauerwas cites the speech of business tycoon Gordon Gekko in the 1987 film *Wall Street* as a manifestation of a philosophy that "greed is good. Greed works."[41] But if one walks around the average American gathering and asks, "Is greed good?" most would probably say it is not and that they themselves are not greedy. This is true insofar as most of them are not Gordon Gekko—that is, they are not in a position of managing a large corporation or massive pools of wealth, and they have not developed the character that such activity may require in our society. The problem is that some let Gordon Gekko types plan their retirements or invest in their companies in order to make a return for . . . what?

The answers here likely reflect the vice of luxury. After all, if you asked Americans, "Is luxury good?" people would be much more likely to answer yes. Take as an example a recent issue of *Money* magazine. A story featured a breathless analysis of five families' retirement savings, breaking down the "fixes" they needed to "reach their goals with ease."[42] Of the five profiles that purported to show a variety of situations, the lowest household annual income was $105,000 (which, for 2009, would put this household in the top 20 percent of all households) and the lowest retirement savings was held by a single mother (making $123,000) who had saved "only" $115,000 . . . by age thirty-nine. A couple just starting retirement in Texas is frantic because they have "only" $978,000. This field of examples clearly suggests that, among those who read *Money*, there is a prevailing sense that retirement savings should be extremely high. While these profiles obscure the many Americans who lack any reasonable retirement savings, and while some concern about retirement savings is rooted in concerns about health care costs, advertising promotions for retirement savings plans are not usually pitched this way anyway. Instead, they appear in terms of the "retirement of your dreams" in which yearning is "unlimited" to the extent that the possible pleasures they could purchase in our economy are unlimited. It is safe to say that the object of desire here is not really gain *per se* but rather the enjoyment of goods and services for which gain appears to be an effective means.

Another rather extreme example of the different though related appearance of avarice and luxury is the recent documentary film *The Queen of Versailles*. It depicts the life and marriage of an older man and his younger wife: the man has become wealthy building the largest time-share empire in the United States. The drama happens when the real estate bubble collapses. The tycoon is unable to escape the drab surroundings of his cluttered home office because he spends every spare minute trying to accumulate money (since he spent the boom years accumulating more and more through leverage), while the wife is unable to care for their expansive house (e.g., clean up after her designer dogs) because the servants are gone. Yet she also can't stop spending money on goods. The tycoon's life looks like one of *avarice*, his wife's looks like *luxury*. Both involve excess, but of different sorts, and the viciousness of these dispositions is evident in different ways. The movie is a kind of parable of how the recent housing bubble involves some actors driven by greed and others by luxury.

One can also understand the difference between the two vices in terms of societies. Much recent literature has pointed to long-term "global imbalances" as the key destabilizing factor affecting today's economy.[43] The largest imbalance is between states that are accumulating huge dollar reserves (the best example is China), in part as a hedge against the boom-bust cycles that affected some Asian markets in the late 1990s, versus states that run large and chronic current account deficits (the United States). The difference between the national interests and policies of China and the United States exemplifies greed and luxury, respectively. China actually "needs" to spend more—that is, allow for a higher level of domestic consumption—and, when it does, the United States will inevitably have to spend less.

Another distinction might be seen in the different relation of each vice to law. Aristotle's emphasis on flat-out violations of law and equity among persons gives the vice of *pleonexia* a more limited, though more serious, scope. By contrast, legal restrictions on luxury, such as sumptuary laws, have proven notoriously difficult to enforce throughout history; part of the reason is that luxury is so broad a phenomenon that a law restricting one thing merely redirects the luxurious to some other outlet.[44] Moreover, the pursuit of *luxuria* can seem quite harmless, even in accord with, judgments of equity—after all, if middle-class people feel that a smartphone is essential, how can the poor be judged for having smartphones? In Hume's perspective (explained later) luxury often leads to an appreciation of others' refinement as well, so that mutual enjoyment seems to ensue. What the law cannot encompass is a sense of *fitting* limits, given the issues described previously: an individual's development toward what is truly noble and a sense that that nobility consists partly in a sense of proportion between public good and private goods. But the inability to legislate against luxury does not mean it is not important, any more than chastity is unimportant for the same reason.

A final reason to differentiate these two vices arises from the nature of consumer society. Consumer society makes a religion not out of accumulation and attachment but of constant *detachment* through the process of continual acquisition and discarding—that is, shopping.[45] Compulsive shoppers seems to be quite different from greedy hoarders or the greedy in the world of corporate governance and finance. True, Gordon Gekko may go to a home or on a vacation that can be described as luxurious, but his greedy activity, which violates justice, seems to differ from his luxurious pursuits. Michael Lewis outlines how the desire for the world's largest sail-boat motivated the initial Netscape stock offering that set off the dot-com bubble—so perhaps luxury still is the root of greed.[46] Luxury constitutes a different sort of vice in relation to wealth and possessions than does greed-avarice. We need language other than "avarice" to make proper sense of our economic virtues and vices.

The Disappearance of Luxury

Regardless of how one parses the terms, the main point remains that both greed and luxury have been consistently portrayed as personally and socially destructive vices. But what happened to the disdain for luxury? Why is it that today Christian ethics still holds greed in contempt but no longer seems concerned about luxury? There are two crucial stories to tell: one is brief, the other more lengthy.

The brief problem involves the gradual assimilation of *luxuria* to sensuality, which becomes synonymous with lust. In a third-century Latin writer like Novatian, the term luxury retains its connection with the material possessions of the rich. He uses the term in denying that St. Paul's permission to eat meats should be taken as a "permission of luxury," and he follows the typical convention of presuming that avarice "follows in the footsteps of luxury."[47] Yet, by the time Gregory the Great's *Moralia* appears, the term *luxuria* is firmly sexual in meaning.[48] This evolution is primarily due to the development of lists of "capital sins," eventually to be numbered seven. While the earliest lists (by Evagrius and Cassian) include eight sins, *porneia* and fornication become equated with the Latin *luxuria*.[49] In Gregory the Great's near-definitive form, *luxuria* (as a substitute for Cassian's *fornicatio*) is listed last; it is understood to be, along with gluttony, a "carnal" sin.[50] This list of sins came to be the major catechetical tool for morality in the Middle Ages, and was not displaced by the Commandments until the Reformation.[51] While the list includes *avaritia*, the overriding concern for excess comes to focus on the carnal sins. It is also reinforced by the occurrences of *luxuria* in the Vulgate New Testament (Eph. 5:18; Tit., 1:6; 1 Pet. 4:4), which render forms of the Greek *asotia* ("licentiousness") rather than forms of *truphe*.[52] (Another part of the story is undoubtedly the fact that Christian society from the sixth to the twelfth centuries was notably poorer, though not as poor as the label "Dark Ages" would make us suppose.[53])

In Aquinas, *luxuria* is understood as lust, based on Isidore. The subject matter of *vitio luxuria* is primarily about sex because "the pleasures that most unloosen the human spirit are those of sex." So *luxuria* is only "secondarily in other pleasures in excess."[54] Aquinas relates the term to wine "because excessive drinking is an incentive to the pleasures of sex."[55] The earliest uses of the English term "luxurie" apply directly to sexuality; it is only in the seventeenth century, after the Reformation, when the English word reacquires its traditional connection to "the habitual use of, or indulgence in what is choice or costly."[56]

Despite the term's disappearance, though, Aquinas (and, more broadly, the Medieval Age) continue to make arguments that in effect reaffirm the critique of luxury. First and foremost, Aquinas follows Aristotle in distinguishing between natural and artificial wealth: the "desire for artificial wealth is infinite, for it is the servant of disordered concupiscence, which is not curbed, as the Philosopher makes clear."[57] Natural wealth simply provides a base of support for human nature and reaches a level of sufficiency.[58] The ancient importance of limits is affirmed. Artificiality applies especially to money wealth—hence, the medieval preoccupation with the evil of usury, which is, "by its very nature unlawful," because money is merely a sterile social convention to facilitate exchange.[59] This critique of usury remains valuable to us today because it is a reminder that transactions should not go on simply because of an intention for profit. However, the single-minded and legalistic emphasis on the absolute norm against usury generated necessary but strange workarounds, as well as accusations of hypocrisy (e.g., when the Church accepted benefits from usurers).[60] The teaching ended up resting too heavily on a kind of "physicalism of money" rather than on an understanding of virtue. Nevertheless, its attempt to place limits on finance remained consistent with a critique of luxury.

A similar recognition of the need to define material excess, as well as the problems when such insight is treated too legalistically, appeared in mendicant controversies over ownership. Writing in the fourteenth century, the Dominican Hervaeus Natalis sought to respond to the idea that perfect holiness meant holding no possessions whatsoever, even possessions held in common.[61] In doing so he drew out key distinctions relevant for naming excess in "temporal things." He writes that "having temporal things does not naturally diminish perfection," so long as we hold "dominion over them" and we hold them only "to a degree sufficient to sustain life according to the common course of nature."[62] Hervaeus is keen to distinguish having things "necessary for life for the sake of God" versus "an inordinate desire for temporal goods beyond a proper measure" (57). Excessive wealth "naturally kindles an inordinate love" (67). Ordinary wealth, even in provisioning for the future, need not be contrary to charity, but Hervaeus cites numerous limits to possession: excessive care for temporal things to the neglect of God and neighbor; preoccupation with remote possible circumstances; an "inordinate love of acquiring"; and "the elation of the mind" that can be associated with temporal things (65–66). All of these relate to the traditional vice of luxury, though Hervaeus does not have the word at his disposal. For Hervaeus, holding goods in common significantly diminishes all these threats, because one is less likely to fall into the cycle of excessive acquisition and inordinate care, and certainly not to "pride" in one's possessions, the worst of all (57). These distinctions can be very helpful for marking out luxury.[63]

Although the term luxury was marginalized in the medieval theological discourse, the concept had not gone away. Sumptuary laws were extensive in Italy throughout the entire period of the Middle Ages.[64] And the language reappeared with force during the Renaissance—unsurprisingly, given the focus on the retrieval of the classical texts, replete with their condemnations of the vice.[65] Diana Wood notes that the combination of labor shortages (due to the Black Death) and the Renaissance idea of humanism "desanctified poverty."[66] But it did not endorse luxury—quite the contrary. In Italy, and eventually in England as well, the "civic republican" tradition retained the suspicion of luxury, particularly focusing on how the pursuit of private wealth and extravagance undermined attention to the common good.[67] Instead, the luxurious are focused on "their own individual or factional interests."[68] The Renaissance Aristotelian Francesco Guicciardini typifies this concern about "luxurious habits," expressing a disgust that "the prevailing 'style of living' amongst 'the people of Florence' is 'such that everyone wants very much to be rich.'"[69] Pocock calls his argument for "the systematic elimination of private satisfactions and appetites" an "almost Savonarolan proposal" that is "nothing less than a polemic against luxury."[70] Similar critiques appeared in English humanists, especially with the rise of "enclosures" that exemplified this concern for keeping material wealth for one's private enrichment.[71]

The major figures of the Protestant Reformation also maintained a severe critique of luxury, holding strongly to an ideal of austerity. Hans Hillerbrand writes: "The plain fact was that commerce and trade were no more receptive to Protestant ethical counsel than they had been to Catholic." Indeed, "the Reformers inveighed against sundry social abuses, such as prostitution, drinking, and luxury in dress as the Catholic authorities had done all along," and sometimes with less of the "practical tolerance" of their predecessors.[72] Perhaps they were less tolerant because, before and during the Reformation, the incongruous gap between the Catholic "religious ideal and clerical practice on wealth was a key concern for both Protestant and internal Catholic critics."[73] In general, the Reformers did eschew begging and "holy poverty" in favor of constant exhortation to lay-led initiatives promoting relief of the poor.[74] Owen Chadwick describes the Reformed ideal: "Though frugal and thrifty, they did not share the medieval ideal of poverty. . . . A good man worked and if he worked he might receive prosperity. . . . But he practiced early rising, days of fasting, temperance at all times, austerity in dress, and he kept few personal comforts in his house." He resisted "trivialities and decorations that diverted."[75] No endorsement of luxury here.

The importance of stewardship was a strong basis for criticizing the misuse of property "for one's own selfish ends." Philip Wogaman notes that while Calvin "was no ascetic," he strongly criticized "self-indulgence."[76] Rather, one's use of property will be accounted for at the judgment, and Calvin goes on: "[R]emember by whom such a reckoning is required: namely, him who has greatly commended abstinence, sobriety, frugality, and moderation, and has also abominated excess, pride, ostentation, and vanity."[77] Wogaman notes that later connections between Protestantism and capitalism are overstated, though he does say that the "readiness to defer consumption" in favor of productive work certainly promoted an attitude indirectly helpful for capital formation.[78] As with other issues assessed during the Reformation, Reformers "differed over the mandates" of the gospel on wealth, especially given some of the extreme community-of-goods experiments of the Radical Reformers.[79] Nevertheless, their general attitude continued the rejection of frivolous material goods.

The Reformers' suspicion of "holy poverty" provided a small space in which wealth might be reconciled with Christian faith. There was a comparable opening in Renaissance humanism, rooted in the observation that some wealthy cities seemed more peaceful than poorer ones while most cities were unable to realize the civic republican ideal. This gap between ideals and reality proved fertile ground for the new insights of Niccolo Machiavelli. Machiavelli shares the traditional belief in the priority of the common good. But he differs in his view of the effects of faction, believing that "class-conflict is not the solvent but the cement of a commonwealth."[80] Machiavelli's novel definition of the ruler's *virtu* still subordinates private interests to the society, but it does so by skillfully *manipulating* private interests, not by eliminating them. Thus, the skillful leader cannot always be virtuous in the traditional sense. Skinner concludes that in *The Prince*, "the concepts of *virtu* and virtue cease to have any necessary connection with each other."[81] Machiavelli's primary tool for statecraft is manipulating others' sense of honor, but the same explanations could then easily apply to property and wealth.[82] This new sort of politics, where self-interest is skillfully manipulated by the leader to bring about social good, represents a strong shift and sets the stage for seeing the pursuit of individual luxury as socially beneficial.

The Roots of the Modern Reversal

While the ancient consensus did not remain entirely intact through the eras of the Renaissance and Reformation, both Renaissance humanism and the Reformers retained much of the substance of the ancient criticisms of luxury. Yet Machiavelli's political strategies preview the second, much more complicated story of the disappearance of luxury. As John Sekora writes, "The changes in the meaning of the concept of luxury represent nothing less than the movement from the classical world to the modern."[83] Wallace-Hadrill agrees with the importance and starkness of this change, noting that today's Roman historians now regard the luxury critique as merely of "historiographical interest" rather than being useful for a contemporary "explanatory framework." Such "automatic and unthinking" rejection of a critique that Romans saw as obvious indicates something has changed at "a deep layer" of the culture. [84]

What changed? A series of changes in the view of the individual and the political order are central, and they form the bridge to this book's constructive argument. Skepticism about either virtue or religion succeeding as the basis for maintaining social order led to urgent questioning: What could be the alternative? Albert Hirschman's narrative traces the emergence of a new distinction between "passions" and "interests." Passions are dangerous and shifting and thus detrimental to both self and society; interests bring a kind of rational, farsighted view of benefits to the self.[85] Individual interests soon became identified with economic and material pursuits, and were contrasted with the passions, which found expression in religious enthusiasm, violence, lust for power, and sex.[86] In this way it was hoped that a political order directed toward enhancing interests could be a realistic one that would tame passions. As Hirschman writes, "the possibility of mutual gain [for self and for social order] emerged from the expected working of interest in politics, quite some time before it became a matter of doctrine in economics."[87] Here we find the groundwork for the "invisible hand." In particular, the French philosopher Montesquieu invented the idea that the spread of commerce was associated with the spread of "gentleness" and a peaceful social order, in contrast to the "disastrously arbitrary rule" of his day.[88] This doctrine of the politically beneficial and peaceful effects of an order based on (economic) interests was also espoused by Sir James Steuart in Scotland. Steuart highlighted the contrast between arbitrary rule by a sovereign, who might be dominated by his passions, to the orderly and mutually implicating rule of law preordained to support men's interests. While subjected to early criticism, this novel approach gained strength and has become almost a kind of common knowledge today.

Notice how this distinction, and its use, undermines the assumptions of the ancient critiques identified earlier. It was still the case that humans were subject to excessive passions that needed to be limited, but the desire for gain through commerce was not one of those passions. Further, in such a situation, the point was not to subordinate self-interested pursuit of private goods to public activity, but rather to engineer the social system so that public order would support (and be seen as supporting) the pursuit of personal happiness. This move also required a significant theological shift, a view Charles Taylor calls "providential Deism" in which the sacramentally present God of historic Christianity is overshadowed by God, the great engineer of an impersonal order who had designed this harmony of interests.[89]

In practice, evidence for the correctness of this new model was seen in the fast-commercializing Dutch republic of the seventeenth century, which deeply impressed observers as a crucial counter-Roman example. Despite their small size, lack of natural resources, and religious pluralism, the Dutch appeared remarkably prosperous and peaceful—a success that seemed to be due to the Dutch commitment to trade and commerce and to an enjoyment of their fruits.[90] As Jan de Vries notes in his study of the "industrious revolution" that preceded actual industrialization, Dutch writers Johan and Pieter de la Court "distinguished what they called Monarchical from Republican luxury."[91] While the former was "unbridled" and invariably led to "excesses and decadence," the latter was properly social, since it was governed and restrained by *amour-propre*, which sought the recognition and regard of others.[92] De Vries roots this theory in the psychology of the Calvinism and Jansenism of the day, keen as they were to focus on the actual passions that motivated human behavior. Like the distinction between violent passions and peaceful interests, this initial acceptance of luxury tried to maintain some validity for the more ancient critique while also distinguishing a "New Luxury" to which the ancient critiques did not apply. New Luxury made men industrious but, above all, was sociable—and identified with "taste" and "refinement" rather than excess and waste.

Thus, both in practice and in theory, the doctrine of "interests" proved to be an appealing alternative as emerging nation-states sought a basis for peaceful social order that was neither religious nor utopian. The Machiavellian idea that the successful prince is one who knows how to manipulate human passions launched a search for "positive passions," and the "new luxury" appeared quite promising, perhaps more promising than Machiavelli's emphasis on civic honors. It also meshed well with emerging social conditions: it provided a boost for the newly wealthy financiers and merchants concentrated in the cities (over against the landed aristocracy) and it supported the trend, outlined by de Vries, toward later and more independent household formation in the midst of rising prosperity and possibility for free economic exchange.[93] (Or, put more simply, there arose more laborers and merchants with money in their pocket to spend on novelties, like the pocket watch.)

However, claims about the gentleness and positive social effects of self-interest always needed to be protected from what we might call "the specter of Hobbes"; his portrait of self-interest being "a war of all against all" unless restrained by a powerful sovereign hangs over this entire era: "Much of the moral philosophy of the eighteenth century, even when it is hedonistic, may be regarded as a revolt against the selfish school."[94] Hobbes, amidst a chaotic age of conflict over legitimate authority, follows rigorously the new scientific method of reducing wholes to their simplest component parts.[95] His novel account of "the individual" presents him as seeking self-preservation via "the desire to dominate and the desire to avoid death."[96] The political theory for such an order is simply power.

Another "scandalous" figure, also opposed by many, presented self-interest as the *unlimited* pursuit of luxury. Demonstrating that an arresting story is worth reams of philosophizing, Bernard Mandeville's *Fable of the Bees* depicted England as a hive of dishonest, prideful, and luxury-seeking individuals whose self-seeking ways made the hive the envy of the world. "Thus every part was full of vice, yet the whole mass a paradise; flatter'd in peace and fear'd in wars, they were th' esteem of foreigners, and lavish of their wealth and lives, the balance of all other hives. Such were the blessings of that State; their crimes conspir'd to make them Great."[97] Schooled in the Dutch line of thought, Mandeville offered two ideas that were to echo for a long time.[98] He noted that in his hive, "It's real Pleasures, Comforts, Ease, To such a Hight, the very Poor Liv'd better than the Rich before" (26). If the goal is to help the poor live better lives, selfishness is the way to go. He also notes that once the hive turns honest, "All Arts and Crafts neglected lie; Content the Bane of Industry" (34).[99] If a nation wants development and progress, it needs discontent and dissatisfaction to fuel the striving to reach it.

Mandeville defines luxury as everything "that is not immediately necessary to make man subsist as he is a living Creature" on the basis that, while it is "rigorous," "if we are to abate one inch of this severity, I am afraid we shan't know where to stop" (107). Indeed, much of his defense of luxury rests on the claim that there is no way to make a reasonable distinction between necessities and luxuries once one admits something, anything, beyond the barest necessities. Socrates's argument indicates that such a distinction *can* be made and it is evident that we do in fact make such distinctions all the time (albeit sloppily). Yet the force of Mandeville's insights remains: contemporary writers suspect that luxury is undefinable and his intuition about the industrious hive is the foundation for the sense that modern economics invalidates ancient critiques of luxury because luxury proves to be economically beneficial for society as a whole.[100]

Mandeville can be read as a satirist, and it appears he is utilizing the satirist's tendency to point to hypocrisy in making his case. As Selby-Bigge writes, "If anyone takes them [Mandeville's paradoxes] seriously and literally[,] nothing but a stick will do him much good."[101] But Jennifer Herdt places him within an emerging "moral Anatomist" position that "achieves a superior position of honesty" by demonstrating the hypocrisy of all claims about public virtue. As she notes: "Ordinarily, satire ridicules vice and folly in order to stimulate moral reform. Mandeville's satire does not fit into this mold."[102] Instead, Mandeville is much more rigorously illustrating that the civic republican tradition is mistaken in its critique that public greatness proceeds from the ancient virtues.[103] As he says in "the moral" to his fable: "Fools only strive To make a Great an' Honest Hive T' enjoy the world's Conveniences, Be fam 'd in War, yet live in Ease, Without great Vices, is a vain Eutopia seated in the brain. Fraud, Luxury, and Pride must live While we the benefits receive" (36).

Many of his contemporaries also took Mandeville's image quite seriously as an extreme option that, like Hobbes, needed to be combatted somehow. Defending luxury was still an extreme position. In response to this belief in human selfishness, which at the time was largely based on appeals to the goodness of the divine design of the world and of human beings, moralists turned "to the plain man's experience of disinterested benevolent affections."[104] For Francis Hutcheson, Adam Smith's mentor, "Mandeville was an obsession," and Hutcheson published a series of articles refuting Mandeville.[105] At times Hutcheson simply mocks Mandeville, but he also insists that proper morality means regulating "our desires of every kind by forming just opinions of the real value of their several objects." He further claims that all see pleasurable goods as subordinate to "kind affections to our fellow creatures, gratitude and love to the Deity, submission to his will, and trust in his providence."[106] Hutcheson charges that Mandeville only makes his case by changing the accepted meaning of terms. Luxury, Hutcheson says, is *not* everything above the barest necessities, but rather is "the using of more curious and expensive habitation, dress, table, equipage, than the person's wealth will bear, so as to discharge his duty to his family, his friends, his country, or the indigent."[107] Anyone (i.e., Mandeville) who attempts such changes in meaning must want to confuse ordinary people so that "they will lose their aversion to moral evil in general and imagine it well compensated by some of its advantages."[108]

Adam Smith's Puzzle as Our Own Puzzle

From both his friend David Hume (a chief defender of luxury, as will be shown) and his mentor, Francis Hutcheson, Adam Smith heard about luxury. It seems he did not quite know what to think.[109] His work acutely articulates the conundrum he inherited, for it expresses the idea that the self-interested search for wealth and possessions is a natural thing, is quite good for society . . . and yet at the same time, a deception in terms of the true good for humans.

Smith *was* clear that Hobbes and Mandeville had gotten it wrong. In surveying systems of moral philosophy, Smith devotes pages to refuting the "offensive" and "odious" doctrines of "Mr. Hobbes" and the "licentious system" of "Dr. Mandeville," which "though perhaps it never gave occasion to more vice than what would have been without it, at least taught that vice . . . to appear with more effrontery and to avow the corruption of its motives with a profligate audaciousness which had never been heard of before."[110] He follows Hutcheson in suggesting that one of the problems with Mandeville's system is the "ingenious sophistry of his reasoning . . . covered by the ambiguity of language," for "everything, according to him, is luxury which exceeds what is absolutely necessary for the support of human nature, so that there is vice even in the use of a clean shirt or of a convenient habitation."[111]

Smith's own moral system emphasized the twin "virtues of sensibility and self-command."[112] The first allows us to enter into others' sentiments, thus increasing our sympathy and fellow-feeling with others; the second allows us to diminish the attachment to our own sentiments, modulating them to the level appropriate for an "impartial spectator."[113] "To feel much for others and little for ourselves, . . . to restrain our selfish, and to indulge our benevolent affections, constitutes the perfection of human nature."[114] He goes on to claim that while our sympathy with others in their sorrow is "more universal," our sympathy in their joy is more genuine: "Our sorrow at a funeral generally amounts to no more than an affected gravity; but our mirth at a christening or a marriage, is always from the heart, and without any affectation."[115] Moreover, when we see someone deeply "sunk in sorrow and dejection" we are apt to "despise him" ("unjustly, perhaps," he adds) and will have to work to overcome our aversion. Smith concludes that "Nature" has "loaded us with our own sorrows" and does not "command us to take any further share in those of others, than what was necessary to relieve them."[116]

Smith's puzzling attitude toward wealth and riches proceeds from this analysis of joy and sorrow; it is from our disposition "to sympathize more entirely with our joy than with our sorrow that we make parade of our riches and conceal our poverty."[117] While "the rich man glories in his riches, . . . the poor man is ashamed of his poverty" and is "mortified." The poor man naturally hides, for when he appears among the rich they "spurn

so disagreeable an object" and "wonder at the insolence of human wretch-
edness that it should dare to present itself before them."[118] Smith makes
frequent assumptions that the shame felt by the poor is appropriate—a far
cry from the holy poverty of medieval beggars.[119]

This admiration of wealth and riches and embarrassment over poverty
has marvelous effects: "Upon this disposition . . . to go along with all the
passions of the rich" is the basis for "the distinction of ranks and the order
of society." We eagerly follow those who are wealthy and we even feel bad
when they are in pain or suffering. Moreover, the public admiration for
the wealthy is also the spur of all ambition to enterprise: "the poor man's
son . . . admires the condition of the rich" and their "numberless artificial
and elegant contrivances for promoting [their] ease and pleasure . . . how
everything is adapted to promote their ease."[120] He avows that "it is well
that nature imposes upon us in this manner," for "it is this deception which
rouses and keeps in continual motion the industry of mankind."[121] Indeed,
such a "palace," with "all the different baubles and trinkets," requires so
much labor that the rich are "led by an invisible hand to make nearly the
same distribution of the necessaries of life which would have been made
had the earth been divided into equal portions among all its inhabitants."[122]

Why, then, is Smith puzzled? Despite all these claims about how much
we admire and pursue wealth, he has termed all of this a "deception."
Immediately prior to this invisible hand passage, Smith claims that people
who lay out money for "trinkets of frivolous utility" actually "ruin themselves," and his story of the ambitious poor man's son is actually a caution-
ary tale in which the son wastes his life and sacrifices "a real tranquility
that is at all times in his power" for "a certain artificial and elegant repose
which he may never arrive at" because these "mere trinkets of frivolous
utility . . . [are] no more adapted for procuring ease of body or tranquility
than the tweezer-cases of the lover of toys."[123] While "necessary for the
order of society," our disposition to admire the rich and successful and "to
despise, or at least to neglect persons of poor and mean condition . . . [is]
at the same time, the greatest and most universal cause of the corruption
of our moral sentiments."[124] Real greatness comes not from these outward
things, but from "wisdom and virtue," despite the fact that "the great mob
of mankind" are "worshippers of wealth and greatness."[125]

So, will the real Adam Smith please stand up? Even in *The Wealth of
Nations* Smith displays this deep ambivalence about luxury. On the one
hand he is forced to admit that luxury not only exists but also leads to
important social benefits. On the other hand he subjects it to much criticism, indicating that it is a weak and impoverishing substitute for building

a nation's "productive stock." The wise man is prudent and frugal, not luxurious, because prudence and frugality engender more development of the means of production.

Smith's puzzle is our own puzzle. We don't quite know whether it is good or bad to gaze on the lifestyles of the rich and famous. We pursue much comfort and convenience for ourselves and our families, believing that we are "helping the economy," yet we recoil at the excesses of celebrities and even those a couple steps above our own location on the economic ladder. We live in a society where achieving one's desired lifestyle seems to be a major motive for industry, and yet we continually tell ourselves cultural stories about how love, family, and friends are so much more important than work and possessions. A similar ambivalence may mark our reaction to the poor and suffering. Most people genuinely want to help those in need, and this spirit is on view most strongly in the response to natural disasters. Yet many also feel the aversion to the poor that Smith describes: we may wish them to conceal their poverty, as we ourselves would, out of shame, and we become unwilling to enter sympathetically, with compassion, into their experience.

Our conflicted response to luxury—is it a problem or a natural desire?—is a legacy of history. Our ancient cultural and religious heritage does not quite mesh with our economic practices and the dispositions we've learned from them. Smith's account shows how difficult it was, even by the late eighteenth century, to retain the ancient critique of luxury. In particular, Smith wrestled with two meanings of "natural": what we ordinarily do in society, and what we ought to do if we follow nature. Smith is half Stoic philosopher, half social scientist. We need to sort through this conflict, first focusing on the philosophical language for understanding what "virtue" might mean, and then reviving a Christian, sacramental language for understanding the conflict between our view of luxury and our view of the God Who is manifest in the poor Jesus Christ.

Luxury: Vice or Virtue?

Smith was not the only eighteenth-century figure who sought some way to contain the excessive potential of the pursuit of luxury. John Shovlin outlines a similar trajectory in eighteenth-century French discourse, in which "Enlightenment apologists for luxury" gained ground in the early part of the century, led by the defense of luxury penned by J.-F. Melon in 1734. Melon claimed that luxury spurred "effort and industry" and destroyed "crude vices" like drunkenness.[126] His effort to defend luxury met an increasing backlash in the latter half of the century, and luxury came to be identified with the "unreal wealth" of merchants and financiers as opposed to the "real wealth" generated by honest trades, especially agriculture. Echoing Socrates, Helvetius compared the *apparent* wealth generated by luxury to "those violent fevers" which confer a short-lived "astonishing strength" only to leave the man much weaker in the long run.[127] The economic collapse that immediately preceded the French Revolution gave credence to this view. The leading French philosopher of the century, Jean-Jacques Rousseau, maintained a severe critique of luxury as epitomizing the destructive effects of *amour-propre* at work in typical society. Rousseau criticizes the rise of luxury by noting that "refinement and politeness" become esteemed over genuine virtue; work is degraded for the poor, while the rich are weakened by the introduction of false, artificial "needs."[128] Dennis Carl Rasmussen notes Adam Smith agrees with Rousseau that "money really can't buy happiness and that the endless pursuit of wealth in fact tends to detract from people's happiness," yet Smith maintains (in his correspondence with Rousseau) that commercial society is better for development, security, and especially liberty than any alternative.[129]

Hirschman notes that some proponents of the civic republican tradition, notably Adam Ferguson in Scotland and Alexis de Tocqueville in France, were not persuaded by Smith's consequentialist argument that the pursuit of self-interest supports political liberty. Quite the contrary: they worried that a focus on one's own affairs opens the door to a neglect of public affairs and even to a despotism that is accepted so long as it promises to protect one's possessions.[130] Ferguson in particular is an important figure who continues to see luxury as a central problem for modern political life. Given our concerns about Smith's portrayal of the poor, it is notable that Ferguson speaks quite differently about the poor. He suggests that serious problems occur "if the disparities of rank and fortune which are necessary to the pursuit or enjoyment of luxury introduce false grounds of precedency and estimation" or if "the mere consideration of being rich or poor" makes people think themselves "elevated" and others "debased."[131] More specifically, he posits that the belief that being poor is a "disgrace" and a "debasement," and that "eminence" is connected to "fortune" (rather than to virtue) leads ultimately to "the desertion of every duty" and "the commission of every crime."[132] The admiration of riches and abhorrence of the poor is not, as Smith put it, a "useful illusion." In fact, it encourages the destruction of society by leading the wealthy to abandon duties of justice in order to procure or protect their luxuries.

Thus, for many in the eighteenth century luxury remained a vice, although with considerably more contestation and ambivalence. Today, despite our aforementioned everyday worries about excessive wealth, the ambivalence manifested in the late eighteenth-century debates over luxury has largely disappeared from the disciplines of ethics and economics, for two chief reasons. First, the philosophical triumph of Hume and the subsequent emergence of utilitarianism meant that the fragile basis on which the luxury critique still rested—that is, some sense of a "higher" or more noble vision of the good life being animated especially by a sense of civic virtue—has faded away. Like the Machiavellian theories of basing the state on self-interest, Hume openly sought to ground philosophy on the way things actually are, not on some theory about how they ought to be: "it is full time" to "reject every system of ethics, however subtle or ingenious, which is not founded on fact and observation."[133]

Second, while thinkers such as Smith maintained the theological belief in God's ordering behind "the invisible hand," the nineteenth century brought forth both an exclusive humanist confidence in human-reforming activity (the Victorians, John Stuart Mill) and a darker view of the natural order (Charles Darwin, Herbert Spencer), both of which made the appeals to benevolent divine mechanism implausible or impossible.[134] As R. H. Tawney notes, the ultimate disappearance of the God-argument for a self-interested economy displayed how inessential the argument from providential order was; instead, the true basis for the self-interest-driven economy was always the notion that "economic rights are anterior to and independent of economic functions, that they stand by their own virtue and need adduce no higher credentials."[135] Tawney's point is that when appeals to the supposed providential social benefits of economic self-interest fail in practice, proponents ultimately fall back into a position where the possession of goods confers a (virtually) absolute right to private use. There are no virtues of liberality and no vices of meanness . . . or luxury. All that remains is "my property." The ancient virtues and vices assume some given function of property for person, household, society, and cosmos. If Tawney is correct, a modern critique of luxury would strike at the very heart of the "acquisitive society". . . if reasonable philosophical and theological bases for the critique can be articulated. This will be the task of the next two chapters.

However, as important as these philosophical and theological changes were in the gradual acceptance of luxury and the disappearance of its critique, the emergence of the modern science of economics also played a powerful role. By gradually separating itself from the classical political economy of a Rousseau or a Ferguson, economics increasingly took as axiomatic the idea that the pursuit of self-interest was simply the way the world worked and was generally for the best. F. B. Kaye argues that Mandeville's argument for "the harmlessness and necessity of luxury" over-against ancient ideals and "ascetic codes," was extremely important—surpassing all previous defenses and providing material for further eighteenth-century defenses[136]—but it remained for the emergent economic science to develop a "scientific" account of Mandeville's insight. Therefore we must also engage the historical evolution of these economic models lest a critique of luxury in terms of virtue ethics and sacramental theology risk avoiding this "damning drawback." The coincidence of self-interest and social welfare turns out to be much more complicated than Mandeville's fable about it.

Notes

1. Martin, *Jesuit Guide*, 195.
2. Ibid., 194.
3. Berry, *Idea of Luxury*, 45. The book, while slim on Christian resources, is the best available study.
4. Liddell and Scott, *Intermediate Greek-English Lexicon*, 822.
5. Berry, *Idea of Luxury*, 47.
6. Ancient criticisms are always posed in the context of a wealthy social elite that constitute a small sliver of the overall population. A contemporary casuistry of luxury will have to consider this difference.
7. Plato, *Republic*, 372d. Further line references in text.
8. Aristotle, *Politics*, bk. 1, chaps. 8–9.
9. In the *Eudemian Ethics* Aristotle offers a list of virtues (1220b–1221a) as means, including excesses like gain (which is contrary to justice), lavishness, and extravagance, as well as "luxuriousness." In this case luxury is contrasted to "submission to evils," with the meaning being the virtue of endurance. As Berry notes, Aristotle here accentuates the sense of luxury as a problem of "softness," therefore aligning it more closely with what we typically now think of as fortitude (*Idea of Luxury*, 58).
10. Some in the ancient world saw *luxuria* as a self-curing disease among the wealthy. See Wallace-Hadrill, *Rome's Cultural Revolution*, 332.
11. Irwin, *Development of Ethics*, 285–87.
12. Berry, *Idea of Luxury*, 64–70.
13. Wallace-Hadrill, *Rome's Cultural Revolution*, 338–39.
14. Thurow, *Future of Capitalism*, 15.
15. Augustine, *City of God*, 35 (bk. 1, chap. 30).
16. Cicero, *Offices*, 458–59 (book 1, chap. 7). On Cicero, who then assumes greed follows from luxury, see Sekora, *Luxury*, 35.
17. Berry, *Idea of Luxury*, 72.

18. Skidelsky, *How Much Is Enough?*, 71. They also cite literature from ancient traditions in China and India.
19. See the many fine overviews of biblical and patristic teachings on possessions, including Blomberg, *Neither Poverty Nor Riches*; Wheeler, *Wealth as Peril and Obligation*; Hengel, *Property and Riches*; J. Gonzalez, *Faith and Wealth*; and L. T. Johnson, *Sharing Possessions*.
20. For a fine, comprehensive overview of Old Testament law on wealth and property, see Baker, *Tight Fists or Open Hands?* While the OT canon does not have things like sumptuary laws (partly because it is oriented to a small, agrarian society), the prophets make clear that the state of affairs of disobeying the law is rooted in and manifests what would be called luxury. Indeed, OT law can be seen as a systematic attempt to prevent the accumulation of excess wealth.
21. For the relationship of almsgiving and idolatry in later Hebrew literature, see Anderson, *Charity*.
22. Blomberg, *Neither Poverty Nor Riches*, 242. See also Wheeler, *Wealth as Peril and Obligation*, 133–34.
23. For further details, see Freisen, "Injustice or God's Will?," which notes James as a critique of the rich who squander gains on self-indulgence (26).
24. Rhee, *Loving the Poor Saving the Rich*, xx.
25. See Rhee, "Wealth, Poverty, and Eschatology."
26. Rhee, *Loving the Poor*, 170. Clement's discourse is relatively mild compared to many of the earlier apocalyptic judgments on riches and wealth. See, for example, Rhee, *Loving the Poor*, 57, on 6 Ezra.
27. Hengel, *Property and Riches*.
28. Prudentius, "Psychomachia," 301.
29. Ibid., 303.
30. Ibid., 305–9.
31. Ibid., 315.
32. Ibid., 317–19.
33. Sekora, *Luxury*, 48.
34. Cicero, "Pro Sexto Roscio Amerino," 188–89. Wallace-Hadrill comments that Cicero is offering "a choice between two models of social dignity" (*Rome's Cultural Revolution*, 355).
35. Livy, "Book 34," 420–21.
36. Berry, *Idea of Luxury*, 67–68. On Sallust, see also Sekora, who links it strongly to the problem of the bounty of war (36).
37. For another example of distinguishing greed and "wicked luxury," see Rhee's comments on Hermas in *Loving the Poor*, 61.
38. MacIntyre, *Whose Justice?*, 111.
39. Ibid., 112.
40. In the *Eudemian Ethics* he connects "the grasper" with one who seeks "disgraceful gain" and is ready "to accept anything" (1232a). Elsewhere, the man who is "greedy of gain" is one "who makes profit from any source" (1221a). The sense here is that *pleonexia* involves a misjudgment about occasions of "gain."
41. Hauerwas, *Working with Words*, 131.
42. "Five Families, Five Fixes," *Money* (January-February 2011), 80–87.
43. See especially Wolf, *Fixing Global Finance*.

44. Wallace-Hadrill suggests this as a main reason for a pullback from a legislative approach to luxury in first-century Rome, though the pullback from a legislative approach did not mean a pullback from the moral critique, which continued (*Rome's Cultural Revolution*, 330–31).
45. For an explanation of a consumer society centered on detachment see Cavanaugh, "Consumer Culture."
46. Lewis, *New New Thing*.
47. Novatian, "On the Jewish Meats."
48. See, for example, *Moralia*, bk. 31, chap. 45.
49. Bloomfield, *Seven Deadly Sins*, 59–60, 69–71.
50. Ibid., 72–73. Isidore uses libido as synonymous with luxury (77). For a detailed recent study of this complex transformation, see McDaniel, "Pride Goes Before," 107–8.
51. Bossy, "Moral Arithmetic."
52. All texts are from the versions available on the German Bible Society website, http://www.academic-bible.com/en/online-bibles/about-the-online-bibles/.
53. See Graeber, *Debt*, 251–52, 282–86. Graeber notes that the disappearance of coinage is taken too readily as evidence for the disappearance of economic trade and activity; rather, he suggests the medieval serf, while not free, was at least not enslaved to feed massive cities and existed within an informal system of credit and debt strongly limited by the teachings against usury.
54. Aquinas, *Summa Theologica* II–II, 153, 1.
55. ST II–II, 153, 1, resp. 2. In II–II, 153, 3, he uses the Vulgate version of Eph. 5:18: "Be not drunk with wine wherein there is lust [luxuria]," reinforcing this connection.
56. See "Luxury" in *The Oxford English Dictionary Online*; http://dictionary.oed.com.
57. ST I–II, 2, 1, resp. 3.
58. An excellent summary of the centrality of this distinction for Aquinas's economic thought in conversation with modern economics is Hirschfeld, "Standards of Living and Economic Virtue."
59. ST II–II, 78, 1.
60. Wood, *Medieval Economic Thought*, 159–83.
61. Hervaeus's text is cited here only to give an example that judgments that in effect mirrored the ancient luxury critique continued to the Middle Ages, even if the specific word had been lost. It is not meant to give an adequate overview of the complex controversy over mendicant poverty.
62. Hervaeus Natalis, *Poverty of Christ*, 55. Further citations in text.
63. The context for this debate was quite distant from any application in day-to-day life. In chap. 3 we will note how such debates presume a two-level ethic of holiness and one that has increasingly been surpassed in contemporary Catholic teaching
64. See Killerby, *Sumptuary Law in Italy*.
65. For the persistence of the critique of luxury throughout Renaissance political literature see Skinner, *Foundations of Modern Political Thought*, 1:42, 149, 162, 170, 175, 276.
66. Wood, *Medieval Economic Thought*, 46–52, here 49.

67. Skinner, *Foundations of Modern Political Thought*, 42.
68. Ibid., 222.
69. Ibid., 163.
70. Pocock, *Machiavellian Moment*, 135. Pocock reminds us that Machiavelli himself and many others regarded Guicciardini as "the only political intellect of a stature approaching his" (121).
71. Skinner, *Foundations of Modern Political Thought*, 226.
72. Hillerbrand, *Division of Christendom*, 428.
73. Chadwick, *Reformation*, 18–19.
74. Hillerbrand, *Division of Christendom*.
75. Chadwick, *Reformation*, 182–83.
76. Wogaman, *Christian Ethics*, 121.
77. Calvin, *Institutes of the Christian Religion*, bk. 3, chap. 10, p. 5.
78. Wogaman, *Christian Ethics*, 124–25.
79. Hillerbrand, *Division of Christendom*, 428.
80. Skinner, *Foundations of Modern Political Thought*, 181.
81. Ibid., 184.
82. On Machiavelli and others as key transitional figures to a new way of thinking about politics as a skillful manipulation of peaceful "interests," see Hirschman, *Passions and the Interests*.
83. Sekora, *Luxury*, 1. Sekora's history, though informative, is marred by the presumption that the critique of luxury is reducible to the maintenance of social class and status.
84. Wallace-Hadrill, *Rome's Cultural Revolution*, 319. He notes that Montesquieu's 1734 essay might be the last serious use of the luxury critique in Rome, and later Montesquieu was converted.
85. Hirschman, *Passions and the Interests*, 32.
86. Ibid., 41.
87. Ibid., 50.
88. Ibid., 70, 81.
89. Taylor, *Secular Age*, 221–98.
90. On the significant power the Dutch example held for the early modern economists, see Appleby, *Economic Thought and Ideology*, which contains an entire chapter entitled "The Dutch as a Source of Evidence."
91. De Vries, *Industrious Revolution*, 59.
92. Ibid., 59.
93. The multitude of details that were revolutionizing the European situation in this age are summarized in Appleby, *Relentless Revolution*.
94. Selby-Bigge, *British Moralists*, xii.
95. Seventeenth-century English history featured a constant stream of massive disruption and war, from the 1630s through to the Glorious Revolution of 1688 against the Catholic King James by the Dutch William of Orange. By contrast, note that the eighteenth century featured almost no wars, only a couple of easily repelled invasions, and political stability.
96. MacIntyre, *Short History of Ethics*, 132.
97. Mandeville, *Fable of the Bees*, 24. Further references in text.

98. De Vries, *Industrious Revolution*, 61–62. Note also that the pro-Dutch position would have been viewed very positively by backers of the Revolution of 1688, whereas Scottish positions would not have (James was Scottish).
99. Both ideas have parallels in the texts of John Locke.
100. One further complication, which we cannot engage here, is that Mandeville and Smith both mounted arguments against emerging mercantilist economic thought. Mercantilists, preoccupied with maintaining a favorable trade balance to gain bullion, saw luxury and especially "imported luxury" as very bad. The fact that mercantilists were wrong about trade need not mean they were wrong about luxury, but at the time it would have been very difficult to disentangle the arguments.
101. Selby-Bigge, *British Moralists*, xv.
102. Herdt, *Putting on Virtue*, 268–69.
103. Ibid., 224–25, 271. She notes here that his work represents a defense of "courtly civility" being transferred to emerging bourgeois life.
104. Selby-Bigge, *British Moralists*, xiii. On appeals to the benevolence of divine design, again recall Charles Taylor's "providential deism."
105. Mandeville, *Fable of the Bees*, cxli; Hutcheson, *Thoughts on Laughter*, which was originally published anonymously in 1724–26.
106. Ibid., 64.
107. Ibid., 80–81.
108. Ibid., 86.
109. For an excellent new study of Smith's ambivalence and its significance for Christian ethics, see McRorie, "Adam Smith, Ethicist."
110. Smith, *Theory of Moral Sentiments*, 318, 313.
111. Ibid., 312. It is interesting that Smith takes this straight from Hutcheson, his teacher, and that Hutcheson's reply to Mandeville also contains a *defense* of a division of labor and of trade, which sound strikingly like Smith's.
112. Ibid., 25.
113. Ibid., 23, 139. Smith's "impartial spectator" is his version of prudence, built on the analogy that we are able to compare things best when we view them from "nearly equal distances and thereby form some judgment of their real proportions" (135). He also seems to equate this idea with the term "conscience."
114. Ibid., 25.
115. Ibid., 43, 47.
116. Ibid., 47.
117. Ibid., 50.
118. Ibid., 50–51.
119. On this point I am indebted to an unpublished paper by Kate Ward on Adam Smith and the poor.
120. Ibid., 181–82.
121. Ibid., 183.
122. Ibid., 184–85. This is the actual context—of two occasions—in which Smith first uses the image of the invisible hand. I thank Daniel Finn for pointing out that a third instance does occur in a treatise on astronomy, where he claims that a moon of Jupiter is held "by the invisible hand of Jupiter."

123. Ibid., 180–81.

124. Ibid., 61.

125. Ibid., 62.

126. Shovlin, *Political Economy of Virtue*, 23.

127. Helvetius, *De l'esprit*, quoted in Shovlin, 13.

128. Rasmussen, *Problems and Promise of Commercial Society*, 28–29.

129. Ibid., 132.

130. See Hirschman, *Passions and the Interests*, 121–23. On Ferguson see also Arbo, *Political Vanity*.

131. Ferguson, *Essay on the History of Civil Society*, 289.

132. Ibid., 292–93.

133. Hume, *Enquiry*, 28.

134. See Taylor, *Secular Age*.

135. Tawney, *Acquisitive Society*, 28.

136. See Mandeville, *Fable of the Bees*, cxxxv–cxxxix.

CHAPTER 2

The Neglected Vice

How Luxury Degrades Us, Our Work,
and Our Communities

In order to understand how luxury is a significant moral vice, we must engage closely the question of how virtues and vices are identified. The goal here is not to argue that luxury is somehow the *worst* vice but rather that luxury is a *neglected* vice. We need to understand why we've neglected it, what we lose when we do, and how we might recover it.

We begin by identifying an impasse, between critics of "the goods life,"[1] which is understood as "an excessive availability of every kind of material goods" in the words of John Paul II,[2] and defenders of consumer society, who see it as economically beneficial and democratically liberating (and who see the critics of luxury as elitists attempting to impose their preferences on others). What's interesting about this debate is that both sides obviously think key ethical issues are at stake. Is *pursuing* the goods life "immoral," or is *critiquing* it "immoral"?

The discussion proceeds in three parts, examining the impoverishment of our ethical language in relation to consumption. The first part explores recent literature in "happiness studies"—specifically, their apparent confirmation that multiplying possessions does not lead to happiness. The findings are important, but they get stuck between a moral logic of utilitarianism that simply sees activity as instrumental to "happiness" and a moral commitment to liberal autonomy that precludes following through on the findings. These studies need a better description of practical reasoning in relationship to consumption. The second part builds this description through a comparison of the contrasting pictures of the luxury life in

David Hume and Thorstein Veblen. Their comparison demonstrates that the moral language of luxury requires what Charles Taylor calls "strong evaluation," especially in relation to work and leisure. Finally, in the third part, the writings of Alasdair MacIntyre on social practices will allow the development of a more precise way to strongly evaluate dispositions (virtues and vices) in order to display the real harm of luxury as a disposition: it undermines practices by conflating internal and external goods.

The chapter concludes in stepping back to show that the contemporary identification of luxury as a vice is significant for two audiences. On the one hand, critics of consumerism often lack the needed ethical precision in making their critiques, and thus leave themselves open to the countercharges of elitism. On the other hand, moral philosophers and theologians who practice virtue ethics have attended carefully to these issues of practical reason but have tended to overlook the viciousness of luxury consumption.

Does the Goods Life Lead to Happiness?

Debating the Goods Life

At least since 1989, with the fall of communism and "the end of history," a certain model of the good society has reigned supreme.[3] Brad Gregory dubs this now-dominant worldview "the goods life." As Gregory explains: "Amid the hyperpluralism of divergent truth claims, metaphysical beliefs, moral values, and life priorities, ubiquitous practices of consumerism are more than anything else the cultural glue that holds Western societies together."[4] These practices assume that "whatever their beliefs about the Life Questions," people "will want more and better stuff" and that "endless acquisition is the highway to human happiness" (236–37). This "cycle of acquire, discard, repeat now makes up the default fabric of Western life" (235), and he suggests that such acquisition should be as unimpeded as possible, particularly by concern for anyone else but ourselves (or, perhaps, our immediate family). The "fundamental cultural assumption" is "that if we have the money or the credit, we are entitled to have as much as we want of whatever we want, when we want it and without obstruction or delay" (240). Gregory's history shows that, while greed and acquisitiveness are as old as humankind, the uniform teaching on the dangerous nature of money and possessions shared by the Scholastics and Reformers constituted a kind of "ethical brake" (262).[5] This brake was gradually but almost totally lost through a series of transformations supporting "the widespread social acceptance among Christians of the counter-biblical notion that the goods life was the good life" (261). Two key transitions leading to this acceptance were the Reformers' detachment of the Christian life from a "teleological virtue ethic" (in favor of an ethics based on the gracious response to God's work) and their "hyper-Augustinian" descriptions of "the insuperable forces of the passions or affections, and the helplessness of human beings to master them" (271). The loss of virtue and the shift to the affections leaves the door wide open for an ethics based on personal desires detached from any given end. This is the reign of "whatever you want, whenever you want it."

But is Gregory's critique accurate? Do people really single-mindedly pursue the endless accumulation of possessions above all else, or does Gregory exaggerate? Furthermore, is our society really in uniform agreement on this point? Writers have met this kind of criticism of consumption with accusations of elitism. Look around, they say: we seem to have built a pretty good world. The pursuit of personal consumption seems to spin off plenty of social good: wealthier countries have less crime, have done more to fix the environment, and do not degenerate into ethnic or religious violence. Contemporary advocates of luxury like James Twitchell chide critics of consumerism as elitist and claim that luxury "is strangely democratic and unifying. If what you want is peace on earth . . . well, whoops, here it is!"[6] If identity and meaning are created through consumption, then they are (theoretically) available to all: "You can buy things. You can't buy ancestry, religious affiliation, or the number of vowels in your name."[7] Consumerism democratizes access to meaning and personal identity and thus is superior to hierarchical systems of social order. The goods life is also "gentle": Gary Cross's study of "the all-consuming century" notes consumerism's shortcomings but admits that "the understanding of self in society through goods has provided on balance a more dynamic and popular while less destructive ideology of public life than most political belief systems of the twentieth century."[8] Deirdre McCloskey, in defending the virtues of the new order, concludes that "our nostalgia for precommercial virtues has been disastrous."[9]

James Livingston's recent polemic, *Against Thrift*, is an excellent representation of this anti-Gregory, pro-consumption position. Livingston argues that "we've reached the point where we have to confront our fears about consumer culture, because the renunciation of desire, the deferral of gratification, saving for a rainy day—call it what you want—has become dangerous to our health. To heal ourselves, we need to spend more freely, to live less anxiously, more easily and generously."[10] Half of Livingston's case is built on economic claims that spending benefits the social order. But the other half is a defense of consumerism as a morally superior democratization of meaning and is especially aimed at showing that consumption "doesn't siphon political energies" but instead "grounds a new politics by animating both new solidarities and new individualities."[11] Consistent with the antipopulist tone of his earlier history of late nineteenth-century American ideas, Livingston calls into question the implied assumption behind Gregory's description of the goods life as shallow and at the mercy of advertisers. [12] Livingston instead extols advertising as "the last utopian idiom."[13] He calls for transcendence beyond "the poiesis of production" in favor of new, creative ways of understanding sociality in a consumer society whose possibilities are "blocked" by "the critique of consumer culture and its intellectual antecedents."[14] Here Livingston extends the "democratization of meaning" claim in a less individualistic direction. It is not just that consumer society allows individuals to freely and creatively construct and reconstruct their identities. This very process creates and sustains human solidarities, which are better than solidarities based on nation or religion or tribe.

How are we to adjudicate these claims? Gregory uses the term "ethical brake" to describe what we've lost on the way to the goods life: "So long as enough acquisitive men and women acknowledged their avarice and vanity as sins . . . an ethical brake remained on the formation of a market-based, capitalist society" (261–62). The image of a brake is both helpful—insofar as it expresses moderation rather than a complete rejection of market society—yet misleading. The story told by consumption defenders has obvious truth; Gregory admits that the modern order produces many benefits he would not want to lose.[15] Indeed, many defenders of market economies are keen to differentiate their defense from a simple endorsement of selfish greed: they too want some kind of ethical brake.[16] For example, McCloskey, a strong advocate of the market, insists nevertheless that "economics has lost its ethical bearings."[17] The problem is that, unlike "the blessed Smith," many economists think of only prudence instead of "a balanced set of virtues." She goes on: "You can't run on prudence alone a family or a church or a community or a foreign policy or even—and this is the surprising point—a capitalist economy. . . . Prudent, economical, market-oriented, capitalist behavior within a balanced set of virtues is not merely harmless—it is virtuous . . . . By contrast, the prudence-only behavior celebrated in economic fable is bad. Bad for business. Bad for life. Bad for the soul. We call it avarice."[18]

Our concern here, however, is that the language of ethical brake betrays a tendency to regard ethics as necessary but *external* to ordinary economic activity. This problematic tendency to externalize ethics is the key to our analysis. Externalizing inevitably leaves critiques of luxury open to rejection as elitist, class-driven moralizing. Andrew Wallace-Hadrill notes that "Modern historians of Rome have found little attraction in the theme of luxury and moral decline," and thus we must ask, "*why it is so self-evident to us* that Roman moralizing discourse was misplaced. . . . When a set of thoughts and a way of thinking that appears self-evidently true to one society then seems self-evidently false to another[;] it becomes interesting to enquire into what has changed at such a deep layer within the culture and the assumptions on which it rests that the rejection becomes automatic and unthinking" (emphasis added).[19] Wallace-Hadrill concurs with John Sekora's major study of luxury in eighteenth-century Britain, that the real issue is not luxury, but class: "The critique of luxury goes hand in hand with a society of rank and hierarchy formally defined by the state. Abandonment of that critique also spells abandonment of a society defined by rank."[20] The Romans were wrong to see luxury as a moral problem, but we can learn that "a society which regards luxury as a central concern is likely to be using it to articulate important concerns about order."[21] Notice Wallace-Hadrill's notion of "using it"—the implication is that some other issue, not luxury, is really what the discourse is about. An "ethical brake" (because it is external) can be seen as a similar attempt by particular social elites to maintain an anti-democratic but unsustainable social order. Notice the similarities to the accusation that critics of consumerism are really anti-democratic elitists who are simply trying to reinforce their place in an unstable social hierarchy. This happens when luxury is used in external ways reflective of cultural order maintenance.

But how would we demonstrate that considering luxury a vice *is* a reasonable moral concern and not just an indirect imposition of class preferences? How do we come to see certain issues about social order as truly "moral" (e.g., democratic egalitarianism) while others are dismissed (e.g., luxury)? Obviously we have a very interesting and difficult question of ethical language here. For the case against luxury to overcome claims that it is merely elitist, it cannot merely cry foul from *outside* the economic game; to show the viciousness of luxury it must engage the practical reasoning necessarily internal to economic activity.

Happiness Studies: Findings and Limits

Where should we look to adjudicate this dispute about "the goods life"? Being moderns, we will begin our search by "trying to find data." One promising site for gathering data on whether a life devoted to unlimited acquisition can be good is the burgeoning field of empirical work known as "happiness studies." While the revival of the language of happiness nods toward Aristotle, its real basis is experimental data on the relationship of life satisfaction (happiness) to various events, pursuits, activities, and the like.[22]

Does pursuing the goods life make people happy, according to these studies? As one author summarizes, "The currently available data suggest that among the truly poor, the relationship between income and happiness is moderately strong. Once one's basic needs have been met, the relationship between income and happiness continues to be measureable but becomes extremely small, and of negligible practical significance."[23] Some studies go further and correlate excessive materialism with unhappiness.[24] While happiness studies do lend some support for a critique of luxury, they run into the limits of our moral language in two ways: one, their utilitarian approach to happiness leads them to look at individual actions as instrumental to *outcomes* rather than to focus on the deeper moral problem of *dispositions*; and, two, they face a difficulty whenever their findings seem to come into conflict with the dominant language of liberalism and autonomy. In both these ways they end up unable to avoid the "latent moral vacuum" that is the political foundation of the goods life.

We see both the promise and the problems of happiness studies in a recent attempt to integrate philosophy and economics. The biographer of the economist John Maynard Keynes, Robert Skidelsky, teamed up with his son, a philosopher, to argue that Aristotle's guidance is needed in order to answer the question of their book's title: *How Much Is Enough?* The Skidelskys' book claims that we have not realized Keynes's vision of economic abundance because we have "lost the moral language to describe what the good life really is."[25] This necessary moral language is that of the Aristotelian tradition, and in particular the recognition that desire for gain threatens to subordinate every other human activity to itself and thus requires language that critiques insatiability.[26] They seek to articulate the language needed if there is to be an alternative to "an ethic of acquisitiveness, which dooms societies to continuous, objectless wealth-creation."[27]

In getting to that language they survey the findings of the happiness literature. What does create happiness? While the studies are not unanimous, Daniel Nettle summarizes some pretty clear findings: relationships and "social embeddedness matter most, as do certain other day-to-day factors: health, autonomy, and quality of physical environment."[28] It turns out that most of us do not adjust to chronic noise and chronic pain all that easily, nor to a constant sense of being controlled by others.[29] Of course, wealth and social class can affect these factors. Members of higher social classes (when social class is correlated to occupation) tend to be happier. But when variables are controlled, it appears that benefits of being in a higher class are the outgrowth of others' deference to higher status, higher work flexibility, and other benefits of the type of occupation, rather than the greater income.[30] The "striking and consistent finding" of the literature is that once grinding national poverty is overcome, collective national economic growth (measured in GDP) does not lead to more happy people.[31] In explaining our misjudgment about the promise of economic growth, Bill McKibben offers a classic metaphor for this error: "Two beers made me feel good, so ten beers will make me feel five times better."[32]

Like the Skidelskys, Nettle suggests that consumerism and our pursuit of material goods is the number one "threat" to happiness in our society.[33] What is the mechanism of this threat? Authors differ: some note that consumerism's emphasis on continual novelty undermines our ability to maintain and find attractive stable commitments, which are especially important for relationships.[34] Others note that consumerism tends to degrade the physical environment, either directly or indirectly, through increasing other sources of unhappiness like commuting times.[35]

Two underlying problems of the consumer economy are particularly singled out. The first, central for the Skidelskys, is that society's pursuit of the goods life leads to too much work. An economy that offered more genuine leisure and less frenzied work-and-consumption would make us happier because it is in leisure (families, friendships, play, etc.) that we find "the things that really matter."[36] The Skidelskys focus on the question of why, given massive productivity increases, Keynes's prediction of the fall in work hours has not happened. While they attribute some of the problem to increasing inequality (with Keynes assuming professionals would be making only three to six times the ordinary worker's pay), they say "insatiability" and the failure to distinguish needs from wants is the main problem. We want to buy too much and so we work too much.[37] They prefer a model already aimed at (to some extent) in most European economies, with European workers every year averaging about 150 to 400 less work hours (or four to ten weeks) than Americans.[38]

Even in the 1940s there was a sense that these were the two alternatives for the future of affluent society. Percival and Paul Goodman describe the options: a frenzied city of constant consumption, festival, and rebuilding, or an economy with a minimum level of work and income that produced basic needs for everyone with an option to engage in further work or not.[39] The latter option, which the Goodmans prefer, is accompanied by an intriguing proposal to divide off a managed "subsistence market" from a free "luxury market" that could "boom and bust" on its own and "no one would starve."[40]

The other major consumerist threat to happiness is our tendency to consistently overestimate both how happy a change will make us and how long that happiness will last. Explaining the basis for the new field of behavioral economics, Daniel Kahneman demonstrates that we ordinarily make significant errors in judgment because we use faulty heuristics in our approach to choices.[41] Among these errors is an overestimation of the happiness payoff from material goods. This failure to deliver is rooted in adaptation: we quickly adjust to the material improvement and it then simply becomes ordinary. In order to recover the fleeting feeling of satisfaction we need to re-up the speed of the "hedonic treadmill." But it never really can go fast enough. As William Cavanaugh observes, consumerism is not about "attachment to things, but detachment," and "this is why not simply buying but shopping is the heart of consumerism."[42]

Happiness studies provide some hint that a life devoted to the accumulation of ever-more material goods is not a path to satisfaction, and may be harmful. They raise some real questions about the supposed "democratization of meaning" made possible by constructing identity through buying, particularly if the "hedonic treadmill" effect means that only the very wealthy can sustain all this shopping. One author even goes so far as to propose that the data should lead us to "applying the ancient virtue of thrift."[43]

However, happiness studies fall short in making a stronger case for the vicious nature of luxury. How so? Such studies face the limitations of any social-scientific study.[44] Correlation and causation are two different things. Findings are generalized and do not apply to every individual. The data itself is subject to debate, especially when it is gathered about such a large and complex subject as a happy life. Happiness studies are social-scientific studies—they tell us something broadly about the majority of people, perhaps, but not every person.

More important, the studies run into two more complicated philosophical problems. First, the studies end up presuming that certain activities are an *instrumental* means to achieving happiness. Happiness studies lead Bill McKibben to call for a "new utilitarianism" that is not based on maximizing economic utility but on real happiness.[45] However, as one author notes, "While happiness is extremely important to people, it is just one of several goals underlying human action," and some of these other goals people "value as ends in themselves, on a par with happiness."[46] Catholic economist Luigino Bruni sees the limits of these studies by saying, "the approach of the psychological economists is still hedonistic (based on pleasure) and not eudaimonistic."[47]

Attempts to get past this problem toward a more substantial account of happiness run into a second, even more vexing philosophical problem: the empirical findings stand in tension with a default ideology of freedom of choice, a tension the authors are particularly weak at handling. For example, Nettle tries to overcome the instrumentalizing problems by distinguishing three "levels" of happiness. Level one is momentary good feelings. Happiness studies attempt to measure "level two happiness," that is, overall life satisfaction." Level three happiness involves a life that "fulfills [a person's] true potential." He claims this cannot be measured because, "at least within any liberal tradition of thought . . . as long as people do not harm each other, then it is their inalienable right to construe their own potential in any way they like."[48] Nettle insists that "happiness should not be moralizing" but this is "an extremely hard balance to strike."[49]

Nettle's "should not" tips off the hidden morality smuggled in here. Insisting that subjective utility is key, the studies end up trapped between the freedom to define utility subjectively and findings that suggest human utility is not subjective.[50] This method is even problematic on its own grounds: as Kahneman in particular shows, our subjective judgments about what decisions will bring us even "level two" happiness are frequently wrong! So these studies might be used to suggest that people can have *too much* freedom for their own happiness, and perhaps that free choice itself is the "ideology" about the good life that is (surreptitiously) being *imposed* by elites.[51]

Using Aristotle, the Skidelskys recognize that happiness studies fall short because they "attach an unconditional value to happiness itself, independent of the various things we are happy about."[52] But even they are brought up short by the modern ideology of freedom. When trying to prescribe exactly how much is enough, they evidence a very modern nervousness. As social reformers trying to make what they consider a virtually revolutionary case, they do not offer the confident moral claims one might see were they dealing with, say, sex trafficking or gender discrimination or same-sex marriage. Perhaps because of their recognition of how their critique is "culturally taboo," they preface potential policy proposals by noting: "The crux of the matter is the extent to which a liberal state is justified in interfering with individual decisions about how much to work and what to consume."[53] They try to thread this needle with what they call "non-coercive paternalism."[54] Put another way, in their attempt to merge Aristotle and Keynes they do not overcome Keynes's own commitments to a form of the good life—the higher pleasures of the arts and friendship—founded on G. E. Moore's intuitionism.[55] Because of this reliance on unsustainable claims about higher pleasures, the Skidelskys (like Keynes) have no way of evading the charge of elitism.

Thus, much of this literature is caught in a contradiction of the modern social imaginary: on the one hand it begins to develop fairly robust empirical findings about what flourishing is, but on the other it can't ever be prescriptive about what such flourishing actually is because that would violate . . . our commitment to the idea that flourishing means choosing our own way to flourish! This contradiction becomes even more acute when the empirical evidence demonstrates that we are often *bad* at such choosing.[56]

All these authors have gotten trapped in what Morris Berman brilliantly terms the "latent moral vacuum" at the heart of our society. In a lengthy description devoted to a critique of technology, Berman offers extensive statistics about the corrosive effects technology has on our ability to pursue the good life. But he then laments the "latent moral vacuum" that is inherent in "the liberal democratic tradition itself."[57] Drawing on Isaiah Berlin's analysis of negative freedom, he notes that in our situation, "it is very difficult to criticize contemporary socioeconomic arrangements or *even find a vocabulary to voice that criticism*" (emphasis added).[58] Such criticism "often comes off as arrogant" and will be viewed as elitist if we have no awareness of any "tradition of excellence."[59] He concludes that he "would come off as some kind of fanatic" in offering such criticisms of technology.[60]

Berman highlights the limits of moral languages that presume the priority of subjective autonomy; the latent moral vacuum of political liberalism sucks up any *substantive* claims about the good life, especially about what constitutes good character. Berman is speaking about attempts to limit technology—a similar project to the consumption limits implied in the critique of luxury—but he realizes that as soon as he starts talking about limits, he starts to sound fanatical.

How can we get past this moral vacuum into which the utilitarian happiness studies fall? Charles Taylor helps us understand the problem by noting, in a critique of both utilitarianism and "formalism" (e.g., Kantian ethics), that certain languages of morality become privileged because "they offer the hope of deciding ethical questions without having to determine which of a number of rival languages of moral virtue and vice, of the admirable and the contemptible . . . are valid."[61] However, modern moral languages end up restricting the domain of the moral, eliminating what Taylor calls "languages of qualitative contrast." These original, complex languages cannot simply be exchanged into the uniform currency of commensurable utility or universalizability. Thus, the effect of this restriction is to create not so much a vacuum as a bifurcation, where certain matters remain in the moral domain while others fall out, especially ones where the "languages of contrast" become "hard to validate."[62]

Taylor suggests that the disappearance of languages of contrast is rooted in "a naturalist account of man" from the seventeenth century, which had the "aim of explaining human beings like other objects in nature." In such naturalistic explanations, "the languages of contrast must be suspect" because "they correspond to nothing in reality" and "appear to designate purely 'subjective' factors." Taylor's insight connects well with Jennifer Herdt's history of the rise of moral anatomists in the seventeenth century, who are "one of the most important seeds of modern descriptive moral philosophy" because they "attempt to understand and describe *how* human character is formed through natural and social *processes*, as distinct from proclaiming an ideal for human behavior or seeking to articulate God's role in bringing about that ideal."[63] Taylor suggests a root for this movement in the rise of modern scientific epistemology; Herdt adds the fact that a "hyper-Augustinian" theology of divine grace makes God's action so mysterious and unknown that a space is opened where action analysis can proceed by simply ignoring it.

On either account, something deeply important is lost from our moral language—and the disappearance of the critique of luxury is Exhibit A for what gets lost. Of all the anatomists, Mandeville is the most devastating and vexing because of his apparent approval of luxury. Luxury is precisely the kind of "language of qualitative contrast" that is lost to systematic ethics—even though, as Taylor points out, "much of human behavior will be understandable and explicable" only by recourse to language that "marks qualitative contrasts." That is, we continue to sense and half-articulate the kinds of problems with luxury, technology, and the like but without the ability to command this language with authority.

Hence, we often get stuck in *quasi*-moral debates over particulars—say, taxing private jets or super-sized sodas—which devolve because of the lack of disciplined language. We endlessly contest luxuries when in fact we should be discussing *luxury*: first and foremost we need the name of a disposition, which only secondarily is connected to any characteristic object or action. Understanding the disposition can teach us to articulate limits on the pursuit of material goods but it is not a critique of items of furniture (or of a particular brand of automobile); it's a critique of persons—of their habits of thought and action—which may be exemplified by what they choose in relation to furnishings (or transportation).

As a disposition, luxury cannot successfully be contested via a simply utilitarian framework surrounded by formal Kantian hedges. Happiness studies can be used to *assist* claims about what is good but it falls short of the full moral argument. What often happens in practice is that happiness studies smuggle in a kind of Rousseauian appeal to "authenticity" that is not explicitly defended and, worse, that is easily countered by defenders of consumerism.[64] Perhaps true authenticity comes from free-wheeling consumption, who's to say?

The critique of luxury is in fact an alternative to the critique of consumer society on authenticity grounds. It focuses on blameworthy *dispositions*, as we do routinely for violent persons or for mean (= malice-driven) persons or (less steadily, but still persistently) for lustful persons. The luxurious person is the concern. To name luxury in this way requires us to turn back to the point where the critique got lost in order to see what happened to our moral language in the process.

The Problems of Practical Reason I: Sentiments and Strong Evaluation

We have seen that a central difficulty can be traced back to seventeenth-century moral anatomists who attempted to prescind from divine commandments and exhortations to virtue in favor of realistic attention to "the processes of character formation that give rise to socially desirable character and behavior."[65] Their claim is to see and understand human action as it really is. The greatest, most ambitious offspring of these thinkers is David Hume.

Hume must be engaged when arguing about the reasonableness of dispositions, perhaps especially luxury. His account of practical rationality ultimately argues that rationality is merely instrumental to the satisfaction of desire, and all we can really know about desires is that people have them, not that they should have them. It is no accident that Hume, the great champion of the passions as the root of morality, is a champion of luxury as well. Any conversation about the ethics of luxury must subject to scrutiny both Humean practical reason and Hume's defense of luxury. This is not because "it is all Hume's fault" or because he is particularly bad. Rather, it is because his account of ethics and of luxury is crucial for understanding why and how our language gets knotted up, making "moral" judgments against "moralizing."

Two knots are in need of untangling: one is Hume's failure to account for his own use of what Charles Taylor calls "languages of qualitative contrast" or (elsewhere) terms of "strong evaluation"—that is, of what is "higher" and "lower" in human flourishing.[66] Hume's work assumes such an evaluation but his own account of morality subverts the possibility of rationally accounting for it. The high value Hume places on luxury and refinement can be traced to an underlying strong evaluation that leisure is more noble than work. I will contest the supposed "naturalism" of Hume's description by offering the stark contrast of Thorstein Veblen's much more hostile account of leisured luxury. Veblen's critique rests on a strong evaluation of a quality he calls "workmanship." Hume and Veblen allow us to see that the case against luxury rests partly on our conflicted strong evaluations about work over leisure.

The second problem with Hume's account can be seen by utilizing Alasdair MacIntyre's approach to dealing with disparate catalogs of virtues and vices via the analysis of practices. MacIntyre's account rests on a key distinction between internal and external goods, a distinction that is unavailable in Hume. Participation in certain practices requires a transformation of our desires from external rewards to internal achievements of excellence in the activity itself, the achievement of which depends on possessing virtue. Many economists now recognize that economic organizations and even whole economies depend on certain dispositions like honesty and trust; MacIntyre can help us see how practices depend also on a resistance to luxury. Luxury names a disposition to goods that are external to practices and corrupts them when it is taken as the end by participants. An analysis of virtue and vice in terms of practices shows that the oft-made claim about the pursuit of luxury leading to social cooperation is ultimately mistaken.

Hume's Account of Practical Reason and Defense of Luxury

Hume's moral philosophy famously challenges the role of reason in human action.[67] It was, obviously, not Hume's discovery that human beings were motivated by their passions. The question of desire and reason is hardly a new one in ethics: "Nothing is more usual in philosophy, and even in common life, than to talk of the combat of passion and reason," and, he adds, to argue in favor of the superiority of reason.[68] What is new is Hume's purpose: "to shew the fallacy of all this philosophy" (413) by arguing that "reason is and ought only to be the slave of the passions" and that "nothing can oppose or retard the impulse of passion but a contrary impulse" (415). Infamously, he writes, "'Tis not contrary to reason to prefer the destruction of the whole world to the scratching of my finger. 'Tis not contrary to reason for me to chuse my total ruin to prevent the least uneasiness of an Indian or a person wholly unknown to me" (416).

Hume's argument is more than just provocative. His demonstrations consistently suggest that the dynamics of human action simply are not like matters of informational knowledge. He does not deny that reason can make mistaken judgments about the means by which to pursue a desire and that reason may uncover "a false supposition" about the relationship of actions to the satisfaction of desires. In other words, information can be useful for motivating action if the information reveals an error in my beliefs about what will instrumentally lead to the satisfaction I desire—but it cannot challenge the desire itself. For example, I may present sociological data confirming that materialism and overconsumption are destructive to marriages, and a student may then change his or her materialistic actions and even desires. But this action results only because of the "contrary impulses" to marriage versus to merchandise.

This form of explaining the dynamics of moral judgments remains powerful today: Jonah Lehrer's popularized version of contemporary neuroscience makes Humean points constantly, particularly in relation to "ethics." Lehrer begins by saying that ever since the ancient Greeks we have assumed that, when making decisions, "humans are rational." But "there's only one problem with this assumption of human rationality: it's wrong."[69] In assessing moral judgment in particular, he notes that our "reasonableness is just a façade" and the "philosophical consensus for thousands of years" is "exactly backward."[70] He reports a psychologist saying that "feelings come first" and "reasons are invented on the fly."[71] But this would hardly be surprising to philosophers: this is Hume in pop-science dress.

Hume was not entirely original in developing this claim about the centrality of sentiments for action. The tradition of Hobbes and Locke had already made the move to founding human action on the individual search for pleasure and avoidance of pain, thus instantiating a debate over how the most obvious passion—that of self-love or self-interest—was to be reconciled with traditional morality.[72] As MacIntyre points out, the tradition of "the moral sense" that Hume received had already moved quite far in grounding both morality and religion in inner states of feelings and sentiment.[73] At the heart of this tradition was a disagreement over the idea that two fundamental sources of behavior exist in human nature: one of reasonable self-love, the other of conscience or altruism. Some writers (Hobbes, Mandeville) more or less reject the claim that a human tendency toward altruism exists. But others (Butler, Shaftesbury, Hutcheson) maintain there are two principles, ordinarily appealing to divine providence, to explain how we are to understand them as harmonious. Crucially, the claim rested on the observation that we experience happiness and pleasure not only at our own pleasure but in our benevolence toward others, and their resulting pleasure.[74] Here, again, Lehrer follows suit: "At its core, moral decision-making is about sympathy."[75]

Hume seeks an account of morality that "delicately positions himself between Mandeville and Hutcheson."[76] He denies that human passions properly described make us into virtual "monsters" of selfishness—the Mandeville position—but also questions the idea that we have some kind of moral instinct.[77] Instead, what we have is a natural sense of pride in what is good about our own lives and a gratitude toward those who grant benefits to us. Through "reflexive self-survey" this pride becomes appropriately subdued in its display, and our sympathy is extended by approving of those who do good to others, even if not directly to ourselves.[78] These virtues, while rooted in the impulses of human nature, do not come from a separate moral sense but are the result of the basic self-regarding impulse properly being trained into social relationships.

Thus, Hume's account of the passions begins with extended treatments of versions of the two principles of "pride" (or "self-love," in the later *Enquiry*) and "sympathy." In what commentators agree is an intentional correction of the somber, dutiful Christianity of his upbringing, Hume praises pride as our experience of pleasure at anything insofar as it relates to and reflects the self.[79] "Can we imagine it possible, that while human nature remains the same, men will ever become entirely indifferent to their power, riches, beauty or personal merit, and that their pride and vanity will not be affected by these advantages?" (281). Central to Hume's epistemology is the idea of associations: the impressions we experience have certain regularities and form certain associations in our mind. The association of ourselves with something fine and excellent is what makes us feel pride (as an indirect passion, in this sense). This pride thereby gives "its possessor a more secure (and positive) sense of identity"—a claim that would warm the hearts of pro-consumption champions.[80]

Hume claims such associations by themselves "have little influence when not seconded by the opinions and sentiments of others" (316). Thus, the remarkable human trait of sympathy, in which we take pride in the esteem of others and, in loving them, take pleasure in their excellences. The real joy is celebrating with other fans when our team wins, or when our work receives praise from others. Eventually, "sympathy must be corrected and extended" from a "steady and general point of view," though its extent is not made perfectly clear.[81]

For Hume, what we take the most pride in and express sympathy about are our possessions: "That's a great outfit," or "Love your new hair style," or "Your kitchen is gorgeous." He claims that one's property is the most common source of pride, and that "every thing belonging to a vain man is the best that is any where to be found. His houses, equipage, furniture, cloaths, horses, hounds, excel all others in his conceit; and 'tis easy to observe, that from the least advantage in any of these, he draws a new subject of pride and vanity" (310).[82] Moreover, Hume insists that our friendships are also based on our pride in our friend's riches . . . or embarrassment over their poverty. Here we should note how vividly Hume accepts and endorses common estimations of the good of riches and the distaste and even *disdain* felt toward the poor. He writes: "As we are proud of riches in ourselves, so to satisfy our vanity, we desire that every one who has any connexion with us, shou'd likewise be possest of them, and are asham'd if any one that is mean or poor among our friends and relations" (307). So, when speaking of love, Hume goes on to say "Nothing has a greater tendency to give us an esteem for any person than his power and riches; or a contempt, than his poverty and meanness" (357). Thus, what Hume means by "sympathy" here is not what we typically mean.[83] Sympathy names our desire to share in the experiences of our pleasures—not just enjoying the thing but enjoying the esteem of others (perhaps via the thing). In his essay "Of Luxury," he asserts: "The more these refined arts advance, the more sociable men become. . . . They flock into cities; love to receive and communicate knowledge, to show their wit or their breeding, their taste in conversation or living, in clothes or furniture."[84]

Hume's moral psychology is shocking but challenging, for two reasons. One is recognizing that he is describing experiences we likely have had, however embarrassing that may be. Some too easily dismiss Hume without coming to terms with how powerful and insightful his descriptions are. We visit a person's new house, perhaps, and they enjoy showing it off, and we enjoy complimenting them. It would be hard to imagine someone in our society who has not shown off their favored possessions or taken pride in them, and have further reciprocated others' enthusiasm. I confess my avid acquisition of a very large music collection was something I was also eager to "share"—that is, display to others for appropriate oohing and ahhing.[85]

A second, more serious challenge is Hume's contention that his description is a more accurate explanation of our *actual* nature than either the utterly selfish Hobbesian individual or the severe and dutiful Christianity with which he grew up. Again, one must give Hume his due. For Hobbes, only fear drives us to get along with others; otherwise, we would take advantage of them at every chance. This is not a very realistic picture. But neither is the noble asceticism—what Hume termed "the monkish virtues"—exemplified in the Christian chastening of self.[86] Hobbes suggests your friend's new kitchen inspires nothing but envy; on the ascetic side, your friend's new kitchen actually fills you with disgust. Neither reaction seems (to Hume) to be what actually happens. And, what do you or I actually do?

This space, between Hobbes and asceticism, is decisive for our topic because it is here where luxury turns from vice to virtue. Luxury is to be differentiated from Hobbesian selfish aggression. It is a "calm" passion that leads to "an increase of humanity from the very habit of conversing together and contributing to each other's pleasure and entertainment."[87] As we saw above, it promotes sociability and advances knowledge. It is not to be confused with excessive self-indulgence. Hume vividly compares the "refinements of cookery" at European courts to the feasting of barbarians, and suggests that it is the latter, not the former, that is indicative of vice.[88] It is seen as a healthy sense of "the finer things," an appreciation that bears much fruit in civilized fellowship. In directly defending luxury Hume makes much of this idea of being "civilized." While aware of the pro-luxury argument from Mandeville's primitive economic analysis, he is moving further toward a defense of luxury consumption on the basis of its civilizing benefits and its ability to foster good human relationships.

Hume is well aware of the long-standing critiques of luxury. In his essay on commerce he denies the concern that a rise in luxury leads to a decline in "the greatness of the state"—specifically, a decline in public military power. He admits that anti-luxury Sparta "was certainly more powerful than any state now in the world consisting of an equal number of people, and this was owing entirely to the want of commerce and luxury." However, Sparta's laws were "peculiar" rather than "natural," and if a ruler were to try to make his nation a "fortified camp," then perhaps it would be good "to banish all arts and luxury."[89] "As these principles are too difficult to support, it is requisite to govern by other passions, and animate the state with a spirit of avarice and industry, art and luxury."[90]

Hume cleverly appears to endorse this ancient view but then suggests it is not very practical: the rejection of commerce often leads to states where people are lazy and poor candidates for martial duty when needed. In countries "where manufactures and mechanic arts are not cultivated," agricultural laborers have no incentive to produce beyond subsistence since they cannot exchange surplus for commodities that serve "their pleasure or vanity. A habit of indolence naturally prevails."[91] (He adds that the compounding state of poverty makes them not good candidates to be taxed, either!) The luxury produced by advances in manufacturing, he insists, do not "soften" people; rather it "adds new force" to both mind and body and develops a "stronger, more constant . . . sense of honor" because it is based on "knowledge and a good education."[92] It leads to industriousness, which is ultimately beneficial in times of war.

Nor is luxury a force of social division. Rome's fall was not due to luxury, but due to "an ill-modeled government and the unlimited extent of conquests."[93] The whole population benefits from luxury, even if not everyone can enjoy it equally. Foreign trade, so often scorned as disposing to luxury, is presented as a good, for it acquaints people "with the pleasures of luxury and the profits of commerce," which then "arouses men from their indolence and, presenting the gayer and more opulent part of the nation with objects of luxury which they never before dreamed of, raises in them a desire of a more splendid way of life than what their ancestor enjoyed."[94] Ultimately, these new desires benefit domestic industry as well. In short, luxuries not only spur polite conversation but larger social cooperation as well.

In Hume's picture all is sweetness and light, as all labor is directed toward this "more splendid way of life." The person who became accustomed to luxury was, on Hume's reading, more sociable than the barbarian and less prone to violence and conflict. The pursuit of one's desires for refined pleasures and comforts, Hume insisted, was normal and natural, and in fact served to civilize and "refine" a person in gentle manners and cordial relations.[95]

In Hume's later *Enquiry* the importance of fine property seems more muted. Indeed, Hume explicitly praises "reasonable frugality," contrasting it with "avarice," a miserly stinginess, and "prodigality" as exhibited by those who have "consumed their fortune in wild debauches."[96] Perhaps reflecting his own aging, luxury's place as a spur both to industry and to conviviality is subordinated to "a desire of fame, reputation, or a character with others," which "is so far from being blameable" and is "inseparable from virtue."[97] This is not "vanity," Hume claims, which is instead "an intemperate display of our advantages, honors, and accomplishments."[98] His praise for "the love of fame" is effusive, for it means we must constantly review our own conduct in relation to others.[99]

Yet Hume's argument for fame has the same structure as the argument for luxury: he takes an external aspiration that has long been the object of philosophical scorn and suggests that it is in fact very good by inspecting our own sentiments and their usefulness in our behavior. But he then makes a distinction and distances himself from a selfish view. Desire for fame is very good so long as it is tasteful and not vulgar in its display. Possessions are good if they are refined but bad if their use is merely a matter of "debauch."

What grounds these linguistic distinctions between good and bad sentiments? This is the problem. As we saw, Hume's friend and contemporary Adam Smith similarly sought to base morality on sentiments. In his survey of systems of moral philosophy within *The Theory of Moral Sentiments*, Smith argues that "it is altogether absurd and unintelligible to suppose that the first perceptions of right and wrong can be derived from reason." While "reason may show that this object is the means of obtaining" this or that pleasing or displeasing object, "nothing can be agreeable or disagreeable for its own sake, which is not rendered such by immediate sense and feeling."[100] Smith similarly draws on the importance of sympathy and makes central the notion of the "impartial spectator," thematizing the importance of reflexive self-survey in Hume.

Smith also claims that "the disposition to admire, and almost to worship the rich and powerful and to despise or at least to neglect persons of poor and mean condition," is "the great and most universal cause of the *corruption* of our moral sentiments" (emphasis added).[101] What has happened here? MacIntyre maintains that "the barrenness of Hume's successors is not accidental."[102] Smith does not solve the problem so much as simply continue the exhortation of Hume's more Christian predecessors.[103] MacIntyre contrasts Hume with Smith, noting that the "moral" Smith is basically a Stoic, and that "when teleology, whether Aristotelian or Christian, is abandoned, there is always a tendency to substitute for it some version of Stoicism" because the virtues no longer aim at some good but rather are their own ends. As we noted, Smith is double-minded, as many of us continue to be: we aim at riches but also tell ourselves that the best things in life are free. But it is Hume who offers the consistent position, at least insofar as it is a claim about utility: luxury is genuinely useful for us and for social relations, and that is all that needs to be said. On what basis does Smith identify it as a "useful *illusion*"?

Strong Evaluations

Yet differences between Hume and Smith call into question Hume's claim that his anatomy of the sentiments surrounding the pursuit of luxuries is more "natural" than Smith's. We should see here that even between two men as culturally and intellectually similar as Hume and Smith, the sentiments evoked by wealth appear to be different. These competing evaluations help create the "latent moral vacuum" described above. The differing sentiments appear arbitrary, though neither Hume nor Smith see them as arbitrary. Indeed, they believe they are articulating a morality that rests on observation of the way human nature is. They believe in their moral anatomies.

The problem here is addressed by Charles Taylor's claim that all moral agency unavoidably contains what he calls "strong evaluations" rather than mere sentiments. What is meant by strong evaluation? Taylor contends that "simple weigher" accounts of human agency—the calculations we make when we weigh pros and cons, or use some other balancing metaphor—inadequately capture how humans operate, and that "the capacity for strong evaluation is essential to our notion of human subject; that without it an agent would lack a kind of depth we consider essential to humanity."[104] By "strong evaluator" he means someone who has "a language of contrastive characterization," of "higher and lower, noble and base, courageous and cowardly" by which he or she can analyze a choice.[105] He notes that we assume such a capacity for "depth" when we view someone as "insensitive" in their choices or "shallow" in their lifestyle.[106] He goes further to suggest that such evaluations are partly constitutive of our identity, such that to lose or contradict these evaluations is "a terrifying experience of disaggregation and loss."[107] A person who simply is a consequence-calculator or a "radical chooser" would essentially have no identity. Indeed, all narratives implicitly rely on a stock of strong evaluations for them to make sense, including Hume's narrative of how we handle our possessions.

Taylor suggests that the mistake of utilitarianism—calculating subjective utility by aggregating all satisfactions—is traceable back to "one of the most fatefully influential passages" of Hume's philosophy: the claim that "our moral sentiments are not ultimately grounded in reason."[108] The problem here, Taylor argues, is not that Hume attributes moral significance to our sentiments but rather his mistake of divorcing sentiments from cognitive perception. There is a difference between what Taylor calls "raw feel" and "emotion": the former is simply a matter of saying, "Boy, that warm shower feels nice," whereas emotions involve much richer "takes" on a particular object. The smell of a particular soap may be nice and may even evoke some kind of feeling of connection to a memory in one's life. The confusion is that "feelings do not just happen; they are not sensations."[109] They are subject to conditioning and cannot be identified apart from cognitive content. Taylor suggests that the distortion introduced here "was to split emotion [sentiment] from its constituent perception and thus assimilate it to sensation."[110]

Ancient philosophers did not exclude sentiments; rather, they had varying takes on how our overall evaluation of "the order of higher and lower activities"—as well as our need to correct erroneous "opinions" within passions (say, the common feeling of rejection and judgment when encountering a contrary custom or other example of human diversity)—meant that passions were already "in-formed" by judgments of perception. "Reason can discern" about these judgments such that "it follows that there is such a thing as getting it wrong." Our subjective responses, however deeply or sincerely felt, can mislead us. But, Taylor says, "Hume denies this model."[111] He defines virtue as "a quality of the mind agreeable to or approved of by everyone who considers or contemplates it."[112] He argues that this approval rests on these qualities being *useful* to self or others, conducive to pleasure, and "cherished in society and conversation."[113]

Hume obscures two ways in which reason, albeit not the "abstract, metaphysical principles" of the kind he constantly rejects, drives his own sentiments.[114] First, he does seem to assume that we can judge passions as reasonable but not according to the discernment of "an order of higher and lower." Rather, reason is "about consequences. . . . The reason involved here is instrumental reason, what causes what?"[115] Hume's revision of the ancients' disapproval of luxury judges the ancients in error, on the grounds they had the instrumental calculations wrong. Correspondingly, Hume's assessment of luxury could be wrong if the personal and social harms of luxury could be demonstrated more clearly. One wonders what Hume would make of the data from the happiness studies.

The second problem, which is crucial for our topic, is that Hume's perceptions *do* involve rational judgments of the sort he tries to deny. That is, in making a distinction between vulgar display and proper concern for reputation, or debauch from refined indulgence, he apparently is making a strong evaluation—but he also presumes everyone shares this evaluation. Hume's claim about "everyone approving" is a smuggling-in of his own strong evaluations: he praises wit and cheerfulness as key virtues, and even more obviously praises the virtue of "decency," which is "a proper regard to age, sex, character, and station in the world. . . . An effeminate behavior in a man, a rough manner in a woman; these are ugly because unsuitable to each character."[116] The point here is not that Hume is sexist; rather, by Hume's own theory one cannot *rationally* challenge such sentiments as distorted. As MacIntyre notes, "what Hume identifies as the standpoint of universal human nature turns out in fact to be that of the prejudices of the Hanoverian ruling elite."[117] Hume approves of the trappings of his desired social class. Smith does as well, and so do both the anti-consumerist critics and the pro-consumerist defenders of democratic shopping for all.

What quickly ensues is Berman's "latent moral vacuum." Since we cannot eliminate these strongly evaluative stories, we instead dissolve their evaluative force by deciding that we have no way of deciding. This is really where the key mistake happens, because in practice we do have real ways of making rational judgments about competing stories and we do rely on the truth of these strongly evaluative stories within our own lives as more than merely subjective preferences (such as, say, the relative meaningfulness of raising a family versus buying a sports car).

Hume's strong evaluations are not necessarily wrong. But how can we know? Frederick Copleston posits that "Hume's philosophy lacks a conception of the practical reason, and of the mode of its operation."[118] So eager is Hume to avoid the dangers of deducing morals from abstractions that he fails to recognize the inevitable place of a different sort of reason in the moral judgments he is making. In particular, Hume obscures the extent to which his "strong evaluations" involve implicit *and rational* claims about the ultimate end of human life. Notice his very strong (yet doubtful) statement that "the ultimate ends of human action can never, in any case, be accounted for by reason, but recommend themselves entirely to the sentiments and affections of mankind, without any dependence on the intellectual faculties."[119]

Veblen contra Hume: Savagery and Workmanship

Hume's particular "strong evaluations" that lead him to favor luxury can be seen and contested by comparing his comments to those of a different observer of the personal and social effects of luxury: the maverick economist Thorstein Veblen. Veblen is especially helpful in this debate because he is remarkably philosophically and theologically innocent. Veblen's work does not provide us with the needed framework of practical rationality that can ground our judgments about dispositions, but juxtaposing his work with Hume's does bring out a crucial moral judgment—a "strong evaluation"—about leisure and work in human life that underlies their different evaluations of the luxury life.

Veblen may seem like an unexpected ally. His enquiries are ill-defined by any academic discipline. Robert Heilbroner, in his history of economic thinkers, portrays Veblen as "a very strange man" and consummate outsider who "walked through life as if he had descended from another world" and to whom the world "was uncomfortable and forbidding; he adapted to it as a missionary might to a land of primitives, refusing to go native, but preserving his integrity at the cost of frightful solitude."[120] Like Hume in both his irreverence and his willingness to be forthright (as well as his provincial background), he is Hume's polar opposite in terms of personal relations, totally disregarding others' praise and approval.

Moreover, Veblen's ideas are critical for explaining why affluent societies are unable to reach a "resting place" of enough, and thus why luxury cannot fulfill its promise to produce a harmonious society. Charles Clark notes that Veblen pioneered the analysis of how "artificial scarcity" is maintained by a combination of leisure-class emulation and "industrial sabotage."[121] Just as Hume is the forebear of consumption defenders, so Veblen is the forebear of consumerist critics (while also lacking attachment to Rousseauian authenticity).[122] Veblen's accounts of emulation and social status match Hume's in candor about how consumption is not just a satisfaction of material needs but also a forging of social bonds. Like Hume, Veblen regards as misplaced the claim that consumption is merely hedonism. Consumption is, above all, conspicuous because it is about social relationships.

But in a stark contrast to Hume, those "civilized" social relationships are portrayed as pathetic, miserable, and savage. Leisure classes develop in societies as the result of a "predatory" claiming of property in order to maintain "the invidious distinction attaching to wealth."[123] Leisure thus becomes the "means of reputability" (132). These are "leisure" classes specifically because of "the requirement of abstention from productive work" (84). Instead, they develop "higher" activities—prowess in exploitation, useless quasi-learning (e.g., dead languages), and especially "manners and breeding, polite usage, decorum, and formal and ceremonial observances generally" (92). Indeed, such social niceties acquire "a sacramental character" and are "a useful evidence of gentility, because good breeding requires time, application, and expense, and can therefore not be compassed by those whose time and energy are taken up with work" (94–95). Veblen carefully singles out these "expressions of status" from "the courtesy of everyday discourse," which is simply "a direct expression of consideration and kindly good-will" (98). He exposes Hume's notions of civility and refinement as foolish. Indeed, the polarity of civilized-savage is strongly evaluative and Veblen reverses Hume's polarity.

Veblen shares with Hume the historical account of society evolving from a structure of hierarchical rank to commercial achievement but challenges the idea that commerce has overcome hierarchy. In earlier societies, the mark of the leisure class was especially seen in the possession of wives and servants, whose behavior demonstrated elaborate deference. As more and more work could be done by machines, and more and more elaborate goods were available, a shift to "conspicuous consumption" and a "specialization as regards the quality of the goods consumed" (116) arose. It "becomes incumbent upon him to discriminate with some nicety between the noble and ignoble in consumable goods. He becomes a connoisseur in creditable viands of various degrees of merit, in manly beverages and trinkets, in seemly apparel and architecture, in weapons, games, dancers, and the narcotics." Such a "cultivation of the aesthetic faculty" turns his life into "a more or less arduous application to the business of learning how to live a life of ostensible leisure in a becoming way" (117). Further resources are used by family members for their refined consumption, "the effects [of which] are pleasing to us chiefly because we have been taught to find them pleasing" (124).

Veblen's dry disdain for this faux-activity in a life of refined consumption is chiefly aimed at "the element of waste" (126). The immoral character of this waste is made evident in two ways. First, Veblen is clear that all this "refinement" can ultimately be traced back to predatory behaviors and continues to rely parasitically on the power held over the productive work of others. Transposed into moral language, this is evidently a kind of critique of luxury based on justice claims.

However, we should focus on the other "alien factor" that rejects this waste but is an idea central to Veblen's entire corpus: "the instinct of workmanship" that "comes into conflict with the law of conspicuous waste" primarily through "an abiding sense of the odiousness and aesthetic impossibility of what is obviously futile" (133). The term "instinct" is potentially misleading; Veblen admits that in the sciences of his day, the term had come into disrepute for its imprecision. His usage, he explains, is as a nontechnical term for "the innate and persistent propensities of human nature," which are "teleological" and "propose an objective end of endeavor." These are elaborated (and potentially distorted) by intelligence and passed-on cultural tradition and habit.[124] The usage is not alien to what the Thomist tradition has meant by "natural inclinations." Veblen is not offering a biologically reductionist account of behavior but rather one that is "in-formed" by both biology and cultural history appropriated and adjudicated by reason.[125]

As is typical of his opaque style, Veblen does not offer a catalog of such instincts. But his study highlights two: the "parental bent" and "workmanship." He indicates they are closely aligned and mutually influential because both conduce "directly to the material well-being of the race."[126] Both instincts involve "that sentimental approval of economy and efficiency for the common good and disapproval of wasteful and useless living that prevails so generally throughout both the highest and the lowest cultures." They are especially seen in relation to concern for the future. As Veblen intones, in an unusually serious moment, "it is a despicably inhuman thing for the current generation willfully to make the way of life harder for the next generation."[127]

What is this "instinct of workmanship"? It involves a satisfaction in itself even as it also aims specifically at "the efficient use of the means at hand and adequate management of the resources available for the purposes of life."[128] That is, it is both a means and an end. It involves proficiency, creativity, mastery of knowledge, and "a proclivity for taking pains."[129] According to its "canons of conduct," it is "efficiency" and "serviceability" that "commends itself," while "inefficiency or futility is odious."[130] Moreover, the instinct of workmanship guides activity that necessarily relies on the build-up of "common stock," that is, common knowledge and processes and even equipment that are required for any individual to perform productive work. Veblen notes that no individual could ever realistically claim to support his or her own life in a self-sufficient manner.[131] So rather than engendering social bonds based on status and the exchange of pleasant feelings, productive work is an honoring of our shared dependence on one another across space and time and leads to both necessary cooperation and necessary gratitude. This relates to MacIntyre's virtue of "acknowledged dependence" that is central to social practices.[132] It seeks excellence in the work of providing for the whole rather than a superior position or share of the prizes of individual work.[133]

What has happened to this workmanship in industrial society? Veblen tells a tale of its great achievements being thwarted by the leisure class. At some point (he speculates that it falls somewhere near the end of the nineteenth century), the evolution of industrial production came to be such that the goal could no longer be to simply produce more.[134] The means of production had become complicated enough that individual or small groups of workmen no longer owned or ran them. The result was "a supersession of free workmanship by a pecuniary control of industry." Run by "captains of industry," these enterprises faced, in market saturation, a significant problem: their own demise—or rather, the demise of their profits. Veblen writes: "The captains have always turned the technologists and their knowledge to account . . . only so far as would serve their own commercial profit, [and] not to the extent of their ability; or to the limit set by the material circumstances; or by the needs of the community. The result has been, uniformly and as a matter of course, that the production of goods and services has advisedly been stopped short of productive capacity, by curtailment of output and by derangement of the productive system."[135] Thus, in Veblen's view it is the business entrepreneur, and increasingly the financier who supports this entrepreneur, who seeks to "sabotage" systematically the possibility of productive abundance based on proper, nonwasteful workmanship.

How is this sabotage carried out? Veblen cites numerous ways. One example is "salesmanship":

> Salesmanship is the most conspicuous, and perhaps the gravest, of these wasteful and industrially futile practices that are involved in the businesslike conduct of industry; it bulks large both in its immediate cost and in its meretricious consequences. . . . It is doubtless within the mark to say that, at an average, one-half the price paid for goods and services by consumers is to be set down to the account of salesmanship—that is, to sales-cost and to the net gains of salesmanship. But in many notable lines of merchandise the sales-cost will ordinarily foot up to some ten or twenty times the production-cost proper, and to not less than one hundred times the necessary cost of distribution.[136]

Of course, the pseudo-skills of advertising and salesmanship are not the only place Veblen directs his gaze. His point, rather, is to highlight the immense waste of a system whose direction is set not by the instinct for workmanship but instead by the continued pecuniary gain of the few. The system is corrupt on both ends, one might say: the leisure class of owners and financiers need to maintain their excessive income from profit and the working class undertakes needless "work" only to spend their pay on unnecessary extravagances—on luxuries!—in their impossible quest to emulate the leisure class.

Luxury and Work

Hume's and Veblen's portraits of the leisure class each imply some strong evaluation of what is noble versus what is base in living out a human life.

The leisure class looks ridiculous to Veblen because the noble life is that of the craftsman and engineer. By contrast, Hume depicts the worker as striving to achieve as much of the refinement and civility of the leisure class as he can get.

This contrast in evaluation reveals a key aspect of the moral contest over luxury: whether the virtuous life is one of leisure or of work. Here we see part of the reason why happiness studies come up short: they often share the assumption that the highest goods are goods of leisure but also define goods in terms of the arts and friendship rather than, say, the pursuit of fashion.[137] This ends up in an impossible discussion about authenticity and elitism, with one side assuming that consumers must be dupes cheated out of what they really want and the other side wondering how we know what other people really want. Consumerism's defenders reply: you like your primitive camping, we like the luxury resort in Orlando. So long as the debate is restricted to being one about competing forms of leisure it is difficult to escape the accusations of elitism.

Interestingly, the preference for leisure over work is a tendency shared by the philosophical and economic traditions. Hume may have rejected the ancient philosophers in many ways, but he agreed that a life of leisure was desirable. While Hume does offer a quick praise of "industry" and "enterprise," both are worthy of praise on the basis of their usefulness for "the acquisition of power and riches."[138] Hume spends only about a paragraph on this idea; compare his much more extensive treatments of the qualities of wit, cheerfulness, magnanimity, amiability, and eloquence. We would not be wrong to depict him as saying: Won't you have better dinner parties, and ultimately better friendships, if you talk about sports and cars and furniture and fashion than if you have debates about who is living the good life? At the very least, develop the skills of good manners and verbal niceties, which are "naturally" seen as agreeable and delightful by others.

Compare the mocking Veblen, for whom manners and eloquence are the leisure class's substitutes for genuine work precisely because only *they* have the spare time to acquire these refinements. For Veblen, the noble life is not centered on good dinner parties but on productive work. In this way he disrupts the conventions of both philosophers and economists. Veblen speaks of the disrespect for labor as "a spiritual fact" which the "predatory culture" has imposed.[139] As Heilbroner writes, "The irksomeness of work, which the classical economists thought to be inherent in the nature of man himself, Veblen saw as the degradation of a once-honored way of life under the import of a predatory spirit; a community that admires and elevates force and brute prowess cannot beatify human toil."[140] Thus, in the course of development, the worker learns to despise his or her lot and (even worse) squanders resources in an attempt to emulate his or her masters. In responding to such a situation, Veblen states that "there is no remedy for this kind of irksomeness, short of a subversion of that cultural structure on which our canons of decency rest."[141] He means that the strong evaluations of work and leisure imposed by the predatory class must be rejected.

We are in a position to draw a first provisional conclusion in our attempt to adjudicate the debate over "the goods life": it rests in part on a difference of strong evaluation, a difference in how one views work and leisure within the good human life. This difference can become invisible when the debate goes on in a utilitarian framework because of that framework's inability to attend to questions of strong evaluation. It is further obscured when the debate degenerates into one between the authenticity of two competing versions of leisure.

Even if the work-leisure debate is kept in view, however, the argument over luxury can still seem interminable because our own culture carries ambivalent and contradictory cross-pressures on this fundamental question, too. Do we honor work, or are we working for the weekend? The critique of luxury ultimately rests on our commendation of good work. It is the same moral judgment we express when we worry about a child becoming "spoiled." The implication is that life can be too easy and that we can and do end up incapable of the noble activity of work. It appears we retain some sense of the moral importance of work.

Yet at other times we seem to treat work as purely instrumental, a necessary evil that makes possible our real enjoyment on weekends, on holiday, and ultimately in retirement. This is because much work in our society has become so degraded. As Daniel Horowitz points out, the "full development of industrial capitalism" required two important transitions: persuading "labor to accept industrial discipline" while also encouraging "consumers to believe in mass-produced commodities and mass culture as the principal means of satisfaction outside work or [as] substitutes for the meaningfulness of labor."[142] Workers need to be disciplined (in a certain way) to meet the demands of large organizations, but then "workers should not be self-denying" outside of work. William Leach tells the story of the massive transformation of American society into one "preoccupied with consumption, with comfort and bodily well-being, with luxury, spending, and acquisition."[143] He argues that it required a re-narration of the key American themes of democracy, independence, and abundance from their original orientation of ownership of productive property toward an ideology of consumption that requires that "everybody . . . would have the same right as individuals to desire, long for, and wish for whatever they pleased."[144] This pattern indicates how the promotion of luxury for all is linked to the degradation of work.

These problems are complex. We want to be free of work when it is bad, degrading work. Ancient lives of luxury almost always rested on the exploitation of many workers—can this also be said of the middle-class consumer abundance we enjoy?[145] Does our desire to buy cheaply a multiplicity of goods create the very degradation of work at discount retailers and third-world suppliers that make us dissatisfied with work? And, if it does, is doing degraded work in order to consume in leisure the output of others' degraded work really a good life? Here the standard questions of justice intersect with questions about luxurious excess.

A further question might be posed by the defenders of leisure such as Josef Pieper, who do not depict it in a Humean fashion. But doesn't all work contain some element of drudgery or toil from which we rightly seek "rest"? Is a kind of all-work, no-play life a picture of the good life? We will revisit this question later in the more detailed casuistry of luxury, but at this point it should be kept in mind that the vice of luxury is a critique of *excess*. It does not reject leisure or material goods but rather some kind of excess regarding them. Combining these questions, we might consider how both work and leisure look different to someone who is pursuing luxury as opposed to someone who is (for example) pursuing the building of beautiful furniture. Implied in Veblen's critique is the idea that luxury consumption neglects workmanship and even systematically undermines it via the businessman who seeks not good products but profits.

The Skidelskys, in an essay published simultaneously with their book, also clarify that their case for leisure should not be misunderstood:

> Let us state firmly that we are not in favor of idleness. What we wish to see more of is leisure, a category that, properly understood, is so far from coinciding with idleness that it approaches its polar opposite. Leisure, in the true, now almost forgotten sense of the word, is activity without extrinsic end, "purposiveness without purpose," as Kant put it. The sculptor engrossed in cutting marble, the teacher intent on imparting a difficult idea, the musician struggling with a score, a scientist exploring the mysteries of space and time—such people have no other aim than to do well what they are doing. They may receive an income for their efforts, but that income is not what motivates them. They are engaged in leisure, not toil.[146]

But, given their examples of people engaged in jobs, why do they then go on to lobby for "a universal reduction of work"? Somehow "work" and "toil" are equated here. In MacIntyre's concept of a practice, the Skidelskys are describing a certain kind of cooperative activity (albeit in individualistic terms) that they denote as "leisure" and which is to be contrasted with (bad) "work." But why the contrast? Why reduce work? Why not instead attempt to *shape* work in such a way that its internal goods are realized? Otherwise, the Skidelskys' use of the term "leisure" suggests that the sculptor and the scientist are merely hobbyists, since there is "no extrinsic end" to their activities. Is it all merely puttering about in one's garden for amusement? Why can't productive farming and crafts be the same? They contrast "an eternity of daytime television" as the alternative to genuine leisure—yet television certainly seems to have no extrinsic end. A kind of strong evaluation is being snuck in here. And, to turn this around, most sculptors and musicians and teachers endure forms of toil within their leisure—in my case I think of grading papers. In short, it sounds like the Skidelskys do not really want a reduction of work activity but a reduction of *toil*—in which case, perhaps, they do not want leisure but, rather, better work.

While such a discussion could be a book in itself, for our purposes we need only to display how the evaluation of the disposition of luxury is deeply connected to competing strong evaluations of work and leisure. Veblen helps us to see that productive work—and its analogous sibling, parental concern—are the most basic of human aims. By contrast, he sees the Humean elevation of personal pride and mutual enjoyment of cultivated pleasures as a wasteful pursuit of a privileged few who are able to engage in such refinement only at the expense of others' real work and who in the process of "learning" leisure become unfit for productive work; they are saboteurs of a society that could direct its knowledge toward the common good, especially of future generations.

The Problems of Practical Reason II:
Practices, Internal Goods, and Social Cooperation

Does this conclusion merely displace the strong evaluation of luxury, or can we further adjudicate these strong evaluations of work and leisure?[147] These questions essentially lead to competing narratives that offer a home for disparate accounts of virtues. One path for resolving these would be to appeal to authority within the Catholic tradition. We could call on the meanings found in the extraordinary encyclical of Pope John Paul II on the dignity of work, *Laborem Exercens*. In it the pope makes clear that work is neither simply toil and punishment for sin nor merely instrumental to meet "objective" needs. Rather, it is commanded by God in Genesis 1 and is the means by which humans constitute themselves as "subjects."[148] Indeed, the parallels of Veblen's instincts to John Paul II's reading of Genesis 1, in which work and parenting are the two fundamental charges of human dignity, are striking. One could cite other Christian arguments for the importance of work as well.

However, philosophically we can dig deeper into the problems with Hume's account (and provide support for Veblen) by turning to Alasdair MacIntyre's account of adjudicating different lists of virtues via the notion of practices. An analysis of luxury as a vice that corrupts practices runs counter to the lengthy tradition of pro-commerce narratives about how the pursuit of these goods produces ideal social cooperation. Ultimately these stories must be called into question, not by appealing to ancient Roman moralists but by a more detailed demonstration of how the disposition to luxury ultimately fosters destructive social competition, not genuine cooperation.

The argument will be developed in two stages: first, in determining what a virtue is and how virtues "make sense" in light of practices (specifically in light of what practices require of our abilities to reason practically), and second, in treating the question of luxury specifically.

Practices and Internal Goods

In *After Virtue*, MacIntyre shows the history of the tradition of virtue as a confrontation among rival and incompatible lists of virtues and vices. How is one to sort these out? In order to do this, MacIntyre develops his well-known concept of a practice: "Any coherent and complex form of socially established cooperative human activity through which goods internal to that form of activity are realized in the course of trying to achieve those standards of excellence" partially constitutive of the activity. Such achievement "systematically extends" both our own "powers" and the goods of the activity.[149] Thus, virtue is "an acquired human quality the possession and exercise of which tends to enable us to achieve those goods which are internal to practices and the lack of which effectively prevents us from achieving any such goods."[150] Practices are not isolated human acts, like throwing a football or punishing a child, but rather human activities, like the game of football or raising a family.

Two (related) elements of his complex, carefully built definition apply here. First, MacIntyre distinguishes between internal and external goods.[151] External goods are only *contingently* related to a given activity and can be achieved in a variety of ways, including by merely simulating excellent activity or even by cheating. He gives the example of motivating a seven-year-old to play chess well by promising candy.[152] The child acts for the sake of the candy, not the chess. She might have some other way to get candy. If the child continues to play chess for candy, she may develop technical skill at chess, but because she seeks the candy, she will only understand the activity as a *means* to this end and so will not develop the attachment to the actual standards of excellence of the activity. And she will likely find a less taxing way to get candy! So long as she is focused on the candy, she will at best develop only technical skill. At worst, she will merely simulate skill or cheat.

A focus on the "candy" of external goods, while characteristic of young children, does not *automatically* go away with age. Here we encounter the second key element: practices and virtues require a transition from an existing desire for an external good to a shared conception of excellence of the activity adopted as our own genuine desire. All human practices require participants to learn a key distinction "between directedness toward their end and directedness toward the satisfaction of their desires," whether that desire is money, fame, comfort, or any other good external to the practice.[153] Everyone initially brings "antecedent desires" to practices (please our parents, earn a reward); but "successful initiation" requires "our desires . . . to be redirected and transformed" toward achieving the objective excellences of the activity. It is moving from founding a microbrewery as a way to make friends or money to doing it for the sake of making excellent beer. Such a process implies learning that "it is never sufficient to explain or to justify our actions by citing some desire."[154] Rather, we must learn to desire the standards for excellence—the internal goods—of the practice.

This crucial transition from external to internal requires a "transition from accepting what we are taught by our earliest teachers to making our own independent judgments about goods, judgments that we are able to justify rationally to ourselves and to others as furnishing us with good reasons for acting in this way rather than that."[155] The process requires a complex form of trusting, cooperative dependence on others, since our ability to make these judgments is constantly vulnerable to both the solicitation of external goods and the errancy of our own desires. This asymmetrical reciprocity requires both power and restraint, and both dependence and independence. It requires a kind of "asceticism" in relation to our own desires, as well as the presence of reliable and trustworthy guidance from those who have themselves made this transition. But it is not simply the *rejection* of desire, which MacIntyre calls a "dangerous phantasy"; it is the *transformation* of desire from goods of effectiveness to goods of excellence, from love of fame or money to "love of the game."

What emerges here is at least a partial account of what being "practically rational"—providing genuine *reasons* for action—means. That is, we need answers to some specific questions: "Is it good for me (or for anyone) to want this or that thing?" and "Should I want it?" and "Do I have good reasons for wanting it?" These questions are at the heart of what we mean by moral agency, which is "the knowledge of how to discriminate among the various objects of attention presented to us by our desires."[156] Being practically reasonable means coming to identify the standards of excellence that are internal to "good" activity, and subordinating the satisfaction of one's immediate desires for external goods to such achievement, in and through cooperation with others. Both the subordination of desire and the relational character of practices are required in the development of the virtues. That is, it is not merely *being* an excellent violinist that necessitates virtue; *becoming* excellent is achieved only by properly subordinating one's desires to one's teachers and maintaining relationships animated by dispositions of trust, justice, and courage (MacIntyre's examples) with other players.

Dispositions in Practices: Honesty and Luxury

If we recall that the point here is to adjudicate lists of dispositions—and luxury is a disposition involving some kind of inordinate attachment to certain kinds of material goods and experiences—does MacIntyre's account of practices show why luxury is a vice? Before looking directly at luxury, it is helpful to examine a relatively noncontroversial example of a disposition that is now routinely accepted as good and necessary for social cooperation in economic activity: honesty or trustworthiness. Economist Partha Dasgupta *begins* his presentation of economics with a discussion of trust and community before turning to markets, because markets (and the productive work on which they rely) simply cannot function without trust.[157] He points out that the success of advanced economies depends on a great deal of "stranger sociality," the disposition to treat strangers and their property with basic forms of honesty. It is striking, he says, that more traditional societies—while exhibiting more "community" in a certain sense—have difficulty developing extensive markets because norms of trust differ depending on whether one is dealing with a family/clan member or not. "Stranger sociality" involves the development of a definite disposition to act in honest ways that are consistent and accord all persons the same due. While our arrangements do depend on underlying enforcement mechanisms of law and contract, such arrangements need to stay largely in the background; if they do not, transaction costs become very high.[158]

It is important to see that the goodness of the disposition is not simply instrumental. It does produce good outcomes but if we are being honest only *instrumentally*, good action would be a matter of knowing when it is best to be honest and when it is best not.[159] In the Humean model the *appearance* of honesty might be beneficial in order to obtain what one desires, but there would be plenty of cases when one might be able to maintain the appearance of honesty while cheating. What is actually necessary for achieving the internal goods of economic practice is that agents possess the real virtue of honesty, or at least a desire for it; a mere imitation of virtue would eventually lead to the collapse of trust.[160] The argument for the necessity of this disposition is based on its key role (backed up by law) in achieving the internal goods of social practices, but which would become problematic if people generally lacked the genuine disposition and sought routinely to counter it (that is, break that law).

How would an analogous case be made for the viciousness of luxury? There are two key ways in which the disposition of luxury impairs the moral development necessary for practices outlined above. First, it is easy to see the viciousness of luxurious desires because they detract from the discipline of initiation into practices described above. If you can't fight off the desire to stay in bed, it's going to be hard to succeed at any economic activity.[161] At this minimal level, an initial case can be made against luxury in terms of possessing the disposition to avoid the discomforts of even minor effort. Adam Ferguson's critique of luxury recalls the ancients here by carefully noting this problem: the error of luxury is one to which people are "perpetually exposed . . . when they are accustomed to high measures of accommodation."[162] A recognition that excessive comfort undermines excellence in practice does not require a militaristic foundation; in our society of constant Internet connection, lack of exercise, and inability to develop even the simplest of skills (e.g., cooking), we can identify examples of how even slight effort is avoided. Are microwave dinners (every night) a luxury? Is taking an elevator when you are perfectly capable of using the stairs indicative of luxury? Luxury can be identified with material goods, especially of comfort and convenience, that impair our ability to do the difficult work of disciplining our desires to achieve the goods of excellence.

However, Hume's definition of luxury is not referring to lying around in bed all day. Indeed, the rejection of pure, vulgar sensual indulgence is at the heart of his distinction between "old luxury" and new.[163] He assumes that seeking luxury actually drives us to activity—an assumption that seems confirmed in much of our society. Let us imagine the person spurred to hard work for all the good things he and his family can enjoy as fruits of that labor.

Here is the second part of the case against luxury: the real distinction between the pursuit of external versus internal goods. MacIntyre's scheme of practical reason indicates that a problem exists when we cannot get beyond the stage of acting for external goods. It does not really matter if what we are seeking is a vacation week in Vegas or a Sierra Club excursion to south Asia. The initial, obvious issue is that any activity done for the sake of luxury consumption appears to be like MacIntyre's playing chess for candy. External goods are not bad in themselves and it is not wrong to want a salary for work. The danger in any type of external reward *as motivational* is how it *instrumentalizes* activity. MacIntyre suggests that his conception of practices and virtues is incompatible with utilitarianism because utilitarianism "cannot accommodate the distinction between goods internal to and goods external to a practice."[164] It systematically instrumentalizes our relationship to any activity, leading us to ask, "What's in it for me?"[165]

Activities that are instrumentalized in this way deform us as persons, deform the activity itself, and deform the cooperation necessary for ongoing excellence in the activity. This is, in a sense, the exact contrary to the claim that Hume makes about how luxury pacifies our character and enhances cooperation. In order to sort out these claims, we first should consider areas in our lives that resist such instrumentalizing logic and clearly exhibit MacIntyre's model. What reasons do people give for getting married? Instrumentalizing answers like "because I want to live longer" or "for the monetary benefits" are likely to be viewed suspiciously. Why, then, is "for the money" considered a perfectly "reasonable" answer—even when one already has sufficient wealth—for choosing this or that job? Here we have to recognize MacIntyre's point that every morality presupposes a sociology—every description of action has a setting that relies on a narrative placed within a large-scale tradition.[166] "To get a new kitchen" can be an answer to "Why are you dating him?" or "Why did you take that job?" but our moral evaluation differs in each case.

This phenomenon of compartmentalization means that different moral logics are in play within different areas of life. Sports and the performing arts are good classroom examples for learning about the internal goods of practices and the importance of cooperation in becoming virtuous. Significantly, few students plan to go on in life and make these activities central, yet neither do many students explicitly intend to go on to become extremely rich. What they want in life is "to be successful"—by which they almost always mean a job that they "like" and that gives them "enough" money to buy things they want for themselves and their future families without worry or anxiety. In other words, they regard their material life—work and consumption—in terms of external goods. The model of activity-as-practice moves to the margins of incentive-based economic activity (work and consumption), while retaining a place in other areas of life (sports and family).

The relevance of these examples of activity-as-practice is that reliance on external rewards undermines, rather than encourages, excellence in cooperative activities. Bribing children may be okay when they are young, but it would be increasingly problematic as a long-term strategy. All forms of monetary support for one's children are not bribery, but we identify bribery when the external good is the primary motivator. As with the development of honesty, our activities may *begin* by motivating people via external goods and coercive punishment but the activity is subject to corruption insofar as moral limits are not internalized as good in themselves.[167]

Based on the important differences between motivation by external versus internal goods, we can name three key ways in which luxury is a disposition contrary to practices and cooperation. (The descriptions here will necessarily be broadly sketched, with the details left for the later chapters of looking more closely at "what counts.") First, luxury can name a desire for excessive, disproportionate *quantities* of external goods. Consider the case of a person who changes jobs, from one that pays enough to one that pays more than enough. Presumably the motivation here could be described as one of luxury. (It could instead be the seeking of prestige or power, or other kinds of nonluxury external goods, of course.) People frequently sacrifice other goods in order to gain consumption rewards that, happiness research shows, are ultimately not satisfying. These goods may be found in other parts of life, like family. But it is important to note that workers may do this, individually or collectively, in ways that sacrifice *internal* goods ignoring excellence in the cooperative activity itself for the sake of superfluous external goods. Employees who demand raises above a living wage, for example, may imperil the whole enterprise. Or high-ranking employees may take pay that leads to sub-living wages for others (the example of skyrocketing ratios of CEO pay is frequently cited). It is economically rational for companies to attract the "best" by staying competitive on compensation, but what if a prospective CEO were motivated primarily not by whether he or she would make $10 million or $20 million but instead by whether the company encourages true excellence in management and (in addition) justice for all its workers? If the CEO is motivated by the extra $10 million, surely we have an example of luxury.[168] Any particular case would require further investigation, but the general problem arises when the drive for "more than enough" external goods overrides the internal goods of the practice.

Second, because external goods are by definition individual, sometimes the search for them means that others *necessarily* will not have them. Such goods are rival and comparative, and luxury can be the name for an excessive desire for such external goods (as well might ambition, arrogance, and avarice). Luxury has always been a comparative category—it (rightly or wrongly) sees material goods as expressions of superior social status and relies on *necessarily* comparative judgments. Only one person can have the corner office.

Many business owners and leaders, both in their rhetoric and (less so) in their practice, acknowledge how counterproductive such status competitions are for the actual cooperative work of the company.[169] One recent study's results published in a management journal sought to identify factors that lead employees to either hide or share knowledge with other employees and teams in the organization. Such knowledge sharing is broadly recognized as important for any organization's overall creativity. The "motivational climate" of the organization makes the difference. Is it a "performance climate . . . characterized by social comparison and intrateam competition"—or is it a "mastery climate" which "values employees' efforts, self-development, cooperation, and learning"?[170] Unsurprisingly, knowledge hiding was prevalent in the former climate, knowledge sharing in the latter. Thus, it is advantageous to adjust the reward structure to emphasize less comparative external status goods. Ideally, such rewards are aligned with actual excellence and are not simply linked to seniority or personal connections. Moreover, they are difficult to fake. As will be discussed in a later chapter, this problem of inherently comparative goods takes on much greater significance in a society of affluence, for more and more activity is devoted to pursuing goods that go beyond necessity. In such situations, the best social outcome turns out to require cooperative collective restraint—that is, a disposition against luxury.

Third, since the focus of such activity is on external reward rather than the activity itself, luxury can name a motivation for material reward that is comfortable with merely *simulating* virtue. Grasping this third problem is more difficult. Consider an example from economist Charles Wheelan, who, like many economists, believes in economic incentives as the best way to fix defective social practices. He criticizes the American education system for its resistance to merit pay ("linking pay to productivity") and the inability to discipline poor-performing teachers and suggests that the data show "the brightest individuals shun the teaching profession at every juncture." The brightest teachers are also the most likely to leave the profession early. While in passing he notes some "gifted individuals" who stay in "because they love it," the "general problem" is that "any system that pays all teachers the same provides a strong incentive for the most talented among them to look for work elsewhere."[171]

This example illustrates not one but two reasons why luxury is a problem. First, Wheelan is correct that low-performing teachers, an embarrassment to the profession, are essentially taking advantage of this system. But surely these individuals do not genuinely care about excellence in their activity; we might inquire whether their aspirations would be characterized in terms of ease, job security, enriching themselves as senior faculty, etc. Aren't their aspirations able to be characterized in terms of luxury? On the other hand, to suggest the solution is to use pay for performance ignores one of the greatest problems of evaluating teaching: how do you measure performance? Couldn't teachers have every incentive to game testing procedures and/or go easy on/bring cookies for their students . . . especially if the students themselves are afflicted by luxury? In this sense, a reliance on external incentives for educational excellence seems to run into potential problems of luxury on either end. A good education system does not primarily need a better incentive system but rather "teachers who love it." Evidence suggests that teachers who love their jobs are *not* going to be living lives preoccupied with luxury pursuits.[172]

Even in the realm of business there are strong indications that external incentives—including ones that appeal to luxury—are ultimately ineffective for achieving excellence. There is considerable debate about whether MacIntyre's model of practices can be applied at all to the modern corporation. MacIntyre is highly skeptical, but Michael Goldberg, in an essay on MacIntyre and business ethics, offers a series of examples of "corporate cults" or "corporate credos" in which highly successful corporations depend on the ability to inculcate a shared commitment to excellent activity. At least internal to the firm, the primary allegiance is to shared excellence rather than to individual advancement.[173] Goldberg rightly recognizes that such a manner of business is becoming more difficult to achieve because of a fragmented social environment and because of the decline of the expectation of long-term employment by a single firm. But this does not invalidate the insight. Rather, it suggests that business activity (like any activity) is affected by larger social dynamics.

In a similar vein, ethicists Helen Alford and Michael Naughton offer a series of examples of businesses that properly order what they call "foundational goods" to "excellent goods." Their distinction is somewhat less dichotomous than MacIntyre's in that, "in some ways, foundational goods, like profits or efficient methods, are the most important because they directly support the economic viability of the firm in a market environment. They are necessities. . . . In other ways, however, our own development and that of others are most important, because as ultimate motivations they inform and render meaningful all of our work."[174] Alford and Naughton crucially recognize that foundational goods are necessary but they must be ordered to higher goods. In their examples, profit is most often the focus: getting it is necessary, but the problem arises when it comes to be seen as an end rather than a means, and when excellence is wrongly equated with maximum profitability. Analogously, we might consider a firm whose employees or managers view the best firm as the one with the nicest offices, or the most employee perks, or the highest salaries. The point here is not to denigrate salaries or offices but rather to suggest how "luxury" might be manifest within a firm: by taking foundational goods as ends in themselves.

Further support is offered in the book-length study offered by Yale psychologist Tom Tyler entitled *Why People Cooperate*. Tyler's data suggests that the tendency of social science in general "to view people as primarily relating to groups instrumentally" and in terms of "potential sources of material rewards" is mistaken.[175] Instead, cooperation is actually achieved through "internal motivations" and involves attachment to others, identification with the whole, a sense of collective participative agency, and the like.[176] Luxury, as necessarily involving relative comparisons, undermines these reasons for cooperating.

Beyond the firm, the idea that the pursuit of luxury makes for a peaceful society runs headlong into the macroeconomic problem of inequality. In a sense this is simply a larger version of the CEO pay problem because arguments over redistribution can be locked into unspoken suspicions about luxury on both sides. For the wealthy, there is a deep suspicion that an overly generous welfare system will be taken advantage of by the poor and that the poor manage what money they have in bad ways—that is, they will spend it irresponsibly on frivolous luxuries. For the poor and their advocates there is the deep suspicion that "tax cuts for the wealthy" have nothing to do with "job creation," but simply enable even more profligate spending by the rich. It would be interesting to compare the debates that go on here to ones appearing in other countries (i.e., Scandinavian ones) in which luxury and "the goods life" appear to be far less central among both wealthier and poorer individuals. Is there greater ability to engage in redistribution (or avoid it in the first place, via a much more compressed system of salaries)?[177]

Observations on the inadequacy of external incentives for cooperative activity should help us recognize that Socrates's concern that luxury creates faction, not social concord, remains a reality.[178] A firm full of workers with the disposition of luxury may not be a good firm and an economy full of luxury-seekers may have serious problems distributing essential resources because of implied mutual suspicion about extravagance. Thus, concerns about luxury should be viewed in the same way economists view dishonesty and social mistrust: they undermine social cooperation aimed at shared excellence. Indeed, insofar as Mandeville himself endorsed both "luxury" and "fraud" in the same breath, it would be odd to agree with him on the one (that luxury is good) but completely reject his case on the other (that fraud is bad). Mandeville's hive is an unconvincing defense of fraud and so, too, is its defense of luxury. An actual analysis of the conditions of practical activity requires us to have some distance on our desires, to order those desires toward other activities in life, and to recognize the importance of acting for good for its own sake rather than merely in response to some incentive.

It's not that incentives are bad; economists are correct to look at systems and figure out how incentives can be better aligned. Indeed, it is to the credit of modern economics that it seeks to manage the ancient problem, also identified by MacIntyre, of aligning external rewards to excellent practice.[179] The point here is not to offer some total critique of modern economics but rather to criticize some of its tendencies. The mistake comes when everything is made to hinge on the *incentives* rather than on people's *dispositions*. Incentives cannot replace dispositions. Both behavioral economics (the locus for much of the happiness studies literature) and the focus on social systems and norms for generating dispositions (like trust and honesty) criticize this reductionism to external incentives. The utilitarianism seen in happiness studies needs supplementation to give an account of goods that are internal to practices, and social norms (and perhaps even laws) are ultimately required not only against fraudulence, but also against luxury. Incentives are good, but not sufficient. Their insufficiency is not simply that "money can't buy happiness" but that external goods don't actually form the kind of virtuous practitioners society requires.

To summarize, MacIntyre's analysis of the practical reasoning and virtues required by practices yields two points that support the view that luxury is a vice. One is that luxury names an attachment to comfort and ease that disables our capacity to discipline our desires, which is a prerequisite for the achievement of virtuous activity. The second, perhaps more important point) is that luxury ultimately distorts excellence in activity because, as an external good or "incentive," it draws our attention away from the realization of internal goods and the cooperation necessary to achieve them.

Luxury and the Recovery of Moral Traditions

This chapter refurbishes the language of luxury as a reasonable language of moral judgment that makes clear the practical rationality of why we should (and in some cases already do) consider luxury a vicious disposition. Two related considerations are crucial: our "strong evaluation" of the nobility of good work and our need for social practices that aim at the goods of excellence—goods internal to practices—rather than merely external goods. But who are "we"? It is important to make a distinction between virtue ethics and American society. Many people who are committed to virtue ethics have neglected seeing luxury as an important vice, especially in the context of our society's consensus on the goods life. Defenders of luxury develop their cases in ways antithetical to the basic moral psychology of the virtue model. Mandeville extols how one "may in a hundred places see Good spring up and pullilate from Evil, as naturally as Chickens do from Eggs."[180] But can virtue ethicists maintain that evil ought to be done for the sake of good? Virtue ethicists reject a Humean account of practical reason yet they do not counter Hume's approval of luxury nor do they recognize luxury as a frequently encountered vice within the richest society the world has ever known. Some virtue ethicists fall victim to the modern tendency of compartmentalization by which persons "move between" many areas that require "different and even sometimes incompatible attitudes" resulting in "a fragmented ethics."[181]

The recovery of language regarding this neglected vice is also instructive for another tradition: the American cultural debate over consumerism and its tendency to be interminable. Such arguments need more precision, in particular about the need to consider deeper claims about practical rationality and teleology (the overall ends of human life). These problems cannot be accessed when the debate remains cast in largely utilitarian terms and further limited by an overarching commitment to autonomy.

Two particular tendencies of anti-consumerist arguments deserve rethinking. One is the tendency to critique social structures rather than personal desires. The language of luxury focuses on personal desire in a way that consumerism may not; like racism or sexism, consumer*ism* suggests a kind of victimhood that creates a stereotypical dichotomy—the lazy corporate rich and the struggling poor—which distorts the actual problems. There are definitely structural issues in our economy, but part of what makes confronting these issues difficult is our attachment to luxury.

The second, the appeal to an argument for leisure against consumerism, is problematic. Hume and Veblen should lead us to see that it is difficult to hold off the allure of refined possessions if one has a lot of leisure. I tend to side with certain figures from the "producerist" tradition—Lewis Mumford, Christopher Lasch, Wendell Berry—who are skeptical about moral arguments for resource redistribution that do not pay more attention to the transformation of work itself. MacIntyre offers one set of pragmatic reasons for this skepticism: the combination of trade unions and the welfare state that supposedly "will enable workers to participate in capitalist prosperity" actually results in "the domestication and then the destruction" of unions, along with the promotion of a "moral individualism" through a liberal politics that is "itself a solvent of participatory community."[182]

Consumer critics might instead recognize that the critique of luxury remains implied in much of American daily life, albeit with much ambivalence and fragility.[183] We only lack a language to make sense of our priorities—the language of luxury. By eliminating this vice *as vice* from our language, we open the door to the unlimited pursuit of a certain way of life that is deeply corrosive but which cannot be identified as such. The remnant of citizens that continue to resist luxury, despite this loss of language, constitute a kind of social and moral capital that we are burning through quickly. Their opposite, a life of leisured luxury, might best be exemplified by the paradigm of "the pure celebrity"—the Kardashians or Paris Hilton—for whom cultural admiration is based solely on their stylish consumption rather than on even *simulations* of virtue or technical skills. Even worse, television shows like the "Real Housewives" series or *Jersey Shore* or house-hunting shows extend this image of unlimited material pursuits into the everyday consumption of ordinary people.

In a broader sense, for both audiences appeals to the virtue of justice should be seen as necessary but insufficient for dealing with our economic lives, both as individuals and as a society. Claims about economic *justice*—which depend on larger narrative frames—become unmanageable social conflicts without presumptions about what economic *temperance* means.[184] Claims about economic temperance and the problem of luxury do feature in some early twentieth-century discussions of the problems of poverty and inequality (see chapter 8). Progressive-era pioneers of the study of poverty often focused on establishing levels of a basic budget for poor workers.[185] It is sometimes forgotten that, besides paying his workers five dollars a day, Henry Ford also sought to form and regulate his workers' lifestyles. "We want to pay the men and pay them well so they can live well, but we don't want to make them reckless," he said. He paired his profit-sharing plan with a team of "investigators" (later renamed "advisers") who sought to help and oversee the home conditions of his workers. They provided help in times of need and crisis (e.g., helping a family stuck in a slumlord's grip with a quick loan, materials, and a cottage of their own) but also kept a close eye on house upkeep, domestic relations, and the like. The goal of living wages and advice was "to protect and build up happy homes," and, as one supervisor put it, the worker who resisted such advice was the one "drinking up his income and beating up his wife."[186]

These examples strike us as paternalistic and I am not recommending fast food restaurants raise their wages to fifteen dollars an hour but then require home inspections and budget controls. However, these notions do manifest a realistic and proper recognition that the economic life of both individuals and society requires more than attention to money distribution. Attention must also be paid to questions of what it is actually good and bad for people to want. A commitment to "the goods life *for all*" is unrealistic economically and unsustainable environmentally; thus, it produces dysfunction within economic activity itself. Economic temperance is a prerequisite for justice, just as some kind of sexual temperance is a prerequisite for love, fidelity, and just procreation. But *saying* this—and saying that it infects rich, poor, and middle class alike—is unfortunately taboo.

Many will remain concerned that a focus on the individual and social need to restrain commerce threatens our social order. This kind of worry indicates that our trust in commerce as the foundation of our way of life constitutes not merely a prudential or pragmatic compromise, but a real *faith*. It is a faith that requires us to make continual sacrifices to the gods of the marketplace and, as a faith, needs to be confronted not merely on a philosophical but also on a theological level. We now turn to this theological level—and the way in which the allure of luxury is given a virtually transcendent glow.

Notes

1. Gregory, *Unintended Reformation*, 235.
2. John Paul II, *Sollicitudo Rei Socialis*, no. 28.
3. Fukuyama, *End of History*.
4. Gregory, *Unintended Reformation*, 236. Further citations in the text.
5. He rightly points out that one of the key effective critiques of the Catholic Church by the Reformers was of its exorbitant wealth, in contradiction to its own teaching.
6. Twitchell, *Living It Up*, 275–76.
7. Ibid., 80. Twitchell also repeats the common economic argument that the system produces the most aggregate wealth (44–47), and has made "many, many millions of people" better off (285).
8. Cross, *All-Consuming Century*, viii. Cross concludes that one key reason why alternatives are not chosen is that they would require a level of self-denial for membership, while consumerism does not (247)—yet he also concludes that the key is not rejecting it, but placing restraints on "a system that naturally has no limits" (251).
9. McCloskey, "Avarice, Prudence, and the Bourgeois Virtues," 334.
10. Livingston, *Against Thrift*, xii.
11. Ibid., xi.
12. Livingston, *Pragmatism*.
13. Livingston, *Against Thrift*, xi.
14. Livingston, *Pragmatism*, xxv, 247–53.
15. Gregory, "Unintended Reformation."
16. Most explanations of the 2007–2009 financial crisis demonstrate that pure self-interested action is insufficient for markets to work well; see, e.g., Cassidy, *How Markets Fail*. Blinder, "What's the Matter with Economics?" notes that economists have done a poor job differentiating the claim about the efficiency of the market system (the "invisible hand") from the claim about the desirability of maximizing self-interest ("greed is good"). This distinction needs wider circulation.
17. McCloskey, "Avarice, Prudence," 318.
18. Ibid., 319.
19. Wallace-Hadrill, *Rome's Cultural Revolution*, 319.
20. Ibid., 326.
21. Ibid., 329.
22. Rubin, *Happiness Project*.
23. Ahuvia, "Wealth, Consumption, and Happiness," 204. Recall Aquinas's distinction between natural and artificial wealth, discussed earlier.
24. Kasser, *High Cost of Materialism*.
25. Skidelskys, *How Much Is Enough?*, 191.
26. Ibid., 75.
27. Ibid., 180.
28. Nettle, *Happiness*, 87. The literature also suggests that there is a biological component of temperament that affects overall happiness. The importance of "autonomy" here is interestingly related to the later point about work, because Nettle notes that what is truly beneficial in life is a sense of "personal control." This varies a lot even within classes, and it's clearly correlated with happiness. For example, members of

the lowest, unskilled labor class whose lives scored high on "personal control" had a happiness score of 7.85 out of 10, whereas professional class members who had little personal control scored 5.82 (74). However, far more professionals scored high on personal control: in the professional group, only 10 percent felt they usually didn't get what they wanted out of life, whereas 34 percent of unskilled workers said this.

29. Frank, *Luxury Fever*, 81–83.
30. Nettle, *Happiness*, 72. For further data see Frey and Stutzer, "What Can Econo-mists Learn from Happiness Research?"
31. Nettle, *Happiness*, 72; Skidelskys, *How Much Is Enough?*, 102–3.
32. See McKibben, *Deep Economy*, 42.
33. Nettle, *Happiness*, 161.
34. Offer, *Challenge of Affluence*; Schwartz, *Paradox of Choice*.
35. Kasser, *High Cost*.
36. This is also the vision of prominent consumer critic Juliet Schor, whose work can be found in *Overworked American*, *Overspent American*, and *Plenitude*.
37. Skidelskys, *How Much Is Enough?*, 33.
38. Ibid., 22, citing OECD Employment Outlook 2011.
39. Goodman and Goodman, *Communitas: Means of Livelihood and Ways of Life*. See Riesman, *Individualism Reconsidered*, 84–99, for a summary of the Good-mans' argument.
40. Riesman, *Individualism*, 95.
41. For a comprehensive account of these errors, see Kahneman, *Thinking Fast and Slow*.
42. Cavanaugh, "Consumer Culture," in *Gathered for the Journey*, 242.
43. Lyubomirsky, *Myths of Happiness*, 149. It is unfortunate that she qualifies her statement by making these recommendations for "individuals on meager bud-gets" who want to "extract the maximum happiness from spending less."
44. Summarized by the Skidelskys, *How Much Is Enough?*, 107–13.
45. McKibben, *Deep Economy*, 45.
46. Ahuvia, "Wealth, Consumption," 216.
47. Bruni, *Wound and the Blessing*, 79.
48. Nettle, *Happiness*, 20.
49. Ibid., 21. He criticizes the well-known work of Csikszentmihalyi, *Flow*, for covertly "smuggling in" level-three assumptions.
50. The two problems here could also explain the data on the negative effects of divorce or single-parenting on children, which (broadly) are strongly demon-strated but whose implications for practice are avoided.
51. Schwartz, *Paradox of Choice*, is the key argument for this.
52. Skidelskys, *How Much Is Enough?*, 107.
53. Ibid., 193.
54. A similar strategy for social change is proposed by Thaler and Sunstein in *Nudge*. A parallel ambiguity crops up in de Graaf's *What's the Economy For*. Relying on happiness studies, they show that the problems with our economy are wrapped up in bad personal consumption decisions, but the concrete proposals in the final chapter focus on government regulation and social service; the idea that indi-vidual people have to change their dispositions disappears.
55. Pabst nicely lays this out in *Crisis of Global Capitalism*, 10–13.

56. The evidence, however, also suggests that life goals make us happier when we feel as though they are "authentic" and genuinely our own. See Lyubomirsky, *Myths of Happiness*, 136, citing, among others, Kasser. This is an interesting "paradox of freedom" that might reward further study.
57. Berman, *Dark Ages America*, 71.
58. Ibid., 73.
59. Ibid., 74.
60. Ibid., 75.
61. Taylor, "Diversity of Goods," 130.
62. Ibid., 139.
63. Herdt, *Putting on Virtue*, 226–27.
64. Herdt's history of the eighteenth century, where Rousseau and Hume represent different responses to the supposed "hypocrisy" of society—equally rejecting of Christianity but virtually opposite in their evaluation of bourgeois society—could be mapped clearly onto the secular debates over consumerism. See ibid., 283–84.
65. Ibid., 221.
66. For this language see Taylor's definitive essay, "What Is Human Agency?"
67. Hume's "subversion" of the moral sense is the central story of MacIntyre's *Whose Justice? Which Rationality?*; in addition, of course, Hume is the classic originator of the so-called fact/value distinction.
68. Hume, *Treatise on Human Nature*, 413. Further citations in the text.
69. Lehrer, *How We Decide*, xv.
70. Ibid., 173. This is a painfully distorted history of how moral philosophy has handled this complicated question, but it usefully fits Lehrer's general "science trumps philosophy" narrative.
71. Ibid., 172.
72. See Macpherson, *Political Theory of Possessive Individualism*, for the classic background account.
73. See MacIntyre, *Whose Justice*, chap. 14.
74. MacIntyre, *Short History of Ethics*, 165.
75. Lehrer, *How We Decide*, 180–94.
76. Herdt, *Putting on Virtue*, 311.
77. Hume, *Treatise*, 486–87, cited in Herdt, *Putting on Virtue*, 309.
78. For a summary see Herdt, *Putting on Virtue*, 308–15.
79. See, e.g., Baier, *Pursuits*, 39.
80. Herdt, *Putting on Virtue*, 312; she cites Hume, *Treatise*, 287.
81. Herdt, *Putting on Virtue*, 312.
82. See also Hume, *Enquiry*, 90.
83. He does treat "pity" or "compassion" later,
84. Hume, "Of Refinement in the Arts" (titled "Of Luxury" in earlier editions), 123.
85. The rise of Internet music, of course, rendered moot the need to develop a vast collection because virtually any song is available on a whim at any time. So much for pride.
86. Hume, *Enquiry*, 111.
87. Hume, "Of Refinement in the Arts," 124.
88. Berry, *Idea of Luxury*, 146, who notes that Hume represents the doctrine of "gentle commerce."

89. Hume, "Of Commerce," 136.
90. Ibid., 137.
91. Ibid., 134–35. Hume concludes his essay by observing that manufactures have not advanced in France or Spain or Italy because agriculture there is "an easy art" where the warm climate "renders clothes and houses less requisite" and removes spurs to industry. Such observations may highlight the fact that Hume's case here rests largely on questionable generalizations and arguments from ancient literature.
92. Hume, "Of Refinement in the Arts," 126. He does add that the labor devoted to manufacturing luxuries can be converted easily to military use in time of need. See "On Commerce," 136–37.
93. Hume, "Of Refinement," 127. He does not apparently make the connection between the need for conquests and the use of economic resources for private luxury.
94. Hume, "Of Commerce," 138.
95. As Charles Taylor shows, this ideal of civility came to have great importance in the rise of exclusive humanist forms of beliefs. See *Secular Age*, 99–114, 216–18.
96. Hume, *Enquiry*, 82. In the earlier essays praising luxury, Hume attempts a similar distinction between "new" and "old" (= bad) luxury.
97. See the recent book by King, *Ambition*, which explains how ambition has moved from a vice to a virtue.
98. Hume, *Enquiry*, 107.
99. Ibid., 116.
100. Smith, *Theory of Moral Sentiments*, 320.
101. Ibid., 61.
102. MacIntyre, *Short History of Ethics*, 177.
103. MacIntyre, *After Virtue*, 233.
104. Taylor, "What Is Human Agency?," 28.
105. Ibid., 24.
106. Ibid., 26.
107. Ibid., 35.
108. Taylor, "Reason, Faith, and Meaning," 14.
109. MacIntyre, "Editor's Introduction to *Hume's Ethical Writings*" 16.
110. Taylor, "Reason, Faith, and Meaning," 13.
111. Ibid., 15.
112. Hume, *Enquiry*, 103. Almost the same definition is given at 117 and 127.
113. Hendel, "Editor's Introduction," xlvi.
114. E.g., Hume, *Enquiry*, 126–27.
115. Taylor, "Reason, Faith, and Meaning," 17.
116. Hume, *Enquiry*, 93, 103, 107.
117. MacIntyre, *After Virtue*, 231.
118. Copleston, *History of Philosophy*, 340. The best way to appreciate what Copleston means here is by reading Daniel Westberg's classic, *Right Practical Reason*, which demonstrates the remarkable complexity and precision with which Aquinas describes the passion-intellect-will psychology of practical rationality.
119. Hume, *Enquiry*, 131.
120. Heilbroner, *Worldly Philosophers*, 218–19.
121. Clark, "Wealth as Abundance and Scarcity," 44.

122. See, for example, Holt and Schor, "Do Americans Consume Too Much?" xv.
123. Veblen, *Theory of the Leisure Class*, 76. Further citations in the text.
124. Veblen, *Instinct of Workmanship*, 2–3.
125. Indeed, Veblen even suggests that these might be referred to as the "spiritual nature" of man, though he quickly notes that he does not mean to make any judgments about the realities of any religion. See ibid., 14.
126. Ibid., 25. Also 48–49.
127. Ibid., 26.
128. Ibid., 31. The notion of "satisfaction in itself" points forward to MacIntyre's account of the importance of internal goods in the next section.
129. Ibid., 33.
130. Veblen, "Instinct of Workmanship and the Irksomeness of Labor," 89.
131. Veblen, *Instinct of Workmanship*, 145.
132. See MacIntyre, *Dependent Rational Animals*.
133. Indeed, in Veblen's view "primitive" societies had very little in the way of such prizes. One author argues that Veblen's basic theory of value is that "tool-using . . . underlies all the achievements of mankind" but that "the exploits by which some men are always seeking to get the better of others are an impediment to workmanship and creative achievement." Ayres, "Coordinates of Institutionalism," 53.
134. Veblen, *Engineers and the Price System*, 36.
135. Ibid., 39–40.
136. Ibid., 68–69.
137. We will see later that Keynes has a similar background assumption.
138. Hume, *Enquiry*, 81, 86
139. Veblen, "Instinct of Workmanship and the Irksomeness of Labor," 94–95.
140. Heilbroner, *Worldly Philosophers*, 232.
141. Veblen, "Instinct of Workmanship and the Irksomeness of Labor," 96
142. Horowitz, *Morality of Spending*, xxii.
143. Leach, *Land of Desire*, xiii.
144. Ibid., 6.
145. Part of the force of the competing pictures of the leisured life is what they do and do not say about where property comes from. In Hume's picture the property is simply there; he ignores questions of how the property was obtained. Veblen, by contrast, indicates that the property of the leisured class is suspect precisely because they are leisured; they did not work for this property but rather appropriated it from others in forcible ways. Of course, luxury defenders will likely point out, "I earned it!" This important digression on the nature of property will be developed further: a crucial element of the Lockean-Humean modern account of property is freeing it from any sense of prior obligation. Premodern accounts of property ultimately saw the right to property as entrenched in a prior set of social obligations or the universal destination of goods required by God.
146. Skidelsky and Skidelsky, "In Praise of Leisure."
147. For a defense of the importance of meaningful work on simply Aristotelian/MacIntyrean grounds, see Beadle and Knight, "Virtue and Meaningful Work."
148. Wogaman, *Economics and Ethics*, 36, makes the goodness of work one of the "theological entry points" into economics, noting that "the theme of peaceful rest

is biblical, but rest is always related to work in the portrayal of human fulfillment." Ratzinger, *Church, Ecumenism, and Politics*, 246, also notes that "idleness is not freedom" and that "the form of work and cooperation appropriate to man leads to freedom"—the right form being one that is "integrated in culture" that allows the work to be formed by "man's deepest questions."

149. MacIntyre, *After Virtue*, 187. For an outstanding overview discussion of the concept, see Knight, "Practices."

150. MacIntyre, *After Virtue*, 191.

151. The secondary literature on this distinction and on its (contested) application to various activities is now extensive. A recent article (Hager, "Refurbishing MacIntyre's Account of Practice") reviews the salient claims and objections and develops examples of blurred lines between internal and external, as well as the heterogeneity of internal goods. But Hager admits that the "morally dubious" trio of "prestige, money, power" that often appears as MacIntyre's prime example of external goods is rightly named. Moreover, Hager and others (e.g., Beadle, "Why Business Cannot Be a Practice") wrestle with MacIntyre's distinction between practices and institutions, a point that might be applicable in terms of luxury. For the purposes of the discussion here, especially in responding to Hume and happiness studies, MacIntyre's basic distinction stands.

152. MacIntyre, *After Virtue*, 188.

153. MacIntyre, *Intractable Disputes*, 46.

154. Ibid., 12.

155. MacIntyre, *Dependent Rational Animals*, 71.

156. MacIntyre, "Recovery of Moral Agency," 118. Elsewhere, MacIntyre, in *Intractable Disputes*, 45–46, identifies the key to practical reasoning is recognizing reasons for action other than simply the satisfaction of our own desires.

157. Dasgupta, *Economics*, 30–71. Contrast this with the absence of any index entry for "trust" or "honesty" in Paul Samuelson's thousand-page *Economics* textbook.

158. McCloskey illustrates this point by comparing her experience in Iowa City to her experience in Chicago. McCloskey, "Avarice," 325. Also, on staying in the background, see Finn, "Social Causality," where he draws on Thomas Wartenberg's conception of "coercion."

159. See MacIntyre's explanation, in *Intractable Disputes*, 31, of how utilitarians will understand the rules of shared deliberation differently because they understand the *telos* of participation differently, i.e., instrumentally. Their participation will necessarily be "qualified and conditional." By contrast, MacIntyre's justification is the ongoing integrity of the practice itself, not the outcomes.

160. Also, the full justification of the virtues may *start* with an analysis of practices, but it does not end there; some account of the good human life overall must also be present. See *After Virtue*, 201–3.

161. This is a non-trivial example: one of the serious challenges of college education today is that many students no longer develop a desire for the internal goods of reading largely because sustained reading requires a more disciplined approach than other forms of communication requires.

162. Ferguson, *Essay*, 285.

163. See chap. 2.

164. MacIntyre, *After Virtue*, 198. It is quintessentially the perspective of individualism and acquisitiveness.
165. There is some evidence from happiness studies that seeking goals "intrinsic" to activities is better for happiness. See the references in Lyubomirsky, *Myths of Happiness*, 276 note 251. However, the use of "intrinsic" here often fluctuates between goals intrinsic to the self and goals intrinsic to the activity. For a non-MacIntyrean account of the insufficiency of external goods, see Laurence James, "Activity and the Meaningfulness of Life."
166. On sociology, see MacIntyre, *After Virtue*, 23; on intelligible action, 206–10.
167. For a survey of empirical evidence supporting these problems with external incentivization, see Kohn, *Punished by Rewards*.
168. Or avarice, but see the discussion of their distinction in chap. 2.
169. For an explicit connection between (some) corporate practices and MacIntyre's account, see Goldberg, "Business Ethics."
170. Cerne et al., "What Goes Around Comes Around," 173.
171. Wheelan, *Naked Economics*, 29.
172. Paul Bambrick-Santoyo's schools in inner-city Newark counter Wheelan's claims (see Bambrick-Santoyo, *Leverage Leadership*). Anyone who goes to one of his schools on the basis that they want to earn an extra $10,000 in pay is not going to work out. There has to be an internal motivation and it is exactly this kind of internal motivation that is required to move students from external to internal incentives for learning. Even their principal's offices are telling in this regard: no secretary, simple table with work chairs. No big desks, no inner sanctums, because one of his central principles is that principals should be out and about in their schools, and office time should be spent meeting constructively with teachers, not acting like royalty welcoming subjects into the throne room.
173. See Goldberg, "Business Ethics," 312–18.
174. Alford and Naughton, *Managing as If Faith Mattered*, 40.
175. Tyler, *Why People Cooperate*, 1.
176. Ibid., 4–5.
177. On a more compressed salaries model, see Sinn, *Can Germany Be Saved?*, 289.
178. Cite chap. 2.
179. See MacIntyre, *Whose Justice*, 24–69, where the tension between achieving excellence in one's role and achieving victory, the rewards, eventually produces an account of genuinely philosophical practical reason in Plato and Aristotle, which makes the fundamental case why the goods of excellence are to be preferred.
180. Mandeville, *Fable*, 91.
181. MacIntyre, "Politics, Philosophy, and the Common Good," 235–36.
182. MacIntyre, "Three Perspectives on Marxism," 153.
183. See Yates and Hunter, *Thrift and Thriving in America*.
184. For temperance as a prerequisite for justice, see Cloutier, "Moral Theology for Real People," 131.
185. Horowitz, *Morality of Spending*, chaps. 2, 4.
186. See O'Toole, *Money and Morals in America*, 172–83.

CHAPTER 3

Neglected Sacramentality

*Why Luxury Blocks a Spirituality
of Material Goods*

The initial impetus for writing about luxury was my experience in teaching undergraduates about Catholic teaching on property. Private property, the tradition consistently maintains, is subordinated to social use; it has a "social mortgage." Such statements are frequently found in the social encyclicals, beginning with Pope Leo XIII's *Rerum Novarum*: "It is one thing to have a right to the possession of money, and another to have a right to use money as one pleases."[1] As John A. Ryan put it, Christians are obligated to use goods "in accordance with the laws of justice and charity," and this obligation toward the common good is "binding directly on individuals."[2] Pope Paul VI, in *Populorum Progressio*, states this idea bluntly: "No one may appropriate surplus goods solely for his own private use when others lack the bare necessities of life."[3] Leo warned, "the rich should tremble at the threatening of Jesus Christ."[4] Do my students tremble? Do I tremble?

Rather than fear and trembling, this teaching is met with a disturbed shock that goes far beyond the reaction to any Catholic sexual teaching. The students are skeptical but unsurprised that the magisterium opposes contraception and premarital sex. However, they are shocked, outraged, and even offended that it might oppose a Corvette. They seem to believe that, so long as it is gained through "work," any property is theirs to enjoy as they please. There is no social mortgage. There is no problem with a life full of luxury goods.

The essential and foundational place of this teaching on property in the Catholic tradition is not in doubt, any more than its foundational commitments to the dignity of life and of marriage. The Catechism's treatment of property portrays the material world as created by God, entrusted to "the common stewardship of mankind," and ordered to "the universal destination of goods" that "remains primordial" over the right to private property. That is, private property is a right only insofar as it serves the "natural solidarity" intended by God.[5] As John Paul II notes, "Christian tradition has never upheld this right as absolute and untouchable"; it is "subordinate to the right to common use, to the fact that goods are meant for everyone."[6]

Yet attacks on the basic principles of the dignity of life and sexuality have received disproportionate attention within American Catholicism. This is particularly striking, insofar as American mainstream culture continues to defend individual dignity and celebrate marriage (albeit with contested exceptions and modifications). But do we have a system where prior claims on and responsibilities of property ownership are acknowledged, even if imperfectly? No, we have "the goods life."[7] This is no accident, since "the most basic change" in the concept of property ownership from old Europe to the United States was a rejection that all land came from a sovereign or higher authority, which thus "implied some form of obligation, to someone higher up the ladder."[8] In America, though land often came from government, property did not come with duties of service or social obligation.

The neglect of the basic teachings on property is even more problematic because many moral failures are "occasional deflections from the way in which [persons] regularly walk," whereas "the luxurious living of the high-minded and earnest among the possessors of wealth is obviously not an occasional deflection of this kind: it is a high-road on which they travel day after day and year after year."[9] That is, as was argued in the prior chapter, the problem of luxury in a society devoted to "the goods life" is one of *consistent vice*, not *occasional slippage*.

However, our theological failure to confront luxury and inordinate possession goes beyond ignorance of the teachings on property or worldly vice; it is our refusal to grasp the intimate, ongoing connection between the material and the spiritual, between creation and God. After all, the covenant between God and God's People is the context for the distinctive Old Testament view of sharing property. Yet all too frequently one hears Christian speech that presumes a strong "dualism" between our material wealth and our spiritual lives. There is a tendency to "spiritualize to death" the inescapable teachings on material possessions found throughout scripture, especially the gospels.[10] This tendency is even more alarming when, at other points, Jesus' teaching is taken with utmost literal-ness. When Jesus counters the rabbinic debate over divorce with a (nearly) blanket prohibition, the disciples respond that "in that case, it is better not to marry" (Mt 19:11). When the rich young man leaves sad after hear-ing that the rich will find it extremely difficult to enter the Kingdom, the disciples say, "then who can be saved?" (Mt 19:25). Despite the parallel responses of the disciples to both of these "extreme" teachings, many read them in starkly different ways. In the former case, Jesus is taken to be say-ing something definite about what we are supposed to do, even if it is dif-ficult: we are not to divorce. In the latter we qualify the idea: "the needle" is supposedly some kind of a gate into Jerusalem, so it's really not that impossible . . . which is actually a still-repeated *fabrication* that first arose in the eleventh century.[11] Or perhaps Jesus just meant "detachment" from possessions. We have to be "ready" to give them away but we don't actually have to give them away. We can be rich and Christian too. Richard Hays is more blunt and more accurate: "For the church to heed the New Testa-ment's challenge on the question of possessions would require nothing less than a new Reformation."[12]

My claim is that the neglect of luxury as a problem requires a better understanding of the relationship between the material and the spiritual, between worldly goods and transcendence. How we handle property should have a great deal more to do with love of God and neighbor. Some Catholics have accepted the proper connection of the material and the spiritual for things like marriage and human dignity but have overlooked it for economic matters. There is a need to recover an *encompassing* sacra-mental ontology as reflected in the treatment of property and the critique of luxury in the early Church.[13] Such a recovery is a necessary challenge to spiritual promises made in today's marketplace by luxury goods and services. While Catholics fall into a dualism about possessions and spiri-tuality, marketers know better—they know that products can evoke true "devotion." The chapter begins by showing how today's luxury marketing presumes a kind of false sacramental ontology, and then proceeds to trace two reasons for the gradual loss of the robustly realistic patristic critique of luxury. We then turn to examine the renewal of a sacramental under-standing of the Christian life, particularly in light of the demise of the so-called two-level ethic in favor of Vatican II's universal call to holiness. Catholic sexual teaching has gone much further in recovering an idea of lay spiritual holiness in daily life, but recent popes, especially Benedict XVI, want to trace a similar trajectory for Catholic social teaching. As this trajectory has developed, it has also become clearer why a critique of personal luxury is necessary if we are to understand what embodied holiness really looks like. Like aspects of our sexual economy that present sexuality in a falsely magical, deceptively spiritual light, our material economy obscures the genuine sacramental possibilities of the material by offering false forms of transcendence—transcendence on the cheap, you might say. The chapter concludes by displaying Benedict's *Caritas in Veritate* as offering a sacramental economy of reciprocity that is a direct alternative to the luxury economy. Paying the "sacramental premium" to participate in relations of reciprocity needs to be favored over the "brand premium" we pay for our taste of luxury.

The Luxury Strategy:
How Luxury Promises Transcendence

The urgency of recovering a theological approach can be observed in how "theological" marketing sounds when selling luxury. Luxury is a very important marketing device, one which (ironically) peddles a "sacramental ontology" of sorts that uses material goods to make spiritual promises of fulfillment and new life. Catholics may ignore the spiritual significance of luxury but marketers know it well.

The terms "luxury goods" or "the luxury market" or "luxury brands" have a more precise definition in the world of business: "goods in each category exceeding a given price threshold, such as $200 for a pair of shoes."[14] But luxury is no longer merely about price. Mark Tungate defines "the essence of the luxury industry" as "an elite brand doing its utmost to provide a personalized service to a high-spending client." These brands have now fallen "into the hands of giant corporations" who seek to expand the market by offering "lower-priced items" that "put luxury tantalizingly within our reach." One can buy a $260 Louis Vuitton monogrammed passport cover "and be treated [at their store] with only slightly less deference than the teenage princess."[15] Luxury thus represents a market segment—albeit one that, in search of more buyers, is constantly trying to expand.

Exactly what causes a "luxury" good to fit into that category? How do you manage to communicate the "right" message about the good or service? To put the marketing question bluntly, what is it that makes people spend $70,000 on a sedan or $800 a night for a hotel room? Why would people pay *that much* for a handbag? Marketers spend a considerable amount of time trying to understand this—and it is pretty obvious why. They are targeting the consumers with the most money and the most discretionary money. These consumers are also the trendsetters for others who aspire to "belong" to this class. Hence, the particular focus on the luxury market in rapidly expanding Asian economies. Britain's *Financial Times* ran an ad for the Walpole British Luxury Summit 2011 on luxury in greater China, which promised "to enlighten, provoke and inspire delegates to make the most of the opportunities that Greater China has to offer."[16]

Companies are eager to find the keys to unlocking these "opportunities." In an episode of the documentary series *Frontline*, the filmmaker arrives at a large seminar hosted at the mansion of an extremely wealthy business consultant, Dr. Clotaire Rapaille, whose latest project is conducting market research to "crack the code on luxury."[17] Companies pay big bucks to get this information. The head of the Luxury Market Council explains, "The premise of the council has been to bring the smartest minds in marketing together and help us all figure out ways to get money from the customers with the most money." Doctor Rapaille is a former psychiatrist who brings theories of the unconscious to his interpretation of focus groups, saying, "It's absolutely crucial to understand what I call 'the reptilian hot button.' My theory is very simple. The reptilian always win [*sic*]. I don't care what you're going to tell me intellectually, give me the reptilian." Rapaille is using a language about one part of the brain, called the reptilian, that is theorized by some to be evolutionarily the oldest and most basic part of our brains.[18] And what exactly is that "reptilian hot button" for marketing luxury? Significantly, the (non-paying) PBS viewer isn't allowed to hear the answer.[19]

More complex analyses than a single hot button are also offered. A group of management scholars complain that discussion of luxury brands "reveals a paucity of definitions of what constitutes a luxury brand. Researchers and authors tend to leave the definition implicit."[20] But they then agree that luxury "is more than a characteristic or set of attributes. . . . No matter how hard you look at a Cartier bracelet you won't be able to identify what makes it a luxury product."[21] Instead, the authors propose that luxury can only be understood in terms of "three spheres": the material, the experiential, and the social. They suggest that luxury can be identified by objective quality, by subjective hedonic experience, and by social status.[22]

The literature tellingly tends to focus on the latter two dimensions as the genuine essence of luxury. It seems clear that whatever luxury means, it does not simply mean product "quality." Central is the subjective experience that is associated with the product. One marketing manual explains that the key strategy for marketing to the "affluent consumer" is to promise not simply a material thing, but rather a "feeling," a "desire to feel special," and an "experience" of "emotionally satisfying goods and services."[23] Jean-Noel Kapferer, one high priest of luxury marketing, explains that "the luxury product corresponds to a dream," and dreams follow a different logic than typical product marketing, which focuses on functionality.[24] Tungate agrees that luxury draws on the basic human desire to dream; it is, as he says, "a way of winning back something against the cruelty of life," and he quotes French historian Jean Castarede that luxury is rooted in "the impulse to single oneself out through ornamentation" and to "seduce others by acquiring or giving rare objects."[25] Luxury accessory brands continually play on any resonance of the product other than functionality.

The priority of the dream and of the status associated with the product overshadows the objective quality dimension. Unlike the desire for something functional, dreams "do not necessarily need to be satisfied" and exist "outside time and often last forever."[26] Lexus, perhaps the king of today's mainstream luxury car field, advertises itself as "pursuing perfection." But Kapferer suggests that Lexus's marketing strategy doesn't quite reach the heights of true luxury because it still emphasizes "super-Toyota" attributes—outstanding quality—*instead of* "the prestige, the intangible, the dream, the imagination."[27] True luxury involves a real "brand myth" and a product that is not "perfect" but rather "affecting."[28] Certain European auto brands have cultivated and maintained this distinction. He notes that Ferrari encourages owners "to send their jewel for an in-depth maintenance check, at the holy of holies, at Maranello. This is the opportunity to possibly come to the very heart of the religion and collect it."[29] Even lesser European brands like Porsche and BMW have maintained a mystique lacking in a Lexus. The transcendent character of the brand can also be cast in terms of other dreams: Robert Frank notes that the designer watchmaker Patek Phillippe urges buyers to think about their watches as family heirlooms, saying, "some people feel that you never actually own a Patek Phillippe. You merely look after it for the next generation."[30]

Perhaps this all is really just about quality? Imagine how well-made a watch is if it can become such an heirloom! Isn't this better than endless cycles of planned obsolescence? This objection is a fair comment and led me to investigate what these watches costs. One discount fine jeweler online has a few women's styles priced at $11,000, but everything else is around $20,000 and up, reaching into the six-figure range.[31] While I am not a watch expert, it is hard to imagine that a high-quality, well-engineered watch that would last a long time needs to cost more than $500 or so.

Of course, luxury brands also want growing sales, which creates a conundrum: How do you maintain exclusivity and still grow sales? After all, most people will never spend $10,000 or more on a watch. Luxury brand companies want to communicate that magic—and its significant price premium—to larger and larger audiences, yet at least part of the magic is exclusivity. One way is to increase turnover. Dana Thomas writes in her study of luxury branding: "With the support of fashion magazines, luxury companies in the last ten years have created the phenomenon of the handbag of the season—the must-have around the world that will catapult sales and stock prices."[32] Another strategy is to introduce this exclusiveness to a wider array of items. Luxury brands since the 1980s have expanded their lines so that "the average consumer" who "certainly can't afford a $200,000 made-to-order couture gown, . . . can drop $25 on a tube of lipstick or $65 on a bottle of eau de parfum spray to have a piece of the luxury dream."[33]

Indeed, lest we think that this whole marketing strategy is really just for the super-wealthy, consultants Michael Silverstein and Neil Fiske outline the importance of what they call "the new American luxury." Far from French fashion designers, this "new luxury" involves "the middle-market consumer who selectively trades up to new and better products and services, trad[ing] down in other areas to pay for his or her premium purchases."[34] This huge market of the top "twenty-one million affluent households control[s] nearly 60% of the nation's purchasing power."[35] Silverstein and Fiske outline the new willingness of midmarket consumers to pay top dollar for things like premium pet food and pet care, "fast casual" restaurants like Panera Bread, and (their leading example) high-end lingerie at Victoria's Secret. These may seem a lot less "magical" than the elite brands discussed above, but the consultants *make the same arguments* for why people will pay $10 for fast food: sure, it's a little better quality, but what is really important is to send "emotional" messages that the product connects "powerfully" to the consumer's "needs" and "unspoken desires."[36] Which are what, exactly? Silverstein and Fiske devote time to issues such as "taking care of me," "questing" for meaning, and "connection" with others.[37] New luxury goods, they claim, are ones that "deliver greater emotional engagement."[38] They cost more—"sometimes a lot more"—than typical products, but they "deliver a lot more value, particularly emotional value."[39]

Not everyone thinks highly of this expansion of luxury to the middle classes. Kapferer is skeptical: "Anything that ceases to be a social signifier loses its luxury status."[40] Thus, there is still a need to retain exclusivity;

the product must retain a sense of marking off superior status. In light of this, a marketing strategy must be developed that "keeps non-enthusiasts out."[41] However, this need not be done through outrageously inaccessible pricing. Kapferer notes that Apple manages a luxury strategy very effectively: no discounts, uniqueness, a myth (including the "creative genius" of the founder), and a virtually religious base of enthusiasts. As the marketing expert Martin Lindstrom outlines in a lengthy chapter on brands, "For its millions of fervent constituents, Apple wasn't just a brand, it was a *religion*."[42] Thus, luxury branding is really about two things: the product somehow being "more than a product" and somehow defining a relationship to others.

The luxury product has what Herbert McCabe terms a "mystique."[43] McCabe is speaking about the phenomenon of "false gods" hiding in today's society. His example is the lottery: we all know that playing the lottery is extremely likely to make you poorer. But the lottery needs you to believe in it rather than in the laws of probability, so the lottery must pretend to be able to deliver something that overwhelmingly it doesn't deliver: riches. No state advertises its lottery in this way: "Play the lottery— most people get poorer, but you might get rich!" Nor do they highlight studies that suggest most winners don't end up happier. For McCabe, all false gods have to construct this kind of mystique, where something is understood to be something other than and beyond what it actually is.

But it would be misleading simply to dismiss the mystique as false. In some sense the belief in the mystique ends up creating its own "reality." A radio segment sought to understand why so many people pay large premiums for iPhones when other smart phones do just as much. One woman commented, "When I see someone who doesn't have an iPhone, I think that either they don't have much money or they aren't cool."[44] The product is really about the relationship with others communicated by the product—in the case of luxury goods and services it is a relationship of superiority over others. While it may be false to believe a phone is actually magic or a car is actually the embodiment of a dream, it is perfectly *true* that these objects create and reinforce certain kinds of perceived relations between the self and other people.

In short, these products make *spiritual* promises: a more-than-material experience for oneself and love and affection from others. Kapferer sums up genuine luxury as moving away from "the domain of having (possession, accumulation, enslavement to the object) toward the domain of being both for yourself (dreams) and for others (recognition, esteem)."[45] His promises are mysticism and *koinonia*! Kapferer actually claims that luxury even "fulfills a fundamental ethical role" of "pacifying society." Through luxury there is peace of soul and peace among people. Such is the marketing promise. It sounds pretty "spiritual," doesn't it?

The Fathers against Luxury

If luxury is recognized as a religious and spiritual reality within the gritty world of business, then how did the Christian tradition come to overlook the spiritual significance of material possessions? Many of my students are more familiar with the intricacies of clothing brands and cell phone models than with the dynamics of the Mass, so how can theological ethics avoid recognizing the *spiritual* meaning of these competing choices? Indeed, one study by marketing experts displays a solidly *positive* correlation between nonreligiosity and "brand reliance"—religious people are less likely to identify with brands. The authors hypothesize that this is because both religion and brands are expressive of identity, "such that when an individual expresses her self-worth via one medium (be it brands or religion), she needs the other medium less."[46]

The initial response is that the tradition doesn't overlook this problem, but there is a story to tell about how the problem of luxury was obscured. The work of some fourth-century Church Fathers, from wealthy urban cities, does make this connection. Their work contains straightforward critiques of luxury excesses, but two key theological shifts reinterpreted and obscured this connection.

It is neither a secret nor an exaggeration to say that the Church Fathers were quite scathing in their views of the rich. Many Fathers made such critiques, but Saints Basil, Ambrose, and John Chrysostom have some interesting similarities.[47] All three were ascetically *minded* bishops—they were not ascetics themselves but their works appeared prior to the institutional formalization of asceticism in the monasticism of figures like Benedict and Cassian.[48] The two-level ethic of the "higher" calling to religious life coupled with the "lower" standard for lay life had not yet crystallized; thus, their works presume a universal call to holiness among members of the Church (a key feature of Vatican II and contemporary moral theology). All three men came from secure, educated backgrounds.[49] All three served in fairly wealthy urban settings. All three worked in that interim period between Constantine's conversion and the decline and fall of the unified Roman Empire. Interestingly, their discourses on wealth can be contrasted with the Father who comes after them, Saint Augustine, for whom luxurious material possessions have less importance. Recovering the argument of these Fathers is particularly helpful because their witness is so easily overshadowed by Augustine's. Their perspectives can be summarized in two ideas: one's use of goods ultimately displays either a recognition or rejection of God as the Source of everything—that is, humility, rather than pride, is the appropriate disposition in relation to ownership; and this humility should lead to an active social solidarity with the poor.

Basil, Ambrose, and John Chrysostom ridicule the idea that the rich are simply keeping what is "theirs." Basil writes: " 'I am wronging no one,' you say, 'I hold fast to my own, that is all.' Your own! You gave it you [*sic*] to bring into life with you?"[50] He goes on: "Whence came the riches you have now? If you say from nowhere, you deny God, you ignore the Creator, you are ungrateful to the Giver. But if you acknowledge they came from God, tell us the reason for your receiving them."[51] Peter Phan notes that in Basil we have the first clear articulation of the universal destination of goods: everything in the created order is a gift from God and therefore belongs ultimately to everyone in common.[52] In claiming that their property is exclusively "theirs," the wealthy are essentially denying the doctrine of creation. Creation names the foundational understanding Christians have of the relation between materiality and transcendence—that all things are made by, and are continually held in being by God, not us. Christian use of possessions should reflect this via use for the glory of God, not for private preoccupations.

Even more important than this humble disposition is that it should lead to an active social solidarity with the poor. Basil, as well as Ambrose, influenced by Basil, both view the use of riches as displaying a fundamental affirmation or rejection of social solidarity.[53] The rich man is one who seeks self-sufficiency. In so doing he denies the idea that "nothing, indeed, is so comparable with our nature as living in society and in dependence upon one another and as loving our own kind."[54] Similarly, Ambrose argues that what is good should be judged by its use for all: "When giving to the poor, you are not giving him what is yours; rather you are paying back to him what is his. . . .The earth belongs to all, and not only to the rich."[55] This social solidarity is a combining of gospel eschatology with the Stoic notion of the unity of the human race. For Basil, "the main cause of hunger and want in the world is the unwillingness of the rich to share with those in need."[56] He writes that the rich "seize what belongs to all and claim the right of possession to monopolise it; if everyone took for himself enough to meet his own wants and gave up the rest to those who needed it, there would be no rich and no poor."[57]

This two-fold view leads to a critique of luxury in the most vivid terms. They heap scorn upon the lifestyles of the rich. Basil proclaims, "What will you tell the judge, you who dress up your walls and leave humans naked? You who groom and adorn your horses and will not look at your naked brother? You whose wheat rots, and yet do not feed the hungry?"[58] Ambrose likewise says, "You give coverings to walls and bring men to nakedness. The naked cries out before your house unheeded; your fellow-man is there, naked and crying, while you are perplexed by the choice of marble to clothe your floor."[59] He goes on to criticize jewelry and gold horse bits. This unnecessary ornamentation is worthy of condemnation, not praise. Even the miser is really only hoping for *future* luxury, for he "longs for the moment when he can squander" his fortune.[60]

No writer brings out the ugliness of the foolish concerns of the luxury life more clearly than St. John Chrysostom. In one homily he envisions the hungry, homeless man who does not know where he will sleep contrasted with the person who is "coming home from the bath, clean and dandy, dressed in soft clothes, full of contentment and happiness, and hastening to sit down to splendidly prepared dinners."[61] The homeless man is completely exposed to the elements, but, "you, if you see a drop of water falling from the ceiling, you would throw the whole house into confusion."[62] Chrysostom makes much of basic questions of how we should eat, dress, and build shelter and shows how they are questions of profound spiritual significance. Not only does he pour contempt on "the luxurious mansions of the wealthy," but elsewhere he compares extravagantly decked-out Christians to prostitutes and laments "luxurious banquets" in the midst of the starving poor.[63] Food, clothing, and housing will be key nexes for contemporary reflection on what counts as luxury.

Manifestations of luxury are a fundamental spiritual betrayal. To these Fathers, God's instructions for right use are clear in Scripture: the wealthy are presented as good to the extent that they are sharing with the poor—in the gospels, the more, the better.[64] This eschatological sharing is in stark contrast to a preoccupation with finery. Chrysostom puts this in the most vivid terms in saying that luxury consumption not only harms the poor but is a counter-witness to the truth of Christianity: "This is the reason why the pagans do not believe what we say. Our actions and our works are the demonstrations which they are willing to receive from us; but when they see us building for ourselves fine houses, and laying out gardens and baths, and buying fields, they are not willing to believe that we are preparing for another sort of residence away from our city."[65] For these Fathers, material goods do have a kind of magical, eschatological significance—but it is not by dying with the most toys or experiencing the most transcending fulfillment of dreams. Rather, these goods have spiritual value when we forsake luxuries for ourselves and devote those resources to the needy. Straightforward reading of passages like Matthew 25: 31–46 is what they believe should be preached to the wealthy cities of their times.

The Christian Critique of Luxury Obscured

What stands in the way of recovering their witness? The meaning of the term *luxuria* was lost during the Middle Ages (as noted in chapter 1), but the difficulty here goes beyond simply recovering a term. There is a larger theological story to tell about what happens to the Christian understanding of the spiritual meanings of possessions. A first barrier to be surmounted in order to restore this connection is the post-Augustinian *displacement* of the material/spiritual connection; the second is a post-Reformation *disenchantment* of the material in favor of a "pure" spirituality.

In the West after the fourth century and the disintegration of the Empire, the most important influences were not these urbane Fathers, but instead the twin forces of Augustine and monasticism, both of which retained a clearly sacramental ontology but shifted and in some ways displaced how the material and spiritual were related. Much might be made about the fact that Augustine's own struggles seem to have more to do with sexuality and worldly prestige rather than with riches. But, and at least as important, Augustine's theology was formed in resistance to Donatism and Pelagianism, which (in different ways) were "perfectionist" movements. Augustine's defense of "mediocre Christianity," or of Christianity as "a lifelong process of convalescence," ultimately sought to cultivate a certain kind of perpetual humility in service of Church unity.[66] Augustine was closing off the "Pharasaic flank" of a critique of riches! Nevertheless, his counter-Pelagian picture undoubtedly lowered the bar drastically. In the context of describing "the man of good works," he notes that he "indulges his incontinence within the decent bounds of marriage" and "guards what he possesses and gives alms, though not very generously." In all this he is "acknowledging his own ignominy and giving the glory to God." This is quite a different picture than what we have seen from Basil, Ambrose, and John Chrysostom.

Augustine's descriptions should be read charitably, for two reasons. One, his immediate context is bound up in resisting Pelagianism. As Peter Brown notes, Pelagian critiques of wealth went *beyond* the ordinary patristic arguments. The Fathers assumed that there were "good" and "bad" uses of wealth—one of the bad uses being "luxury."[67] But the Pelagian critique treated the rich not as fools in danger but rather as "criminals."[68] They came close to seeing material goods as inherently evil. Augustine was resisting a view that had gone to the other extreme.

Second, Augustine's realistic descriptions of our struggle cannot help but ring true to our ears, however earnest we might be. The context of his portrait should be noted: rejecting the "insidious pride which ruptures community."[69] We'd like to believe that we are not seduced by worldly concerns (only others are!) and that we are generous people who are not wrapped up in the sins of consumerism (only others are!). But, in fact, we embody a grudging and guarded attitude toward basic almsgiving all the time. Augustine's approach has the merit of disrupting our temptations to self-deception about our own generosity.

In practical terms, there also wasn't much of an audience left for the prior critique. The social infrastructure that had sustained surplus wealth had fallen apart. After the early fifth century, the collapse of Rome and near-disappearance of large, wealthy centers of urban culture coupled with the new preeminence of institutionalized monasticism reoriented the ways in which the material and the spiritual intersect. As Peter Brown explains, Western Christendom migrated northward in the following centuries, and even Christendom's lay forms had become deeply intertwined with centers of monasticism.[70] Brown writes: "What was lost . . . was a true leisured class, and the styles of culture and religion that went with such a class."[71] Brown shows that the concern for using wealth correctly—that is, for transcendence—was embodied in key practices, chiefly the endowment of monasteries by the nobility.[72] But this constituted a shift in how one was to understand the use of goods for God's glory: the sacramental, holy use of possessions was moving toward a still material but more separated sphere.

Yet possessions still existed under a "sacramental mortgage." Charles Taylor explains that the medieval system retained what he calls "ambivalent complementarities"—worldly life and monasticism, the power of spirits and divine remedies—making for a social order that was still "enchanted."[73] This was notably also seen in the "enchanted" character of the beggar and "an aura of sanctity around poverty."[74] For all its weaknesses, the Augustinian synthesis retained this enchanted relationship between the material to the spiritual. While we today would criticize aspects of it, we should also recognize that the "social imaginary" presumed by the earlier Fathers was still partially in force. Treasure on earth still needed to be "converted" into treasure in heaven.

Now, this kind of sacrality was always treated with a certain ambivalence. Was it merely a "pagan" cultural remainder that needed to be overcome? Brown shows that "reformers" who sought to bring a kind of intellectual and clerical order (and control) over these semi-idolatrous tendencies existed as far back as the eighth century.[75] Moreover, such an orientation ended up creating the wealthiest institutions in the society. As one monastic observer put it, "Discipline produces wealth, and wealth destroys the discipline."[76] The corruptions of ecclesiastical pomp and splendor proved profoundly damaging to this way of thinking sacramentally about material goods. On the eve of the Reformation, plenty of voices (and not just future Protestant ones) recognized the extent and character of this unintended problem of sacramentalizing possessions by giving them to the Church.[77]

This brings us to the second significant shift. While the Protestant Reformation led to varying treatments of the question of wealth and possessions (though all rejected luxury), the underlying dynamic of the material and the spiritual unified nearly all of them: the sacramental synthesis of the Augustinian age, of holy objects and holy beggars, of holy alms and treasure in heaven, of monks and purchased Masses, was rejected. These were a fundamental human distortion of the true Gospel.

Taylor offers a very powerful account of the semi-intentional "disenchantment" of materiality that resulted. Seeking to de-paganize the "ambivalent complementarities" more thoroughly, Reformation religion redefines God's providence and moves it from a notion of enchantment to a notion of divine ordering or design. This move initially makes for a different kind of enchantment—with Calvinist believers anxiously trying to discern whether their wealth is a sign of God's election, for example. But as the emphasis in Christianity becomes more and more anthropocentric, the goal of simply being a good human within the given designs of the universe "can begin to seem" to be something "that we can encompass . . . with our unaided forces. Grace seems less essential. We can see where exclusive humanism can arise. The stage is set, as it were, for its entrance."[78]

Taylor's narrative expresses his own ambivalence at this dissolution of the enchanted material world. What was supposed to happen was the replacement of pious church donations (and clerical excess) with agapic love. But, he says, "what we got was not a network of agape, but rather a disciplined society in which categorical relations have primacy and therefore norms."[79] As an unintended result of this laudable desire to reform clerical and lay abuses of sacraments and other material realities, and to focus instead on a life of true ethical agape, the connection of the material to the spiritual became weakened and was eventually lost. Instead, the modern social imaginary is constituted by immanent abstractions like "the economy" and "the state." Spirituality becomes privatized.

To put it in more straightforward (and admittedly less-than-nuanced) terms, the endgame of this second turn is Adolf Harnack's "God and the soul—nothing more."[80] Such a spirituality may be extrinsically connected to using one's material possessions for the poor, but material goods have lost real sacred resonance. An excess of concern for material goods may compete with one's spiritual growth, but they are like two separate projects; the only concern is to make sure one does not intrude on the other.[81] Taylor's disenchanted world is another way of saying that the genuinely sacramental understanding of material goods and relations runs counter to our very way of understanding what religion is. Many Christians may seek to recover a concern for the poor and needy. But even when this happens, the connection is modest—one may seek detachment, enlightened philanthropy, maybe something akin to Andrew Carnegie's plan of giving every penny away before he died. None of these strategies are likely to revive the patristic claims about golden bits and marble floors—such rhetoric might hurt the philanthropic giving, after all. But it is unfair to suggest that our tacit endorsement of luxury consumption is merely designed to avoid giving offense; the deeper issue is that many simply do not think it is a problem for a Christian to have a Lexus or a granite countertop. We do not see the material and the spiritual clashing *in this way*, because we have passed through these two barriers: the Augustinian shift to material goods as sacred if devoted to piety and the Reformation criticism of such piety that then developed into a dualistic and individualistic spirituality.

The Recovery of the Sacramental in Catholic Ethics

The Augustinian two-level ethic and the tendency to spiritualize and individualize Christianity, then, seem to be the two key reasons why Catholics are scandalized to hear that the Church might be opposed to their acquisition habits. They understand the importance of not stealing and perhaps retain some sense of the need to do charitable and church giving. But even the minimal Old Testament ideal of a firstfruits tithe is likely to be greeted by disenchanted grumbling . . . even by those who have sufficient money to spend more than 10 percent of their income on upscale goods.

Yet the modern Church has not only retained the basic teachings about the universal destination of goods that animated the pre-Augustinian

Fathers, but since Vatican II has moved far *beyond* mere minimalistic ethics like tithing. Magisterial documents have vitally reclaimed both the inherently social nature of faith (over against a spiritualized individualism) and the recognition of a universal call to holiness in all areas of lay life (over against a two-level ethic).[82] *Lumen Gentium* is the foundation of such a revitalization of the material/spiritual relationship, though it cannot be separated from the liturgical revitalization of participatory Eucharist as the "source and summit" of life (not an escape from it)[83] and the missional revitalization of the Church's necessary service to and for the world (rather than merely a fortress to protect against it).[84]

At the center of these transformations is the idea of a renewed yet traditional sacramental ontology. What do I mean by using the term "sacramental" here? Hans Boersma defines the sacramental ontology that animated the ressourcement theologians as a recognition of "the mystery inherent in the created order" such that "historical realities of the created order served as divinely ordained, sacramental means leading to eternal divine mysteries."[85] Boersma relates how this worldview, recovered from the Fathers, was a reaction against a variety of problems: the rigid dichotomies of neo-Thomist theology, the juridicizing of the sacraments and the Church itself, the secularization of Western society. It sought to recover and reconnect the supernatural with the natural, and grace with nature—not just in the sacraments but in the whole of Catholic life. Boersma contrasts the "sacramental imagination" with a "rational mindset" in the ways each deals with "narrative, symbols, and practices."[86] Matthew Eggemeier describes the sacramental imagination as "grounded in a distinctive approach to the relationship of God and creation" that "sustains a vision of creation in which all of reality manifests the grace of God."[87] Given this understanding, "the proper disposition toward the gift of God's presence" in created reality "is one of gratitude, praise, wonder, and thanksgiving."[88]

This sacramental ontology has had some effect on moral theology, particularly in elevating the beauty and value of marriage, but there is a parallel (if slower) development of this sacramental ontology in the papal social encyclicals of Paul VI, John Paul II, and especially Benedict XVI, which fully blossomed in *Caritas in Veritate*. As with the revitalized understanding of marriage as a vocation of holiness and service (and not just a natural-order phenomenon centered on regenerating the race), so, too, social ethics—especially economics—should be understood as a worldly site where lay people can and should live out the vocation to a "maturity" that "will allow each man to direct himself toward the destiny intended for him by his Creator."[89] The universal cooperation of all for the development of peoples stems "from a brotherhood that is at once human and supernatural."[90] As Eggemeier notes, a sacramental imagination "is an important corrective to the vision of the world dominant in contemporary culture, in which creation has been reduced to a mere commodity for human use."[91] Following hints in John Paul's encyclicals, Benedict fully "theologizes" the Catholic social tradition and appeals for an economy based on "charity in truth" in which even economic transactions themselves must contain "quotas of gratuitousness."

What does this have to do with the category of luxury? Besides rerooting Catholic thought in an imagination closer to the world of the patristic writers, Benedict is proposing an alternative to the luxury economy as described earlier. In the luxury economy the "grace" embedded in material goods is primarily concerned with one's own social status and personal experience, but its economic benefit is directed toward the corporate shareholders and managers of the brand. In this way the real possibilities of beauty are distorted and destroyed. There is an analogy in a comparison between the beauty of eros—which promises much but which cannot fulfill its promises apart from the mutual self-giving of marriage—and the beauty of material things. The "sacramental premium" implied in Benedict's work can be contrasted with the "luxury premium" in the contemporary market's way of making luxury goods and services sacred.

Reenchanting the Family:
The Development of Catholic Sexual Teaching

Certainly the question of the relation of the material to the spiritual is encountered in the messy but blessed materiality of our sexuality. The trajectory of the relation of sexual behavior and Christianity passes through the same two problems explained above. As with the normativity of reluctant almsgiving in the context of a two-level ethic, Augustine's theology long offered a standard solution to the problem of sex: celibacy was preferable but marriage was still a good—indeed, a sacrament—even if always endangered by the recalcitrance of sin. While the Reformation "disenchanted" marriage, Catholicism retained the Augustinian solution. And while it is overly simple to accuse Augustine of vestiges of neoplatonic dualism, it is clear that he was more anxious over the potential negative influence of sex gone awry than he was in propounding a positive vision of marriage and sexuality as an actual path to holiness.[92]

However, such reticence has receded in twentieth-century Catholicism.[93] The tradition has taken giant steps towards developing a genuinely sacramental ontology of the material realities of sex, marriage, and family. Personalist theologians like Dietrich von Hildebrand began to develop positive accounts of marital love despite official resistance. The Second Vatican Council offered a unified vision of marriage as "an intimate union of [the spouses'] persons and of their actions," a "community of love" that finds in children its "ultimate crown."[94] Arguably, the pinnacle of this development of reenchanting sexuality was Pope John Paul II's theology of the body. He went far beyond a positive assessment of marriage in arguing that the (proper) experience of bodily communion is in fact a reflection of divine love. Elsewhere he makes clear that vestiges of the two-level ethic—in which a vocation to family might be *contrasted* with a vocation to ecclesial mission—are to be rejected: marriage is an ecclesial vocation with specific missions of growth in holiness and service. The family is not simply a "saved community" who "receive the love of Christ"; the family is "called upon to communicate Christ's love to their brethren, thus becoming a saving community."[95] He goes on to show how the family participates in Christ's offices of prophet, priest, and king, the offices used to organize the mission of the whole Church in the first section of *Lumen Gentium*.

This development represents an example of how twentieth-century Catholic theology has developed a novel way of bringing together materiality and transcendence that is fully sacramental. This is to say that, properly understood, the entire reality of marriage and family—including sexual intercourse—is understood in terms of a sacramental, and not simply natural, *telos*. Marriage does not have two natural ends *plus* an additional sacramental end. Rather, marriage's natural ends are transformed from within and given their genuine telos by being taken up within the larger story of communion with God. In *Familiaris Consortio*, rather than use the traditional ends of marriage, John Paul II identifies four "tasks" of the Christian family that define the full scope of families "becoming what they are": fostering communion, serving life (which includes not just procreation but education), building up the larger society, and serving the mission of the Church.[96]

This understanding of the supernatural transformation of the natural is also fundamental to Benedict XVI's understanding of love. Writing about the relationship of natural and supernatural love, he says: "The first thing needed here is to ward off a tendency that would separate eros and religious love as if they were two quite distinct realities. But this is to distort both of them, because something wanting to be purely 'supernatural' love becomes powerless. . . . The creator and the redeemer is one and the same God. In redemption he does not take creation back but rather makes it whole and raises it up."[97]

While seemingly unending conflicts over normative sexual issues can obscure it, there is virtually universal acceptance of this century-long development. Debates about norms occur within a context where the presumption on both sides is that the *material* relationship of marriage and family is an essential *spiritual* practice, that is, a practice of holiness in the world. For three reasons it is not surprising that this renewed understanding of materiality and transcendence should develop first in sexual ethics, even despite the earlier Augustinian suspicion. First and foremost, the sacramental character of marriage could not be denied insofar as the Church affirmed marriage as one of the seven sacraments. An account of this temporal reality as an effective sign of grace *had* to be given. Sacramental ontology could not be avoided. Second, as Gene Burns notes, the rise of the modern secular state and the loss of the papacy's temporal power tended to push the Church's juridical structures toward a focus on marriage and sexuality where it could still attempt to name and exercise control over specific violations. He says acerbically, "It is rare for Rome to identify and condemn specific violations of social doctrine, and excommunication for such violations seems not to be in the realm of consideration."[98] Third, the rise of romantic love provided a kind of "secular analogy" for the transcendent significance of sexual matters. Moderns may have given up their enchanted understanding of nature or the state but they still held on to a pretty elaborate "mysticism" of romantic love. As my work has argued elsewhere, the appeal, for good and ill, of the theology of the body (and much post–Vatican II marriage theology) is rooted in appeals to a still-common enchanted sensibility about what married love should be.[99]

Reenchanting the World: The Development of Catholic Social Teaching

Sadly, it has become all too common to narrow the application of these developments about sacramental living to marriage and family. As Luigino Bruni notes, "agape has in fact been relegated to one part of the private sphere, in families or spiritual or strictly intimate relationships."[100] The intertwining of materiality and transcendence, as embodied in lay holiness in the world, is also properly applied to economics and politics. The restriction of renewed lay holiness to the sphere of sex and the family artificially reproduces within theology a public/private split that has no proper place in the Christian worldview.[101]

Despite a lack of wider awareness, the encyclical tradition has consistently moved in this direction of speaking about economics and politics in theological terms, too. The writings of Pope Paul VI mark an important point in this development. Prior to Paul VI, modern popes robustly taught the importance of the universal destination of goods as well as the need for charity. But these teachings followed a fairly strict two-tiered structure rooted in Thomist natural law principles, with charity appearing as extrinsic to justice.[102] With Paul VI, however, a subtle change appeared. In introducing a concept of "integral" or "authentic" development, the lines between what is natural and what is Christian or between justice and charity start to blur.[103] International brotherhood is "at once human and supernatural," and so "necessary technical competence must be accompanied by authentic signs of disinterested love."[104] Peace is ultimately possible because "we are all united in this progress toward God."[105] The tasks of justice and charity are no longer neatly divided and the entire process of development is instead discussed in a fully theological context.[106]

The encyclicals of John Paul II enhance this development. First, as noted earlier, *Laborem Exercens* develops a rich theology of work that should be understood as the economic parallel to John Paul's theology of the body—they are twin theological expositions of the two original commands of creation for the persons created in God's image: "have dominion" and "be fruitful." The pope provides a detailed reading of Genesis on work, and most notably focuses on the "subjective dimension of work," and the idea that human beings realize their own "humanity" in the "image of God" through work.[107] Of course, the opposite is also true: under degrading conditions of instrumentalization, they come to be seen as objects.[108] In economics (as in sexuality), John Paul II argues for "the primacy of persons over things" and an understanding that workers are not to be understood as "dependent" on capital except and insofar as this is a dependence on other persons and ultimately on God. Notably for our discussion of luxury, "the error of economism," which asserts the primacy of the material over the spiritual in economic activity, arises due to "the greater immediate attractiveness of what is material."[109]

In *Solicitudo Rei Socialis* the pope builds on Paul VI's language of a "civilization of love" to mount a social vision centered on the virtue of solidarity. Solidarity means that "we are all really responsible for all"; it involves "a firm and persevering determination to commit oneself to the common good."[110] While solidarity essentially includes traditional notions of justice, it trends in the direction of love with the understanding that even distant social relationships have deep theological significance. As Meghan Clark writes, John Paul roots solidarity not only as "the human person as imago Dei" but also as the unity of the human race as a reflection of God's communion "based on our faith in the Trinity."[111] The pope is clear that this solidarity requires "conversion" and a change in "spiritual attitudes" in order to confront "structures of sin."[112] The problem of international inequality (his focus) is not simply a matter of technical failures but of faith. This spirituality of development also involves the prophetic denunciation of "superdevelopment" and "crass materialism" that are associated with "the *cult* of 'having'" (emphasis added).[113] As in *Laborem Exercens*, structural sins are traced back to a vice that sounds much like luxury: the *attractiveness* of having lots of stuff.

Finally, in *Centesimus Annus* John Paul makes the striking claim that the failure of communism was not simply due to "the inefficiency of the economic system" or "the violation of the rights of workers" but rather "the spiritual void brought about by atheism, which deprived the younger generations of a sense of direction."[114] Could contemporary capitalism be accused of exactly the same thing? John Paul explained that consumer choices and investments are always moral choices, and concluded that any society is "alienated" insofar as "its form of social organization, production and consumption *make it more difficult to offer this gift of self* and to establish this solidarity between people" for which God created us.[115] The language of self-gift is thus not restricted to the private sphere. Benedict's encyclical *Caritas in Veritate* can be read as developing John Paul II's theological critique of communist totalitarianism but as it applies to "godless" globalized market societies. Benedict notes directly that "*every economic decision has a moral consequence*" and that "my predecessor John Paul II . . . saw civil society as the most natural setting for an economy of gratuitousness and fraternity, but did not mean to deny it a place in the other two settings [i.e., the market and the state]."[116] Francis is continuing this direction in his *Evangelii Gaudium*: he reads contemporary society not by "an allegedly neutral and clinical method" but in terms of "evangelical discernment"; he notes that "behind" the attitudes of global capitalism stands "a rejection of ethics and a rejection of God."[117]

Benedict XVI's Sacramental Social Teaching

In *Caritas in Veritate* we see the systematic extension of these ideas to the entire economy as well as to the natural environment on which it depends.

Benedict is viewed with suspicion by some social justice advocates because of his role (as Cardinal Ratzinger) in publicly disciplining liberation theologians.[118] It is important, however, to look carefully at the content of his criticisms, which reveal how deeply "theological" Benedict's social thinking is. His problem with liberation theology was not that it made faith political, but rather that it made faith political *in the wrong way*. Ratzinger himself notes that "the error" in some liberation theologies "would not have been able to wrench that piece of the truth to its own use if that truth had been adequately lived and witnessed to in its proper place." Indeed, as he states, the reason for his 1984 *Instruction on Certain Aspects of the "Theology of Liberation"* was because noting the error is all the more important "the greater that grain of truth is."[119] In other words, the Church had been neglecting teaching and living out its social justice message and liberation theology was so powerful because it called attention to the seriousness of this neglect. The problem with liberation theology is not *that* it links faith and economic praxis, but rather *how* it does so.

So, what is this correct relationship? In an earlier essay Ratzinger foreshadows the emphases of *Caritas in Veritate* by noting that, "[t]he practical alternatives have hitherto been insufficiently formulated and have in many cases remained without political reverberation *because Christians have no confidence in their own vision of reality*. They hold fast to the faith in their private devotion, but they do not dare to presume that it has something to say to mankind as such or that it contains a vision of man's future and his history" (emphasis added).[120] Liberation theology fills the void of this insufficient Catholicism of private devotions and individual morality. Their confident critique of privatism is correct. But, in Ratzinger's judgment, liberation theologies are too tempted to allow purely material categories to determine their theologizing of the struggles of history.[121] In fact, as he goes on to explain, what Christians have is a comprehensive historical vision that actually constitutes a full-scale *alternative* to Marxist and liberal-capitalist models of history and progress.[122] This "Christian alternative" (241) possesses a correct understanding of social relations because it is rooted in a correct understanding of the human person.

Whether or not this accurately assesses liberation theology, the major point is that Ratzinger's response to liberation theology should not be understood as a retreat to personal morality. Ratzinger's vision is a full-scale social vision and one that is not "individualistic" (239) but involves "learning to understand and live Christianity in its totality as an alternative to the liberation mythologies of the present" (242). He claims that Marxist and Enlightenment ideas of freedom—not Christianity—are in fact the unrealizable mythological ones. They imagine a pure freedom of "doing everything one wants and of doing only what one would like" (242), but this kind of thinking leads to instrumentalizing others depriving them of their freedom. Real freedom means commitment to reciprocity: a person "cannot arbitrarily call for the other when he happens to appear useful. He cannot arbitrarily let him go when he does not like him, precisely because the other is a self and not a means for anyone" (244–45). Nor is their view of history coherent: Marxism and capitalism both assert that freedom is their goal, but then devise a means—in one case, the revolutionary state, in the other, the free market—that is understood to work and progress "mechanically" in history. Ratzinger counters this mechanism with salvation history in which Christ forms "a new people" that "is taking shape [and] that has a place among all peoples; it does not abolish them but forms a force for unification and for liberation in them all" (250), functioning as a harbinger by which the theological vision of gift and reciprocity animates the "historical program" that is progressively articulated in Catholic social teaching (251–52). Moreover, Marxism and capitalism justify short-term injustice and suffering in the name of future freedom. They accuse Christianity of utopianism and social irresponsibility, but it is Marxist and capitalist utopianism that instead "displace[s] the kingdom into the future, for its future has no present, and its hour never comes" (254). Recall Kapferer's discussion of the ever-deferred "luxury dream." By contrast, the Christian attitude of faithful eschatological trust thereby rejects short-term evil and makes a necessity of doing good—and only good—in the here and now.

The idea that Christianity offers a full-blown social alternative to existing ideologies—and therefore a thoroughly theological perspective on handling possessions—flowers in *Caritas in Veritate*. Its understanding of reciprocity and gift at all levels of social life is the culmination of the trajectory of theologizing Catholic social teaching. At the center of the encyclical is this concept of reciprocity or fraternity.[123] Stefano Zamagni explains how this principle is distinct from both "pure charity" and the traditional notion of contractual "exchange of equivalent values."[124] In contractual exchange, agreement on price precedes the exchange and if the parties do not fulfill the exchange, they can be obliged by coercion. There is freedom prior to the agreement but not after. By contrast, reciprocity involves doing or giving something with an open-ended and unenforceable expectation of some future response, either to the self or to some other party. It is thus "fragile" and necessarily "interpersonal." Further, the reciprocal exchange need not be a matter of value equivalence for it begins in someone's desire "to make a gift, not to make a deal."

Luigino Bruni also notes Marcel Mauss's distinction between *munus* and *donum*; the former involves networks of obligation and commitment while the latter is merely a "gratuitous gift" that is considered outside any network.[125] What fraternal or civil economics tries to recover is the *munus*. Bruni seeks to argue, in line with the pope, that in our world, "*communitas*" disappears in favor of "*immunitas*" in order to protect ourselves against the potential betrayals and harms of the *munus* system. That is, networks of genuine reciprocity are sources of both "the wound and the blessing": if we simply act to protect ourselves from the possibility of wounds in ongoing reciprocity we will also lose all the blessings.

The possibility of enacting and sustaining fragile reciprocity depends on what Benedict calls "the astonishing experience of gift," that is, the experience that "expresses and makes present this transcendent dimension." What is this experience? The description is complex. It begins by noting three aspects of the phenomenon: it is something we receive, it is "something not due to us," and it is "a force that builds community."[126] By contrast, in other experiences we are not receptive because we grasp or are closed in on ourselves, we demand or give simply what is due, or we act in ways that foment conflict.

The encyclical calls our attention to such "quotas of gratuitousness" within our economic activity. Benedict rightly notes that "without internal forms of solidarity and mutual trust, the market cannot completely fulfill its proper economic function."[127] To act as if we are simply and purely self-interested, fulfilling minimal obligations, paying no attention to the divisions we might cause would in fact wreck the economy. One need not look very far to recognize all sorts of gift-like behavior in the economic sphere.[128] Most people "work beyond contract." Friendships and connections facilitate job switches. Everyone pitches in to help out when an employee is called away to deal with an emergency involving children. The fundamental mistake condemned here, as Zamagni notes, is the "absurd idea" that there is a "dichotomy between the economic and the social sphere."[129]

The encyclical has been critiqued by some for offering fluffy or even misguided language that lacks clear application to the actual practice of economics.[130] But, rightly understood, Benedict's message *should* seem incomprehensible to those who insist on seeing the market economy as simply a mechanism. It is not a mechanism; it is a set of human relations. To deny this is not simply theologically wrong. It is in fact foolish on a purely natural level, much less within a supernatural context.

Thus, what Benedict offers is a basic breakthrough in our understanding of the relation of the material and the spiritual, a relationship that is parallel to the personalist revolution in Catholic sexual ethics. Like personalism it does not reject nature; rather it seeks to understand its full supernatural potential—its *sacramental potential*. That potential does differ from the standard accounts available in modern society, although the difference is not one of simple opposition. Instead, the economy functions within a human and theological context of relationship rather than freedom, of covenant history rather than triumphal accounts of advance, of eschatological limitation and trust rather than hubris and evil for the sake of future good. The proper application of this framework can become a fruitful topic for Catholic social ethics—but what is evidently rejected here is "embrace" and "ghetto," which are the terms Ratzinger uses to describe two incorrect ways of understanding Vatican II.[131] The goal is not to merely embrace economics nor to reject it wholesale. The goal is to place it within a framework where the spiritual potential of the material can be realized—where sacramental holiness can be practiced in everyday life.

Reenchantment and Luxury: Purifying Economic Eros

How do these developments in economic theology allow for a renewed critique of the problem of luxury? We can draw a parallel with the development of sexual ethics and extend it to the economic sphere. Luxury functions in the modern economy by appealing to an "economic eros" much as appeals to sexual eros function in the contemporary sexual economy. Like the myth of romantic love based on eros, the myth of luxury promises to produce social bonds "magically" out of the pursuit of individual self-interest. Like sexual eros, the luxury myth builds on the genuine goodness of creation; there is great beauty and pleasure to be found in material goods. But, like the promises made by sexual eros, luxury in the long run fails to produce stable, lasting social bonds even if it yields some kinds of mutuality in the short run.[132] The alternative to the erotic appeals of the luxury economy is the realization of beauty in the practices of economic reciprocity that are rooted in the experience of gift. This kind of "sacramental economy" is the true fulfillment of the erotic promises of material goods, whereas the luxury economy makes false promises of joy and harmony that end up being aimed at self-fulfillment and the enrichment of luxury's priesthood.

Luigino Bruni's work suggests this analogy with sexual eros. He explains that modern economics has a particular view of how the common good comes about, as "a non-intentional result of the actions of single individuals."[133] Following Adam Smith, Bruni explains how Smith believes that "the emulation of the rich and powerful by other citizens lower in the social order is the principal mechanism, indirect and unintentional, that leads to the common good" (4). Yet as noted earlier, Smith sees this passion toward "opulence and well-being" as "a deception of which individuals are victims unaware: the idea that the rich are happier" (4). However, even if this end is illusory, it does, "when well-ordered and regulated," bring about common good (5). Bruni explicitly makes the analogy between eros and contract: a contract is based on getting what I want, just as eros is based on an initial lack "that wishes to fulfill itself by means of another" (3). Just as nature makes use of eros to bring about "the propagation of the species," so too does "economic eros" aimed at self-fulfillment bring about social bonds.

However, sexual eros is insufficient by itself to bring about the stable bonds actually needed for families. Eros promises communion without effort and liberation without promises. Eros "needs help," as C. S. Lewis put it, if its promise of "selfless liberation" is to last "a lifetime" instead of "hardly for a week."[134] That is why eros was constrained by various types of social limitations in most premodern societies. In many ways the modern rise of romantic love and (subsequent) sexual freedom is the story of privatizing sexuality so as to free it from these types of social constraints.

Notice the analogy with the ancient critique of luxury. Luxury was constrained in premodern orders both by overt social rules and by strongly evaluative conventions, both of which insisted that excess goods were not a private matter. The rise of free economies centered on the individual pursuit of self-interest has been the same story as the progress of *privatizing consumption choices so as to free them from social constraints*. Like the rise of eros-based marriage as normative, luxury is assumed to bring about social happiness by allowing individuals to seek their happiness unfettered by obligations. The promise of perpetual luxury of a constantly renewed stream of material goods is the economic version of the promise of perpetual eros for the genuine love needed for marriage. Neither promise can ultimately deliver on either self-fulfillment or social good. Marriage names the real fulfillment of sexual eros; economic reciprocity names the real fulfillment of the "economic eros" of the allure of material goods.

In making the analogy of unbounded eros and luxury, we should note two important dynamics. First, like sexual eros, luxury consumption does indeed generate some short-term benefits. The mistake comes when one undertakes to build an entire economy on it without attention to the necessary "quotas of gratuitousness" or *agape* that must in fact be present for the whole thing to last. In this sense the practice of marriage is in far better shape in the contemporary world. The scale of familial relationships tends to make clear the need for ongoing selflessness. Indeed, the experience of raising children still tends to be deeply formative for many people because it moves them from eros to mutual self-giving. A friend once said to me, "Having kids meant seeing that I could no longer be selfish." Moreover, even when it is detached from its religious foundations, the modern myth of romantic love continues to contain strong agapic elements. Modern fables of sexual freedom such as the television series *Sex and the City* continue to cultivate "endings" in which agapic relationships (almost magically!) materialize out of erotic chaos. That is, the sexual sphere continues to contain a teleology toward a love that is not simply erotic even as that belief frays under various pressures. By contrast, few stories of modern economics insist on the continued role for agapic moments or endings—other than the story expressed in the film *It's a Wonderful Life*. We are far more likely to be addicted to the short-term benefits of the illusion of luxury than to the illusion of pure eros.

Second, this analogy brings us back to our original conundrum over materiality and transcendence: while a pure materialism is problematic, so, too, is the anti-sacramental distortion created when the spiritual and the material are separated or connected only extrinsically.[135] While Pope John Paul II's work in sexual ethics tries to avoid this, critics have noted his "spiritualizing of the body" leads to a kind of extraordinary and unrealistic purity in the descriptions of total self-giving in his discussions of sex.[136] In the economic sphere we can similarly dichotomize the material and the spiritual—either by making the material irrelevant for spiritual life or by rejecting the material for the "purity" of the spiritual.[137] Both distort the material/spiritual connection: on the one hand, "to enclose love in the finite . . . is to falsify even earthly love," while on the other, to "attempt to live the new love . . . while ignoring or going against nature would necessarily degenerate into a caricature of this love."[138] As is seen in Benedict's treatment of eros and agape, any either/or choice is rejected; so, too, should economic materialism and dualistic economic spiritualism be equally rejected. This is the all-or-nothing approach to possessions mentioned earlier.[139] The larger point is to engage in a kind of "consecration" of creation for the new creation but the chronic problem is mistaking the "counterfeit divinization" and "divine intoxication" of eros/luxury for the real thing.[140]

A critique of luxury should not be a brief for a total asceticism nor even for a strict rejection of *any* excess. Much like eros, delight in fine material things may have its *occasional* place in, for example, occasions of communal celebration (see chapter 8). The problem comes when we take a subordinate characteristic and allow it unproblematically to assume the lead role. Hence, renewing the critique of luxury is a way of avoiding either completely vilifying or simply embracing the economic processes of our society. It is a kind of middle way.

However, it is *not* a middle way in the sense of simply splitting the difference. Instead, it alerts us to how "economic eros" on its own can mislead us and distort our sense of the genuinely "magical" (that is, sacramental) purposes of the economy—that is, how our economic activity can truly be a sign of and effective service to God. In other words, economic eros is a real manifestation of divine goodness so long as it is directed toward "the tree of reciprocity" without which societies "are doomed to decline."[141] The problem with the modern marketing of luxury goods is that it promises transcendence. In rejecting these promises we should not then suggest that material goods are *irrelevant* to transcendence. Rather, luxury should be seen as a *false form* of transcendence that blocks the *genuine* ways that material goods and our economic relations with others in producing and acquiring them can in fact show forth transcendence. Like eros and agape in the sexual sphere, the point is not to separate the two but rather to have our ordinary material needs and wants become reoriented and transformed toward their genuine telos: showing forth and bringing about love of God and neighbor. We must reject its tendency to masquerade as the real thing. A critique of luxury is not a rejection of material goods, but rather a way to name their tendency to overshadow "the real thing": economic agape or "gratuitousness."

Sacramental and Idolatrous Economies

Benedict invites us to see "magic in the marketplace" in a different way than is seen in the luxury marketing of products. If our economic transactions should prioritize people over the self-gratification and prestige of luxury items, then we must face the tradeoffs we make by spending on goods and services that are personally gratifying and status-reinforcing versus spending on goods and services that involve the kind of reciprocity described in the encyclical.[142]

Earlier, we saw the marketing promises made on behalf of luxury goods and services. Do people genuinely "believe in" these promises? Does their attachment constitute a parallel to the "worship" that was insisted upon for ancient gods? Are the marketers really the clever "priests" of such a god? This is a difficult question, but a very real one. As Herbert McCabe notes, as moderns we tend to believe that we no longer have idols and that we are "past all that." But, as he suggests, our idols may simply have gotten a bit more abstract.[143] When a person makes a "pilgrimage" to visit a sports team, builds a "shrine" of autographed memorabilia in his basement, or even seeks to be buried in the "vestments" of his team, is that idolatry? What is really going on there?

The phenomena of "belief in" and "trust in" are tricky ones. Three possible ways exist by which our contemporary desire for luxury can trend toward idolatry. One is the simple belief that this or that *particular* material good is essential for happiness and fulfillment, especially when that good or service is highly specific. Does it really matter if a phone is made by Apple or a coffee is brewed by Starbucks? Brands seek to cultivate trust and "relationships" of a sort—and when they do so in terms of a reputation for basic quality they are surely not seeking to be worshiped. But the "magic factor" increases significantly in some areas, and for some goods and services; it is here where one should begin to worry about luxury.

Another more abstract level of idolatry can be attached not simply to this or that good but rather to the whole endless *process* of shopping and consuming. This is parallel to the idea that, in sexuality, some people are "in love with being in love." As Lewis notes about sexual eros, "the real danger seems to me not that the lovers will idolise each other, but that they will idolise Eros himself."[144] Luxury can name the never-ending pursuit of "fashion," that requires a stream of stimulating new clothing or furnishing or, more recently, digital technology.[145] Such shopping easily becomes ritualized, alerting us to the presence of idolatry.

At the deepest level, however, the danger is that consumption is really a matter of worshipping the *self* and making the self the god in whom one believes. Notice that so much advertising plays not on the objective qualities of a product but rather on how the product is "all about you." The rhetoric connects a commodity with the uniqueness and potential of the self: for example, an ad for Sprint smartphones boldly proclaims "I am unlimited." As marketers have recognized for decades, consumption is driven by trying to keep up with others. Yet one must tweak the message so that the product doesn't seem to represent social conformity instead of individual distinctiveness and expression.[146] The full extent of this occurs when the body itself is made into an object of continual attention and modification. Shocking amounts of resources may be spent on hairstyling or plastic surgery—aren't these particularly blatant examples of luxury? The body, whose flourishing depends on basic diet, exercise, and rest, must be turned into something more than that.

There may be no way to test precisely "how much" of modern consumption is driven by this building and maintenance of personal identity (as opposed to the fulfillment of genuine human needs for, say, functional quality). Both luxury critics and luxury defenders maintain that the amount is significant; in monetary terms, developing a brand identity is worth a great deal to companies and is a cost they pass along to consumers. Recently, Adidas signed Derrick Rose to a $185 million, thirteen-year endorsement contract. Adidas sells only $25 million of basketball shoes a year in the United States, while its rival Nike sells $90 million, driven by LeBron James's $93 million endorsement deal. Based simply on US numbers, Rose's contract amounts to over 50 percent of the wholesale cost of each pair—though, of course, the idea is that his name will help them sell more shoes. Nike's deal ends up giving LeBron somewhat under 20 percent of each pair's wholesale cost.[147] These can be great deals for companies if they gain significant market share and are able to charge a significant price premium. As one expert noted in relation to another famous brand, "Porsche has the largest margins in the world."[148]

This willingness to pay the "branding premium" is one of the major critiques of luxury. But the sad thing about all this idolatry is that the genuine potential to produce "magic" is overlooked—if the premium were directed not to the delights of the self but to the real sustenance and flourishing of those who produce necessary goods and services. Nothing is so emblematic of idolatry than a stream of spending along the lines described earlier (e.g., premium-priced gym shoes) accompanied by the insistence that one cannot buy food (or gym shoes!) produced in a just manner because it is "too expensive." This is to refuse one premium in favor of another and prefer luxury to the relationships of reciprocity. Justly produced and priced goods command an appropriate "sacramental premium" that should be understood differently from a brand premium. Whereas a brand premium is paid out of self-interest, a sacramental premium is paid out of interest in the processes that make possible one's own consumption. Notably, the cost of the more expensive price is probably distributed among your neighbors and not poured into the coffers of Derrick Rose or LeBron James.

I use the term "sacramental premium" to suggest a contrast with the acknowledged "brand premium" and a way to think about the goods and services that the marketplace might offer if we were serious about seeking an economy of reciprocity rooted in gift. One can imagine paying a sacramental premium in a variety of ways to fulfill the "quotas of gratuitousness" seen in Benedict's encyclical. We could seek out the personal reciprocity of informal economies of sharing and barter.[149] Certainly these economies can be "money saving"—but what they really are is "money *exposing*." It becomes clear who has excess resources in such systems and who might "share" more than others. Ideally, such informal economies really do enable the support of poorer neighbors, rather than their isolation, and pushes us toward thinking about what we buy in ways oriented to communal sharing. Shared goods and services tend to lead us away from luxury (see chapter 8).

Or we could consider why one might pay more to patronize certain establishments even as one is not "getting" more. I pay more to my independent mechanic for oil changes and more to my small bank for checks than I would by frequenting a chain oil-change place or a big bank. In the larger scheme of things, I can "afford" this—it is not a choice about whether the electric bill will be paid. The premium also benefits me: the mechanic has more skilled workers than the ten-minute lube place, and the local bank manager (who knows me personally) has proven helpful in a crisis situation of identity theft. So, too, a small-classroom college education often costs more, though one can see the benefits to self. What is happening in these situations is that the money is fostering workplaces of relationship and reciprocity. It is true that sometimes small businesses can be terrible.[150] There is no merit in small per se.[151] One can ignore those establishments and not patronize them. It takes work on the consumer's part . . . but so does keeping up with following fashion or reading ads to find the best deal so as to buy more and more unnecessary things. (Of course, it may also be work that one devotes to raising one's children—the question of the value of convenience will be explored in later chapters.)

Even larger organizations could attempt to provide a "sacramental premium" in and through their "brand premium." A brand need not be constructed upon celebrity endorsements or personal dreams; a brand can be built on images of genuine reciprocity. The food retailer Whole Foods gets derided as "Whole Paycheck"—in a clever retort they produced reusable bags that displayed the slogan "Whole paycheck . . . for farmers!" One may dispute the truth of this claim in relation to this or that product in their stores (e.g., Whole Foods now sells a considerable percentage of conventional produce rather discreetly mixed in with prominently signed organic or local), but the idea is correct. The "magic" Whole Foods promises is for the farmer and for a food system of reciprocity.

Daniel Finn notes that one of the limitations of Benedict's encyclical is its focus on small-scale "hybrid enterprises." He suggests that reciprocity finds "partial embodiment" in larger ordinary firms as well, and that attention to reciprocity in these contexts would improve "the accuracy of the discipline of economics" as well as help firms "envision and embody a deeper form of daily economic interaction."[152] Difficult but interesting questions are raised at this point, particularly about corporate structures (e.g., Are large, privately held businesses better at attending to these concerns?) and about the shape of market incentives (e.g., Could firms be encouraged in this direction if investing dollars were driven by such concerns?). In all these cases, though, firms will ultimately depend on both workers and consumers with particular dispositions, and a key reason to critique luxury is to show how Christian consumers can and should adopt different sorts of dispositions in working and consuming to seek sacramental reciprocity, not luxury, with their dollars. Many systemic reforms in ordinary firms could make more headway were the employees and customers of the firm not disposed to luxury. The attachment to luxury blocks moves to reform.[153]

Ultimately these sorts of concerns are also ways of addressing the question of the poor, the "premium" most highlighted in the early Church. The displacement of low-wage work by globalization and technology sometimes provokes yet another polarizing debate. Catholic social thought has not taken one side or the other; it has traditionally dealt with the problem of work in terms of a just wage and other basic rights. If we are to move toward a more sacramental vision of economic relations, a sole focus on worker rights overlooks key issues about luxury and quality when analyzed in particular cases. It may be that, whether at a Whole Foods or at a local food cooperative, what we are doing is paying a premium to support "high-skill" versions of work. Farming, banking, car repair, food preparation—these need not be low-skill professions. They can and should provide skill and dignity. Does that mean we need not worry about regulations of justice, or that "the old-fashioned way" is always better? By no means. The point is simply to call our attention to matters of scale in relation to work. Recognizing that the right scale for work—a scale that involves growth in the "subjective dimension" of the worker—might require us to pay a premium. Paying more for this purpose is a sacramental alternative to the luxury premium.

The attempt to pay attention to this sacramental premium in larger systems is not easy. In a mental exercise dealing with file sharing and retail stores, frequently a group of students will say that stealing from some big box store is fine (if you don't get caught) but that they'd feel bad stealing from Uncle Joe's Hardware down the street. The students are calling attention to the ways in which the impersonal, commodity market seems to bring out a different moral identity than a more face-to-face one does. Nevertheless, large companies have become quite skilled at cultivating "brand relationships," an affection for and loyalty to the impersonal entity of the corporation. Such strategies can become problematic vehicles of "sacred meaning." But there is no reason in principle that brands cannot use these strategies to foster identity rooted in an economics of reciprocity and gift. Organic Valley, itself a cooperative of small farms and thus significantly not at the mercy of impersonal shareholders, has aggressively identified its brand with its actual farmers as owners. They call themselves a "family of farms" and their labels depict actual farmer-owners in stylized pictures who hail from a particular region.[154] The brand "re-presents" the person. Many food companies are rushing to capitalize on the fondness people have for such images, and in this way, again, consumers and their proxies must figure out which brands are "real." The critique of luxury seeks to shift brand relationships in this sacramental direction.

But isn't shopping at Whole Foods and attending small liberal arts colleges totally about luxury? Isn't Organic Valley milk expensive? This sort of question must be examined more concretely in chapter 7. Here it is simply worth noting that the ancient concern for the poor can and should be manifest in the marketplace, not in the search for goods and services that make "magic" for you but which shine with the radiance of good production. The early Church Fathers took luxury to be a sign of idolatry and of neglect of the poor. Our descriptions, particularly of Benedict's economy of reciprocity rooted in gift, should help us recognize that in our modern economy we must relinquish idolatry and attend to the poor not simply outside our market transactions. We must direct our transactions toward "forms of economic activity marked by quotas of gratuitousness and communion."[155]

Benedict also states that this direction is exactly what "civilizing the economy" means.[156] Notice the use of the term "civilize": this is the same term used by Hume to defend the rise of luxury. Obviously, when contrasting the economy of communion with that of luxury we are looking at two very different accounts of what "civilized" means. The economy of luxury focuses on the acquisition and enjoyment of sensual, status possessions. The sacramental economy focuses on actively seeking to do good via spending; the method of making and acquiring our possessions can be genuinely sacramental and genuinely an effective sign of the unity of the human race.

"Smart shopping" is often defined as finding exactly what you want or finding the lowest price, or both. There is a certain logic of what "smart" means, but it is not the logic of the gift. We could be "smart" by figuring out how to do the most good connecting ourselves with others through our purchases; call it "sacramental shopping." This is most easily done in personalist or mutualist contexts, such as co-ops, local goods and services providers, and the like. Many companies are eager to advertise themselves as doing good for their employees and for the environment so it is important to penetrate through the hype and identify what is actually true. In so doing, we shun luxury on the basis of rejecting idolatry and recognize a different "magic" in the economy. In so doing, we notice the poor—which is to say we honor and give what is due to those who do this kind of good work.

I do not want to equate good grocery shopping with opening a Catholic Worker house. But we need to concretize the basic Catholic theological vision of property and decide what economic holiness of life in the world looks like beyond the classic, Francis-like models of voluntary poverty. A critique of luxury and the proposal of a sacramental alternative offers a form of economic practice for Catholics that overcomes the classic dichotomy between simply going along with the consumer economy versus "dropping out." Resisting the mystique of luxury and reorienting one's resources toward building more sacramental economic relationships that embody the economy of reciprocity as described in *Caritas in Veritate* offers at least one way the use of possessions can embody our theological commitments.

Notes

1. Leo XIII, *Rerum Novarum*, no. 19. Cf. Pius XI, *Quadragesimo Anno*, nos. 47–51; John XXIII, *Mater et Magistra*, nos. 119–21; John Paul II, *Centesimus Annus*, no. 30; and Benedict XVI, *Caritas in Veritate*, nos. 7, 43. See also *The Catechism of the Catholic Church*, nos. 2402–7, which quotes *Gaudium et Spes* no. 69.
2. Ryan, *A Better Economic Order*, 149, 151.
3. Paul VI, *Populorum Progressio*, no. 23.
4. *Rerum Novarum*, no. 18.

5. See *Catechism*, nos. 2402–3.
6. John Paul II, *Laborem Exercens*, no. 14. This is consistent with many particular Old Testament laws rooted in the vision of all things as coming from God. See Baker, *Tight Fists or Open Hands*, 307–14.
7. I am not challenging the importance of secure ownership of property over against arbitrary confiscation for commerce and daily life.
8. Banner, *American Property*, 5.
9. Sidgwick, "Luxury," 2.
10. Stassen and Gushee, *Kingdom Ethics*, 417.
11. Ibid., 417, citing Garland, *Reading Matthew*, 401. Such a reading even grates against the disciples' shocked reaction, which clearly indicates the radical character of Jesus' suggestion. Otherwise, perhaps Jesus simply could have responded, "I mean *that* gate, you dummies!"
12. Hays, *Moral Vision of the New Testament*, 468.
13. The term "sacramental ontology" is used by Hans Boersma, *Nouvelle Theologie*, pointing to the work of the twentieth-century writers in the *ressourcement* tradition. The term can be understood more broadly to encompass a sensibility like David Tracy's "analogical imagination" or Andrew Greeley's "Catholic imagination." Other resources: Milbank, *Being Reconciled*; Anderson, *Charity*; Wirzba, *Food and Faith*; Eggemeier, *Sacramental-Prophetic Imagination*; and Smith, *Imagining the Kingdom*.
14. Frank, *Luxury Fever*, 18–19. Note that the threshold here is given for the late 1990s.
15. Tungate, *Luxury World*, 2.
16. For a complete study see Chevalier and Lu, *Luxury China*.
17. "The Persuaders," 2004, available in full online: http://www.pbs.org/wgbh/pages /frontline/shows/persuaders/.
18. On this, see "The Brain from Top to Bottom," at http://thebrain.mcgill.ca/flash/d /d_05/d_05_cr/d_05_cr_her/d_05_cr_her.html.
19. All quotes from online transcript: http://www.pbs.org/wgbh/pages/frontline/shows /persuaders/etc/script.html.
20. Berthon et al, "Aesthetics and Ephemerality," 46.
21. Ibid., 47.
22. Even within these categories the authors insist that luxury brands are of four different types—"classic, modern, postmodern, and wabi sabi"—plotted on axes of aesthetics and ephemerality. See ibid., 51–53.
23. Michman and Magee, *Affluent Consumer*, 105, 148.
24. Kapferer and Bastien, *Luxury Strategy*, 160–62.
25. Tungate, *Luxury World*, 5–6.
26. Kapferer and Bastien, *Luxury Strategy*, 160. This is also why luxury brands must maintain a certain kind of "distance" from clients and hold "a position of superiority with respect to its client" (19). That is, it does not serve the client but rather shows to the client what true meaning really is.
27. Ibid., 47.
28. Ibid., 52, 162.
29. Ibid., 60.
30. Frank, *Luxury Fever*, 16.

31. http://www.alanfurman.com/patek-philippe/. Accessed on January 16, 2015.

32. Thomas, *Deluxe*, 4.

33. Ibid., 11.

34. Silverstein et al., *Trading Up*, viii.

35. Ibid., 10.

36. Ibid., 67–68.

37. Ibid., 72–95.

38. Ibid., 291.

39. Ibid., vii. For further evidence, see Matthews, "Ritzy Retail" and note the success of upscale shopping malls anchored by the likes of Nordstrom and Blooming-dale's, compared to the "dying" of more conventional malls.

40. Kapferer and Bastien, *Luxury Strategy*, 19.

41. Ibid., 62.

42. Lindstrom, *Buy-o-logy*, 121. The shrine-like character of its stores, which are necessarily few, require a pilgrimage and present the objects for sale in startlingly "pure" and "holy" ways; this is only the most glaring example.

43. McCabe, "Truth about God," 30–31.

44. NPR, Marketplace, June 11, 2012.

45. Kapferer and Bastien, *Luxury Strategy*, 298.

46. Shachar et. al, "Brands" 93.

47. For a broader survey of the early Fathers on these issues, see Gonzalez, *Faith and Wealth*; Rhee, *Loving the Poor*; and Finn, *Christian Economic Ethics*. For accessible excerpts, see Phan, *Social Thought*.

48. Chrysostom spent some time trying to be an ascetic and wrecked his health doing so. Basil was drawn to asceticism, but eventually he sought a more communal form and then was drawn into ecclesiastical leadership. Ambrose was simply an educated layman when he famously was picked as a compromise candidate to be bishop.

49. Kelly, *Golden Mouth*, 1–6; Harrison, "Introduction," 11.

50. Homily on "I will Pull Down My Barns," in Phan, *Social Thought*, 117.

51. Ibid.

52. Phan, 109.

53. See Gonzalez, *Faith and Wealth*, 187–88, and Frend, *Early Church*, 212.

54. "The Long Rules," in Phan, *Social Thought*, 119.

55. On Naboth, in Phan, *Social Thought*, 173.

56. Gonzalez, *Faith and Wealth*, 177.

57. Homily on "I will Pull Down My Barns" in Phan, *Social Thought*, 117.

58. Homily in "Divites," quoted in Gonzalez, *Faith and Wealth*, 178.

59. On Naboth, in Phan, *Social Thought*, 175.

60. Ibid., 171.

61. Homily on 1 Corinthians, in Phan, 152.

62. Ibid., 153.

63. Kelly, *Golden Mouth*, 97–99.

64. These Fathers employed a distinctive approach to "reading" biblical texts, one that differed from some of their contemporaries. Elizabeth Clark contrasts three ways of reading the material commands against riches that are so frequently seen in the Old Testament. John Chrysostom's strategy was one of "embracing it as the

Christian present" (*Reading Renunciation*, 153–54) and reading it as binding on Christians. By contrast, Jerome, and in an even stronger way Origen, seek to allegorize or bypass entirely the "carnality" of these commands. Other Fathers, like Clement and Augustine, also come to Christianity via Platonic paths rather than Stoic ones, thus encouraging spiritualizing.

65. Homilies on the Gospel of Matthew, in Phan, *Social Thought*, 141.
66. Markus, *End of Ancient Christianity*, 54.
67. Brown, *Through the Eye*, 311. Interestingly, in the entire "debate" over wealth in the early Church, no one takes a pro-luxury position. The question is usually the appropriate degree and practice of renunciation.
68. Ibid., 316.
69. Markus, *End of Ancient Christianity*, 54–55.
70. Brown notes that cities in the east retained wealth for some time, so that two different dynamics developed. In the west, bishops and monasteries generated secure Christian towns that looked out warily at the pagan countryside, but in the east, "God-fearing farmers" populated a Christian countryside against urban "enclaves of profane living." Brown, *Rise of Western Christendom*, 116–17. Brown further notes the deep decline of trade and contact among regions (218) and the dearth of learning and books (a library of three hundred books was the largest in existence north of the Alps, 217).
71. Ibid., 135.
72. Ibid., 157.
73. Taylor, *Modern Social Imaginaries*, 49.
74. Ibid., 42.
75. Brown, *Rise*, 260–72, narrates the extensive attempts of Willibrord and Boniface to bring order to this tendency to merge pagan and Christian symbols and idioms. They anticipate what Taylor (in *Secular Age*) describes as the impulse to "reform" that drives the West, in both Protestant and Catholic forms, after the Reformation.
76. Pieper, *Guide to Thomas Aquinas*.
77. Gregory, "History of Christianity."
78. Taylor, *Secular Age*, 244. The idea that notions of humanly beneficial divine design provide the key bridge from the world of 1500 to the world of 2000 is central to Taylor's entire argument and his preferred alternative to "subtraction stories," which simply try to say that science supplants faith.
79. Taylor, *Modern Social Imaginaries*, 66.
80. Lohfink, *Jesus and Community*, 2. Harnack takes this from Augustine, but it is not Augustine's mature view, which is considerably more ecclesial.
81. Even worse versions of this dualism appear in evangelical Protestantism, where creation itself is going to be destroyed anyway. This is not a marginal view: a recent Pew poll shows that nearly half of American Christians believe Jesus will "definitely" or "probably" return in the next forty years. http://www.pewforum.org /Christian/US-Christians-Views-on-the-Return-of-Christ.aspx.
82. *Lumen Gentium*, nos. 38–42, in Abbott, ed., *Documents of Vatican II*, 65–72.
83. *Sacrosanctam Concilium*, no. 10, in Abbott, ed., *Documents of Vatican II*, 142.
84. *Gaudium et Spes*, no. 3, in Abbott, ed., *Documents of Vatican II*, 200–01.
85. Boersma, *Nouvelle Theologie*, viii, 289.

86. Ibid., 13.
87. Eggemeier, *Sacramental-Prophetic Vision*, 8.
88. Ibid., 10.
89. Paul VI, *Populorum Progressio*, no. 15.
90. Ibid., no. 44.
91. Eggemeier, *Sacramental-Prophetic Imagination*, 10.
92. For a contemporary reappropriation of Augustine on this, see Bennett, *Water Is Thicker.*
93. Cloutier, "Marriage and Sexuality."
94. *Gaudium et Spes*, no. 48, in Abbott, ed., *Documents of Vatican II*, 250–52.
95. John Paul II, *Familiaris Consortio*, no. 49.
96. Ibid., no. 17.
97. Ratzinger, *Yes of Jesus Christ*, 88–89.
98. Burns, "Abandoning Suspicion," 73.
99. See Cloutier, "Heaven Is a Place on Earth?"
100. Bruni, "Common Good," 6.
101. Thus, my project argues for a unity of Catholic sexual and social teaching, though it is beyond the scope of this text to develop that argument except for identifying a common tendency toward the universal call to holiness and the insertion of the Catholic moral life within a context of lay holiness, liturgy, and mission.
102. Note, for example, the strongly sequenced treatments of justice (paras. 15–17) and charity (paras. 18–20) in *Rerum Novarum*.
103. Paul VI, *Populorum Progressio*, no. 14.
104. Ibid., nos. 44, 72.
105. Ibid., no. 80.
106. For a pathbreaking article that makes the connections between *Populorum Progressio* and *Humanae Vitae* and displays the consistency of this shift to holiness in both areas, see McCarthy, "Procreation."
107. John Paul II, *Laborem Exercens*, no. 6.
108. This realization/degradation dynamic could be seen as parallel to the one explained in the theology of the body contrasting love and lust.
109. John Paul II, *Laborem Exercens*, no. 13.
110. John Paul II, *Sollicitudo Rei Socialis*, no. 38.
111. Clark, *Vision of Catholic Social Thought*, 31–32.
112. John Paul II, *Sollicitudo Rei Socialis*, nos. 38, 36.
113. Ibid., no. 28.
114. John Paul II, *Centesimus Annus*, nos. 23–24.
115. Ibid., nos. 36, 41.
116. Benedict XVI, *Caritas in Veritate*, nos. 37–38,
117. Francis, *Evangelii Gaudium*, nos. 50, 57.
118. For a sober and detailed look at the underlying issues about theory and praxis at stake in Ratzinger's qualified critique of liberation theology, see especially Kroger, "Prophetic-Critical and Practical-Strategic Tasks."
119. Ratzinger, "Liberation Theology," 217. See also Congregation for the Doctrine of the Faith, "Instruction."
120. "Freedom and Liberation," in Ratzinger, *Church, Ecumenism, and Politics*, 241. Further citations of this important chapter are in the text.

121. See also Milbank, *Theology and Social Theory*, chap. 8, for a similar critique in terms of a well-intended but misguided "naturalizing of the supernatural."

122. Benedict expands on the notion that individualistic eschatology leads to a ceding of history to scientific (whether capitalist or socialist) understandings of historical progress in his encyclical *Spe Salvi*.

123. For details on this language, which is unfamiliar to most Americans, see Zamagni et al., *Handbook on the Economics of Reciprocity*.

124. For all the following see Zamagni, "Fraternity, Gift, and Reciprocity," 156–57.

125. Bruni, *Wound and the Blessing*.

126. Benedict XVI, *Caritas in Veritate*, no. 34.

127. Ibid., no. 35.

128. See Finn, "Reciprocity."

129. Zamagni, "Fraternity, Gift, and Reciprocity," 157.

120. For a complete rundown of reactions to the encyclical, including criticisms, see Blosser, "Pope Benedict XVI's *Caritas in Veritate*."

131. See Ratzinger, "Review of the Postconciliar Era," 391.

132. For an excellent treatment of the problematic history of the eros/agape dichotomy, as well as an approach to overcoming it via friendship, see Wadell's classic, *Friendship and the Moral Life*, esp. 70–96.

133. Bruni, "Common Good," 4. Further citations in text.

134. Lewis, *Four Loves*, 114–15.

135. "Extrinsic connection" is something like what Helen Alford and Michael Naughton, *Managing as If Faith Mattered*, 13–15, name as the problem of "spiritualizers," who see the fruits of economic enterprise as to be used to foster private religious devotion and charity and family, but who do not see agape as necessary within economic activity.

136. See Mattison and Cloutier, "Bodies Poured Out in Christ."

137. The latter might involve an excessive "puritanism" or an asceticism that is not actually conducive to mission.

138. Ratzinger, *Yes of Jesus Christ*, 88.

139. Reference back to chap. 1.

140. Benedict XVI, *Deus Caritas Est*, no. 4.

141. Zamagni, "Fraternity, Gift, and Reciprocity," 164.

142. All three of my constructive chapters recognize the problem of luxury in terms of making certain tradeoffs: in the virtue chapter, the tradeoffs involve leisure/work and external/internal goods; here the tradeoff is between magic for the self versus magic in the reciprocity of the economic relationship. In the following economics chapter, the tradeoffs are with investment, redistribution, and among different consumption goods.

143. McCabe, "The Truth about God."

144. Lewis, *Four Loves*, 111.

145. Gonzalez's excellent *Shopping*, 16–17, makes excellent points about the allure of quick-turnover fashion.

146. For example, see the excellent *Frontline* program on advertisers' "cool-hunting": http://www.pbs.org/wgbh/pages/frontline/shows/cool/etc/hunting.html.

147. Saporito, "What's in a Name?" Contracts: Rose: 185 mln/13 yrs = 14.23 mln/yr = 56.9% of $25 mln wholesale income (for basketball shoes); James: 93 mln/7 yrs =

13.285 mln/yr = 14.8% of $90 mln wholesale income. The percentage estimates are rough and do not consider international sales, since it is hard to know how NBA endorsements affect those sales. Regardless, they do demonstrate how much of a price premium we are paying for the "high priestly" endorsements.

148. http://www.nytimes.com/2015/01/16/business/in-the-falling-euros-shadows
-bargain-hunting-for-luxury.html?ref=business.
149. See McCarthy, *Sex and Love in the Home.*
150. Livingston, *Against Thrift,* 20–25, reminds us that small businesses can often be the worst practitioners of labor abuses, of environmental carelessness, and the like, as well as lacking efficiency.
151. MacIntyre, "A Partial Response to My Critics," 302, rightly distances himself from the "contemporary version of Romantic politics which glorifies the small-scale and local as such."
152. Finn, "Reciprocity," 77.
153. One might also consider the oft-reported "arms race" that colleges are forced to engage in, toward ever-more deluxe residential amenities that will impress students on their ninety-minute tours.
154. One farm family depicted, the Zwebers of Minnesota, also appear in Cavanaugh, *Being Consumed.*
155. Benedict XVI, *Caritas in Veritate,* no. 39.
156. Ibid., no. 38.

CHAPTER 4

Neglected Positionality

Why Luxury Does Not Always Help the Economy

The last two chapters have developed a philosophical and theological case that offers firmer ground for morally problematizing luxury. Luxury's status as a vice is not merely a reflection of class perspectives; it rests on the real harm it does to social practices, especially work, and to the Christian life, all while masquerading as a false alternative to building a more sacramental economy.

Nevertheless, the economic objection remains potent: isn't this a critique that reflects class comfort and ignores the economic harm that would happen if people stopped consuming so much?[1] Isn't it true that the widespread pursuit of luxuries produces an economic system where wealth "trickles down," even to the developing countries making the goods that fill our stores? Most potently, doesn't the ancient critique of luxury rest on a fundamental economic mistake: a zero-sum model, where one person's gain (of private luxuries) represents another person's loss (of daily bread)? As economist Juliet Schor puts it more bluntly at the end of her critique of overconsumption, "will consuming less wreck the economy?"[2]

Recent historical episodes seem to confirm this worry. By the Great Depression year of 1933, GDP had plunged "to half its 1929 level" and industries "dependent on discretionary spending had all but gone out of business."[3] The plunge in both consumption and investment led to unemployment of 25 percent. During the Great Recession of 2008–2009,

Federal Reserve Chairman Ben Bernanke noted that the 5 percent decline in GDP experienced in the United States in 2009 translated into a loss of 8.5 million jobs.[4] At the center of that decline was a collapse in two major consumption markets, housing and automobiles. Auto sales dropped to unheard-of lows, from nearly 17 million sold in 2005 to just over 10 million in 2009, with the result that two of the three major American automakers had to be put on government support lest a huge swath of workers be put out of their jobs.[5] New home construction—which topped 1.5 million units a year at the height of the earlier boom—fell to below 300,000, a number far below any year since before statistics started being kept in the postwar period (and, remember, in earlier years the population was much smaller than today).[6] New homes and new cars: these might well be considered luxuries since the collapse in demand came from people merely caring for cars and houses already in existence, or forgoing these private goods for other purchases. As Bernanke explained, the housing decline also meant a decline in the many goods that are bought for new houses: appliances, furniture, and the like.

Christian ethicist James Nash, in his attempt to revive the virtue of frugality, calls this the "damning drawback." Frugality is an important virtue, he says, but it "is a formula for market depression."[7] He explains: "Frugality implies significantly less economic stimulus. Thus, it would likely result not only in less production and fewer goods, but also smaller investments, lower profits, lower wages, reduced revenues, decreased philanthropy, and higher unemployment. The social, not to mention the psychological, consequences could be serious, particularly for the poor and unemployed. Equitable distribution would become an enhanced imperative but probably not an easier task. Internationally, the repercussions could be no less serious, particularly for poor countries dependent on affluent countries for export markets and economic assistance."[8]

Railing against the excesses of consumerism from a tenured academic position could be the worst sort of moralizing unless these economic questions are confronted. This chapter responds to this objection responsibly; there is a credible economic case for questioning the standard objection, that an attack on luxury amounts to an attack on our overall economic well-being. Such a case must be made carefully. It cannot simply be made by attacking capitalism or "the market"—instead, the case will be made from within the basic logic and structure of modern economics. Nash's "damning drawback" assumes the basic Mandevillian perspective, that excess consumption is good because it leads to economic growth—and that any attempts to curb this consumption will lead to economic depression.

But critiquing *luxuria* need not be seen as an attack on consumption as a whole; rather, it is a critique of certain kinds of consumption and therefore an argument for shifting consumption and spending. Crucial to this response is a more nuanced treatment of the economics of consumption, not only in terms of *what* is consumed but also of the *context* of that consumption. Economic "truths" are always dependent on conditions and circumstances, which obviously can and do change. What held true about the social benefits of luxury consumption in Adam Smith's time may no longer hold so clearly under our current conditions. A nuanced treatment of consumption will help us have a better, richer model for analyzing the economics of particular spending choices.

First, we must consider the historical evolution of modern economics as a discipline in order to understand why the problem of luxury drops out. After all, not everyone in the seventeenth and eighteenth centuries praised luxury like Mandeville did. In one sense this is a story of the triumph of the powerful metaphor of the "invisible hand."[9] Defining two revolutions in economics will help us understand why the question of interrogating individual consumption decisions gets pushed to the margins of the discipline or even gets ruled out of bounds altogether.

A second important contemporary economic challenge to the Mandeville/invisible hand model must be considered: Fred Hirsch's treatment of the social limits on economic growth. Hirsch suggests that the invisible hand model works but only to a certain point and under certain conditions. Particular economic insights are often said to be true *ceteris paribus*—that is, if all other factors are unchanging. The mistake is to presume economic insights (like the invisible hand) apply at all times to every economic decision in every circumstance. Efforts by economists to name more precisely where and how the invisible hand picture is inadequate interestingly converge with traditional moral concerns about luxury, and in particular the ancient insight about the social conflicts produced by *widespread* luxury. A more nuanced picture emerges that supports the idea that luxury—as a *widespread* disposition to excess—no longer produces so much benefit and may indeed produce much more social harm and waste. The issue is not spending versus hoarding; the ancient traditions criticizing luxury all come out against hoarding. The issue is good and bad spending. It turns out that even economics can suggest the need for distinctions between the two—and therefore can provide support for a measured critique of luxury.

How Economics Forgot Luxury: A History

Competing Intuitive Models

Modern economics is a science of sophisticated models.[10] It is reasonable to say that there is in reality no such thing as "the economy." Rather, there are myriad social processes of material provisioning and servicing that are interrelated and follow patterns, and these patterns can be represented by models. The word "economics" comes from the Greek word *oikonomia*, which refers specifically to the household and underscores the idea that the household is the proper site for this provisioning.[11] But the household is hardly the only model. For example, many contemporary economists become exasperated when government officials speak of governments having to "tighten their belts in hard times" just like households do because the model is misapplied in a number of ways.[12] Government spending, because it pays bills in currency it issues, must be modeled differently. On a broad level, to speak of economics is to speak of the implicit and explicit models we use to understand the relationships of provisioning by which we live.

Just as natural scientists point out, the practice of model-making is complex. The elements of the periodic table are sufficiently complex that proton-neutron-electron models oversimplify reality. Light exhibits behavior that suggests both a wave model and a particle model. Model-making for social processes is even more complex. Indeed, one of the more potent critiques of centralized economic planning is that such planning requires information for modeling that no person can actually possess.[13] Yet, critics of planning also have an economic model that allows for some human ability to grasp and regulate markets (e.g., definitions of and restrictions on fraud).

The supposed "damning drawback" of criticizing luxury rests on a model that largely remains true to Mandeville's intuitive metaphor of the beehive: desire for luxury and material advancement spurs overall economic activity and produces more wealth overall. Much of the work laying the foundations of modern economics was done in the seventeenth and eighteenth centuries as thinkers began to grapple with a number of significant changes in the world of material provisioning, which seemed to demand new models. Inflation pushed prices outside their traditional fixed limits, causing pain to landlords and wage-earners but simultaneously leading to great and growing wealth for merchants and innovators. Trade became much more widespread and seemed to produce vast riches.

Countries like Spain, which seemed to gain great "treasure" from explora-tion, ended up falling behind nations like England and Holland, where trading, finance, and production seemed to be creating more wealth. In short, significant changes were actually happening that did not seem to conform to the workings of traditional models that had largely limited eco-nomic activity according to moral laws and customs.[14] Longer-distance trade and surplus production for market exchange, once a minor sideshow to the dominant economic activity of local subsistence, increasingly took center stage. As Joyce Appleby writes of the period, "No longer visible and tangible, the economy generally became incomprehensible."[15]

The "traditional model" presented luxury spending as a waste of resources that could be put to "better" use. As the disciples say to Jesus when a woman anoints him, "What is the point of such extravagance? This could have been sold for a good price and the money given to the poor" (Mt 26:8–9). The same model, as we have seen, is offered in the ancient and patristic literature: spending on private luxuries is bad because it wastes resources that could be better used.

The school of thought now called "mercantilism"—which sought economic growth through the accumulation of precious metals by main-taining a favorable balance of trade, especially by promoting exports and limiting imports—was one effort to make a new model for what general prosperity might look like.[16] Mercantilism sought to manage the new, wider economy by involving the sovereign in regulating the expanding trade just as authorities had used law and custom to shape economic trans-actions in the more limited feudal economies.

Yet, as economies expanded and became more intertwined, this model encountered problems and hints of a different model appeared based on a new question: What if economic transactions were not subordinated to social laws but rather followed "natural" laws of their own?[17] Mandeville's metaphor of the beehive, along with Smith's "invisible hand" (however overblown it became in the work of later writers), suggested this different, more challenging insight: that economic prosperity for all, including all nations, lay not in regulating or limiting economic activity but rather in letting individuals freely pursue their own interests. How did this work? After all, the traditional model seems obvious: feed the hungry *or* buy fin-ery. Restricted trade seemed just as obvious: give your money to the local poor (or employ them) or give your gold to foreigners for novel luxuries.

Smith's work is best understood as an extended argument against the mercantilist model in favor of a different "system of natural liberty" rest-ing on solid property law and the "natural instinct to truck, barter, and exchange," which would produce outcomes that would be mutually beneficial.[18] In Smith's model, "the wealth of a nation consisted in the value of its produce"; such a value could increase via free trade and other loosening of economic restrictions.[19]

It is important to remember that Smith distanced himself from the Mandeville position. Even beyond his moral objections to luxury, Smith limited even his economic endorsement of luxury: luxury spending was a second-best route to development and the "frugal nation" that saves and invests its surplus is preferred over one that consumes it in "prodigality" because "capitals are increased by parsimony, and diminished by prodigality."[20] Consequently, he favors luxury taxation.[21] As Charles Clark notes, Smith, like most "classical" economists of the late eighteenth and early nineteenth centuries, had "a well-being, material-production view of wealth."[22] Neither piling up gold nor piling up luxuries produced a wealthy nation; rather, productive investment that produced more corn or textiles was key. Smith hoped for nations to approach "a full complement of riches" and this did not mean endless expansion; it meant enough food and manufacturing to support the population plus the necessary transportation to export surpluses.[23]

Smith's muted endorsement of the insight about the importance of self-interest did not necessarily lead to Mandeville's inversion of traditional vice and virtue. After all, while the Dutch may have lavished attention on their homes by adding new items amidst prosperity, they also were "notoriously frugal" in other ways.[24] Moreover, Dutch prosperity "hit a plateau" in the eighteenth century in the forsaking of advances in agriculture and manufacturing in favor of becoming "the great financiers of other countries' ventures and follies. . . . Many a Dutchman and woman found ways to enjoy the good life as a rentier . . . [and] turned their attention to acquiring status and enjoying the good life by investing in land or becoming bankers, or doing both."[25] By forsaking workmanship for an easier life, the Dutch themselves fell victim to a form of luxury and then found themselves surpassed by the industrious English. Mandeville's fable about the economic goodness of luxury possessed some short-term plausibility but did not seem sufficient as a model for the whole economic story.

Did such a model exist? Neither Smith nor any other thinker of the late eighteenth century gave a definitive answer, in part because they focused their attention on issues of international trade, aggregate national wealth, and questions of production. Their focus was not primarily on what are now called microeconomic choices—that is, on understanding the "adding up" of individual consumer choices to collective economic benefit.

The development of the modern discipline of economics followed other disciplines and pushed toward the scientific. Gradually thinkers began to emerge who sought models that were theoretically and mathematically effective in explaining economic activity and did not need to be presented in a rambling eight-hundred-page book like Smith's. The discipline slowly became distinguished from ethics (where Smith stood) and even "political economy." While economists sought better models, what counted as "better" requires a historical narrative of development that clarifies why certain questions and approaches are vindicated and others disappear.

Such a history is itself full of contestation. Any description must be oversimplified, lest our inquiry get lost in the weeds. In particular, the historical narrative can be simplified by focusing on a particular problem: through the end of the nineteenth century, economists continued to engage and debate the question of luxury in their economic models, yet in the course of the twentieth century the question has virtually disappeared. Why? Two key modeling "revolutions" occurred in the discipline, both of which systematically pushed this question to the periphery.[26] These two revolutions are often invisible in philosophical and theological work on economic ethics because they are either assumed or ignored. While a review of them will necessarily contain technical material, the point of the technical material is to display how the modeling revolutions worked to exclude considerations of luxury and implied that such considerations would likely have negative economic impacts.

The Marginalist Revolution

The first of these is known as the "marginalist revolution." Jonathan Schlefer refers to marginalism as the "smart shopping" model because it assumes that for all aspects of an economy, markets exist to find the prices where supply and demand will balance to best satisfy ends, given scarce resources.[27] We open the Sunday advertisements, merchants call out and adjust prices, and we shop around to make the most of our resources. In marginalism, "the economy as a whole . . . can be viewed as one big rational resource allocation process" that reaches optimal equilibrium of supply and demand, as both producers and consumers make decisions "at the margins" to shift their decisions according to the fluctuation of prices.[28] The result is, ideally, the most efficient allocation of scarce resources to their most valued uses.

Marginalism did not appear as a completely formed model in any one theorist's work but resulted from the convergence of multiple factors and individuals.[29] For our purposes here, the formulation of the principle of "marginal utility" proved a breakthrough for understanding the activity of individual economic agents (businesses and consumers). It explains "the equilibrium of the consumer" as the state by which he or she "so distributes his expenditure that the marginal utility of each good acquired stands in the same proportion to its price."[30]

Since no ordinary person ever thought to talk this way about his or her choices, it might seem strange to think that this is a good model, so let us try to describe it carefully. The technical problem of price determination is described by Frank Knight as "the pivotal new logical idea" that marks a break with the classical economists (e.g., Smith, Ricardo, Marx).[31] Classical economists sought to model price primarily (though not exclusively) based on the cost of production, but Peter Danner notes that "marginal utility completely reversed the explanation of value" by shifting attention from production to consumption.[32] Value is not "inherent" in things, but rather it is "imputed."[33] Demand, much more than cost of production, determines value.

What causes people to demand things? This is where the "marginal" part comes in. For most goods, our desire for more of them diminishes as we acquire units of them. The value of a single glass of water may be very high, but the value of subsequent glasses falls. We will pay less for the next one, and so on. Thus, "the ratio of exchange [= price] of any two commodities will be the reciprocal of the ratios of the marginal utilities of the quantities of goods available for consumption after completion of the exchange."[34] We will buy more and more of product A until the extra utility per dollar we gain from having more A falls below the extra utility per dollar gained from having more of products B, C, D, etc. We maximize our utility overall when the extra (marginal) utility per dollar is the same for all products. Prices are set in a market by the utility of the *marginal* unit of a good, that is, our demand for that unit in relation to our demand for quantities of other goods we want.[35] Thus, at different possible prices for product A, consumers will demand different amounts—at a lower price they may want more; at a higher price, less. Aggregating these demand curves produces an overall model of what the demand of a product will be at certain prices.

The marginalist solution to the problem of consumer prices was also turned around and applied to the prices paid by businesses for the factors of production (wages, capital, and rent).[36] "The right story about production could turn it into smart shopping."[37] John Bates Clark told a story about how a "natural" wage was set by what unskilled labor could command from large industries in a free market.[38] Parallel to diminishing marginal utility in consuming different products, producers experienced diminishing marginal productivity. For example, workers are added to factories or fields to the point where the additional production from another worker is not worth the additional wage. Perhaps it is then better to spend extra money not on more workers but on expanding the size of the factory. Producers buy inputs (buildings, workers, machines) in the same way consumers spread their resources among products. A producer reaches "equilibrium" when a firm cannot increase production by adding or shifting resources among inputs. Thus, at different prices for each input, firms supply different quantities to the market. Setting prices for different mixes of inputs can do the same thing. For example, a recent article highlights an auto parts manufacturer who makes decisions about using workers or a machine to do a process based on whether the machine will cost less than two years' worth of the wages for the workers doing the work manually.[39]

By combining these ideas about consumers and producers seeking maximum marginal utility and productivity, the marginalist revolution led to a model of market prices as the price where the number of units consumers were willing to buy and the number of units producers were willing to produce met. This provided an elegant and comprehensive view of why markets worked so well overall, even though both individual consumers and producers were trying to get the best deal for themselves. One can see why a marginalist model of economic behavior could explain the connection between individual maximizing choice and large-scale social benefit.[40]

However, marginalism's power proved attractive for another, less intuitive reason: it seemed so deeply "scientific." In nineteenth century economics, political economy kept slipping into seemingly nonscientific modes. A prime example: John Stuart Mill's classic *Principles of Political Economy* seemed to lurch from quantitative mechanical analysis to qualitative description and evaluation in ways that seemed unscientific. By contrast, marginalism promised to make the entire economy, both consumption and production, into a mathematical mechanism that could be readily displayed via calculus. John Medaille describes Clark's achievement thusly: "Mandeville's paradox . . . is given a mathematical form."[41] The marginalist model puts at its center the notion of equilibrium.[42] The best economy is Pareto-optimal; it is an equilibrium where there is no way to improve any one person's situation without harming someone else's.

In what way can this be understood as "best"? Here the attempt to purify scientific economics from moral considerations gets tricky. A description of how markets work best (economists acknowledge that they do not always work in this way) shouldn't be seen as equivalent to a claim that markets are always *morally* best. Strictly speaking, the problem is not the marginalist model per se, but rather the temptations the model offers in defining what is best. The removal of any questions about the content of individual consumer choices from scientific economic models offers a temptation to believe that what is best in terms of the model is best, simply speaking. Giving into such a temptation then fundamentally excludes talk about luxury.

Early marginalists (Marshall, Pigou) continued to make arguments for redistribution following the ideas of earlier utilitarian economists (Mill, Sidgwick), to whom it seemed obvious that a dollar is more useful (= produces more value) for a starving person than a rich one. But as the marginalist revolution hardened into what is known as "neoclassical economics," which forms the basis for most contemporary textbook economics, the science increasingly sought to exclude any such consideration.[43] "Modern neo-classical economists mostly reject" interpersonal comparisons "on the ground that it is impossible to make objective comparisons of utility across individuals."[44] Lionel Robbins offers the classic definition: "Economics is the science which studies human behavior as a relationship between ends and scarce means which have alternate uses."[45] It prescinds *any* judgment about ends, and instead limits its attention to the most efficient use of various means to meet given ends. The point of economics is not to judge my desires but rather to articulate the best way for me (and everyone else) to get the most possible of whatever I value most. The entire model labels the "best" outcome only to the extent that we reject any possible interpersonal comparisons of subjective utility. That is, if I say I want a thousand cheap paintings for my thousand dollars and my neighbor wants just one perfect painting, we don't judge at all which is "better." We just set up the economy in such a way that everyone's wants are met to a maximal extent possible: I get my thousand, my neighbor gets her one. This is "best." In this model, utility judgments are inherently separate, individual, and subjective and the work of economics is not to critique them but rather to articulate a system where everybody's wants are maximally satisfied. In effect, efficiency is substituted for morality, becoming the uncontested but dominant "highest good" in the model similar to how happiness studies defaulted into wanting a value-free model that privileges autonomy as the highest value.[46] Speaking critically about luxuries is simply declared beyond the bounds of economics.

But it is not out of bounds altogether unless we adopt this theory of the consumer in what Mark Nixon calls its "ideological form."[47] As one contemporary writer explains, "Economists cannot prove that taking a dollar forcibly from Bill Gates and giving it to a starving child would improve overall social welfare. Most people intuitively believe that to be so, but it is theoretically possible that Bill Gates would lose more utility from having the dollar taken from him than the starving child would gain."[48] It is technically correct that economists cannot prove this, but it is easy to (mis)read the statement as saying that no such rational judgment could be made on *any* basis. Of course, we could make such a judgment if we named some reasonable basic standard of necessities—for example, a standard the Church Fathers applied when they shamed the rich for their fine clothing while others lacked any clothing. That would require understanding utility in nonsubjective ways, with the most obvious being a distinction between which are necessary material goods for a human life and which are superfluous. Nixon also notes the ideological form of consumer theory would need "to modify its axioms" in order "to view the individual as a communal creature" and avoid the temptation to become "a normative social philosophy."[49] That is, the marginalist model tempts us to believe that there are no objective standards for utility and that my judgments about the relative utility of goods have nothing to do with my neighbor's judgments.

Thus, a certain ideological form of the marginalist model *creates* the "damning drawback" when what is best according to the model is understood to be the best, per se. Recall that the "damning drawback" refers to how frugality and the critique of luxury would hurt the economy. One cannot deny this, if by "hurt" is meant that overall utility is defined simply by aggregating the individual utility judgments of everybody, whatever they may be. But this definition of hurt implies the impossibility of completely untangling the economic rationality from the moral rationality. As one essay puts it, "Economists usually deny that economic theory presupposes any ethics, but they freely admit that it presupposes a great deal about rationality. However, economists cannot have it both ways."[50] Is it a "drawback" if a critique of luxury means that wealthy persons have fewer superfluous goods?

The Keynesian Revolution

Before going further with critiques of the marginalist model, a second revolution needs to be examined in order to understand the disappearance of luxury in economics: the Keynesian revolution. Here again the topic is complicated and subject to many interpretations. But overall there is agreement that John Maynard Keynes's seminal work, *The General Theory*, especially as implemented after World War II, constituted an important corrective to the failures of the marginalist model to deal with the problems of chronic unemployment that plagued developed economies in the first third of the twentieth century.[51]

Keynes's work is historically rooted in the development of "welfare economics" by his British predecessors, Alfred Marshall and A. C. Pigou. Marshall's 1890 text, *Principles of Economics*, "was perhaps the most influential text of the marginalist revolution."[52] But Marshall also sought to "develop what he considered an improved measure of economic welfare" that would avoid "naïve laissez-faire views" and identify "factors that might cause individual satisfaction to diverge from national income."[53] Pigou, Marshall's successor at Cambridge, pushed the work further by distinguishing the "marginal net social product" and "marginal net private product" of economic activity.[54] Pigou highlighted the real difference between "economic welfare" and "total welfare," and while it was often the case that the two moved in the same direction, "any rigid inference from effects on economic welfare to effects on total welfare is out of the question. In some fields the divergence between the two effects will be insignificant, but in others it will be very wide."[55] One case where Pigou noted a significant divergence was in the socially "debasing" or "elevating" effects of private consumption choices—certainly this is an echo of the concern about luxury.[56] The ideas put forth by Marshall and Pigou were early attempts to model what have become known as "market failures," where self-interested activity seems to lead to obvious bad social effects; they combined the adoption of the new tools of marginalist microeconomics with the Victorian British penchant for social reform and sought to combine mathematical acuity with actual social improvement.[57] They resisted the temptation to identify "best" simply within the marginalist model.

Keynes developed within this tradition, but he also revolutionized it. Keynes's most famous "general theory" has many moving parts, but at base it tries to make sense of why depressions can happen and are not self-correcting as typical equilibrium models assume. What happens when your paintings aren't selling? In the marginalist model you drop the price and more buyers emerge. Or there are too many paintings so you stop producing them and make something else; and eventually people buy up the remaining paintings, leaving room to return to producing them once the supply drops. This model assumes that the market cannot ever really stay out of equilibrium. Keynes agrees that the economy will find an equilibrium—but with the significant qualification that such an equilibrium may be far below what an economy is capable of producing. Why? His crucial move was to reject the traditional economic axiom called "Say's law": the idea that supply creates its own demand.[58] In fact, Keynes argued: (1) supply does not create effective demand, and (2) the capitalist system itself tends to erode demand over time, due to the fact that "winners" accumulate savings because their "marginal propensity to consume" declines. That is to say, only the possession of wealth creates *effective* demand, and as wealth concentrates, those who have it are less and less likely to use the extra dollar on consumption and are more inclined to save it. Thus, an economy can find itself in a situation with a lot of wealth and a lot of people seeking work . . . and no production. Why? Because of a lack of effective demand, and in particular of lack of *investment*, which is what actually drives changes in income (and therefore consumption). Keynes identifies the "paradox of thrift" as the more people and governments save in hard times the less they invest, and the harder the times become.

Keynes's deeper analysis, typically brilliant and subtle, ultimately suggests that there are two drivers of demand in this situation, with one more "mechanical" than the other. One is the benchmark rate of interest, which is the ultimate determiner of whether money will be invested.[59] If the interest rate is high and demand is low, why would a businessperson build a new plant? He or she won't, and will instead simply save at the current interest rate. (This is why, for example, the recovery from the most recent recession has been spurred on by a virtually-zero interest rate policy.) But the other driver is "animal spirits": the propensity to invest and to consume always involves risk, and people's economic choices are often driven by whether the spirit of the times is optimistic or pessimistic.[60] In pessimistic times, what is needed is optimism—yet the rational, self-interested response tends to be more pessimistic and risk-averse.

What is the importance of this revolution for analyzing luxury? First and foremost, the above discussion shows why Keynesian economics is often described as demand-side theory or "demand management"—one gets the economy going by stimulating demand, particularly by stimulating investment. As will be noted, Keynes *himself* is much like Smith in that his work also contains philosophical-but-partly-economic rejections of frivolous "needs." But Keynes *as typically received* is behind the idea of government stimulus in difficult times, and even the idea that such stimulus comes from things like tax rebates or lowering taxes to allow people to buy more things. Some suggest that Keynes "saved capitalism from itself" by offering a model in which the failures of self-interest could be "managed" without abandoning the fundamentals of self-interested behavior. In the Keynes system, "motivation could be subordinated to results."[61]

This pro-consumption reading of Keynes tends to assume that all spending is good spending, luxury spending included, particularly when an economy is sluggish or depressed.[62] Keynes himself, a master of the story, famously wrote:

> If the Treasury were to fill old bottles with banknotes, bury them at suitable depths in disused coalmines which are then filled up to the surface with town rubbish, and leave it to private enterprise on well-tried principles of laissez-faire to dig the notes up again (the right to do so being obtained, of course, by tendering for leases of the note-bearing territory), there need be no more unemployment and, with the help of the repercussions, the real income of the community, and its capital wealth also, would probably become a good deal greater than it actually is. It would, indeed, be more sensible to build houses and the like; but if there are political and practical difficulties in the way of this, the above would be better than nothing.[63]

If such an absurd scenario is nevertheless beneficial, then surely luxury spending would also seem to be. In formal terms, "Keynes taught that expenditure generates income and employment, and after him it became recognized that *when income and employment are unduly low*, public or private thrift ceases to be a virtue" (emphasis added).[64] Therefore, the formal statement of the paradox of thrift: "The more virtuous we are, the more determinatively thrifty, the more obstinately orthodox in our national and personal finance, the more our incomes will have to fall *when interest rises relatively to the marginal efficiency of capital*. Obstinacy can bring only a penalty and no reward" (emphasis added).[65]

However, these "when" clauses are often neglected. Keynes's attention here is ultimately on the problem of the rate of interest (still "obstinately" tied to the gold standard, at least ideally for some). His further statement explicitly limits the paradox of thrift: "If the rate of interest were so governed as to maintain continuous full employment, *Virtue would resume her sway*; the rate of capital accumulation would depend on the weakness of the propensity to consume."[66] Thus, under a different set of economic conditions, thrift is beneficial.

Under what conditions would that be? Full employment and low interest rates. Here we see a different Keynes, one acutely aware of the problems of luxury. Far from promoting endless economic expansion, his own model sought to "increase the stock of capital up to a point where its marginal efficiency had fallen to a very low figure."[67] This would eventually accomplish "the euthanasia of the rentier"—the end of the class of people who drew an income without productive contribution.[68] Thrift is a key element for an economy to reach maturity and abundance. For now, he warns, "we must pretend to ourselves and to every one that fair is foul and foul is fair. . . . Avarice and usury and precaution must be our gods for a little longer still."[69] Yet the *goal* is to be "free . . . to return to some of the most sure and certain principles of religion and traditional virtue—that avarice is a vice, that the extraction of usury is a misdemeanor, and the love of money is detestable."[70] The path to this goal lies less along the lines of income redistribution and much more along the lines of coordinated, semipublic management of savings and investment.[71] As one writer put it in the 1980s in defense of Keynes in the midst of the Reagan revolution, "Keynes saves."[72]

Hyman Minsky and Duncan Foley explain that Keynes's long-term vision of capital abundance is not pro-consumption; rather, it assumes a ceiling on our material desires such that they could come to be met with cheap, easy processes and technologies—enough clothing and dishes, say—at which point capital would no longer command a premium above wages. Minsky summarizes Keynes's vision as requiring "the prior achievement of a state of disciplined wants, a stable population, and a lifting of the burdens of war. None of these conditions have been fully satisfied—and of these conditions, it may well be that the disciplined-wants requirement is furthest from sight."[73] Indeed, "a world in which an endless accumulation of gadgetry and weaponry is the desire of man is not a world in which full investment will soon occur."[74] Foley notes acerbically that "the retail mall is a powerful capitalist immune response" to the prospect of any kind of state of productive abundance.[75] That is to say, without a disciplining of wants there is always something more to buy, which means there is always something more on which capitalists will earn a return on their capital.

However, these anti-luxury aspects of Keynes's ideas are usually ignored. As one writer put it, "policymakers and journalists are enthralled by the 'paradox of thrift.' Like many of Keynes's formulations, the concept has been Americanized to extol consumption pure and simple" while ignoring his emphasis on communal savings and thrift.[76] In America, Keynes's work is transformed into an ongoing macroeconomic countercyclical indefinite growth engine that does not disturb cultural values of consumption and leaves us squarely in the "foul is fair" period, sidelining any concerns about luxury just as surely as marginalism does, though in a different way. Indeed, insofar as these two revolutions in economics essentially govern the standard Econ 101 textbook—awkwardly (many say) connecting "microeconomics" (marginalism) and "macroeconomics" (Keynesian management of demand)—Keynes is often reduced to a guide for policymaking and legislating amidst the business cycle, while firms and individuals go on maximizing their individual self-interest as in the marginalist model. Thus, both models end up being taught as denials that the best economic state requires sharing and sacrifice of wants. Rather, the promise of post–World War II economics is that the combination of free markets and expert demand management will meet everyone's constantly expanding wants. Both sides say: The economic problem isn't your wants or your neighbor's wants; the problem is structural. For marginalism, the economic problem stems from various artificial restraints on the market; for pro-consumption Keynesianism, the economic problem stems from insufficient government help for the market. In both cases the problem is not that some people "have too much" or "want too much." The problem is mechanical, not moral. Econ 101 is relieved of the task of critiquing individual consumer excesses—as is, to a large extent, the discipline as a whole.

The Critics: The Limits of the Dominant Models

One should not dismiss these "mechanical" problems; the more one reads of economics, the more one appreciates the enormous wisdom built up within the discipline. However, disentangling the mechanical from the moral is not really possible in reality (note that Keynes has anti-luxury elements in his work). A full appreciation of the problem requires turning to another set of critics who seek to identify weaknesses in the treatment and measurement of consumption in these models and resist the temptation to simply equate private consumption with public benefit. Steven Medema's history portrays a "to-and-fro relationship" in economic analyses of self-interest's relation to social benefit: "Those writing economics have been wrestling with the impact of self-interested behavior on social and economic outcomes for more than two millennia, and Nobel Prizes continue to be awarded for work that furthers our understanding" of this problem.[77] It is too simple to portray economics as simply embracing the Mandevillian claim that self-interest leads to social benefit.

One perennial criticism of these models is handling externalities—a term that refers to positive or (more often) negative effects of market practices that occur in the lives of persons not directly involved in the economic exchange that generates them.[78] Often, though not always, these are difficult to account for in terms of monetary gains and losses. The history of this problem dates back at least to the work of John Stuart Mill, who defended individual liberty in economic action except in the case of "spillover," where "there is a definite damage or a definite risk of damage, either to an individual or to the public" such that liberty should be limited if someone makes "himself a nuisance to other people."[79]

Does luxury consumption produce negative externalities? Environmental concerns are the most prominent externality in today's world, and they are obviously related to luxury. But other externalities may be even more directly related to luxury consumption. We saw that Pigou viewed certain kinds of private consumption as having negative externalities. But a detailed analysis of such consumption externalities is found in the work of Fred Hirsch, who in the late 1970s sought to explain what he termed the "social limits to growth."[80] Economic growth, in the form of improved productivity, has always held out the promise of providing basic goods for all and overcoming the dearth that plagued human life from time immemorial. Hirsch agrees that at this level of increasing output of basic goods, productivity growth for all is in fact spurred by self-interest. However, he notes that as societies become more affluent and move past immediate concerns over the scarcity of basic goods, an "increasing portion of consumption takes on a social as well as an individual aspect" (2). In particular, he suggests that the elaboration of goods and services beyond necessity becomes increasingly "positional": the value of a given house is not simply its function for shelter, but rather its relative position in relation to other houses and their features (and neighborhoods and schools, etc.). Luis Carvalho and Joao Rodrigues nicely summarize Hirsch's model:

> Following Roy Harrod's distinction between "oligarchic wealth" and "democratic wealth" (Hirsch 1976: 23–24), the economy is composed of two sectors: the material and the positional. The material sector comprises the production of goods and services that can be quantitatively increased without losses in quality, and with continued productivity gains. In the positional sector, individual consumption is influenced by consumption and/or fruition by others, involving goods, services or, more broadly, social relationships, that are subjected to physical or social scarcity, or prone to congestion by means of extension in use. Traditional economic growth solves the problems of the material economy but not those of the positional economy. In fact, Hirsch suggests that

economic growth may even exacerbate the problems of the positional economy, since material affluence contributes to the intensification of "positional competition". The individual quest for goods, services and social relationships, which by their very nature cannot be shared by all and thus possess positional attributes, forces those same individuals to spend an increasing amount of time and/or material resources to attain, or simply to retain, a certain position in the social hierarchy: "More wealth of the kind attainable by all paradoxically means an increased scramble for the kind of wealth attainable by some" (26).[81]

It is the nature of positional goods that everyone cannot have them since their value is based on some kind of "getting ahead." Thus, an increase in economic resources devoted to positional goods is largely "zero-sum" (52)—everyone spends more, with the effect that everyone maintains position.[82] Indeed, positional goods may in fact be "negative-sum" because such competition "involves additional resource costs" (52). Our economic measures of success are "only appropriate for truly private goods" (7). Growing GDP may produce more food overall, and thus "growth," but if increased spending and production is for positional goods, there is no overall advance even though such positional competition also increases overall GDP. Robert Frank, who follows Hirsch's analysis, calls this expenditure arms race "smart-for-one, dumb-for-all."[83] For example, it is smart for one person seeking the good of their children to pay a considerable premium for housing in order to move into a "better" school district, but it is dumb for everyone to do it because doing so simply pushes up the price of housing overall and no one is in fact "better off." Spending is simply "defensive" and an attempt to hold relative position. Frank identifies many such conflicts, from military arms races to "appearance competitions" like high heels and cosmetic surgery. Spending increases GDP but without any relative gain. However, it is also dangerous for the individual to eschew the competition because of the potential to suffer real loss.

Hirsch's argument forces us to recognize that consumption is not of goods in isolation, but of goods that exist "with certain characteristics and in a certain environmental framework or conditions of use" (108–9). Given this fact, Frank levels one of the basic critiques against the marginalist model of consumption:

> In traditional economic models, individual utility depends only on abso-
> lute consumption. These models lie at the heart of claims that pursuit
> of individual self-interest promotes aggregate welfare. Recent years have

seen a renewed interest in economic models in which individual utility depends not only on absolute consumption, but also on relative consumption. In contrast to traditional models, these models identify a fundamental conflict between individual and social welfare.[84]

Several aspects of the positional goods model need to be clarified. First, positional goods are not simply a distinct set of goods because many consumption goods have both positional and nonpositional aspects to them. A house is, in one sense, a necessary shelter with certain functionalities (e.g., a kitchen needed for food preparation). In another sense a house is the quintessential positional good—not everyone can have the mountain view, the park across the street, or the "best" schools. Hirsch highlights the desires prevalent during the 1970s for a more tranquil suburban existence apart from the city that is lost when everybody moves out to the suburbs—or, rather, when people are forced to move farther out to (re)gain the position they desire (with consequent harm in a longer commute, etc.) or when zoning laws restrict development to ensure tranquility but at the cost of bidding up the now-scarce available housing to much higher prices than the houses themselves would otherwise fetch. The key insight: what people want is not simply "a house" (a good that is subject to productivity gains) but a "quiet, tranquil house still connected to the city" (a good that is scarce by definition and lost if too many others want it).

    Hirsch and Frank are not merely reiterating Thorstein Veblen's classic analysis of "conspicuous consumption," where people consume particular status goods "uselessly." Such consumption could certainly be seen as economic waste. The problem here is more systemic: our desires for legitimate goods (e.g., a better school for our children) cannot be satisfied—or can only be satisfied with constantly escalating "expenditure cascades"—because the nature of the goods we seek are partly social and our personal consumption of them embroils us in what economists call a collective action problem. Collective action problems typically involve "public goods," or goods that can be obtained only through common action (e.g., public defense and safety) and not through individual maximization of choices.

    How does this work for positional consumption goods? In light of their social character, the actual goods people seek (e.g., a good education for their children) turn out to be achieved only through some common restraint . . . yet this restraint is not in any individual's particular interest to heed unless others also restrain themselves. Hirsch notes studies of how neighborhoods "tipped" during the 1960s: "Individual behavior on the basis of given preferences produces a chain of reactions that works itself out only after culminating in a pattern that no single individual would himself choose" (89). Many residents may have wanted integrated neighborhoods, but individual choices culminated in a complete "tipping" of the neighborhood. Hirsch notes many other examples in which individually rational choices led to undesired collective outcomes: the local store went out of business, public transportation grew worse as more people were forced to buy cars, etc. He makes the crucial point that "in practice, the individual is confronted with choices only on a piecemeal basis and has to take as a fixture the relevant conditions of use" (90). This is to say, individual market choices do not present us with the choice of the actual state of affairs that we would most desire—though collective action could do so.

"Positional waste" becomes significant under conditions where larger amounts of the population are involved in the competition. In early capitalism, most of the economy was directed toward providing necessities. Hirsch notes the baubles and trinkets of the rich mentioned by Adam Smith did produce social benefits "because effective demand for them was so small on the part of others whose far more urgent needs went unsatisfied." The prices paid "at this stage in history far exceed[ed] their opportunity cost to the rest of society" (65). As Smith himself notes, "Great nations are almost never impoverished by private . . . prodigality and misconduct," but this is because "the profusion or imprudence of some" is "always more than compensated by the frugality and good conduct of others."[85] In Smith's world, only a few can be luxurious, so the harm cannot be very great compared to the distribution benefit of such spending to those it employs. However, Hirsch counters that "as general standards of living rise, demand for luxuries becomes more extensively diffused throughout the population" (66) and developed economies devote more and more of their resources to these goods and the competition for them becomes stiffer and stiffer—and more and more expensive, but with no overall social gain. We create a situation which Smith couldn't imagine: private prodigality on a mass scale.

Worse, in these kinds of circumstances people have come to expect never-ending social advance; when it does not materialize, individual competition and frustration actually intensify despite the general affluence. As he bluntly summarizes: "Thus, to see total economic advance as individual advance writ large is to set up expectations that cannot be fulfilled, ever" (9). These frustrated expectations explain in more sophisticated terms why Plato's "luxury city" ends up in conflict: under conditions of affluence the paradoxical increase of individual competition to get and stay ahead and "keep what is mine" erodes the social morality of cooperation that preexisted the competitive economic order. As more people focus on getting more than just basic goods, they become more ruthless in their competition for the inherently limited "ahead" spots because they have been taught that self-interested behavior produces better outcomes for all . . . though in reality it doesn't. Under conditions of abundance, then, cooperation in consumption for overall social benefit is more needed but in reality is less and less possible.[86]

Hirsch is critical of American-style Keynesianism because it ignores this erosion. The individualistic mentality of market competition and choice erodes the informal social norms that previously restrained choice and in effect constituted a kind of collective action that held down this positional competition among all except the very rich. As luxury increases and informal norms of frugality diminish, a tipping point is reached where they end up having to be legislated or contested legally, a very difficult task. Daniel Finn notes that a key element of the "moral ecology of markets" is "the morality of individuals and groups" whereby "most of us, most of the time, can count on our neighbors, co-workers, and friends to be generally truthful, to offer help when needed, and to show the ordinary signs of civility and cooperation"—and, we might add here, restraint.[87]

Hirsch and Frank point toward the ultimate problem, beyond Keynes, in marginalism: the ongoing need to manufacture artificial scarcity in a situation of apparent affluence. As Charles Clark trenchantly points out, marginalist analyses of economic maximization appear on the scene just as "real scarcity ceases to be the main economic problem facing capitalist economies"—instead, "artificial scarcities" must be created (i.e., more positional goods) "in order to maintain the rate of return on wealth and the social power that attaches itself to 'scarce' wealth."[88] But Hirsch and Frank propose that this isn't simply a matter of "evil capitalists." Instead, individual consumers become participants in the cycle due to the nature of the goods sought. The result is the paradox of a more heated economic scramble in an economy that seems more affluent. Clark points out how all of this is rooted in marginalism's elimination of "any possible critique of individual use" by means of the tautology, "Individuals maximize utility by choosing goods, and the proof that the goods maximize utility is that individuals choose them."[89]

The point of explaining Hirsch's work is to recover economic terms that help analyze consumption choices and their effects in social, rather than exclusively individual, terms. Mark Nixon notes that "significant and interesting new understandings of the theory of the firm have resulted from specific consideration of institutional factors, such as organizational structure, contracts, and agency."[90] These insights need to be translated into economic theories of the consumer. Once we recognize the social nature of consumption we can pose real questions about the social benefits and harms of various consumption choices. Above all, we are able to recognize *the collective economic value of social restraint in consumption.*

Once we restore this element of economic analysis we can doubt the supposed "damning drawback" intuited by Mandeville and reinforced by the marginalist and Keynesian models. There might actually be "economically bad luxury." A critique of luxury is not necessarily anti-consumption; rather, it asks how our consumption might shift. We shouldn't presume that economics and ethics will automatically give opposing answers. Rejecting luxury can and should mean embracing *better* consumption—which need not hurt aggregate demand.

Toward a Better Economic Analysis of Consumption

The idea that all types of consumption are not created equal in terms of their social benefits is hardly new. Francis Hutcheson's original reply to Mandeville's pro-luxury contentions did precisely this: even in the eighteenth century Hutcheson could imagine numerous consumption possibilities other than luxury ones. He points out that intemperate, luxurious eaters probably die of ill health at an earlier age. They spend on themselves what they could spend on their families or friends, or even their posterity. Consumption should be conscientiously shifted elsewhere, not rejected. Unless "all mankind" is provided with "all necessities" and "all innocent conveniences" there need be no loss of overall production if consumption is shifted away from luxuries.[91]

Therefore, economics has ample room to escape the damning drawback by modeling consumption in an affluent society in ways that might better take account of genuine material welfare.[92] As Ben Fine explains, "consumption with economics is almost always treated abstractly without reference to specified items of consumption . . . it is hardly surprising that the nature of consumption goods and of consumption activity cannot be addressed."[93] In practice and even beyond Hirsch's critique, the marginalist model faces a large and expanding literature (called behavioral economics) that demonstrates countless ways in which individuals make tradeoff choices in much more complex ways.

Fine argues for taking a "vertical approach," where consumption is analyzed within "systems of provision"—that is, "explanations around consumption must be specific to particular commodities or groups of commodities" such as "a clothing system, an energy system, housing system, food system."[94] Such a fine-grained analysis fits nicely with the casuistry of luxury that requires attention to the qualities that people actually seek (a nice place to live and not just "a house") and the "social properties" of these consumption choices. Consumption must be first and foremost analyzed in terms of some basic standard, some "standard of living," that is deemed good or necessary for all (including the self). Such a standard must be socially determined, partly because what determines it will be what is required by others or by certain structures such that a car or frequent Internet access or regular access to clean bathing facilities may be deemed necessary in order to seek decent employment. One could critique any given social standard but could not establish a standard that did not attend to the simple fact that human life is social.

These specific analyses would recognize the social harms involved in luxury that arise from socially shaped but individually chosen consumption tradeoffs—the kind of fruitless positional competitions identified by Hirsch that leave no one better off.[95] Because an individual spends excessively on a positional good—say, a luxury automobile or expensive housing in order to obtain a better education for their children, they then look for the "best deal" on their food or clothing—a deal that is often provided by exploiting workers or using resources in unsustainable ways. Insofar as the issues of a just wage and environmental stewardship are matters of justice, we might not see the relevance of the vice of luxury. But the example suggests that unjust spending choices may be traced to the disposition toward luxury that drives the original tradeoffs rather than a disposition to treat workers unjustly. As is the case with many of Hirsch's illustrations, the exploitation of third-world laborers making our basic goods is not something that most people would choose but it is never presented as a direct choice. Instead, many people buy cheap goods because we either buy other expensive luxuries or because so much of our income is tied up in maintaining reasonable positional goods. We often criticize corporations for injustices against workers, but as long as we are driven toward "cheap" goods—whether cheap luxuries or cheap necessities required to be cheap so that we can buy luxuries—consumer desires must be seen as part of the problem.

The crucial insight for this more sophisticated analysis is being able to recover the sense that economic well-being and overall well-being are related in complex ways and that maximizing the former does not necessarily maximize the latter. Some better measure of aggregate economic benefit is needed beyond the single measure of GDP. A critique of luxury might indeed "hurt GDP" but that doesn't mean society is also "hurt." The question of how quality-of-life variables—work, family, the environment—might be included in our economic calculations has led economists to seek alternative measurement tools for decades.[96] Paul Samuelson and William Nordhaus outline a measure (developed by Nordhaus and others) of "net economic welfare" that makes adjustments to GDP in order to account for things that are not measured, such as leisure time and activity; "underground" barter activity (including criminal markets); and environmental damage.[97] Such a measure suggests that there is *some* correlation between pure GDP growth and actual adjusted growth, although actual growth is less robust. Herman Daly and John Cobb point out, however, that over shorter periods of time, some measures can go in opposite directions (just as Pigou would expect).[98] They outline another measure—the Index of Sustainable Economic Welfare [ISEW], containing twenty-three different measures—that "indicates a long-term trend from the late 1970s to the present [1994] that is indeed bleak. Economic welfare has been deteriorating for a decade."[99] Their measure indicates that peak ISEW was reached in 1972 or so and experienced a decline of 10 to 15 percent overall in subsequent years, despite GNP increases of about 30 percent.[100]

It may be true that there is simply no way to use a single "scoreboard number"—whether GDP or, even worse, stock market averages—for measuring economic progress. Once we are beyond a scoreboard number, though, the relevance of identifying luxury becomes evident. For example, a multivalent approach to the economic state of a society might place the highest emphasis on a sustainable material base for the society, looking at sector-based economic data over time to understand where problems are and then moving on to other essentials—such as family stability or health—that ultimately are not reducible to economic quantities but which can in fact be measured in various ways. Even Daly and Cobb note that if sustainability is defined as the ability to meet present needs without preventing future generations from meeting those same needs, "there is the question of distinguishing 'needs' from extravagant luxuries or impossible desires. If 'needs' includes an automobile for each of a billion Chinese, then sustainable development is impossible."[101] An accurate measure cannot follow Lionel Robbins's edict that normative considerations must be banished from economics. Rather, a proper economics itself requires some degree of moral judgment in order to determine how an economy might understand itself as more or less successful.

A recognition of the social character of consumption can lead to solutions many view as problematic. Luxury taxes are notoriously hard to enforce and often lead to mere substitutions. Laws regulating consumption, from zoning regulations to bans on large sodas, often produce rancor and may not even be effective at achieving the social ends they seek. But this is precisely why having *social norms* against luxury performs such valuable economics work. Without requiring the precision of a law, inculcating a norm against luxury would serve to discourage the useless and wasteful economic competitions by limiting the extent to which people will go to achieve some kind of social positioning.

A viable critique of luxury need not be stuck in the damning drawback of consigning us to economic decline or impoverishment. Economics does not provide arguments in favor of luxury; rather, it may be that social restraint—that is, a sense of the vice of luxury—is needed to make the promise of modern economics (abundance for all) actually possible. A careful economic analysis helps us see the complexities that should lead us to characterize luxury spending as economically ambiguous. The moral and theological cases are still the issues of primary concern, but it cannot be said that modern economics poses a damning drawback for them.

Notes

1. See, for example, Elizabeth Warren's strident critique of the "overconsumption myth" plied by Schor and Frank (*Two-Income Trap*, 15–54).
2. Schor, *Overspent American*, 169.
3. Kennedy, *Freedom from Fear*, 163.
4. Bernanke, "The Federal Reserve."
5. http://www.calculatedriskblog.com/2013/04/april-vehicle-sales-forecast-to-be .html. The Cash for Clunkers car incentive program was much less focused on environmental impact and more focused on keeping these numbers from collapsing even further; http://news.yahoo.com/why-cash-clunkers-hurt-environ ment-more-helped-024848694.html and http://www.nytimes.com/2009/08/21 /business/21clunkers.html?_r=0 .The housing market was also supported with the brief, large tax credit for house purchases; http://www.nytimes.com/2010/04/27 /business/27home.html.
6. http://www.calculatedriskblog.com/2013/04/new-home-sales-at-417000-saar-in-march.html.
7. Nash, "Toward the Revival," 158.

8. Ibid., 158.

9. For an excellent history of the ups and downs of this idea in economics, see Medema, *Hesitant Hand*.

10. Schlefer, *Assumptions Economists Make*; Morgan, *World in the Model*.

11. For example, Aristotle, *Politics*, book 1, chaps. 8–10.

12. See, for example, Clark, "Catholic Economics 101," where he states bluntly: "Anyone who says that the federal government is like a household, that its spending should be limited by its revenue (tax collections) does not understand our economic system."

13. This is the "Austrian school" critique, represented by Friedrich Hayek. See his classic, "Freedom and the Economic System," esp. 193–203.

14. For a quick summary see Medema, *Hesitant Hand*, 6–10.

15. Appleby, *Economic Thought and Ideology*, 26.

16. On mercantilism see Viner, "Mercantilist Thought."

17. Appleby, *Economic Thought and Ideology*, 47–48.

18. On Smith's rejection of mercantilism and revision of French physiocracy theory, see Medema, *Hesitant Hand*, 17–19.

19. Smith did believe in strong restrictions on monopoly, however, and was suspicious of large corporate enterprises, which could function as de facto restraints on trade when acting in their own interests.

20. Smith, *Wealth of Nations*, 321. Smith spends the entirety of book 2 chap. 3 in laying out the importance of frugality for a nation's capital accumulation, though he interestingly suggests that some private consumption of durable goods (e.g., fine furniture) has a much better effect on overall wealth because it endures and is passed on to others. While Smith did not grasp the idea of services as "goods," this does not undermine his focus on the key to the economic engine of growth, which is on productive investment.

21. Ibid., 823.

22. Clark, "Wealth as Abundance and Scarcity," 41.

23. Smith, *Wealth of Nations*, 346, 348. He noted: "Holland is near this" (96).

24. Appleby, *Relentless Revolution*, 43.

25. Ibid., 52–53.

26. The simplicity of the story in particular glosses over the work of American Institutionalists of the early twentieth century, many of whom were concerned with improvident consumer spending (see chap. 7).

27. Schlefer, *Assumptions Economists Make*, 90.

28. Foley, *Adam's Fallacy*, 160.

29. For the story, see Spiegel, *Growth of Economic Thought*, chaps. 22–25. It is telling that Spiegel's treatment of this movement covers four separate chapters focusing on four different ways in which attention to different aspects of economic activity resulted in marginalist models becoming accepted.

30. Ibid., 518.

31. Knight, "Economic History," 50. The technical advance was the recognition that "the classical rejection of use-value as a cause of price had been an error, because the economic value of a good reflects the use-value of an increment (acquired or given up), not that of the commodity in the abstract." Moreover, the value of additional increments of a particular good diminishes because the wants for

any particular good are satiable, even if wants overall are not. These observations surpass Smith's famous "diamond-water paradox," which made it appear that use-value did not cause prices (water is useful but virtually free; diamonds are not useful but expensive).

32. Danner, *Ethics for the Affluent.*
33. Spiegel, *Growth of Economic Thought*, 534.
34. Ibid., 519.
35. Ibid., 525–26.
36. This had the added value of disrupting the extant labor theory of value and the support it seemed to give to the Marxist model. Late nineteenth-century econo-mists worried that the labor theory of value made dangerously plausible the idea that capital owners were thieves.
37. Schlefer, *Assumptions Economists Make*, 102.
38. Clark, *Distribution of Wealth*, 84–94.
39. Davidson, "Making It in America."
40. It not only provided a seemingly rational system of rationing resources to their most valued uses, but it also revealed a "consumer surplus," where one is able to obtain goods for less than one would otherwise be willing to pay because produc-ers are also selling to those whose desires for the same good are less fervent.
41. Medaille, *Vocation of Business*, 67. The problem of the over-mathematicization of economics is chronic in many areas of the discipline. Paul Volcker notes that a "basic flaw" that plagued the "financial innovation" behind the market crisis of 2007–2008 was the belief that "thinking embedded in mathematics and physics could be directly adapted to markets" ("The Time We Have," 12–14) .
42. Described by Knight, "Economic History," 55: "At equilibrium, simultaneously all consumer expenditures would buy at the margin equal increments of satisfac-tion and all productive resources would yield (marginally) equal increments of value product, all prices being equal to costs (ignoring monopoly). . . .The main economic decisions are made formally by entrepreneurs, . . .but they are finally responsible to consumers and owners of productive agents," and so (in theory, at equilibrium) entrepreneurs "have no power at all."
43. See Robbins, "Interpersonal Comparisons," 637, where he describes his initial disappointed reaction to the discovery that "economics as a science could say nothing by way of prescription." Suzumara, "Social Welfare Function," points out that "The old welfare economics originated by Pigou was constructed on the sup-position of interpersonally comparable and cardinal welfares" (418), a supposition harshly criticized and rejected (successfully, it turns out) by Robbins.
44. Foley, *Adam's Fallacy*, 172. Foley notes that the marginalists also rejected Smith's praise of thrift and instead suggested that the rich will invest or consume based on marginal utility.
45. Robbins, *Essay*, 16.
46. For the substitution of efficiency for morality, see George, "Reflections on *Caritas in Veritate*," 212.
47. Nixon, "Satisfaction for Whom?," 39.
48. Wheelan, *Naked Economics*, 60.
49. Nixon, "Satisfaction for Whom?," 55, 45.
50. Hausman and McPherson, *Economic Analysis and Moral Philosophy.*

51. For a description of what changed before and after Keynes, see Spiegel, *Growth of Economic Thought*, 611–12: "Before Keynes, economic analysis was concerned with the efficient allocation of resources, a matter treated under the headings of price theory, value and distribution, and partial and general equilibrium. After Keynes, these theories were supplemented by the analysis of the determination of total output, yielding income and employment theory."

52. Medema, *Hesitant Hand*, 54.

53. Ibid., 54–55.

54. Ibid., 61.

55. Pigou, *Economics of Welfare*, 1, 12.

56. Ibid., 1, 10.

57. Marshall himself famously described the process of developing economic ideas as involving a later stage where you "burn the mathematics." See Skidelsky, *John Maynard Keynes*, 223.

58. More precisely, as Duncan Foley summarizes, Keynes saw that Say's Law "is completely out of date in economies with a highly developed financial system" because in such systems the intermediation of savings to investment is complicated and often quite long term. See Foley, *Adam's Fallacy*, 186.

59. Keynes, *General Theory*, 136–37.

60. Ibid., 161.

61. Hirsch, *Social Limits to Growth*, 119.

62. Keynes, *General Theory*, 46: "All production is for the purpose of ultimately satisfying a consumer."

63. Ibid., 129.

64. Spiegel, *Growth of Economic Thought*, 612.

65. Keynes, *General Theory*, 111.

66. Ibid., 112.

67. Ibid., 375.

68. Ibid., 376.

69. Keynes, "Economic Possibilities," 372.

70. Ibid., 371. A few pages earlier he even calls the love of money "a somewhat disgusting morbidity, one of those semi-criminal, semi-pathological propensities which one hands over with a shudder to the specialists in mental disease" (369).

71. Keynes, "End of Laissez-Faire?," 313, 318.

72. Kuttner, *Economic Illusion*.

73. Minsky, *Keynes*, 155.

74. Ibid., 154.

75. Foley, *Adam's Fallacy*, 212.

76. Garon, *Beyond Our Means*, 358. Garon points out that "genuinely Keynesian economists" focus specifically on government spending on long-term public goods in times of sluggish demand.

77. Medema, *Hesitant Hand*, 4.

78. Other strands of critique might be identified in the history of American institutionalist economics, or in heterodox figures such as Gunnar Myrdal, in *Challenge to Affluence*, who adamantly opposed even the possibility of an "objective" economics that ignored "explicit value premises" (vi).

79. Mill, *On Liberty*, 147, 101, quoted in Medema, *Hesitant Hand*, 35.

80. Hirsch, *Social Limits to Growth*. Further references in text. A comparable insight is offered by Catholic economist Peter Danner's analysis of how "abundance creates scarcity" in his *Ethics for the Affluent*, 25–39.
81. Carvalho and Rodrigues, "On Markets and Morality," 333.
82. The zero-sum characteristics are taken up in more detail by Thurow, *Zero-Sum Society*, who concludes (in 1980) that "Wants become necessities whenever most of the people in society believe that they are in fact necessities" (198), and that, under these conditions, "our society has reached the point where it must start to make explicit equity decisions if it is to advance" (194). Instead, what happened post-1980 was the avoidance of the problem (temporarily) through debt and low-wage globalization.
83. Frank, *Luxury Fever*, 148–51.
84. Frank, "Are Concerns about Relative Income?," 137.
85. Smith, *Wealth of Nations*, 324–25.
86. Frank identifies a related problem of what he calls "winner-take-all markets," where it becomes more and more possible for a small number of firms to capture huge parts of markets. The effect? Increased scramble of competition to make sure you can get into the "winner's circle" and walk away with a disproportionately large prize. At the other end of the scale, smaller businesses and menial jobs become less and less skilled or disappear.
87. Finn, *Moral Ecology*, 136.
88. Clark, "Wealth as Abundance and Scarcity," 43–44.
89. Ibid., 43. Clark's work points beyond the scope of this project, to the question of how to model an economics of abundance or adequacy. Economists in history—Malthus or Marx, Ricardo or Keynes—seem to have been simultaneously fascinated and flummoxed in approaching this problem. For other extended work toward an "economics of enough," see Schor, *Plenitude*; Coyle, *Economics of Enough*; and Skidelsky and Skidelsky, *How Much Is Enough?*. Catholics in particular might take more seriously the forgotten work of economic thinkers like Heinrich Pesch and Peter Danner, both of whom insist that "moderate use" is an essential element of economic success. On Pesch, see *Ethics and the National Economy*. On Danner, see the festschrift from O'Boyle, *Looking beyond the Individualism*.
90. Nixon, "Satisfaction for Whom?," 55.
91. Hutcheson, *Thoughts on Laughter*, 89–95. Hutcheson reinforces his case with a series of amusing analogies, such as medical quacks being the cause of religious faith (because their dishonesty converts souls who encounter an honest, caring clergyman). Hutcheson insists that it is the industrious, not the luxurious, who are good.
92. In addition to the examples mentioned here, in chapter 8 we will look at a number of economists for whom defining something like a "standard of living" is really the key need for the discipline (e.g., Sen; American institutionalists).
93. Fine, "From Political Economy to Consumption," 127.
94. Ibid., 139.
95. One of the few classic economics articles to do so is Leibenstein, "Bandwagon, Snob, and Veblen Effects." Leibenstein's idea is to identify the ways demand from one individual is not independent from what is demanded by other individuals,

which would mean that the overall market demand curve cannot be derived simply from summing up each individual's demand curve.

96. For a recent extensive analysis see Stiglitz, Fen, and Fitoussi, *Mismeasuring Our Lives*.

97. Samuelson and Nordhaus, *Economics*, 117–20. Danner, *Ethics for the Affluent*, 55, also points out the large increases in "household services" that are now included in GDP but were not previously, and which do not necessarily add anything to productive activity overall.

98. Daly and Cobb, *For the Common Good*, 79.

99. Ibid., 507.

100. Ibid., 462–63. Again, it should be noted here that these numbers necessarily involve contestable judgments about how to quantify things that can't be quantified. This does not mean they are somehow less "real" than GDP, but rather they indicate how partial and unreal GDP itself also is.

101. Ibid., 76.

Part II

CHAPTER 5

Luxury Defined

The last three chapters have developed a systematic case for the vicious and sinful character of luxury. For most of Western history, luxury was assumed to be a moral problem even though this characterization often remained quite unsystematic. Thus, the critique of luxury proved fragile. By placing the topic in the context of debates about consumer society ("the goods life") and about the marketing of "luxury" as an experience of transcendence and unique social identity, a strong evaluation of the good of work and an analysis of work and social cooperation in terms of MacIntyre's category of practices provides a philosophical basis in virtue ethics for seeing "the goods life" and the pursuit of luxury as morally problematic. Theological developments in Catholic social teaching, in particular Benedict XVI's notions of gift and reciprocity, show how a sacramental economy challenges and functions as an alternative to the dominant marketing language of luxury. In terms of both natural and supernatural virtue, economic choices made in the pursuit of luxury appear contrary to the genuine good. However, some might still retain the classic objection rooted in modern economic models that luxury, whatever its "moral" effects, is economically good for society. Yet the actual complexities of assessing properly the supposed "benefits" of luxury spending can be seen by attending to the incomplete assumptions and frameworks that would support such a claim. These philosophical, theological, and economic arguments all help make the case that luxury is a problem.

But what, exactly, *is* luxury? To be sure, this concept represents some kind of disposition regarding *excess*—excess attachment to comfort, excess attachment to goods that are external to practices, or excess attachment to experiences and social identity that such goods appear to bestow. But defining "excess" begs the question of what counts as reasonable . . . a question that has not yet been answered.

It would be tempting at this point to defer to prudential judgment and leave it at that. However, there are good reasons to proceed further in specifying the problem. In discussing the eighteenth-century British controversy over luxury, John Sekora calls it a "chameleon of a concept" because its usage was trapped in variation and imprecision.[1] Sekora notes how his subject, the novelist Tobias Smollett, uses luxury to explain dozens of contemporary problems, from "careless architecture and shoddy construction" to "high prices" to increases in "tea drinking" to the "debauchery of farm boys" to "stupidity and corruption."[2] This imprecision, Sekora contends, means the concept was really functioning as a "scapegoat" or "verbal placebo" for distressed nobles seeking to defend the "necessity and hierarchy" of their favored social order.[3] On the other side of this debate, Mandeville's writings defend luxury by including anything and everything beyond bare survival. Such imprecise identification robs the concept of coherence and contributes to its disrepute and disappearance. We need a provisional definition of the vice in order to develop, in subsequent chapters, categories to evaluate the ordinary consumption by all of us and to devise criteria by which we can prudently and faithfully see where luxury might be present in our own lives and in society.

Defining Luxury: Identifying Surplus and Tradeoffs

First and foremost, recall that luxury is a disposition, a vice that disposes us to choose and act in certain ways. A proper definition of the vice focuses not on individual items but on what disposes people to prefer them to other goods.

Two post-Humean moralists, Henry Sidgwick and Adam Ferguson, attempted to define the concept even while accepting key points made against the ancient definitions. Sidgwick, a key transitional figure, was a moral philosopher whose work also stands at the headwaters of modern economics.[4] In an 1894 essay on the topic of luxury Sidgwick argues that "what we should agree to call luxurious expenditure is a source of considerable perplexity to moral persons who obviously find themselves in the possession of an income obviously more than sufficient." While "they cannot deny that they live in luxury," Sidgwick claims that "it can hardly be denied that luxurious living is commonly thought to be in some degree censurable. We should be surprised to hear an earnest and thoughtful man say, except jocosely, that it was part of his plan of life to live in luxury."[5] In his major work, *Theory of Political Economy*, Sidgwick questions whether "the system of laisser-faire" [*sic*] even leads to the greatest production of wealth, much less the greatest overall welfare. He notes that judging an economy based on "the production of maximum wealth" means that "we have to assume that utilities valued highly by the rich are useful to the community in proportion either to their market price or to the pecuniary gain foregone in order to obtain them." Sidgwick has not foresworn inter-personal utility comparisons, as modern economists have. Among these utilities valued highly by the rich are "the love of ease and all the whims and fancies that are wont to take possession of the minds of persons whose income is far more than sufficient to satisfy ordinary human desires." But he objects: "It is only by this strained extension of the idea of social util-ity" that such production "can be said to have even a general tendency to reach the maximum production possible."[6] Both morally and economi-cally, Sidgwick saw luxury as a problem.

Sidgwick's essay makes a distinction between "comforts" (i.e., protec-tions against minor annoyances and inefficiencies) and "luxuries" (sources of positive pleasure): a thick coat on a frosty day is a necessity; a railway rug (to cover the lower legs) is a comfort; a fur cloak is a luxury. Such distinc-tions are first and foremost governed by custom, but the judgment of cus-tom can be challenged. On what grounds? He makes four key arguments: that there is a distinction between "inconvenient conveniences" that are useless and preoccupying, as opposed to those which truly serve function; that some luxury may lead to harming health; that while the *prospect* of luxury may be an incentive to work, luxury itself may not (that is, some things are luxuries because they hamper work); and (in good utilitarian fashion) that the particular item may provide less happiness than could be gained by using the resources for someone else. Sidgwick exempts "the advance of knowledge" and "the advance of beauty" from his critique, since he claims that students and teachers would be fine if "costly luxury" were eliminated.[7]

In *An Essay on the History of Civil Society*, Adam Ferguson, writing in the late eighteenth century, devotes an entire chapter and parts of others to luxury. He shows some appreciation for Hume's arguments, in particu-lar the claim that much of what could be criticized as luxury is in fact social refinement and the mark of becoming more civilized. However, he hastens to add that the "apprehensions of the severe in every age" are not "groundless and unreasonable." Indeed, "luxury, considered as a predilec-tion in favour of the objects of vanity, and the costly materials of pleasure, is ruinous to the human character."[8] And, as he notes, we are "perpetually exposed to the commission of error in this article."

How so? Ferguson's response makes three key claims. First, that luxury is a problem for people "wherever they shrink from small inconveniences and are incapable of discharging their duty with vigour."[9] Second, this disposition can lead to improper admiration of "paultry distinctions or frivolous advantages"; the honor due to real goodness is dissolved into "mere pageant" when luxury becomes admired.[10] Third, the disposition considers "these conveniences as the principal objects of human life" and prefers them to "friends, to a country, or to mankind." Since he is not a utilitarian in approach, Ferguson focuses more on the disposition by noting that the critique is not meant to single out "particular species of lodging, diet, or cloathes" but rather to contain these "trifling accomodations" to wherever they currently are and avoid spending energy and resources trying to enhance them at the expense of "the higher engagements of life." He thus accepts that societies may progress in what "the mechanical arts" have made available but rejects the temptation to admire and strive for more than the standard. A wealthier society need not be a luxury society; or, as Ferguson puts it, "the mere use of materials which constitute luxury may be distinguishable from actual vice."[11] Nevertheless, the wealthier society needs to be *more* disciplined in its practice of virtue, not less. It must not make intentional pursuit of these objects important, nor should one spend time, energy, or resources striving for eminence in regard to them. Rather, one must simply rest with the "mere use of accomodations and conveniences which the age has procured."[12]

Matthew Arbo's recent book-length appreciation of Ferguson as one of "the earliest modernity critics" summarizes Ferguson's concerns: "The goals of modern commerce and the methods used to achieve them generate irresolvable moral and political antinomies" by undermining "the very political institutions intended to sustain commercial life."[13] Ferguson's critique of luxury anticipates the problems of positionality (see chapter 4) insofar as he sees that an attachment to luxury makes greed and envy "necessary" for survival for individuals and nations, which in turn undermines the possibility of genuinely free and equal relationships. As Arbo puts it, "Luxury is premised on inequality, and so long as luxury remains part of capitalism's project, the level of social equality required for genuine democratic order will never be reached."[14]

These descriptions offer insights that we can use to distill an initial definition of luxury offered in the form of a Thomistic description of vice: *The disposition of using surplus resources for inordinate consumption of private goods and services in search of ease, pleasure, novelty, convenience, or status.* The first part of this definition suggests the "object" of the disposition.

Habits, Aquinas states, can be distinguished by their "specifically different objects" (I–II, 54, 2). The problem of luxury occurs in connection with a specific situation: where there is surplus. The term "surplus" itself has a complex history within economics. The nontechnical use here is in rough terms "having more than I (or we) need." Thus surplus can only be understood in relation to some account of necessity, both individually and socially. Sidgwick's description highlights the "whims and fancies" of those "whose income is far more than sufficient to satisfy ordinary human desires." While appreciating the point made earlier, that because luxury is a disposition, one may be luxurious even though one does not have the economic capacity to satisfy one's outsized desires, even this idea is really only possible in a social situation where one has had exposure to these excessive goods. Luxury is measured relative to some kind of standard even if it is not a fixed standard through time. Insofar as these standards are social, Socrates was correct to identify it as a characteristically social vice.

The definition also states that luxury is "inordinate." The term "inordinate" is common in Aquinas's discussion of vice and sin. A vice involves "being disposed in a manner not befitting [a thing's] nature" (I–II, 71, 2), which for humans involves something "contrary to the order of reason." Nearly all the potential objects of luxury are not objects that are always to be avoided; rather, the vice consists in desires for these objects as greater goods than others, that is, desires that are out of their proper order. So far we have been largely concerned with fleshing out the disordered tradeoffs we make when dealing with surplus resources. Such tradeoffs can be examples of what Aquinas calls "sins of malice," the most serious sorts of sins. Since we never will evil *qua* evil, sins of malice occur when the will "loves more the lesser good" and is willing "to suffer some hurt in its regard, in order to obtain a good that one loves more."[15] While we might never will evil directly, we are willing to allow greater goods to suffer for the sake of lesser goods. As John Langan puts it, Thomas "is relying on the distinction between what is directly chosen and what is indirectly chosen."[16] Thus, to sin by certain malice is to will directly as a greater good what is in actuality a lesser good and thus indirectly to set our will against an actually greater good. Or, as Aquinas puts it in *De Malo*, it is to will "a particular good with an associated evil."[17]

Such tradeoffs are often encountered in nonsurplus situations. To use a gruesome example, one can imagine selling a child into slavery in order to obtain funds to feed one's other children. These sorts of lifeboat dilemmas often take up a disproportionate amount of the time of ethicists. Of course, that disproportion can be justified because the dilemmas often involve very high stakes. On the other hand, critics of quandary ethics have further suggested that the importance of such situations even in light of this is exaggerated and distorted because situations are portrayed atomistically and without sufficient attention to character.[18] Be that as it may, we have developed an extensive (if debated) language for dealing with types of nonsurplus tradeoffs.

Luxury presents a peculiar challenge to our moral language specifically because it is concerned with the right and wrong of *surplus* tradeoffs. That is, a focus on luxury assumes that tradeoffs made with surplus are morally significant (both for individuals and for a society) and that "luxury" names the vice of making such surplus tradeoffs badly, in disordered ways contrary to reason. Both Sidgwick and Ferguson identify luxury not by an absolute standard but rather in depicting what "higher" goods might be sacrificed in choosing to devote extra resources to luxury. They instead adhere to a reasonable shared standard of living. This fundamental point about surplus tradeoffs and their moral significance is illustrated by all of the preceding chapters: at the core of each chapter is the identification of tradeoffs—whether purely economic ones (investment versus consumption, positional consumption versus nonpositional consumption), moral ones of "strong evaluation" (work versus leisure, internal versus external goods), or theological ones (sacramental gift versus various forms of personal and social gratification).

The notion of tradeoffs can get oversimplified by utilitarianism's inability to establish anything but a quantitative or aggregate ordering of goods. On the other hand, utilitarianism's moral significance is dissolved by the idea that such tradeoffs are purely subjective or a matter of "personal preference," as in marginalist economics. Luxury is a key moral concept partly because it refuses both of these reductions in our capacity of moral judgment. It necessarily relies on some sort of strong evaluation (Ferguson's "higher engagements"), a qualitative sense of (relatively) noble and base goods, of (relatively) higher and lower or better and worse ways of making these tradeoffs. Furthermore, it assumes that these tradeoffs have a moral weight rather than it solely being a matter of something as simple as choosing corn flakes or raisin bran. Surplus resources continue to have moral obligations attached to them—they need to be directed toward proper ends.

The latter part of the definition offers a constellation of terms that suggest the disordered ends at which luxurious tradeoffs aim. Both Sidgwick and Ferguson hover around this area and name it in terms of "love of ease" or "whims and fancies" or "costly pleasure" or "vanity." They both recognize that luxury can make one too susceptible to petty inconveniences and minor discomforts, and Ferguson in particular highlights how luxury puts too much weight on "paultry distinctions." Luxury names the intuition we have that we can in fact be "too comfortable" or "too status-conscious." But when is that? The right level is not absolute, but the disposition is exposed when we sacrifice more important goods for lesser ones. As Sidgwick says, we sacrifice health or the pursuit of knowledge; Ferguson points out that we shirk social duties. Thus, luxurious tradeoffs harm the self and injure social solidarity.

We should stop here to draw an example that demonstrates both the moral relevance and the challenges involved in evaluating surplus tradeoffs, particularly ones sought for the sake of ease and convenience. Instead of money, let us focus on time.[19] Time is finite (though, as with production, there are efficiency gains to be had), and so the tradeoff structure of time is more fixed. It is readily accepted that many modern developments are adopted and justified because they are time-saving, though many social commentators often wonder whether this "saving" makes us better off. We are all familiar with the complaint of feeling stressed out because there are not enough hours in the day. However, for a country that claims to be stressed out, we do spend an enormous amount of time watching television. Lester Thurow derides the rise of "TV man" and suggests that he is destructive to the economy because such behavior "inculcates a set of anti-production values."[20] Compare the time survey data for 1934 and 1966, which shows dramatically more time spent on meals, on walking, and on reading in the pre-television era.[21] The latest US time survey data indicates that the average American spent at least 2.5 hours of every day watching television, with considerably higher numbers for weekends; if we screen out the 20 percent who did not watch at all, the average television-watcher tops 3.5 hours a day.[22] The data is even worse for children. Children spend an average of over 4 hours a day on television, and a particularly troubling 7 hours and 38 minutes every day consuming all forms of media (except texting, which if included circa 2010 would add another hour).[23]

How much television-watching is the right amount and how much is too much? Most would acknowledge this question as significant despite the difficulties of arriving at precise numerical specifications. To a certain extent, "watching television" is an insufficient specification of the action in question. We would have to ask about what is being watched and why, whether it is a shared activity that generates communal spirit and discussion, and what other responsibilities might be pressing but ignored. I do not have cable television, so I watch virtually nothing. But at the end of the semester I like to go out to a local video store (that still exists) and rent three or four movies or a season of a television series as a break at the end of a day of grading. It even requires some kind of judgment about one's own dispositions. The main reason I would get cable is to watch baseball games and I do miss watching them. But I know from experience that the lure of baseball available all summer would end up sucking up a lot of my time—and that the more I watch, the more I will want to watch.

However, even in light of all these circumstantial questions, can we reasonably judge that the aggregate numbers cited above are "too much"? Can they at least call into question the claim that modern life is too busy and full of stress? While we don't have a number to specify exactly where "television excess" would begin, we do have some sense that there is an excess point and that being able to answer some questions would help us determine what would count as excessive. A similar set of judgments might be made about using smartphones and the Internet. Recent studies have highlighted both the neurological and the social effects of our attachment to web-access devices.[24] The point is not to suggest that the Internet is evil; rather, it is to claim that there are morally significant judgments about "web excess" that we can and need to make.

The examples of television and Internet excess can be seen as aspects of a disposition to luxury. Who among us does not get stuck "wasting time" on the Internet or "vegging out" in front of the television? These are generally easy, comfortable, undemanding forms of relaxation and only on rare occasions (at least for television) can we make a case for their necessity, particularly in relation to other possible activities, whether that is in reading, prayer, exercise, or socializing. Yet, especially in the case of the Internet, we are likely to be able to distinguish quite easily the difference between using it well (e.g., to gather data and sources for a book or to send work email) versus using it excessively (e.g., looking up unrelated baseball statistics or reading baseball blogs). Even further distinctions can be made as well: college professors recognize that some students use the Internet as an excellent research tool while others use it in a way that only simulates doing research. Trying to specify this distinction is sometimes maddening, especially if the student doesn't actually want to believe in the distinction. But, however imprecise, the distinction is both real and important.

In moving toward a moral specification of luxury we cannot simply draw lines to determine certain things as good and others as bad, just as television or the Internet should not be seen as good or evil. Yet we also must resist Mandeville's temptation to regard luxury as so amorphous that its specification simply melts away. Rather, we must be attentive to how consumption choices of all sorts involve dispositions toward certain kinds of immediate, pleasurable, and private rewards that are chosen at the expense of more complex and important goods. It requires clarity on what exactly is being chosen with attention to the personal and social circumstances within which the choice is being made. That is, we need more adequate action descriptions.

Specifying Prudence

Being able to identify the vice of luxury also requires an exercise of the virtue of prudence. Prudence is fundamentally misunderstood if it is assimilated to opinion or a purely subjective judgment. Aquinas is clear that prudence involves a judgment of *reason*; it is a virtue because it can be done well or badly. A brief look at some of the requirements of prudence will set up the key questions of the final chapters.

William Mattison defines prudence as "the virtue that disposes us to see rightly the way things are in the world around us, and to employ that truthful vision to act rightly."[25] This definition helpfully compacts what is indisputably a complex treatment in Aquinas. Aquinas's treatment wrestles with different, overlapping lists of parts and "quasi-integral parts" of prudence, many of which can be sorted into Mattison's two-part definition.[26]

"Seeing rightly" turns out to involve a number of different elements.[27] Some, like understanding and reason, involve clarity and accuracy. Some, like memory and foresight and circumspection, involve using knowledge about the past and future well. Some, like docility and *eubolia* ("good counsel"), focus on our reliance on others in seeing and choosing accurately—an ability that is "completed" by the spiritual gift of counsel which, as Aquinas says, gives us a kind of "God's eye view" of the particulars. ("Really, would God make that purchase?") It is important to note that the Church can be a crucial community of discernment on these issues. James Halteman rightly points out a major reason why the Church "is so silent on consumption": because of "the ambiguities of determining what is luxury, what is need, and when things are too important. 'Everything is relative' can sidetrack any preacher brave enough to suggest restraint of lifestyle." But, he also says this is the "most compelling reason" why the local church community is crucial.[28] Finally, some of Aquinas's categories, like the slippery *synesis* ("right judgment" or "good sense") and *gnome* (also "good judgment," but within the context of a certain set of circumstances), involve recognition of a kind of synthetic ability or skill to put together all these elements and even to discriminate when the "common sense" course of action doesn't apply.

Until now we have built up resources for "seeing rightly" the prudential judgments involving consumption. We studied history, we delved more deeply into economics, and we explained how luxury is marketed. Even more particular knowledge—especially about employing the vision to act right—is still to come, but there we are also turning to the question of "employing the vision *to act rightly*." Specifically, three areas must be explored for the understanding of luxury to be applied prudently. First is the further development of the notion of *surplus* resources, looking broadly at our social context in order to recognize how luxury has to function differently than it did for the ancients. In particular there are significant changes in the questions of who has surplus and knowing when we are in positions of tradeoffs. Here we develop more circumspection, foresight, memory, and the like.

Second is the perennial question of distinguishing necessities from luxury, both in terms of unnecessary "extras" and (often) the inordinate consumption of those necessities. General principles (understanding) and their connection to the existing processes and structures in our society (reason) will be developed. Prudently judging necessity also requires considerable "good sense," particularly when looking at the overall patterns of consumption present in American society. While we depend on the insight that we do (sometimes somewhat lazily) recognize, both individually and as a society, some common sense principles for making this distinction, we also often refrain from stating these principles clearly and critically.

Finally there is the question of our consumption beyond necessity. We must assume that a situation of surplus means some consumption would not be identified as necessary but still might be seen as good. But how do we sort out such "good excess" from luxury? What are the proper ends to pursue if they are not ease, pleasure, or status? We must focus on our lives as ordered to a natural and supernatural common good and how to sort out the differences between, say, a public park and a private patio or a fancy dinner to celebrate one's wedding anniversary and a fancy dinner every weekend night. Here, *gnome*—the element of discriminating where and when excess and celebration might be acceptable—enters quite strongly, as does the gift of counsel, by which we attempt to see our excess resources not as future pleasure for ourselves but from God's point of view, that is, as resources to foster the sacramental economy of reciprocity.

Notes

1. Sekora, *Luxury*, 19.
2. Ibid., 16.
3. Ibid., 72–73.
4. For the significance of Sidgwick as the immediate predecessor to Alfred Marshall and the Cambridge school of economics, see Robert Skidelsky's chapter in *John Maynard Keynes*, 26–50.
5. Sidgwick, "Luxury," 1.
6. Sidgwick, *Theory of Political Economy*, 404.
7. Sidgwick, "Luxury," 15–16.
8. Ferguson, *Essay*, 286.
9. Ibid., 285.
10. Ferguson, *Essay*, 239, cited in Arbo, *Political Vanity*, 135.
11. Ferguson, *Essay*, 294.
12. Ibid., 286.
13. Arbo, *Political Vanity*, 7, 12.
14. Ibid., 143.
15. ST I–II, 78, 1.
16. Langan, "Sins of Malice in the Moral Psychology of Thomas Aquinas," 188.
17. Aquinas, *On Evil*, q. 3, a. 14.
18. A representative classic critique of quandary ethics is Pincoffs, *Quandaries and Virtues*.
19. Economists are fond of noting that time is the ultimate "scarce resource" since we cannot produce more of it.
20. Thurow, *Future of Capitalism*, 317–18.
21. Scitovsky, *Joyless Economy*, 163
22. See the American Time Use Survey data from the US Census: http://www.bls .gov/tus/current/leisure.htm The average for religious and spiritual activity during the week is 4.2 minutes—but this is a result of only 6.1 percent of the population doing anything at all. The ones who did do activities spend more time on them. Comparatively, almost 80 percent of Americans watched some television on an average weekday.
23. Lewin, "If Your Kids Are Awake." Just in case anyone is interested, the time spent reading books is twenty-five minutes a day. We could conduct further discussions about how such preoccupations lead to an aversion to work and effort, and how not all media consumption is "equal" in the sense that some television is more "worthy" and some is just "trash." Notice how these categories tend toward the analysis we are developing of luxury. Also see Friedman and Mandelbaum, *That Used to Be Us*, 127–29.
24. Carr, *Shallows*; Turkle, *Alone Together*.
25. Mattison, *Introducing Moral Theology*, 98.

26. Aquinas's general definition—a disposition which "applies universal knowledge to particulars which are objects of sense" (ST II–II, 49, 1)—involves both knowledge and application, but Mattison's definition highlights the key component of accuracy.
27. These are discussed as "quasi-integral" (II–II, 49) and "quasi-potential" (II–II, 51) parts of prudence. "Integral" parts Aquinas describes by comparing them to the walls, roofs, and foundation of a house; "potential" parts are "connected" but "secondary," like "sub-virtues" ordered to the operation of the virtue itself. See II–II, 48. For our purposes it is sufficient to consider these qualities simply as various aspects or dimensions of exercising prudential judgment well.
28. Halteman, *Clashing Worlds*, 72.

CHAPTER 6

Luxury and Social Context

Who Has More Than Enough?

In the late fourth century the wealthy Paulinus of Nola renounced his riches in dramatic fashion and in the process became an example widely cited by others. Augustine, in *The City of God*, praised him: "Our Paulinus . . . who, from being rich as rich can be, made himself extremely poor."[1] While income continued to come in, Paulinus devoted it to the shrine of Saint Felix in his adopted town of Nola, where eventually he became bishop. Most strikingly, Paulinus emphasized "his new poverty" by rejecting what Peter Brown calls "the practice of splendor." Brown writes: "To possess and to show splendor — éclat — was what being rich was all about. . . . [I]t had everything to do with how one looked, how one dressed, how one ate, how one traveled, and last but not least, how often one bathed. Wealth sheathed the bodies of the rich with a set of unmistakable signals of prosperity and good fortune. By contrast, with Paulinus and Therasia, that splendor was well and truly dowsed."[2]

What were these "signals of prosperity" and how were they changed? Expansive villas were replaced with "cramped cells." The refined company of friends and dependents was replaced with "close contact with the drab masses." Walking replaced coach travel. Their clothing was "dark, coarse, and drained of all color." They ate plain food from pottery with wooden utensils — "no silver was to be seen." And, "above all, they were enveloped in the dull smell of the underbathed. This was the sure mark of poverty in the ancient world."[3]

The particulars of Paulinus's life offer us a way of beginning to reflect on the difficult question of what counts as luxury and illustrates the complex nettle of personal discomforts and social renunciations we might face. It also raises pointed challenges: are our bathing habits an example of luxury? The daily hot shower is still something not readily accessible for much of the world's population. Yet, speaking personally, this is surely one of the last things I could imagine giving up. (However, as one reader pointed out, even here lines can be drawn: a standard water-conserving shower is different than a rainforest showerhead in a bathroom reconfigured as a spa.[4]) Moreover, we may rightly be concerned by the potential "designer poverty" of this kind of dramatic example.[5]

We must begin with a key recognition: we live in a different world than Paulinus did. When considering his example we should notice key similarities but also key differences of context. True, like Paulinus we can be seduced away from helping and associating with the poor by our desire to maintain a lifestyle of status and relative ease. We certainly can recognize that, like Paulinus, our pursuit of luxury is deeply entwined with the status-conscious social relationships we express in our choices of diet, clothing, and personal appearance.

For many of us, however, the vice of luxury will be something that seeps into our lives in gradual and small but continual ways, unlike a wealthy Roman nobleman born and socially entitled to such wealth. Thus, the most important difference is who should be "targeted" by a critique of luxury. The "native context" of the ancient critique of luxury was a few vast aristocratic fortunes in a society filled with the poor. We have a picture of the quite different contemporary context. Some in our society exist in the same stratospheric universe of wealth that Paulinus possessed (albeit with splendors far beyond Paulinus's most extravagant possibilities—imagine what he would have thought of a private sleeping suite on a transcontinental jet!). Does that mean the rest of us are exempt? Yet we too are conscious of the same problems he confronted: these were problems of personal ease and status markers being sustained by surplus wealth. For example, being underbathed continues to be a sure mark of poverty.

Our task here is to develop a better understanding of the shifted context of the "we" susceptible to luxury before turning to specific consumption choices later. Specifically, we need to compare and contrast our social stratification with that of premodern societies. The luxury critique depends on the existence of a social stratification, with surplus resources at the top and a lack of basic necessities at the bottom. Our society surely has this stratification. Yet our reality does look considerably different from the premodern one. We also must address some underlying problems with the portrait of our society as luxurious which in themselves point to long-running mistaken tradeoffs that are indicative of the vice.

The Context of Surplus

As Socrates argued, a society as a whole can be said to be infected by luxury.[6] Is this true of the contemporary United States? Are we under the spell of luxury—which is to say, are we using surplus wealth badly? We must figure out whether the United States does in fact have surplus and, if so, who has it. At first glance it seems obvious that US society has a great deal of surplus wealth. Economists routinely point out that since the late nineteenth century, overall GDP per person has risen at a steady rate such that the average person of today is many times "better off" than the average person of 100 to 150 years ago. Greg Mankiw's textbook assures us that "the typical American enjoys much greater economic prosperity than did his or her parents, grandparents, and great-grandparents"; he shows a real rise in per capita GDP from $3,752 (in 1870) to $44,260 to prove it.[7] Since 1930 alone, per capita GDP has risen six-fold due to increasing efficiency and capital investment.[8] This increase has not gone to the better-off alone. In inflation-adjusted dollars the 1948 median household income was $26,500 compared to $62,200 in 2012—which is another way of saying that today's median household has more than *twice as much* purchasing power at its disposal.[9] One need only look at the mounds of inserts in the Sunday paper to see how many things are produced in the unending competition for this increased purchasing power. Economists commonly state that today's average person is better off in absolute terms (though not necessarily in relative ones) than even much wealthier persons of earlier ages. Mankiw offers a comparison with the life of John D. Rockefeller, who despite his riches, "couldn't watch television, play video games, surf the internet, or send email." Nor did he have air conditioning. For much of his life he didn't have the use of a car or the option of air travel, nor did he benefit from many medicines. Mankiw opines that, given these comparisons, maybe our prosperity is *underestimated*, even in light of the explosive growth in the statistical measures.[10]

Given all this, why does society continue to struggle with poverty and economic insecurity? For some, this seems like a simple matter of injustice. There are very wealthy people who don't or won't pay their fair share but who make and sustain great wealth via the exploitation of others. Considerable wealth accumulation in the modern era was made possible through expropriation, colonization, slavery, plainly inhumane labor conditions, cheating, and many other forms of inequality.

Nevertheless, a considerable population (including, I suspect, most readers of this book) have shared in the benefits of aggregate economic growth and presumably they want to identify some amount of our increased productivity as compatible with justice. So a proper understanding of the situation requires a bit more inquiry. We are not facing a simple situation where the wealthy (including many of "us") are wealthy solely because of direct exercise of unjust power and violence. In this sense the tirades against global financiers and corporate moguls, however justified, are insufficient for assessing our situation of wealth. Most especially, a focus on origins can distract from what may be the more pressing question: What to do now? After all, many biblical stories, such as that of Zacchaeus the tax collector (Lk. 19:1–10), demonstrate the centrality of repentance and forgiveness even in situations of unjustly acquired wealth. The injustice of the accumulation process must always be kept in mind; at the same time, the responsibility associated with surplus wealth, however acquired, must be the priority for an economic ethics that seeks to realize the common good in the present and future.

Social Stratifications through Time

The fact that most people in the ancient world were quite poor didn't stop ancient moralists from suggesting that society could be captured by luxury. Critiques of ancient Roman society must have been critiques of a particular section of that society that was mishandling surplus wealth. What and who was targeted by the ancient critique of luxury? According to recent studies, even the relatively wealthy late Roman empire of the third and fourth centuries was still a place of immense socioeconomic stratification. Wealthy aristocrats made up perhaps 3 percent of the population, with a small percentage of these possessing truly stratospheric wealth. A small, somewhat variable group (7 to 15 percent) possessed some spare resources beyond subsistence. Over 80 percent of the population existed at or very near subsistence levels: around 25 percent of the whole was fairly stable near subsistence level while well over half the population lived a truly precarious existence.[11] In such a context, the critique of luxury had both obvious bite (there are so many truly poor) and obvious targets (the small number of wealthy). Moreover, the wealthy were assumed to have obligations of magnanimous giving. Luxury was not simply about being rich; it was about being rich and failing to practice magnanimity.

If we move forward in time, this basic stratification and its obligations remain. Christopher Dyer's study of standards of living in the mid-to-late Middle Ages in Britain show both similarities and differences from the Roman picture. The wealthy nobility were a very small sliver of the population (again, with a very steep gradient up to the very few whose resources were immense). Dyer estimates the truly wealthy were around 2 percent of the population.[12] As in ancient Rome, the feudal order in place meant certain customs of magnanimous hospitality were expected. But the picture lower on the ladder is somewhat different: the less-centralized feudal society meant that a larger percentage of households, mostly small landholders, actually generated a measurable surplus—around a fourth of the population before the Black Death in the mid-1300s and half or more after it, as labor became scarce and land was abandoned. Dyer's study details what a late medieval yeoman might be able to accumulate. The more prosperous could accumulate some land, animal stock, and tools ("capital"), as well as household goods like bronze cooking pots, chests to store extra bedding, and even a riding horse or a chess set.[13] The later Dutch Golden Age which so impressed eighteenth-century economists showed even further expansion: probate inventories suggest a steady increase in the number of possessions as well as a shift toward items made from more breakable materials and more fashionable design (e.g., an enthusiasm for Asian porcelain).[14] Thus, there was certainly *some* increase in the number of households having what we would call disposable income. Yet the ancient categories mostly hold: only a few had anything resembling *a lot* of spare resources.

By 1900 the world had changed in many ways, but snapshots of American society in this era continue to reveal a similar pattern: a majority of persons (at least) lived at near-subsistence levels, either on farms often wracked by economic cycles and persistent deflation or in slums and tenements in swelling industrializing cities. The data is often sketchy, but one author suggests that in the United States of 1870, "the poorest half of the wealth distribution own virtually no wealth beyond housewares and furniture."[15] This is not much different from late medieval England. Income data is sparse, particularly before the institution of the income tax in 1913, and even then only the very wealthy filed reports.[16] Application of any kind of "poverty line" is also problematic. By one estimate, in 1918 only 14 percent of persons had income over $2,000, a level around which budget experts of the time estimated reasonable comfort but little else (see the next chapter for more details on these budgets; for reference, 6 percent have incomes over $3,000).[17] The same survey shows only 28 percent overall above $1,500. At best, this group, at and around these levels, could be compared to English peasants with a few nicer pots and outfits.[18]

Thus, considering the question of surplus resources, a reasonably clear three-tiered structure persists into the early twentieth century: a very small percentage of households with significant spare resources, a relatively larger group who have some (but not many) spare resources beyond bare minimums, and a much larger group that has virtually no spare resources whatsoever (or worse). We also have social systems where hierarchical networks, rather than free labor markets and government activity, play a significant role in distributing resources. Furthermore, "subsistence" often means either direct dependence on a wealthier household or on direct production of most of one's own goods.[19]

Does today's social context fit into such a threefold model? This question is immediately complicated by the challenges of global poverty. As Paul VI said so eloquently in his encyclical on international development, these challenges demand "great generosity, much sacrifice, and unceasing effort on the part of the rich man" because "the superfluous wealth of rich countries should be placed at the service of poor nations."[20] Yet, a consideration of the threefold structure in our society immediately raises two issues that will help us understand the prudential challenges for the luxury critique today.

One consideration is the difficult question about what subsistence looks like in a wage-driven economy, especially one with developed systems of social welfare. What percentage of the American population today live like beggars did in ancient cities? Or how many live like peasant farmers, entirely dependent on an adequate harvest to avoid starvation? In one sense almost no one in contemporary America lives in such an utterly precarious position, or in the position of hundreds of millions in impoverished nations.[21] In another sense, however, "precariousness" may look different in a society where paying rent, fixing a car, and checking out at the grocery store all demand regular payment: we lack the subsistence opportunities and social supports that might be afforded in rural societies or societies with more developed clan structures.[22] Thus, imperfect-but-approximate measures like the poverty threshold are developed. The poverty rate stands at around 15 percent.[23] But the rate at which households begin generating surplus, according to the Bureau of Labor Statistics (BLS), is the $40,000–$50,000 income range—below which over 40 percent of households fall.[24] Households below this threshold spend more than they make but are supported by tax credits, welfare expenditures, informal economies, and debt. If the category of luxury has something to do with what one does with a surplus, then perhaps few households making $40,000 or less really have any surplus at all. At best they are making ends meet from month to month; "a bad harvest" for them is an unexpected bill that falls outside the norm. While a lack of resources does not by itself rule out a disposition to luxury, it certainly limits action on it.

The second and more challenging issue raised in our modern context is the need to determine where and how to differentiate between the upper two categories: those with what we might call "small surplus"—the "bronze pot" owners—and those with "significant" surplus. In an incisive article, Steven Thorngate indicates how many Americans like to think of themselves as middle class. By his thinking, if "rich" only begins at $250,000, and "poor" is poverty level, then over 80 percent of Americans are middle-class.[25] But is a household with two professionals earning $75,000 apiece really living a life comparable to owning a bronze pot or two? What, exactly, is "middle"? Thorngate's article offers instructive examples of the problem: an Episcopal minister who makes $65,000 annually self-identifies as "lower middle class" (which may be true among Episcopalians), while a DC mom blogger identifies herself as "middle class" at $100,000 and another person defines middle class using the $48,000 qualifying line for Pell Grants. If we looked for a "middle third" on the household income scale, we'd get a range between $32,000 and $76,000. In 2010, the median family income was $62,301.[26] That same year, the average of the fourth income quintile of families (that is, *approximately* the top 30 percent) was $94,893. Is "top 30 percent" still in the "middle"? Thorngate points out that the oft-used $250,000 designation for tax hikes on the "rich" to pay their "fair share" is problematic. He suggests more realistic thresholds for the rich, "who can afford to pay more taxes," as above $186,000 (the top 5 percent of households) or even $101,000 (the top 20 percent). Backing up this claim, we can look to BLS expenditure data: households in the $120,000–$149,000 range generate an average annual surplus of income above expenditures of $47,000, even after contributing a good deal more to pensions (which is counted as spending) *and* spending more than lower-income households in nearly every category of good and service.[27] In other words, this group already buys many more bronze pots. But, even beyond that, it generates a *surplus* that nearly equals the median household's *overall* income. They seem to qualify for the "significant" surplus resources category!

A chart depicting these various stratifications illustrates the change in distribution over time:

Table 6.1. Economic stratification in different eras

	Ancient Rome	Late medieval England	Turn-of-the century US	US today
Significant surplus resources	3%	2%	6%	20–40%
Small surplus resources	7–15%	25%	22%	20–40%
No surplus resources	80%	60–70%	72%	40%

Of course, such income data is inevitably imprecise data—and doesn't differentiate between, say, cost of living in different areas, household size, whether a couple is retired, whether they own a house or not, and so on. But before exploring these details further in the next chapter, we must get a general sense of who might be considered in the top category because these are the folks who are the primary target of the critique of luxury. They probably don't feel like Paulinus, but at this raw level there is a case to be made that they have significant surplus resources. A general conclusion would be that the top class contains far more members than it did in earlier societies. When asking the question about luxury as a problem in our society, it is not only the existence of the extremely wealthy (the 1 percent) that might come into view, but a much larger group.

Who Has Surplus Today? Richistan and the Rest of Us

An important distinction must be made between the 1 percent and the rest of us. As Clive Crook notes, in drawing on a classic image from economist Jan Pen, an hour-long "parade" of individuals whose heights are proportionate to their incomes (average height = average income) would begin with many people so short as to be barely visible. But "the weirdness of the last half minute of today's American parade—even more so the weirdness of the last few seconds, and above all the weirdness of the last fraction of a second" would be striking because of the skewed nature of economic gains over the past few decades.[28] The parade would end with people reaching far into the clouds and, at the very end, a few people with the soles of their shoes "hundreds of feet thick."

In his profile of the lives of the super-wealthy, Robert Frank suggests that because of the explosion of wealth at the top end, it's like they live "in a different country." No longer are there just a few "clubby enclaves" like it was "before the late 1980s."[29] He calls their world "Richistan." Frank tours us through the enormous expenses of this luxury lifestyle: at a school for butlers the most important rule is "never to judge their employers, whom they call 'principals.' If a principal wants to feed her shih-tzu braised beef tenderloin steaks every night, the butler should serve it up with a smile. If a principal is in Palm Beach and wants to send his jet to New York to pick up a Château Latour from his South Hampton cellar, the butler makes it happen, no questions asked."[30] But he also describes how anxious these principals can be about their security and about what they *don't* have in comparison with those who are richer. In Richistan, having enough wealth to feel "secure" means "twice their current wealth," whatever that might be.[31] Within all of this, the rich "love to say they're simple middle-class people."[32] One interviewee, "for all his wealth," says he "hates being labeled 'rich.' Rich people, he says, are stuffy, pretentious and outof-touch. Richistanis like to think of themselves as ordinary people, albeit with extraordinary fortunes."[33] Even Richistan has degrees, though. Frank divides them into "lower Richistan" (with a net worth between $1 and $10 million; about 7.5 million people), "middle Richistan" (between $10 and $100 million; about 1.4 million), and "upper Richistan" (over $100 million). The lower group, being so much more prevalent, sets spending standards for many "non-Richistanis."

In the context of the previous discussions, the people of Richistan face some stark tradeoffs that proceed in ways much like those faced by Paulinus of Nola long ago. While it is certainly important to point out that these residents pay taxes and often make large charitable donations, the question still remains: Why they do not pay *more* taxes (given the need) and make *more* charitable donations (again, given the need)? One recent newspaper story featured a pharmaceutical millionaire who realized he'd given $34 million to charity since 2000 and had just spent $34 million on a luxury yacht. He says that the spending on the yacht does as much good as the charity, citing how the order for the yacht saved a custom manufacturer during the Great Recession.[34] The embarrassing logic on display here is evidence for how deeply we deny the problem. The residents of Richistan need not and should not live the way they do; there are plenty of other (creative) ways to dispose of millions of dollars that do far more good. Catholic social ethics is today too unwilling to make this obvious claim.[35]

But if this critique is merely about the excesses of people who build themselves $34 million yachts, it wouldn't be very worthwhile. The profound difference in our own society is that so many of us strive to imitate the habits of Richistanis while not living in Richistan. Unfortunately, the spending patterns of middle-class, non-millionaire households often aim at simulating as much of the luxury lifestyle as possible . . . and with far more economic impact. The $34 million yacht is a drop in the bucket compared to the aggregate surpluses of the many. The social impact of the consumption choices of those in the top two quintiles (excluding the 1 percent) is much larger than that of the 1 percent—more than three times greater.[36] Moreover, "the 39 percent" has approximately thirty-nine times the number of votes with which to influence social policy.

Furthermore, as we saw in Hirsch's analysis of the social limits of growth, luxury becomes a different sort of problem when it becomes a legitimate aspiration for large swaths of society. There has been a Richistan in every age, but in our society the problem is the increasing number of people competing for inherently scarce positional goods and commodifying and bidding up these goods in ways that waste resources to gain private positional advantage or even merely "positional protection."[37] More and more economic and social resources become tied up in this seeking of relative advantage, which eventually has bad collective consequences.

While it is easy to maintain the luxury critique for today's 1 percent, it is considerably more important to understand its relevance for "the 39 percent." That relevance isn't concerned with private yachts and jets; it requires further specification of the distinction between luxury and necessity as the most "common-sense principle" for our prudential judgment of consumption. It is possible to speak of an appropriate increase in standards of necessity for goods and services that can actually be provided in greater amounts (via productivity gains). But, as Hirsch's analysis shows, the positional and crowding problems associated with other goods and services limit such expansion. Everyone can have clothing and education but not everyone can have "stylish clothes" (insofar as style is defined comparatively) or the "best school for their kids" (by definition this is comparative). Everyone can in theory have a "good school" or "decent clothes"—but these terms necessarily imply basic standards that are identified in noncomparative ways. Developing the luxury/necessity distinction with more precision is vital. Here we can simply conclude that our society still contains a significant stratification of wealth (on which the luxury critique

depends) while also recognizing that the critique is made more complicated in our times.

The Fragility of Affluence?
Debt and Natural Degradation

Before we turn to the question of defining necessity, some qualifications
should be added to the above picture, which is largely based on income
measures. One simple observation is that relying on income measures
alone obscures the accumulation of capital. An elderly couple on Social
Security may have a relatively low income but they also may own their
house outright, have ample furniture, possess two serviceable cars, etc. In
a similar way society obviously benefits from the accumulation of existing
goods. A wealthy society is a society that not only has high income but also
has accumulated a large stock of productive resources. Thomas Piketty's
recent book suggests that the inequality of capital accumulation is even
more dramatic than income inequality, with socially distorting effects.[38]
Since this project focuses on the disposition related to an *ongoing* lifestyle
supported by wealth, most attention should be paid to income measures
but the further question of accumulated resources is also relevant.

Two other observations complicate, rather than add to, the picture of
social surplus: debt and the degradation of resources. Debt can often make
obvious the vicious character of luxury as a disposition: to have difficulty
restraining desires makes times of cutting back much more painful. Traditional restrictions on usury were a "supply side" approach to the problem, but the easy availability of consumer credit (often given on usurious
terms) creates problems with luxury throughout the socioeconomic ladder.[39] Some who struggle with debt in our society are caught in a trap
where, having only spotty income below subsistence level, they rely on
high-interest borrowing (multiple credit cards, payday lending) to hold
their lives together. While anyone can benefit from being more frugal, the
primary villain here may be the greed of the usurer.

However, the "middle class" and the relatively wealthy can fall into a
similar pattern of spending beyond their means, with perhaps more blame-
worthiness because the wants are more frivolous and the attachment to
luxury more clearly visible. Shira Boss tells the story of a successful work-
ing-class couple, Dan and Tammy, who start a family with frugal practices
but move when Dan is transferred to a new management position. When
buying a new house they became attached to buying in a more upscale

neighborhood that was "something of a reach." Well-manicured grounds, bricked walking paths, a clubhouse—these luxury features seemed worth the extra money (as did "nicer schools"). What they had not anticipated, however, was that moving into this neighborhood also meant a whole new social group, where it was "expected" that one joins the country club, sends kids to expensive camps, and engages in lots of recreational shopping and expensive dining experiences. In order to keep up with their new social peers Dan and Tammy started using credit cards, then home equity loans; eventually they could not avoid bankruptcy.[40] The story helpfully illustrates the problem of debt and luxury as well as the intertwined individual and social forces that drive the disposition.

Is the society that as a whole lives beyond its means in some sense playing out a macro-version of Dan and Tammy's luxury lifestyle aspirations that outstrip incomes? Many signs indicate yes. While government debt gets a disproportionate amount of attention, *overall* debt load and persistent trade deficits are more important signals of the unsustainable situation.[41] In the run-up to the housing crisis in 2007, newly generated debt constituted over 18 percent of total US GDP; the subsequent collapse was only softened by the sudden spike in government debt. By comparison, in 2009 debt was under 10 percent of GDP, and in nearly all categories debt actually shrank—the number only remained as high as it did through massive federal borrowing, which clearly provided a floor for demand.[42] Is it sustainable to generate 18 percent of overall demand via new debt creation? Historically this is certainly far above the norm for creating stability. As one expert observed in an NPR report, this unprecedented level of overall debt means "we've been living very high on the hog. Our living standard has been rising dramatically in the last twenty-five years. And we have been borrowing much of the money to make that prosperity happen."[43] Or, as another writer put it more bluntly before the crash, "we're a society living way beyond our means and seemingly helpless to save ourselves."[44]

What is a reasonable level of debt for a society to have? A functioning credit system is important for generating so-called good debt—the kind of borrowing that supports asset acquisition and "pays for itself" in the long run. A reluctance to take on debt can harm a business and limit its ability to expand and develop. Similarly, mortgage debt in reasonable amounts and at low rates is a sensible way to support middle-class wealth development, since homes constitute a significant "savings." The same might be said about reasonable debt for education, which is a kind of asset development for the self; however, there are arguably better ways to finance education.[45] Yet of most concern is the persistent extension of consumer credit, which not only creates problems for families like Dan and Tammy but also threatens to crowd out more important (but less lucrative) borrowing for business investment.[46]

The US problem of overconsumption is linked to a long-term and persistent trade deficit.[47] Over the past couple decades much-discussed "globalization" has had many effects, but it is undeniable that it has vastly increased the amount of imported goods that we consume—in 2004, 21 percent of consumer spending (excluding petroleum) was on imports—and double the percentage in 1980.[48] The economy theory that free trade is a matter of comparative advantage where goods are produced where it is most advantageous to produce them only works if significant factor immobility (e.g., the inability to rapidly close plants in one area and open them in another) is involved; moreover, the theory was developed at a time when wages were assumed to be pure subsistence.[49] Far from rejecting trade, concern about persistent trade deficits is simply a recognition that over time a society must either function like a household in its relation to other countries or face unpleasant possibilities. As Adam Smith himself recognized, a negative trade balance may not be a concern, but a "very different" balance, that of "annual produce and consumption," must be maintained lest "the expense of the society . . . exceeds its revenue, and necessarily encroaches upon its capital."[50] Of course, a society facing persistent trade deficits does have a "solution" that households do not: inflate the currency. But an inflation solution creates significant problems and faces resistance from many quarters.

How can the United States continue to spend more than it earns? It enjoys a kind of protection because the dollar functions as the world reserve currency. Countries wanting to secure themselves against external crises accumulate dollar reserves by lending money to the United States, which is used to manage the demand gap left by the trade deficit. As Robert Skidelsky ably summarizes, "For developing countries as a whole, foreign exchange reserves rose from 6 to 8 percent of GDP during the 1970s and 1980s to 30 percent of GDP by 2004. Developing countries hold such high reserves of foreign exchange to insure themselves against destabilizing runs on their domestic currencies and to avoid the intrusive IMF [International Monetary Fund] supervision that befell the countries caught in the East Asian crisis of 1997–1998. East Asian countries also keep their own currencies undervalued to promote their countries' exports. Countries use their reserves to buy American Treasury bills. This enables the US to consume more than it produces, to the tune of nearly 7 percent of its GDP."[51] Eliminate 7 percent of GDP and you get a downturn worse than the recession of 2009 (see chapter 4). David Graeber speculates that China is in effect making us into a client state by first "showering us with gifts"![52]

This process cannot continue indefinitely, according to most analysts. At some point some other plan for reserves will be forged by those who have the reserves, and the United States will no longer be able to borrow on extremely attractive terms. On a collective level we could suggest that the phenomenon of debt confirms what some ancients said about luxury: it was surely a vice, but it was self-curing.[53] If the United States is a luxury society today, it likely will not be one in a century from now. Sadly, the social aspect of debt accumulation means that today's luxurious individuals may not end up being the ones who pay the eventual price.[54]

A second signal of social luxury would be a reliance on unsustainable resource use. All consumption processes rely on natural resources to varying degrees.[55] Pope Benedict was particularly prophetic in noting the "scars which mark the surface of our earth: erosion, deforestation, the squandering of the world's mineral and ocean resources in order to fuel an insatiable consumption."[56] Economic models indicate that one positive element of functioning markets is that they promote substitutability of raw materials—if one resource is running low and thus becomes more costly, there are incentives to discover and switch to other resources, which in turn promotes efficiency in resource use overall. In the abstract, substitutability is assumed to be infinite; in reality, there are limits. Agriculture may be a small sliver of overall GDP but we can't respond to crop failures by eating our surplus T-shirts. Oil prices in particular have a disproportionate effect on our overall economy, because while a family or a business might substitute different materials at the dinner table or in the manufacturing process, there are no ready substitutes for oil.[57] Daniel Yergin, the leading scholar on energy, notes that in 1850, 94 percent of the world's energy came from humans and animals, whereas by 1957, 93 percent came from coal, oil, and natural gas; it is still over 80 percent today.[58]

The idea of infinite availability and substitutability of natural resources is both mistaken and dangerous, plus it fosters the illusion of mass luxury. Thomas Freidman describes our society as running up a "carbon debt," and much could be said about the unsustainable rates of use of water, soil, and minerals as well.[59] As James Garvey notes, it is simply a "deluded thought" to imagine we can continue like this, considering the sheer quantity of what he terms "luxury emissions."[60] We inadequately measure these problems in our economics and we harbor the illusion that developing countries can aspire to the "middle-class lifestyle" that we take for granted. A combination of increasing scarcity and waste absorption limits is appearing as a result of profligate use. It is important to note that we have developed sufficient knowledge to both use renewable resources in ways that could continue virtually indefinitely and "store" nonrenewable resources so that they could last virtually indefinitely. We could decide, as a society, that we'd like to power our computers and our emergency vehicles with our own North Dakota oil and gas for the next thousand years, and we could allot a certain quantity of those resources to be used gradually so they would last. To do so, we would have to distinguish necessary uses from luxury ones. Luxury enters the picture here when we believe that somehow there will always be more because there has always been more in the past. In particular, we have spent so much building an infrastructure for housing and shopping that is entirely car-dependent that we now have a large amount of sunk costs in the proposition that oil will always be readily affordable for virtually everyone.

These observations might plausibly be thought of as further "symptoms" of a society with a "luxury disease." Just as in individual cases, a society of luxury initially may appear as innocent when in fact it actually involves attachments that over time lead to living beyond one's means. There are strong reasons to be concerned that our society has this disease of excess. As with any complex disease, individual symptoms in isolation might be attributed to any number of possible underlying conditions. Taken together they are indicators of unsustainability, like the person who has high blood pressure, is thirty pounds overweight, and lives on a diet of fast food. Heart disease may hit very soon or not for a while, but the patient is well-advised to recognize the strong possibilities on the horizon.

Chronic debt and environmental depletion often receive an analysis on the basis of justice. This is not incorrect, but it does seem incomplete. Regarding inequality, justice does matter, but so do the luxurious spending patterns of both rich and poor in a consumer society. In some cases the problem of excessive debt is a structural one by which basic needs could be put in jeopardy unjustly, such as by an unexpected medical bill. In other cases debt involves a pursuit of too many and unnecessary goods and services. Confronting these problems requires attention to more than justice alone; it also requires restraining the vice of luxury. In effect, justice-based solutions that do not attend to our dispositions toward luxury pretend that problems can be solved too easily. Consider that the above problems have a great deal to do with a reliance on cheap imported goods and on imported oil being generally available for everyday use. Both of these are matters of ease and convenience that could be otherwise if we—rich and poor alike—had not accustomed ourselves to a pattern of consumption that

204 · *Chapter 6*

we are loathe to break. In short, an inability to confront these problems is not separable from our reluctance to confront the lifestyle assumptions of "the 39 percent"; these lifestyle assumptions themselves create norms for success that infect the rest of the population. Which among these ideas of "success" might be reasonable and which might be excessive? What is a necessity and what is a luxury?

Notes

1. Brown, *Through the Eye*, 217.
2. Ibid., 219–20.
3. Ibid., 220.
4. I thank Tom Shannon for this insight.
5. Brown, *Through the Eye*, 219.
6. See chap. 1 this volume.
7. Mankiw, *Principles of Economics*, 549–50. The earlier caveats about GDP as a measure should be noted; nevertheless, it would be impossible to deny that aggregate wealth is considerably higher.
8. See Posner, "9 to 12." Also Gregory, *Unintended Reformation*, that income has increased eightfold in real terms during the twentieth century, and yet no acquisitive ceiling has appeared. Also Danner, *Ethics for the Affluent*, 26, has a comparison of the years 1880 to 1976 that shows an almost-eightfold increase in real per capita GDP.
9. See Friedman, "Who Stole the American Dream," 36.
10. Mankiw, *Principles of Economics*, 554.
11. Rhee, *Loving the Poor*, 9–10, summarizes a variety of studies.
12. Dyer, *Standards of Living*, 29–32, with examples of the wildly steep gradient, where distinguished earls made one hundred times or more the income of the lesser gentry.
13. Ibid., 170–74.
14. De Vries, *Industrious Revolution*, 126–30.
15. Pope, "Inequality," 136.
16. See Plotnick et. al., "Twentieth-Century Record," 254–72.
17. National Bureau, *Income in the United States*, 137.
18. Of course, in 1900 only 39.6 percent of the population was classified "urban," so some subsistence agriculture escapes these numbers. In 1990 this number is 75.2 percent.
19. On the difficulties once factories and enclosures removed the possibilities of the household acquiring "extra" income via cottage industry and using the commons, see Boyer, *Economic History of the English Poor Law*, and Snell, *Annals of the Laboring Poor*.
20. Paul VI, *Populorum Progressio*, nos. 47–49.
21. An annual HUD report to Congress identifies over 600,000 homeless at any given time, with around 1.5 million experiencing homelessness in a given year. See

http://en.wikipedia.org/wiki/Homelessness_in_the_United_States. While these numbers are depressingly high, they still represent less than 1 percent of the total population.

22. However, for examples of the modern informal economy, see http://www.npr.org /templates/story/story.php?storyId=8928346.

23. See the official report for 2011: http://www.census.gov/hhes/www/poverty/data /incpovhlth/2011/highlights.html. This number has remained stubbornly fixed for decades, falling only a few points during economic surges. In 1980 it was 12.6 percent, rising briefly to 15 percent in the early 1990s, before falling to an all-time low of 11.3 percent in 2000 and then resuming a climb. *World Almanac 2012*, 52.

24. http://www.bls.gov/cex/2009/Standard/income.pdf.

25. Thorngate, "Defining the Middle."

26. Mishel et al., *State of Working America*, 65.

27. http://www.bls.gov/cex/2009/Standard/higherincome.pdf.

28. Crook, "The Height of Inequality." For a detailed comparison of the gains made by different income groups since World War II and since 1979, see Frank, "Why Do Americans Save So Little," 425–26.

29. This is a different Robert Frank than the economist discussed in an earlier chapter. *Richistan*, 3.

30. Ibid., 16.

31. Ibid., 50.

32. Ibid., 25.

33. Ibid., 75.

34. http://www.nytimes.com/2014/07/26/your-money/seeing-a-supersize-yacht-as-a-job-engine-not-a-self-indulgence.html?ref=business.

35. Fr. John Ryan, the early twentieth-century American social thinker, was considerably more willing to do so.

36. As of 2009 the top two quintiles started at an annual income of $61,801. See Census Bureau Historical Tables H-1 and H-3. According to a CBO study that highlights the extent to which income gains of the last twenty-five years have gone largely to the top quintile, and especially "the 1 percent," the share of national income (after taxes and transfers) of the top 1 percent was 17 percent ; of the next 19 percent, it was 36 percent; and of "the 39 percent" (that is, everyone from the sixtieth percentile to the ninety-ninth) it was 59 percent. See p. 8 of the full report at http://www.cbo.gov/publication/42537.

37. Hirsch, *Social Limits to Growth*, 109.

38. Piketty, *Capital in the Twenty-First Century*.

39. See Manning, *Credit Card Nation*, for the rise of this in the 1970s.

40. Boss, *Green with Envy*, 45–80.

41. Friedman and Mandelbaum, *That Used to Be Us*, 166, quotes former Fed vice-chair Alan Blinder: "The nation took leave of its fiscal senses and simply stopped paying for anything during President Bush 43's eight years," a concern that will be amplified in coming years with the demographic reality of Baby Boomer retirement.

42. Fed Flow of Funds.

43. Davidson and Blumberg, "Taxpayer Beware," *NPR Morning Edition*, February 27, 2009.

44. Colvin, "We're a Nation Helpless," 52.
45. The state of Oregon has passed a measure so that students can attend school tuition-free but also has assigned a fixed percentage of their future earnings to pay back the university system over time.
46. Hyman, *Borrow*, 253. For other comments see Farrell, *New Frugality*, and Garon, *Beyond Our Means*. The addiction to debt even extended to Richistanis like those in *The Queen of Versailles* (see chap. 2); the business philosophy is "Why have an asset that doesn't have a mortgage when you use money to make money."
47. There is considerable controversy over this issue. For strong, detailed cases of the problem of global "structural imbalances" in trade, see Roubini and Mihm, *Crisis Economics*, and Wolf, *Fixing Global Finance*. The problem is that America has been able "to finance its imperial pretensions" (Robert Skidelsky, review of Wolf) and still consume far beyond its means because of the "exorbitant privilege" (Roubini, 253) of having the world's reserve currency, producing what has been described as a "balance of financial terror" with China (Phillips, *Bad Debt*). Others insist that such concerns are overblown. In a detailed 2013 study, Michael Pettis, *The Great Rebalancing*, rejects the term "exorbitant privilege," instead suggesting that the American situation is an "exorbitant burden" because the import of foreign savings necessarily must decrease US savings, leaving the United States stuck with the choice of increasing unemployment or increasing the debt burden (156). However, Pettis puts more of the onus for the imbalance on China's government-directed investment growth policy, which holds down Chinese consumption. Pettis criticizes "the inanity of moralizing," insisting that these tradeoffs follow from government policy. But this overlooks the extent to which government policy is itself constrained and shaped by entrenched consumption habits. For example, Pettis suggests that in the United States a consumption tax or a tax on the wealthy would help immensely (186) but it is surely our attachment to spending that makes such a move politically unpalatable.
48. Uchitelle, *Disposable American*, 227.
49. The quick movement of capital stock by multinational corporations makes comparative advantage into a "race to the bottom" for labor. For a more substantial case for why comparative advantage does not work under today's conditions, see the detailed case in Daly and Cobb, *For the Common Good*, 209–35.
50. Smith, *Wealth of Nations*, 464. Keynes astutely saw the problems of these imbalances and at the end of World War II proposed a system that would control them. "The Keynes plan was designed to provide for symmetrical adjustment by creditor and debtor countries. Central banks would hold their international reserves—i.e., their assets in gold or foreign currencies—in an International Clearing Bank. The balances held by creditors would be automatically available in the form of "overdrafts" to debtors up to an amount limited by the "quotas" they had been assigned. Persistent credit and debit balances would face a rising tariff of penalties. This would "incentivize" countries to shrink their balances to zero over the course of a year. This ingenious scheme was designed to achieve what the gold standard was supposed to do automatically through movements of gold between surplus and deficit countries." See R. Skidelsky, "Inventing the World's Currency,"
51. R. Skidelsky, "Gloomy about Globalization." He notes further that this is a unique situation: "Under the classic gold-standard regime, a deficit country like

the United States would have been forced to curtail its living standard in order to regain competitiveness. In the present nonsystem, it can live for years beyond its means, at the sacrifice of its competitiveness. This is because the dollar is the world's main reserve currency. America is in the happy position of being able to write IOUs for purchases of goods and services that destroy American jobs."

52. Graeber, *Debt*, 369–72.
53. Wallace-Hadrill, *Rome's Cultural Revolution*, 332.
54. While the European situation differs, it has similar issues with imbalances even more difficult to manage because they are among the Euro countries themselves: imagine political debates in the United States in which New Jersey had the power to deny dealing with an economic mess in Nevada. See Rogoff, "Europe's Debt Wish."
55. See Dietz and O'Neill, *Enough Is Enough*, and Schor, *Plenitude*, for recent evidence that there has been little "decoupling" between economic growth and the use of natural resources.
56. Benedict XVI, "Address to Young People."
57. Recent production boosts in oil and natural gas haven't lowered the price because these finds are only viable at $100 per-barrel prices. In fact, the price has been "lowered" from what it would be if we didn't have the new oil, which will eventually prove more and more expensive to extract. On this, see Walsh, "Future of Oil," 28–35. The unexpected decline in prices in late 2014 will likely shut down some of the new production.
58. Yergin, *Quest*, 3–4.
59. Peppard, *Just Water*; Gorman, *The Story of N.*
60. Garvey, *Ethics of Climate Change*, 111, 139.

CHAPTER 7

Luxury and Necessity

What Is Enough?

Economist Lester Thurow wrote in 1980 that the problem with what he called "the zero-sum society" is that "wants become necessities whenever most of the people in society believe that they are in fact necessities."[1] Long before John Paul II condemned "superdevelopment" and "the excessive availability of every kind of material goods," early twentieth-century Benedictine theologian Virgil Michel criticized this expansion of necessity as "the bourgeois spirit."[2] Calling it "the enemy of all believers, students, scholars, soldiers, and saints," he describes this spirit as involving "a constant solicitude for the future, not merely in regard to the necessaries of life, for it was not satisfied with such a moderate goal, but in regard to the ever greater accumulation of material goods."[3] It "knows nothing of denying oneself the comforts and goods of this world for the sake of growth in spiritual things or for the sake of another world."[4] A man possessing such a spirit has an unreasonable abhorrence of physical pain and yet "lives for work," believing in "a maximum of individual and social privileges but coupled with a minimum of personal and social obligations."[5] He therefore approaches "all his environment as legitimate prey"; to do this effectively, his life must be "full of shams."[6] Michel suggests the problem comes from failing to limit one's strivings to necessities therefore displacing the genuinely higher spiritual strivings with "the comforts and goods of this world."

John Ryan is similarly critical of what he calls "the 'higher-standard-of-living' fallacy."[7] He insists that social reform requires that we "put away that false conception of life and values which permeates all classes of contemporary society, and which holds that right life consists in the indefinite expansion of material wants."[8] He offers many suggestions on what could be cut, saying that "the importance and necessity of this kind of individual action can scarcely be exaggerated."[9] He goes on to complain about the "evidently false" theory of life behind the constant desire to "better one's position."[10] This "indefinite striving after indefinite amounts of material satisfaction is not an accidental feature of modern existence" but rather the "natural outcome" of a theory of life that elevates "the scientific knowledge of nature" as the "loftiest object," not "for itself but because of the abundance of material goods that it will put at his disposal."[11] Like Michel, Ryan suggests the problem is not simply a matter of going a little bit overboard; rather, it is a whole style of life that endlessly seeks novelties and comforts—i.e., luxury—and knows nothing of genuinely "higher goods."[12]

Michel and Ryan suggest that striving for an ever-increasing standard of living is a serious spiritual problem. While they avoid using the term "luxury," they are surely targeting it. The remedy requires the identification of a reasonable standard, an appropriate limit on material goods. But where does that limit lie? People live in vastly different contexts, in different family situations, and within changing cultural norms and technological standards. Yet defining luxury requires a clearer identification of necessity; so, too, does the Catholic Catechism's moral principle for the proper use of property: for "basic needs" and then "natural solidarity."[13] We must undertake the task of delineating reasonable judgments about standards of living and develop categories for the exercise of prudence. These standards will help put flesh on the Catechism's category of "basic needs." Once these are defined, we can then move to developing a contrast between "luxury" and the use of goods for "natural solidarity" sacramentally oriented to the Kingdom of God. Naming necessity proceeds in three stages. We start with studies of the standard of living by economists in the era of Virgil Michel and John Ryan. During this period in which widespread surplus first developed, defining a "standard of living" and household budgeting were seen as integral parts of economic science, a proper complement to economic efforts to improve production and allocation mechanisms. Economists of the Institutionalist school combined ambitious statistical collection with the reforming zeal of the Progressive era and were emboldened by their experience of planning during World War I. While they rejected socialism, these economists nevertheless sought to develop various kinds of flexible plans for wages and prices aimed at meeting the needs of all. The task could not be accomplished, of course, without first defining those needs, a task that proved quite arduous and freighted both by the complexity of the economic problem and the political sensitivity of evidently normative judgments. Many social reformers and economists unfortunately turned to other ways of evaluating and enhancing social welfare. Despite their limitations, these earlier studies attempted a necessary task and provided two enduring insights about necessities that should be recovered.

Second, critics indicate the task of defining a standard of living for today is hopeless, but they are far too pessimistic. Evidence suggests that though absolutely rigid lines cannot be drawn, communal judgments about relative standards are widely shared at any given time and place. Indeed, various social policies cannot avoid such judgments, which involve an implicit moral claim about what constitutes luxury. If we are to develop such prudential judgment about the range and limits of spending variation, we need to be able to "see" spending accurately, and in fact several approaches for determining standards for necessity converge.

Finally, categories of basic goods themselves often present particular prudential problems of what is reasonable and what is excessive. Though it would be impossible to exhaust all the details involved in making such a judgment, a few brief examples can help illustrate common questions. Saying that all people need a certain amount of food is likely uncontroversial; in principle we have more than enough food to feed the nation. But is the "cheap" food supply distorted? Is it "luxury" to spend more on higher-quality food? What about meat consumption? How do we analyze these tradeoffs, especially when the vice of luxury and the virtue of justice may prompt outwardly similar actions (e.g., buying local)? A two-dimensional model for adequate prudential judgment is developed to name both the social interdependence of consumption and the individual tradeoffs we make. Several recent Christian writers echo Michel and Ryan in suggesting strategies for placing a monetary ceiling on our basic consumption. Refusal of such limits is ultimately rooted in our attachment to luxury.

The Standard of Living in Early Twentieth-Century Economics

The problem of luxury retained a place in the writings of late nineteenth- and early twentieth-century mainstream economic thinkers like Henry Sidgwick. In the midst of an era of rapid social change, the language of luxury still functioned in a critical way. In 1910 pioneering home economist Ellen Richards of MIT could still urge the emerging middle class "to avoid the debilitating effect of luxuries."[14] Instead of the "temptation to spend for things pleasant but not needful," the "higher aspirations . . . of the intellect and of the soul" should be cultivated with newly procured wealth.[15] Richards believed that "to preserve its values and sustain its place in American society, the middle class had to sacrifice luxury."[16] In 1927 Stuart Chase could still spend an entire chapter classifying and criticizing the role of "super-luxuries" in the economy and explicitly rejecting the idea that they could be economically justified because they "make work."[17] He sought an analysis of the economy that distinguished between the production of wealth and the production of "illth."[18] The 1921 lectures of Catholic social economist Valère Fallon, SJ, of Louvain, include a chapter on luxury, criticizing expenditures as "morally at fault" insofar as they require "the destruction of goods greater than the utility derived from them; in other words, whether the part of wealth and of labor used tends to reduce that which should be reserved for other more important needs."[19] Fallon simply assumed—as did many non-Catholic economic thinkers—that the problem of luxury remained an integral part of the economic analysis of society.

Yet this discourse faced a difficult time in Muncie, Indiana. In their well-known 1920s book *Middletown*, Robert and Helen Lynd remark on "the diffusion of new urgent occasions for spending money in every sector of living" (giving a long list of those sectors), and observe that "both business men and working men seem to be running for dear life in this business of making the money they earn keep pace with the even more rapid growth of their subjective wants."[20] A number of factors converged to challenge traditional practices of restraint. Perhaps the most important was the increasing shift from small proprietorship to wage-earning and management. The Lynds note that "in the quaint county seat of the middle eighties [1880s] men lived relatively close to the earth and its products. In less than four decades, business class and working class, bosses and bossed, have been caught up by Industry, this new trait in the city's culture that is shaping the pattern of the whole of living."[21] They point out the transition from seeing work as a source of pride, skill, and social solidarity in the 1890s to a mechanized, mindless routine requiring little training in the 1920s.[22] A foreman candidly admits that machine runners can't really get pride or satisfaction from their jobs.[23] The rise of scientific "Taylorism" in management further turned workers into little more than cogs in a sped-up operation.[24] James Barnes suggests that, during this era, the ordinary American "found his world turned topsy-turvy" because in the past "he owned a business in whole or in part" where he could "gloat over its prosperity or grieve over its losses." But by 1929 he had lost this sense of ownership and "only in his immediate home could he display that which was purely private property."[25] The Lynds characterized Middletown's turn to consumption in terms of people who "looked hungrily to the consumer marketplace for compensatory fulfillment" because work and community life had been robbed of "genuine satisfactions."[26] Daniel Horowitz notes that even social reformers of this era "recognized the difficulty of deriving a sense of meaning from industrial labor" and so shifted their attention to "ways to make leisure the character-building activity they once hoped work would be."[27] This shift in the nature of work was accompanied by a number of other dramatic changes, such as the rapid growth of urban centers and the appearance of new amenities like movies, amusement parks, and department stores.[28]

Were these changes to be viewed as beneficial or disruptive? For some the consuming life was really an attempt at compensation being pushed by those interested in selling for a profit; this was "the vacuum created by the demise of meaningful work."[29] For others who were more accepting of mass production, the important problem was a matter of ensuring that this affluence be devoted to "higher" goods, not commercialized ones that (in the words of Progressive economist Simon Patten) depended "upon debasing appeals to pent up passions" in order to reap private profits.[30] For still others (like home economist Richards), public extravagances like museums and libraries were little better than nickelodeons and saloons; resisting luxury meant running a frugal, scientifically informed home of sanitation and sobriety. While insisting that her ideal middle-class budgets continue "strict control of food costs," she allowed ample spending for "elevating leisure" that could be enjoyed in the home itself, especially goods that served education and piety.[31]

Yet amidst these differing responses there was a unified theme: the attempt to delineate appropriate living standards *continued to treat the problem of distinguishing luxury and necessity as a serious economic question*, especially as it related to overcoming poverty. Economists of the Progressive and Institutionalist schools, in recognizing the existence of poverty amidst enormous production, sought to make provision for all—and such "provision" needed to be defined. The most ambitious attempts of the era, arising in the midst of the Great Depression, moved quite close to a planned economy.[32] Mainstream economists tended to be more cautious: they carefully parsed household budgets in the hope that compilation and dissemination of data by experts would lead to better choices by everyone. Leading Institutionalist Wesley Mitchell sought a new "professional class of Doctors of Domestic Science" through whom households could be managed as expertly as health was managed by the medical profession.[33] This kind of management by experts could be seen as paternalistic, much as Henry Ford's decision to accompany his higher wages with social worker visits to his workers' households.[34] In another sense, institutions like the Consumers Union performed exactly this function, exposing scams, testing products, and standing as an honest, knowledgeable guide through the maze of modern consumption.[35] Perhaps unlike the Consumers Union, however, these explorations were not merely fact-finding missions. Rather, they sought to establish objectively what people would "really need." For example, one survey of government employees in Washington spends several pages delineating precisely how much and what kinds of "extra" clothing might be acceptable for a wife in this position![36]

This level of detail indicates the difficulties these kinds of studies would encounter in determining a reasonable living standard, all while economics sought to become more and more "scientific" and average consumers found more and more goods within their reach. Nevertheless, the broad lessons of this literature remain instructive. The studies mark the period where meaningful surplus is becoming widespread beyond the elite. In 1875, one of the earliest "budget studies" found that a mill laborer had to work "all the time" *and* put his 12- and 10-year-old sons to work in order to afford a decent four-room tenement, poor but useful clothing, and bread and butter for two of three daily meals. Beyond food, clothing, and rent, less than 5 percent of income remained as potential for saving or spending.[37] There was little possibility for luxury. By contrast, the budgets of unionized typographers in 1920s San Francisco showed nearly a third of income remained after paying for food, clothing, shelter, and home operation.[38] Even budgets for lower-income workers showed that 20 percent of income might remain after these basics.[39] While many barely scraped by, many more found themselves with some extra disposable income.

Two particular lessons stand out. The first is the importance of recognizing and naming a "middle ground" notion of comfort that recognizes the real benefits and advances of modern life while continuing to require restraint. The studies sought to name "restrained comfort" in urban, wage-labor living situations not unlike many today and their efforts assist prudence in seeing luxury accurately. The second lesson is their consistent reliance upon the distinction between "lower" and "higher" pursuits as a way of distinguishing among different possibilities for using surplus wealth. The advances of modern life are accepted, but not indiscriminately. In teaching both of these lessons, we find thinkers trying to identify the middle ground: not a back-to-the-land agrarianism or Franciscan radicalism, but also not an unlimited pursuit of personal desires either. These studies manifest the conviction that the new situation of surplus should call forth new moral and economic categories of discernment. These new categories retain the critique of private excess and the need for limits central to the concept of luxury.

Let us turn to the specifics of these lessons. The first is the delineation of some sort of "middle ground" between necessity and luxury; this is an appropriate response to a more productive economy. Appleby notes that in early American discourse, "the word comfort began to figure as the happy mean between biting necessity and indulgent luxury."[40] The benefits of genuine economic progress could be enjoyed but the traditional lessons of restraint could still apply—insofar as a term remained for the extreme. Sidgwick distinguishes "comforts" (protections against minor annoyances and inefficiencies) and "luxuries" (sources of positive pleasure) and most of these surveys sought to identify similar issues, often with significant rigor. In one 1909 study, a household with "meagre" possessions had little more than beds, tables, and upright chairs, whereas a "comfortable" household was marked by things like rugs, mirrors, and comfortable easy chairs— items such as a piano were reserved for a level beyond comfortable.[41] The tradition of identifying such distinguishable levels of consumption continued: a series of Bureau of Labor Statistics (BLS) studies in the 1960s calculated "lower, moderate, and higher" standards of living, all of which differed from a strict poverty minimum.[42]

Such efforts show that "necessity" need not be reduced to bare-minimum survival. As ordinary experience would suggest, some aspects of our consumption seem less superfluous than others. The aforementioned study of Washington government employees differentiates two standards: poverty was a "minimum of subsistence" (that "allows little or nothing for the needs of men as social creatures"), and "decency" was a "minimum of health and comfort" that allows at least some "comforts" beyond strict subsistence.[43] The task of delineating some reasonable though limited modern comfort illustrates how dramatically our spending has grown and diversified, even compared to the "comfortable middle-class" of the early twentieth century. The family of five was allowed "simple amusements, such as the moving pictures once in a while, occasional street car rides for pleasure, some Christmas gifts for the children, etc." In monetary terms, $20 was allocated for an entire year's amusement, out of a total household budget of $2,262.47— less than 1 percent. For a family making $60,000 today, this would be $600 for the entirety of annual entertainment, including Christmas gifts—an amount that falls far short of the bill for most cable television packages alone. No vacation is included, and no car—the total transportation budget for work and shopping for the family is $45, at 2 percent of the total, went entirely for streetcars.[44] A newspaper was allowed "because it is desirable that every citizen should read a daily paper," but other reading material was excluded since it could be had from the library.[45] Lee Rainwater's overview of the 1960s standard of living studies distinguishes a lower standard (that includes a car and a washing machine—only the truly poor must rely on buses and laundromats) from a moderate "package" that includes home ownership, a color television, a window air conditioner, and a clothes dryer. (The lower standard included a washer but also a clothesline in the backyard.)[46] Developing such standards simply requires thinking through reasons for this or that decision, especially insofar as the reasons for self-ownership should apply to what it is reasonable for other people to have too. In sum, the life of the middle class might have been comfortable, but comfort remained distinguishable from luxurious excess.[47]

The second lesson, which is evidenced in the claim about the "necessity" of a daily newspaper, is the need to make a distinction between "higher" and "lower" pursuits and uses of wealth. Studies of the standard of living continually make judgments between "proper" and "improper" uses of funds beyond the obvious categories of food and shelter. As with the middle category of comforts, the distinction between higher and lower pursuits created room for a critique of luxury. Wesley Mitchell, in his essay "The Backward Art of Spending Money," summarizes this line of thought by noting: "To spend money is easy, to spend it well is hard."[48]

The higher-lower distinction appeared even in the mainstream development of British economics. While not identical to the meaning of luxury, the distinction is important because it provides a richer moral language of evaluation that persisted in the central stream of the development of contemporary economic analysis. It was (rightly) assumed that economics must be concerned with material goods contributing to overall human welfare. Alfred Marshall begins his classic textbook, *Principles of Economics*, by noting that the study of economics is "the study of mankind in the ordinary business of life." Therefore "it is on the one side a study of wealth; and on the other, and more important side, a part of the study of man."[49] He provides a stirring set of statements in which the elimination of slavery is precedent for the true goal of economics: "the hope that poverty and ignorance may gradually be extinguished."[50] Economics was not just about goods or markets; it was aimed at social improvement: "Most economists agreed that there was a very large expenditure by the rich which contributed little toward social progress and conferred only unworthy satisfactions on the spenders."[51]

Perhaps the most advanced and careful articulation of this assumption appeared in Arthur Pigou's classic *The Economics of Welfare*. Pigou's work was an ambitious attempt to combine the developing Marshallian science of economics with the classic (utilitarian) moral concern for overall social improvement. He argues that the innovative Marshallian tool of supply and demand curves reflects only private costs and demands, but that there can be extensive divergence between maximizing private product and maximizing social product. Such externalities should be taken into account. The divergence is rooted in the difference highlighted between "economic" and "non-economic" welfare with which Pigou begins his book. His work displays an anthropology that is far from *homo economicus*:

> Human beings are both "ends in themselves" and instruments of production. On the one hand, a man who is attuned to the beautiful in nature or in art, whose character is simple and sincere, whose passions are controlled and sympathies developed, is in himself an important element in the ethical value of the world; the way in which he feels and thinks actually constitutes a part of welfare. On the other hand, a man who can perform complicated industrial operations, sift difficult evidence, or advance some branch of practical activity, is an instrument well fitted to produce things whose use yields welfare. The welfare to which the former of these men contributes directly is non-economic; that to which the latter contributes indirectly is economic.[52]

Pigou describes here a normative anthropology—or, possibly, two normative anthropologies in some tension—similar to what is seen in Smith and Keynes.[53] With this distinction in hand, Pigou notes that a relationship exists between economic and non-economic welfare, but it is not always a positive one. A negative one can develop when labor is degraded but also in certain circumstances of consumption:

> Non-economic welfare is liable to be modified by the manner in which income is spent. Of different acts of consumption *that yield equal satisfactions*, one may exercise a debasing, and another an elevating, influence. The reflex effect upon the quality of people produced by public museums, or even by municipal baths, is very different from the reflex effect *of equal satisfactions* in a public bar. The coarsening and brutalising influence of bad housing accommodation is an incident not

218 · *Chapter 7*

less important than the direct dissatisfaction involved in it. Instances
of the same kind could be multiplied. The point that they would illustrate is obviously of large practical importance. Imagine, for example,
that a statesman is considering how far inequality in the distribution of
wealth influences welfare as a whole, and not merely in its economic
aspects. He will reflect that the satisfaction of some of the desires of
the rich, such as gambling excitement or luxurious sensual enjoyment,
or perhaps, in Eastern countries, opium-eating, involves reactions on
character ethically inferior to those involved in the satisfaction of primary physical needs, to the securing of which the capital and labour
controlled by the demand of the rich would, if transferred to the poor,
probably be devoted. On the other hand, he will reflect that other satisfactions purchased by the rich—those, for example, connected with
literature and art—involve reactions that are ethically superior to those
connected with the primary needs, and still more to those derived from
excessive indulgence in stimulants. (italics added)[54]

Note that in his initial observation Pigou distinguishes "equal" subjective "satisfaction" from actual welfare. He correctly sees that the agent's
immediate satisfaction is not an adequate guide for human flourishing and
certainly not one for achieving the welfare of society as a whole.[55] Some
consumption activities may indeed have "positive" economic effects, but
the non-economic externalities— gambling, for example—have negative
effects on persons and the society. He applies the same sorts of distinctions
in his treatment of the relief of poverty. In another example he clearly favors
"in-kind" spending for the wider population (funding public parks, schools,
and libraries) as well as general social subsidies for "elevating" activities
(he cites the German practice of sponsoring many inexpensive orchestra
performances) rather than simple distribution of transfer payments.

At this juncture we are likely to run up against accusations of "moralism." Who is to say that orchestra concerts are to be favored over jazz
combos? Or music over sports? Or any spectator activity over participatory activities (e.g., a community garden)? [56] Horowitz critically notes that
WASP-ish American Progressive suspicions of "drink" and "the saloon"
often misunderstood or overlooked the complex social functions this space
performed for immigrants.[57] By contrast, progressives praised poor workers
for spending on sprucing up their homes. But how did new or matching
rugs get designated as more "elevating" than convivial social gathering
spaces like the pub?

Bye-Bye, Budgets: The Disappearance of Standards of Living

Today such distinctions earn scorn from economists. Robert and Edward Skidelsky note that the economist's dictum of "the givenness of wants" means that "desire is no longer, as it was for the ancients, an arrow capable of hitting or missing its mark." If desires are simply not able to be evaluated, then the distinctions between needs and wants, between necessities and luxuries, is lost.[58] Yet we need not look at the ancients for support of reasonable limits; enlightened, progressive economists of the early twentieth century found these judgments reasonable. What happened? A brief history of the development from Pigou and the Institutionalists to the present is needed here.

Not long after Pigou's theories came on the scene, welfare economics abandoned this language; it is standard to cite Lionel Robbins's 1932 *Essay on the Nature and Significance of Economic Science* as a key document marking most economists' abandonment of such judgments.[59] Robbins rejects the idea of economics as "the science of material welfare" because any such "science" would have to predetermine people's ends in order to satisfy the criterion that "scientific generalizations . . . must be capable of being stated exactly."[60] Institutionalists are criticized harshly for trying to aggregate historical data into a science by "the mere multiplication of observations."[61] Robbins opines: "[S]cratch a would-be planner and you usually find a would-be dictator."[62] He instead gives the definition of economics as "the science which studies human behaviour as a relationship between ends and scarce means which have alternative uses."[63] Thus defined, economics merely analyzes relationships; "ends as such do not form part of the subject matter. Nor does the technical and social environment."[64] Economic theory is also split from particular political questions and cannot "furnish a set of norms capable of providing a basis for political practice," since that would require an interpersonal utility comparison that is impossible to make because "there is no means of testing" it.[65] He concludes, "Economics deals with ascertainable facts; ethics with valuations and obligations. . . . Between the generalizations of positive and normative studies there is a logical gulf fixed which no ingenuity can disguise."[66]

The desire to evade normative questions about rugs versus saloons was not limited to academic economics. As Thomas Stapleford shows in his exhaustive study of the history of cost-of-living indices, political actors also played a role in effecting this change. Disagreements between unions and government statisticians over how to measure a living wage led unions toward an easier argument for wage increases: underconsumption.[67] As productivity increased, workers needed to earn more in order to keep consumption up. Wage increases were "good for the economy," in the now-ubiquitous phrase. Not only was this tidier than arguing over measures like what belonged in a "health and decency budget," but, as Stapleford indicates, it marginalized the mostly female economic voices who studied such matters.[68] The prospect of union bosses and their predominantly male membership being overruled in their economic judgments by women was hardly palatable. Moreover, such arguments were obviously more welcome by businesses themselves. As Emily Rosenberg summarizes, "[A]dvertisers began to voice a refrain that soon become a hallmark of their profession: the prosperity and stability of the nation (and then of the world) depended on their skill in stimulating ever-higher levels of purchasing and consuming and therefore of jobs and prosperity."[69] Her essay nicely demonstrates the unsustainability of that strategy for more than a couple decades.

Finally, the rising expectations that marked the post–World War II economy—and, frankly, the relief from decades of turmoil and scarcity—seemed to make obsolete the idea of frugality and budgeting. Only in the area of overcoming poverty did budget studies continue to play an occasional role, and even here many normative implications were often avoided. The development of the official poverty level during Lyndon Johnson's War on Poverty ended up eschewing lengthy and controversial budget studies in favor of Mollie Orshansky's "arbitrary" estimate of it being three times a reasonable food budget. Such a measure could avoid normative arguments by "grounding her threshold in the one section of household spending where something akin to the natural sciences (nutrition) could be used," and "relying primarily on empirical observation [for the multiplier] instead of judgments about adequate housing, clothing, and so forth."[70] It screens out many of the positional concerns by tying the economic value measurement of food being defined in terms of nutrition standards without any consideration of positionality.

The Case for Necessities

In his study of the idea of luxury, Christopher Berry claims that giving any kind of "fixed or determinate sense" to the idea of necessity "is unsustainable" today.[71] But the problems addressed by the early-century studies don't go away; in fact, the flight from politically sticky normative judgments about consumption hasn't stopped the cultural battles between the "greedy" 1 percent and the "profligate" poor. Such arguments are often filled with scorn, anger, and frustration—and far less often with clarity, precision, and a sense of shared standards for the common good, all of which animated the earlier studies. Perhaps the Institutionalists were right in their belief that normative analysis of household consumption patterns is an integral part of understanding and improving the overall economic system in the context of an industrial economy based on wage labor. The early-century studies supplement the case that, based on the increasing importance of positional competition and the interdependence of wants, differentiating consumption is important for understanding how the economy is working. Problems of distribution and poverty cannot be separated from judgments about luxury.

Even so, can such judgments be made reasonably? The best case that a distinction between necessity and luxury can be made rests on two important observations: the enduring and well-supported idea that satiability is a characteristic of human flourishing; and the ongoing (though often unacknowledged) distinction of necessity/comfort/luxury within the everyday life of individuals and societies.

Even if we no longer conceive of human nature in a purely static way, we still generally believe that someone who is "insatiable" has a problem. John Medaille notes how artificial it is to dismiss satiation, and argues that "it takes a tremendous amount of miseducation" to "move the security and wealth lines 'northwards' so that people will always feel insecure and poor, and hence will devote more of their time to paid work and more of their money to consumer products." Since we have little experience of an affluent society without advertising, we simply don't know if satiation in relation to material goods might be normal. Advertising and social manipulation create false social hierarchies, but they also misallocate billions of dollars of resources and degrade work itself by emphasizing the "external goods" that such work secures.[72] Medaille's analysis suggests that everyone has implied judgments about what would count as economic "security" (i.e., "comfort") and actual "wealth" (i.e., abundance to enjoy)—but we often do not have an appropriate *language* to articulate where these might lie and how to subject them to critical analysis. Therefore they tend to exist as a constantly moving target. (Interestingly, we make an exception for people who are "insatiable" in certain pursuits—perhaps in a desire for discovery or a quest for new adventures—but this may be a reflection that judgments of "higher" and "lower" ineradicably operate in the background.)

As the Skidelskys note, nearly every wisdom tradition supports this ideal of satiability.[73] One need not appeal to the Greeks or the early Christians. Take the wisdom tradition of modern psychology. Barry Schwartz depicts two types of consumers: the maximizer, who is always looking for the best and the newest; and the "satisficer," who simply wants to acquire something that is "good enough."[74] He suggests that "satisficers" are much happier but that our world is increasingly set up to cater to and encourage the maximizers. Schwartz is not trying to maintain some kind of absolute standard; he is concerned that maximizers lack standards of "enough" and end up dissatisfied because of their high expectations. They trade their time and attention in favor of activities like doing research and shopping at multiple stores in the search for refinement, but they also pay less attention to intrinsically more satisfying nonconsumer activities.[75] Schwartz later suggests that there might be areas of life in which making the absolute best choice is wise, but we need to differentiate these from most consumer choices. Schwartz here relies on exactly the two lessons we learned from the early-century economists: in daily life people must establish a restrained comfort level of "good enough" and they must distinguish between higher and lower goods. Perhaps consumerism should be classified as a psychological disease!

The desirability of maintaining moderate restraint, and therefore a satiation point, is further supported by the phenomenon of the "hedonic treadmill." This is the idea that "once you have a certain new experience, you need to keep on having more of it if you want to sustain your happiness."[76] This tendency to adapt unfortunately means that the pursuit of novel pleasure—a key component of luxury—actually requires stronger and stronger "doses" in order to sustain the original enjoyment. As the ancients rightly thought, material goods are not in fact very interesting or fundamental to human flourishing (compared to friendship or wisdom or community) so one must run faster and faster on the "treadmill" of purchasing in order to sustain the illusion that they are. Such an idea is supported by the prevalence in spiritual traditions of periodic fasting, which is rooted in the recognition that material appetites "are like children who clamor constantly for attention and who, if indulged, will in short order run the house."[77] This tendency of material wants to increase faster and faster can also be identified, as Peter Danner does, with the classic Catholic doctrine of *"fomes peccati,"* or "the tinder of sin" in which "mild forms" of luxury—a constant seeking of bodily comfort, say, or a restless insistence on perfectly beautiful surfaces, or an addiction to regular pleasure routines—must be held in check intentionally so that they do not become occasions of genuine sin.[78] We may not be able to define exactly how much concern for comfort is too much, but there does seem to be a limit. Luxury is what happens beyond that limit.

Another reason to believe that the necessity/luxury distinction is real is seen in our continued implementation of social policies that rely on just such a distinction. Communities continue to operationalize this distinction through policies that imply that some goods are necessities and some are "higher" than others. We designate welfare support for certain goods and not others, and even subsidize certain community goods ("the arts") but not others (the movie theater). Economists now call them "merit" and "demerit" goods.[79] While fluid, the necessity/luxury distinction is manifest in government policies of taxation and welfare: "[T]axation of consumption goods is a case where the definition of luxury is made socially explicit, when some goods are either exempted from or, conversely, specially selected for such a tax. Poverty is a case where it is the definition of need that is made socially explicit."[80] For example, many US states exempt food and (less frequently) clothing from sales taxes. Some jurisdictions have gone further by reinstating taxes on things like candy, take-out food, or clothing priced above a certain level—presumably with the idea that these things are luxuries. The WIC (Women, Infants, and Children) supplemental nutrition program for pregnant women and new mothers defines food "needs" by restricting recipients' choices, in terms of both type and price.[81] Poor families may receive subsidies for some things (e.g., rent, heating costs) but not others (e.g., gasoline, car insurance).

The mistake here is to believe that, because the standards can shift somewhat over time, they are *completely* illusory. This is a false premise and relative shared standards continue to be operationalized in practice. The simple fact that such definitions are tied to cultural norms and somewhat fluid over time does not mean that we don't make them and act upon them. The mistake is exacerbated when Catholics become preoccupied with a limited set of "moral absolutes." One does not need eternal fixed categories in order to identify important shared moral judgments. John Ryan knew this, insisting that Pope Leo XIII's standard of "reasonable and frugal comfort as" set out in *Rerum Novarum* is "a practical and tangible conception" because of "the remarkable level of agreement" among various studies and estimates.[82] In writing a 1964 comprehensive study on Catholic teaching in economic life, Father John Cronin could still recommend such prudence: "While there may be some elements of the subjective in such terms as poverty, frugal comfort, and luxury, there are nonetheless sufficient objective standards to warrant some conclusions about proper standards of living."[83] The agreement among studies noted by Ryan largely continues today.

Despite economists' reluctance to acknowledge it, the distinction between necessity and luxury survives in political practice because it rests on relatively strong consensus judgments of average citizens. Consider a British survey from the early 1980s that listed 35 items and asked respondents to identify each as either "things all adults should not have to do without" or "things which may be desirable, but not necessary." A large degree of consensus, over 75 percent, occurred on the following items: accommodations with plumbing, heat, and a non-leaky roof; a decent coat and pair of shoes; public transport; bedrooms and three meals a day for each of one's children; and a refrigerator. By contrast, only 51 percent said a television was necessary, only 43 percent identified a telephone as such, and only 22 percent selected a car.[84] Such distinctions are evidently contingent on circumstances, but they do suggest a substantial consensus in any given context (hence, also, the typical laws about minimum standards in apartment housing). The authors break down the responses by socioeconomic class and show strong convergence; the few that diverge (64 and 61 percent of the lower classes said television was a necessity, while only 38 and 37 percent of the higher classes did) often turn out to be differences in claims about necessary leisure. (By contrast, 74 percent of the top class said that "a holiday" was a necessity, compared with only 57 percent of the lowest class). Circumstantial variables affect such a listing in different times and places, but the general consensus indicates that a baseline is not impossible to set.[85]

Moreover, the distinction continues to be made not simply between different categories but also within particular categories as well. As Berry notes, luxury is not only a matter of a particular distinctive class of goods. Rather, it is a way of elaborating basic human goods. As an example, he outlines four categories—food, clothing, shelter, and leisure—all of which are touted in an ad for a weekend spa getaway.[86] Luxury may involve not some purely novel good but rather a particular "refinement" of some basic human need. Yet, often enough, those "refinements" are seen as a problem if they go overboard. Christine Hinze notes the story of a woman in 1992 who defined "comfortable" as being able to buy an $80 blouse or a $250 suit, while also claiming it would take $100,000 to 150,000 to be "comfortable." But this same woman did think there was "extravagance" in $1,000 suits.[87] So, too, are "we" likely to view the 70,000-square-foot house built by a Microsoft founder as simply "too much."[88] The reaction to the German "luxury bishop" of the Diocese of Limburg, who was disciplined by Pope Francis for building a $42 million residential complex, is an unmistakable sign that people make these judgments;[89] so, too, the reaction to the residential building projects by Archbishops John Myers and Wilton Gregory.[90] People do make these judgments—and they should make them more carefully about their own choices as well. Even if we lack reflective and socially explicit standards, we are still likely to operationalize the necessity/luxury distinction in practice. Perhaps having children is the remedy: their pleading for particular goods might push us to make the distinction explicit.

The inability to eradicate this distinction arises even in technical economics: "luxury goods" are formally known as "those goods for which expenditures rise more than proportionally with income."[91] Flipped on its head, necessities or "needs" are goods that "are relatively impervious to changes in price."[92] The empirical observation of differing elasticities for different goods is not a moral distinction, nor is it equivalent to the broader moral discourse about luxury. But it does indicate some empirical basis for understanding different types of goods—and that people want different goods in different ways with some regularity—and suggests the plausibility of people making a real distinction between necessity and superfluity.

Developing Categories of Necessity: American Spending Patterns

Because of evidence for the appropriateness of satiability and for the resilience of a necessity/luxury distinction in social policy and individual judgment, it seems quite reasonable to believe in the distinctions made by early twentieth-century economists—but also quite unreasonable to imagine that persons or societies do not operationalize standards of restrained comfort and a differentiation of "higher" goods that imply judgments about luxury. But this is only half an answer. That is, we've established a reasonable case for the *existence* of relative standards; however, can reasonable cases be made to adjudicate between better and worse identifications of the *content* of the standards?

A further development of consumer prudence requires more general information about common patterns that will help frame a reasonable judgment about necessities—and thus raise questions about spending outside this realm. Questions about variations or exceptions to the basic pattern can then be engaged; that is, an inductive approach to necessity seems more reasonable than a deductive one. Setting a reasonable standard doesn't mean criticizing all spending beyond basic needs. Rather, it means that going beyond the standard will require some kind of explanation about the intention of such spending: will that explanation be one that evidences a disposition to luxury, or will it proceed from some other disposition?

I want to suggest three stages for such prudence: the first identifies reasonable convergences in overall living budgets and allows for a broad understanding of what is reasonable spending on necessity; the second explores the details within specific categories of budgets to identify social structures and individual choices that may involve luxurious excess; and the third recommends further prudential discernment best undertaken within local communities.

Prudence requires accurate "seeing": what would a necessities budget look like in today's society? The main distinction for establishing reasonable parameters for a standard of living is choosing between people's actual expenditures and estimated budgets prepared by experts. The first identifies what people actually spend, on average; the second makes judgments about what they should spend and is based on surveys of what things actually cost. As shown in a historical study by David Johnson, John Rogers, and Lucilla Tan, BLS studies until 1981 followed the latter "expert budget" method, which the authors dub the "prescriptive method." But, as they note, "[b]y the late 1960s, BLS was increasingly uncomfortable with its role of making the normative judgments that were the basis of the family budget cost estimates. In 1969, BLS Commissioner Geoffrey Moore, wrote: 'I do not think the BLS should set itself up as an authority on what is adequate or inadequate, what is a luxury and what is not, etc., no matter how reasonable the position may seem to us.'"[93] In 1980 an expert committee was convened, whose purpose "called for a radical departure from past practices, such as abandoning attempts to derive detailed lists of goods and services that were intended to represent norms or standards in favor of estimating total budgets directly from expenditure survey data."[94] This moved the measurement to what the authors call a "descriptive method": "The standard designed to reflect the level of living achieved by the typical family would be set at the median expenditure of two-parent families with two children and be called the *Prevailing Family Standard* (PFS)."[95] The new standards of living were presumed to be determined by whatever the median household spent. Further standards were set as a percentage of the PFS—a "lower standard" at two-thirds, a "social minimum" at one-half, and a "social abundance standard" at 50 percent higher. While the PFS is an empirical judgment, the establishment of other categories ("social minimum") using benchmarks still suggests some normativity.

Each method has advantages and disadvantages. Since the goal of this chapter is not social-scientific precision but rather the exercise of prudence, we can approach the problem by bringing together the two methods and making comparisons. Consumer expenditure data is readily available from the BLS Consumer Expenditure Survey (CEX); "expert budgets" are available in the form of many "living wage" calculators that make normative judgments about what to include and what to exclude, and at what level, in determining an adequate wage. The use of multiple calculators and an examination of their assumptions yields more data for better prudential judgment.

The first question to consider is which categories of spending should be included as "necessary." Four categories—food, housing (including utilities), transportation, and medical care—are typically included. All living-wage calculators use them, and according to CEX data, even households making $125,000–150,000 devote over half of their spending on these.

What do the two methods reveal about actual spending? Complexity is introduced because each method deals differently with the data. The BLS spending data aggregates households in many different circumstances; for comparison, Lawrence Mishel's detailed breakdown focuses on family income, noting that in 2010 the average *family* income for the "middle fifth" income bracket was $62,268—the comparable number when nonfamily households were factored in was $50,865. Even here, as Mishel notes, average "family" size has decreased over time, and "family" still includes units like retired couples.[96] On the other hand, living-wage calculators necessarily make assumptions not only about what categories to include but also about certain key decisions that may not apply to all households (e.g., child care expenses may be reduced or eliminated because of informal familial care arrangements or marital status, or transportation costs may be reduced by proximity to work or carpooling). Many calculators add a "miscellaneous" category to deal with other obviously necessary but relatively minor expenses (e.g., basic clothing, cleaning supplies) that may vary for personal and life-cycle reasons but which must nevertheless be included.

If differing assumptions about certain expenses are factored out, significant convergence is seen in the living-wage studies. Alongside the current data included in table 1, Jared Bernstein's exhaustive book-length study of over twenty different living-wage budgets constructed by different organizations in the mid-1990s provides evidence for this convergence. Bernstein carefully notes the assumptions of each budget and provides an overall average: $44,610.51 in 2014 dollars for a family of one adult and two children; and $53,561.21 in 2014 dollars for two adults and two children.[97]

Table 7.1. Comparison of current cost-of-living data

	EPI Living wage, family, MD	JOBS NOW Living wage, family, MN	CEX 2009 Income 40K–50K[a]	CEX 2009 family	CEX 2009 Income 100K–120K[b]
Food	$9,048	$8,280	$5,384	$9,827	$9,622
Shelter+Utilities	$15,012	$13,440	$11,990	$19,141	$18,808
Transportation	$7,284	$5,460	$6,393	$9,988	$12,378
Medical	$4,554[c]	$5,448	$2,937	$3,460	$4,385
Misc. spending	$6,156	$3,804	$12,849	$27,913	$30,947
Total spending	$42,054[d]	$36,432[e]	$39,553	$70,329	$76,140

Note: For all examples, "family" is a four-person household. The JOBS NOW calculator i for the state of Minnesota (metro Twin Cities): see http://www.jobsnowcoalition.org/calc lator/calculator.html. The Economic Policy Institute (EPI) calculator can be customize to any US location. The Maryland numbers here are for Baltimore: http://www.epi.or /resources/budget/. The BLS data is available at http://www.bls.gov/cex/csxstnd.htm.

a. This income bracket includes an average household with 2.5 persons, 1.3 of whom work and 0.6 children. For a larger household the numbers would be predictably smaller tha these estimates.

b. This income bracket includes an average household of 3.0 persons, 1.9 of whom work and 0.8 children.

c. The EPI calculator assumes no employer subsidy for medical insurance. For compariso purposes only 25 percent of the number is used, to represent a typical employer-subsidize plan share. The JOBS NOW calculator includes subsidized employer insurance. The CE data measures only direct medical spending. Thus, the comparison here is difficult.

d. The total here is less than what the web calculator shows (the estimator includes chil care, whereas the JOBS NOW calculator assumes no direct child care expenses for a fou person family). Child care expenses have been omitted from all the data for now, for eas of comparison.

e. The JOBS NOW database assumes that this family will have a negative income tax bil and their income needs are thus lowered. The EPI, strangely, has a *substantial* positive ta bill. Since CEX data measures income and spending before taxes, taxes are not include in either wage calculator.

Since an "average" budget combines many differing assumptions, Bernstein also constructs his own family budget for a two-parent, two-child family living in Baltimore: the total before-tax budget is $45,214.78 in 2014 dollars.[98] In Bernstein's own estimate, a miscellaneous expenses category is about 12 percent of the overall budget; in constructing the budget he makes deep spending distinctions (e.g., the family can rent an occasional movie but doesn't go out to the movies) instead of simply stating a percentage estimate. He notes that his own estimates "make the conservative choice to omit" a whole series of items, which implies real "hardships and difficult choices" for those living by his basic standard.[99]

Comparing these converging expected estimates to actual spending is more challenging. Table 1 provides several illustrations of segments surveyed in the CEX. The average spending for households consisting of husband, wife, and two children, with the oldest child 6 to 17 years (the closest BLS category to a two-parent, two-child household), is $70,329 from an average income of $94,302.[100] "Average" is notoriously unhelpful here, since it obviously includes the income and spending of very wealthy families. The BLS data does allow us to look at the average spending of households by income bracket as well—so the average income for households in the $40,000–$50,000 bracket is $44,733, while average spending is $39,553 and nearer the point of the wage calculators. Keep in mind that these households vary significantly in size, state of life, and geographical location. Significantly, the $40,000–$50,000 income bracket is the lowest bracket having pretax income higher than expenses; households making less spend more than their incomes.

How might we utilize these various forms of observation in answering our question about the definition of basic needs? The point here cannot be to establish fixed, absolute standards; rather, the best that can be done is to offer some guidelines for discernment that we might fruitfully compare with our own spending. An effective judgment about surplus may also be assisted by a guideline number that would represent an estimate of where surplus might begin. It is not unreasonable to suggest that a number around $50,000 is today a reasonable proxy for a basic standard of living for a household of four; that estimate runs slightly above the calculators and presumes that some small amount of ongoing saving for life events and discretionary spending is reasonable. (The question of retirement savings will be addressed later.) This "proxy" number can be adjusted slightly upward or downward for household size. It also can be adjusted for the cost of living in different locations, which varies most significantly as related to housing. But even this variance need not be large. According to the Department of Housing and Urban Development, fair-market rents in major cities for two-bedroom apartments varied from $740 per month in Cincinnati and $772 in Pittsburgh to $1,412 in Washington, DC, and $1,610 in San Jose.[101] Even at the full DC rent, the (spartan) living-wage budgets require an income just over $45,000, so perhaps $55,000 would work as a reasonably safe estimate. Pittsburgh rents are several thousand dollars a year lower, so perhaps $45,000 would work in Pittsburgh. Still, this is not a wide range.

A guideline number is useful for recognizing poverty as well as recognizing luxury. As is well known, many in our society work and earn much less than this range. Joseph Stiglitz provides a rough calculation of $16,640 a year for a full-time worker getting $8.50 per hour.[102] Average annual wages for many low-skill positions in our society are well below $30,000.[103] Bernstein suggests that the actual expenditures of low-income families are somewhat lower than the experts recommend in living-wage studies, as households scrimp on necessary expenses—or acquire these goods outside of ordinary market exchange.[104] Our guideline number for necessity confirms the concern about a lack of living wages in our society.

On the other hand, what about those above the guideline number? In an affluent society it is not unreasonable to expect to live somewhat higher than a "basic needs" standard. The expansion of the production possibilities frontier is real. While one may rightly pursue a vocation to holiness of life through more intentional asceticism and renunciation, John Paul II nevertheless says that "it is not wrong to want to live better."[105] (As he quickly makes clear, however, the decisive question is whether this is directed to "the quest for truth, beauty, goodness and communion with others for the sake of common growth" or simply to "enjoyment as an end in itself." This distinction is central to the next chapter.) Critiquing luxury is an alternative to an all-or-nothing approach. Here we might draw on the earlier distinction between being comfortable and pursuing luxury. Studies over a substantial period of time indicate that a level understood as comfortable in a given social setting could be set at 50 percent higher than a "getting along" or "adequate" standard.[106] That would offer a rough guideline for comfort-without-luxury to be $75,000 in annual expenditures for the four-person family. Again, these are not absolutes, but rather guidelines for prudence. (And, again, I have omitted certain considerations, most notably college and retirement savings, issues that are complex given the odd tangle of public and private provisioning.)

There is no doubt that many professional positions pay substantially more than the above numbers, and that many families making $100,000 feel like they are just getting by.[107] Yet it would seem that considerable amounts of this spending would require some kind of justification. If $45,000–$50,000 is the place (roughly) where surplus begins—a place at or below which about half of American households fall—then it is here where the questions about luxury should be asked. This is not to say all surplus spending is bad, nor that someone making $30,000 is not subject to the vice of luxury (although at that level such a person will likely pay a heavy toll for indulging the vice). It is simply the area where prudential judgments about luxury come into play. If these seem like surprising numbers then the reader cannot help but realize their position of social privilege. It is not "normal" by any general social standard to be making and spending $100,000 a year, much less $300,000. But labeling excess income as "privilege" does not mean to suggest that it is bad. Rather, it simply requires answering these questions: What should those with such privilege do with it? What responsibilities attach to this wealth and income? As noted earlier, the moral problem denoted by luxury is not a rejection of surplus wealth per se. Instead, it is a claim that excess wealth can be used well or badly, in ways that are well-ordered or inordinate.

A vivid example of this problem is given by a recent *Washington Post* article about a family in the Virginia exurbs.[108] Their dicey economic situation is profiled as an example of how the middle class are still struggling despite the economic recovery. Both parents are employed, and their income is nearly $90,000, but they still talk about the financial problems they have and their struggles to pay all the bills. When asked how much they would need to feel secure, the wife immediately responds that $150,000 would be needed. Yet the extensive online comment boxes on the article reveal the doubts many readers feel about how this family spends its money. Thanks to low-interest-rate refinancing, their mortgage payment is low ($700 a month) so many commenters with much larger mortgage payments wondered where all that income is going. The point of this example is not to make light of a well-intentioned family's economic struggles. Rather, it is to illustrate the larger point about the need for prudence to be able to make reasonable judgments about necessity, so that families like this one in the 39 percent—that is, the upper two quintiles of household incomes—assess their situations accurately and constructively, particularly in relation to the larger population that makes so much less.

The suggestion of a particular level of income, or at least a reasonable range, should hardly be shocking. As noted earlier, John Ryan forthrightly suggests that in the 1910s, "the majority of families that expend more than $10,000 per year for the material goods of life would be better off in mind and character if they had kept below that figure."[109] The 1919 study of Washington workers offered the number $2,262.47 for families with three children, and a similar study found $2,143.94 as the standard for those living in small towns.[110]

In using monetary numbers to establish spending levels, we cannot avoid the difficult interface between judgments about goods and the money cost of those goods. The easiest way to determine a standard level for needs is to identify the amount of money that is needed, but at some point this money amount must link up to a qualitative judgment about the goods themselves. Even more challenging is the fact that each of our four basic categories exists within markedly differing market-delivery systems. Consider transportation costs: these vary substantially based on the reliability and fuel consumption of a given vehicle, and the choice (or lack of choice) of housing affects the amount of driving and the need for constant availability of a car. As we know, the use of marginal networks of public transportation may be possible and cheaper but arduous. In this last example, is a car a luxury or a necessity? Or is it luxury to purchase more expensive housing that is close to efficient public transportation? Is buying a reliable car ultimately worth the extra expense? The exercise of making these judgments prudently invites further consideration of two issues that were encountered earlier in the discussion: the interdependent, social characteristics of consumption and the importance of understanding consumption in terms of individual tradeoffs.

Regarding the social character of particular necessities, Amartya Sen's capabilities approach to establishing a standard of living can be helpful. Referring to the difficulties encountered by Pigou, Sen notes that the concept of an "objective minimum of conditions . . . has a good deal of immediate plausibility" but runs into problems when "taking stock of commodity possession" becomes the measuring stick.[111] Instead, the standard of living "is really a matter of functionings and capabilities, and not a matter directly of opulence, commodities, or utility."[112] Sen focuses on questions like: "Can they take part in the life of the community?" and "Can they appear in public without feeling disgraced?" and "Can they visit friends and relations if they choose?"[113] As one author puts it, while the capabilities approach "produces a host of difficult, often normative, questions" and "raises innumerable operational problems," it also suggests that *social participation* is the standard that should and does guide prudential judgments about the necessity level for commodities.[114] This accords well with the Catholic social principle of dignity as participation in society.[115] This sort of analysis is not suited to one-size-fits-all templates, but it can helpfully shape thoughts on prudence. Transportation can be seen as a necessity, for example, but what is specifically required will vary not simply by individual preference but also by measuring what is necessary for ordinary social participation.

Another interesting example would be a household Internet connection. Much social participation now relies on an Internet connection . . . but perhaps not the super-fast ones.

Sen's capabilities approach was anticipated in the work of Institutionalist economist Hazel Kyrk. Kyrk argued that standards of living for consumption are social phenomena. They are ends "which it is incumbent upon one to realize"; the failure to do so "causes a feeling of insufficiency and of privation" (176). In many cases socialized consumption involves not simply individual survival needs but "prestige values" (225)—such as the desire for "respectability" or "distinction" (202–3)—or for a "group of values which make life interesting, enjoyable, or worthwhile" (229)— such as excitement, play, creativity, and community. She notes that these beyond-physical-survival needs are not able to be disentangled from simple material consumption. Most goods do not serve only one good or another; rather, they are "bundles of utilities" that serve overlapping ends. An exercise group may be an occasion to achieve health but it also may serve as a mark of a "worthwhile" life in our society. On the flip side, it can also be an occasion to display to others the latest in high-tech exercise gear or the leisure time one has available to devote to exercise.

Kyrk's key point, seen especially in her rejection of the theory of marginal utility, is that these standards for consumption are not "haphazard" variations among individuals: they are defined strongly by society and groups within it.[116] Problems happen when standards surpass income and/ or productivity gains. She says: "An interesting element . . . is that if the 'simpler life,' the lowered mode of living, is known to be voluntary, or if 'everyone' else is adopting the change in question, the disagreeableness is partly removed."[117] That is to say, if the standard for public presentability in dress is lowered, then "necessity" becomes easier to achieve for all. She is making a point we have made throughout this book: standards of consumption can be vicious because they aren't properly portrayed as innocuous individual wants but rather shape and are shaped by the standards of others. Consumption is a collective activity, not simply a private one.

Nevertheless, the social interdependence of some items of consumption does not close off a second area for prudence: individual judgment about various tradeoffs. Why buy the stylish car if you can buy the reliable one? Why live in the larger house with no walkability when the smaller, slightly more expensive one would be okay—and also consider saving money by owning only one car and using it less? Do large houses necessitate the purchase of extra furnishings and raise energy costs? Why buy $5 lattes yet complain that sustainably produced and traded food is too expensive? In other words, what counts as necessary is in part a matter of social standards, but achieving that functioning also involves prudent individual choices. Kyrk rightly notes, "There is abundant evidence that expenditure and buying are more and more coming to be regarded as problems requiring skill and thought."[118]

Examining Consumption: Social Interdependence and Individual Tradeoffs

A basic-needs budget is a starting point, not an ending point, for reflection. A further two-dimensional analysis would examine both the structures of social interdependence—which can tend toward luxury when collective-action problems of shared restraint are ignored—and individual tradeoffs—which themselves can aim at the various aspects of luxury (i.e., ease, convenience, novelty, status). Examples could fill many books. Here, some general patterns and a few instances where the problem of luxury arises are identified.

Food and Clothing

Over the course of history, much of the rise of the standard of living was a matter of devoting a smaller and smaller share of wage income (and time) to securing the most obvious necessities of food and clothing, with a corresponding increase in available discretionary time and income. Francis Hutcheson's eighteenth-century estimate was "in a nation of any tolerable extent of ground, three fourths employed in agriculture will furnish food to the whole."[119] David Ricardo's fight against the Corn Laws in favor of free trade was a recognition that rent-seeking landlords having the ability to prevent the importation of cheaper food was a major drag on economic growth.[120] The data bears out the extraordinary reduction in the percentage of national and household income devoted to food purchases. The early twentieth-century studies include subsistence-level budgets in which 44 percent of income is devoted to food alone, whereas Jared Bernstein's aggregate of living-wage budgets in the 1990s show that just over 15 percent went to food.[121] The BLS's history of consumer spending affirms this steady drop, as do other sources.[122] For all consumers, food and clothing represented 22 percent and 10 percent, respectively, of total consumer spending in 1950, compared to 7 percent and 3 percent in 2010.[123]

The achievement of inexpensively produced necessities seems like a great benefit of our economic system, and to some degree lower-cost goods are the result of production efficiencies, which markets incentivize well in situations of wide consumer choice. For example, the amount of labor to grow agricultural commodities has dropped by shocking amounts: 100 bushels of wheat took 106 labor hours to grow in 1910, but in 1980 it took only 7.[124] On the retail side, Marc Levinson tells the story of "the great A&P," the first and biggest grocery chain, whose expansion had the effect of lowering the entire nation's food bill. A&P leveraged its size to gain discounts from suppliers (eventually becoming its own wholesaler), implement company-wide efficiencies, and accept lower margins (which was possible at a larger scale).[125]

However, there is a shadow side to this achievement. Analyzing necessary spending on food and clothing runs head-on into what Ellen Shell calls "the problem of cheap." As she notes, "'Everyday low prices' are built on everyday crummy lifestyles, not only for Mexican cloth cutters and Thai shrimp farmers and Chinese toy makers, but for all of us."[126] "Cheap" means that while extremely low-cost goods are available, such goods may be of questionable quality and durability and their cheapness may depend on labor and environmental practices that contradict basic principles of Catholic social teaching. In this case, our food and clothing use may look disturbingly similar to the uses by the luxurious rich of earlier times, who could carelessly dispose of goods and rely on slaves to keep on producing.

In this context, judging ordinate desire and avoiding luxury may not be a matter of spending less money—that is, price may not be the primary marker of luxury. Choosing more expensive food and clothes could be a matter of prudence and justice, not of luxury. However, what we often do is spend more for reasons of luxury (e.g., convenience and status considerations) and then demand unjustifiably cheap goods for other necessities. That is, we demand cheap in some areas but are perfectly willing to spend in others—for luxury reasons, not for justice ones. How exactly does this tradeoff work? Consider the $5 coffee concoction, a nearly everyday purchase for many Americans. It embodies a certain excess: it is often high in calories, it is not nutritious in any way (it's almost all sugar and fat), it is highly profitable at its price point. It might be readily recognized as a luxury by someone trying to "cut back" in a family budget. It is often a target of consumer critiques in part because it is commonly desired among those who otherwise find critiques of consumerism appealing—for example, some think a cartful of goods at Walmart is consumerism run rampant but their mocha lattes not so much.[127] The latte is also a product that is imported from poorer countries (coffee, chocolate, sometimes sugar), which raises serious questions about exploitation despite the high profit margin. Yet the combination of pleasure and convenience (someone else probably prepares it, even though it could be made at home at a much lower cost) is often irresistible to many who otherwise consider themselves conscientious consumers.

This is not to say that the $5 coffee by itself is a significant moral problem, although whether one should consider it as an occasional treat rather than a daily item is a question. But many people who pay $5 a day for it also resist paying the $6 price attached to a gallon of organic, sustainably farmed milk instead of the bargain-basement-priced milk. How is this tradeoff to be justified? Here is an example of how legitimate justice concerns get sidelined in favor of private pleasures—that is, seeing these consumption choices together, the resistance to justly produced food is clearly a matter of the disposition to luxury, of preferring certain private goods and pleasures to important considerations of the common good.[128] The disposition is displayed in the effective tradeoff involved in two choices: cheap milk, expensive coffee drink. The important issues of food justice and faithfulness in sustainable food production fail here . . . but not because people are seeking injustice. Rather, they are disposed to luxury and end up tolerating injustice. An early-century budget study particularly advised limiting "outside meals" and "out-of-season foods" as luxuries; despite significant changes in our food economy, it still may be the case that we opt for the luxuries of eating out and year-round asparagus but then don't pay what justice requires for other parts of our nourishment.

Clothing follows a similar pattern. Notoriously, much of our clothing is made under suspect, often deadly conditions, as was illustrated by a series of factory disasters in Asia in late 2012 and early 2013.[129] One wonders what the "real cost" of a T-shirt might look like if one sought to implement the basic expected labor and environmental standards that are applied to American workers, even the inadequate standards of large-scale American dairies that produce the cheap milk. One study cited by Nelson Lichtenstein indicated that the implementation of fair labor standards at one Reebok factory pushed the wholesale cost of a pair of shoes from $7 to $11.[130]

Somewhat more expensive clothing might not be a problem, considering the fact that we already have way too much. As a society we might consider clothing as the single most obvious category where we have actually reached "nonscarcity." Pietra Rivoli describes the scene at a Bethesda, Maryland, Salvation Army drop-off site: "they need to clean out their closets to make room for new stuff" and "they shake their heads, not sure how they ended up with so many T-shirts." For the Salvation Army, "the supply now so far outstrips domestic demand that only a fraction of the clothing . . . stays in the United States." The rest becomes part of an ever-increasing mound of used clothing exports that have risen from around 100,000 kg in 1989 to nearly 350,000 kg in 2003.[131] At least that mound is not thrown away: Rivoli notes that "the average American throws away about 68 pounds of clothing and textiles a year."[132] A visit to the local Goodwill, if not to one's own closet, will convince easily that we really have pretty much all the clothing we need. Unlike food, clothing ought to be relatively durable and, except for the case of growing children, the level of sufficiency can seemingly be reached quite easily with minimal expenditure for replacement.

Because we don't "need" clothes, we are resistant to price increases (at least on basic items) and manufacturers respond in two ways. One way is by relentlessly cutting production costs.[133] As with food, some cost-cutting comes simply from "mechanization and technological progress."[134] But as one advocate put it in the wake of the Bangladeshi factory disasters, "Quite honestly the most effective things that consumers can do is really educate themselves about how the things we buy every day are made and ask ourselves do we need 20 T-shirts."[135]

Producers also support prices and their income by catering to our desires for convenience, novelty, and status. As Michelle Gonzalez explains, the real issue with clothing in today's society is that "the value of fashion is entirely constructed."[136] The fashion industry supplies "disposable clothing" that "individuals purchase and wear one or two times because it is (1) too trendy to wear more than that; and (2) because its quality is so poor it often begins to fall apart after a few wears."[137] Juliet Schor notes that it is "almost unfathomable" that clothing can now be bought by weight for less than rice, driven by companies' desires to turn clothing into a commodity like toothpaste or detergent, a "fast-moving consumer good," disposable and constantly changing.[138] But the strategy has been incredibly financially successful: the average consumer purchased 34 new clothing items in 1991 but almost double that number (67) in 2007.[139] End it, don't mend it, as the saying goes from Aldous Huxley's *Brave New World*.

The "designer T-shirt priced at $300" that Gonzalez mentions is on the other extreme. With little evident distinction in functionality, or even quality, clothing prices can escalate rapidly, particularly in terms of brands with cultivated luxury images.[140] Clothing remains a crucial social status marker in these ways. Outside of fast fashion or haute couture, our social norms also seem to dictate an unnecessary variety in dress. We encounter clearly our tendencies toward luxury, both in terms of social standards (people would notice if you wore the same 4 shirts all the time) and individual tradeoffs (preferring to pay for a stockpiled variety instead of durability and justice).

Housing and Transportation

Shelter and transportation markets have notably different dynamics from those of food and clothing. The cars we drive and the houses we live in were probably manufactured in just ways (although some of the underlying raw material supply chains might have problems). A comparison of older budget studies shows that the proportional amount spent in these areas has not decreased over time—indeed, to some extent spending in these areas has increased. As noted previously, transportation was around 2 percent of the 1920 government employee's expenses; today, transportation makes up around one-sixth of the $40,000–$50,000 household budget.

However, the expansive disposition for luxury—for comfort, convenience, and status—has created disorder of a different sort. The American dream of the post-1945 era is centered on the aspirations to a single-family house and a personal automobile.[141] Strictly speaking, neither of these can be considered as necessities in the way food and clothing are. Since most production (particularly of food) has moved outside the home, extra land and household square footage is now dedicated to additional consumption. Our standards for house size have changed radically over the past century and in fact, the *average* American new home size has more than doubled since the early 1950s.[142] This average dwelling is over 1,000 square feet larger than the standard dwelling in most European countries, and many more European units are semi-detached.[143] Even the early postwar suburbs featured houses that would now be scorned: the tidy Cape Cods of iconic Levittown were "down-to-earth and unpretentious," with a simple layout of a 12 foot x 16 foot living room, a kitchen, a bathroom, and two small bedrooms.[144] Moreover, those lot sizes were from one-fifth to one-tenth of an acre; today, many buyers desire "privacy" (read: luxury) which in turn drives the expansion of lot size (and sprawl). Larger home sizes also promote more and more furniture buying; as Juliet Schor notes, the physical amount of imported furniture in the United States *doubled* from 1998 to 2005, without any decline in domestic production.[145] Many Americans could easily live in smaller houses with smaller lot sizes—and reap a consequent environmental and cost benefit as well as a benefit for sociality. Smaller dwellings mean closer neighbors and more use of facilities and opportunities outside the home.

The excesses of our built environment have become intertwined with the "need" for a certain kind of transportation: a personal vehicle which is, as Jeff Speck puts it, a prosthetic device rather than an optional convenience.[146] Broadly speaking, transportation is a human need, but it is an instrumental one: one does not seek the car ride but the destination. Thus, social standards that undercut shared transportation significantly increase consumption resulting in special burdens for the poor. Bernstein notes that one living wage study focused on Washington, DC, budgets only 2.1 percent of expenditures for transportation, because it assumes that a household can forgo a car.[147] This particularly highlights the significant private economic burden imposed by social settings that virtually "require" the costs of car ownership. Of course, what is considered necessary in a car can mirror the unnecessary expansion of house size. Particular car choices, perhaps more than any other consumption good, involve expressing status—which is why so many cars (and houses and apartments) are advertised as "luxury."[148]

Houses and cars are quintessentially positional goods, that is, they are strongly influenced by relative considerations that go beyond status. Many people buy large vehicles in order to be safe in a crash; as Frank notes, when everyone does this no one is better off. Similarly, many people flee to "protected" suburbs and upscale housing enclaves for the safety and education of their children—but when everyone does this the effect is merely to bid up prices for the same relative position. These decisions are "smart-for-one, dumb-for-all"—private goods whose value is significantly determined by relative patterns of others' consumption even at the level of simply wanting a house or car that is somewhat "nicer" (a determination that will always be determined by what is the average). Enticing advertisements for positionally advantageous features of cars and houses like granite countertops and on-board computers leave the inevitable pricing effects to do the positional sorting.[149] Thus, these are areas where everyone's adoption of a simpler standard (in Kyrk's terms) or a shared "downscaling" (in Schor's terms), or perhaps even Frank's progressive consumption tax could produce significant redirection of economic energy and lessen unnecessary costs that proportionally fall most heavily on the poor.

Other "Necessities"? The Need for Communities of Discernment

Finally, one might wonder about what is being left out of the previous discussions. Aren't savings required for retirement? What about some form of vacation?[150] What about education, a service that lower-income households spend very little on but whose cost shoots up disproportionately for wealthier households?[151] Are they spending money on private schools for luxury reasons or for the sake of "higher goods"? For example, what about the Jesuit high school in the rich suburb that I was able to attend thanks to my parents' thriftiness . . . and their knowledge that there was "no way" I was going to a Chicago public school in the late 1980s? As with other categories, significant interdependence and tradeoffs are involved. My parents undoubtedly sacrificed some of their own ease and comfort in order to send my sister and me to a Catholic school; they also benefited from the childcare blessing of having my grandmother living in a condo a few blocks away. She never had a driver's license, which meant they kept us in the city (on a small lot) in an age when many had left for the suburbs. My family didn't really have family vacations when we children were in junior high and high school and we also never paid for television. Today the average Comcast subscriber pays nearly $150 a month for cable and Internet connection, a number that has increased at twice the rate of inflation for seventeen years, according to the FCC.[152] While we certainly didn't live in poverty, real tradeoffs were made in eschewing certain choices to enable others.

Once the discussion reaches this level of questioning, it will be beneficial to assess communal discernment with neighbors who share moral commitments to restraint. James Halteman, an economist teaching at Wheaton College, advocates local communities discerning the range beyond which one would need serious reasons to go.[153] He defends this kind of practice, saying that otherwise, "the church is forced into the position of saying that the rich and the poor, in many areas of life, do not have the same needs, or that the rich should be allowed to consume above their needs in areas of luxury."[154] He sees no biblical grounds that could be used to justify such a difference. Crucially, this point saves the consistency of the moral argument for *all* people to restrain their consumption because if one remains within this range, one accepts that any other member of the community should not be denied the standard chosen. Such shared communal discernment about one's money is modeled by the Lazarus at the Gate program discussed in the opening chapter.[155] One might in

Table 7.2. Categories of disproportionate spending by top earners

	Percent of overall spending for these goods by the top 20% of households
Floor coverings	58.6
Other lodging (hotels)	58.5
Education	56.4
Entertainment fees and admissions	56.2
Other vehicles (boats, campers, etc.)	53.1
Household personal services (cleaning, etc.)	51.6
Public and other transportation (bus, rail, air)	51.3
Mortgage interest and charges	47.4

Source: BLS Consumer Expenditure Survey, 2012; http://www.bls.gov/cex/2012/aggre
gate/quintile.pdf.

particular consider BLS data that reveals which categories of goods and services are disproportionately occupied by earners in the top 20 percent (see table 7.2).

John Ryan makes a similar point about discerning the living wage at a workplace: while paying a living wage does not require that a business be bankrupted, it does mean that if employers are already earning "a decent livelihood" then they "have no right to take from the product one cent more" until all have a living wage. Doing otherwise would wrongly imply that "the right of the employer to the means of indulging in luxurious living" is somehow "morally superior" to the employee's basic living needs.[156] In both cases the standard of living for all must be seen as having moral priority over anyone's luxury consumption. Trading off in the other direction—prioritizing one's luxuries over another's necessities—might be justified on the basis of an account of property rights as absolute, but not on a biblical or Catholic account of property and equal human dignity.

Such communal prudential discernment nicely accords with the recognition that luxury is both an individual problem and a social problem. Because the standard of living is genuinely a social standard, addressing excess is in part a problem of addressing social structures. These may be "structures of sin," where the relevant underlying vice is luxury. Standards for things like communication and transportation are inevitably based on what is expected for shared participation. As any parent knows, it is hard to deny a child a particular good if by doing so you cut the child off from his or her peer group. The effect, Mary Hirschfeld explains, is that "as those standards of living rise, even practitioners of economic virtue will feel socially compelled to raise their own standards of living."[157] Writing in 2006, Hirschfeld notes that cell-phone holdouts might consider what it is like to try to contact people who have held out against answering machines.

In discerning these choices, we should keep in mind two important problems: first, we as a society have lost our collective ability to discern what actually counts as an "advance." We too easily assume that new products mean better living. Clive Crook makes a common argument when he states that the complaints about "the stagnation of real incomes" of the middle class "[seem] belied by a steadily improving quality of life." As he says, "Who really believes that ordinary Americans are barely any better off in material terms than they were in the early 1970s? There were no cell phones back then, no video games; few homes had microwave ovens. There were no iPods, if you can imagine."[158] Recall economist Greg Mankiw's comment that average Americans today may be "richer than Rockefeller" because of everything from television to email to air travel to air conditioning.[159] Elsewhere, Mankiw illustrates the quality of life of economically growing societies by showing us three pictures of families with all their possessions outside their homes: one in Britain, one in Mexico, and one in Africa. The superiority of our economic system is supposed to be demonstrated by the extent to which the British family's possessions spill out all over their front yard.[160]

Is such a depiction or list really evidence of substantial improvement? Is it correct to measure economic success by the amount of stuff we can drag out onto our lawn? John Paul II rightly states that, "[t]he manner in which new needs arise and are defined is always marked by a more or less appropriate concept of man and of his true good." Driven especially by the need for corporate profit and expansion, the creation of new "needs" may be the single most lucrative business plan available. It may be a trivial consideration in terms of introducing a new brand of toothpaste but a quite different question when it comes to introducing new home designs, automobile features, or technologies. One can only imagine, with a shudder, what this could mean amidst possibilities in biotechnology. The importance of distinguishing "the good" from "the novel" cannot be overemphasized.

Second, as a society we have increasingly developed systems that assume and promote private independence over interdependence. From individual-sized frozen dinners to detached single-family suburban homes to cell phones for each individual person, material progress has come from adopting strategies that maximize personal choice and minimize potential cooperation and interdependence. Every 1980s teenager remembers the challenges of phone conversations when the phone was a shared household resource.

The biblical and patristic material we have encountered previously insists repeatedly that wealth is a problem specifically because of the ways it promotes notions of self-sufficiency and minimizes dependence on God and on others. Many students cite oversimplified versions of God's providence—"everything happens for a reason"—but who can deny the importance of chance encounters and forced cooperation for hearing the voice of God rather than listening to our own internal volitional monotone? Some of these developments might rightly be considered luxury insofar as they are chosen and used in order to make ourselves independent of others and/or mark off our status from others.

Perhaps the most vivid living illustration of the possibilities of social refusal of certain material standards comes from the Old Order Amish. The Amish practice careful (and sometimes communally divisive) discernment about limits that goes beyond simply saying yes or no, all while keeping in mind genuine human goods and, in particular, the overall good of the community and its traditional culture of work. For example, some Amish use a specially designed "classic word processor" advertised by its Mennonite developer as "made specifically for the plain people" and offering "unequalled safety": since it is not connected and has no sound or graphics it is "just a work horse for your business."[161] Shared phone shanties are common, rather than private lines.[162] Individual dress, houses, and vehicles should not be used to display income: "Incomes vary but it should not be that a person from the outside can walk into our homes and make a distinction between those who make $50,000 a year and those who make $250,000 a year."[163] Imagine if other Christian communities could even approximate such an ideal. The point here is not to recommend Amish rules, but rather to show communal prudence being exercised in a direct attempt at avoiding economic excess, specifically for the purposes of good work and communal solidarity.

Other Approaches to Necessity

Many people lack an awareness of what they are spending, how their spending relates to typical expenditures in our society, how society's expenditures might compare to those of the past, and what dynamics contribute to what is available at what price in a given market. Thus, the discussions above are meant to be aids for prudential judgment, not absolutes. Simply by gaining knowledge about these matters we are likely to make better judgments and recognize excess where it occurs, both in our individual tradeoffs and in our collective thinking about how personal consumption depends on collective social decisions.

We have approached this issue by making a broad argument for creating a baseline budget that assumes a range of categories are necessities and making judgments within categories by considering social participation, expert estimation, and a recognition that both individual and social choices can shape the achievement of basic needs. Further inquiry illuminates the decisive importance of the problem of luxury. For example, achieving a nutritious, even environmentally sustainable diet on the given food budget is quite possible, but one may fail in the attempt because more expensive healthful items are traded off in favor of junk food or prepared convenience food.[164] Such a tradeoff may be a sign of the disposition to luxury—that is, favoring spending on comfort, convenience, and/ or status over other priorities.

The ability to identify luxury via a particular budget with categories that are interrogated on both an individual and a social level is complementary to other approaches that provide different guides for prudential restraint of spending. Ronald Sider's well-known graduated tithe is a nice example: one gives 10 percent of a number that represents a basic standard of living and also gives a progressively larger percentage of everything above that amount.[165] While this differs from an emphasis on prudently analyzing consumption categories, Sider's approach manifests the fundamental notion of luxury as a problem: there exist moral claims on one's excess income, and acting on these claims requires some identification of basic standards in one's own life. Following Sider's advice inevitably would push households to constrain their excess spending, since more and more of it would have to be devoted to giving.

David Platt's evangelical bestseller, *Radical: Taking Back Your Faith from the American Dream*, also maintains that "we have in many areas blindly and unknowingly embraced values and ideas that are common in our culture but are antithetical to the gospel [Jesus] taught"—values like "self-sufficiency," "individualism," and "materialism."[166] Platt articulates the importance of the need "to connect the blessing of God with the purpose of God."[167] He advocates, among other things, "simple caps on our lifestyles" that would free us "to give the rest of our resources away for the glory of Christ in the neediest parts of the world."[168] Perhaps most power-fully, Platt has actually led his mega-church congregation in Birmingham, Alabama, to practice communal discernment—what he calls a "multiply-ing community," where spare resources are added together to address dire needs—on what he calls his "Radical Experiment."

Laura Hartman has recently developed another, more impressionistic approach to discernment, which she describes in her book *The Christian Consumer*. Hartman sets out "an effective and explicitly practical ethics of consumption" via four primary considerations: avoiding sin, embrac-ing creation, loving the neighbor, and envisioning the future.[169] Within each of these themes she develops a moderate, balancing approach that pushes people to a closer examination of daily consumption choices. All of her categories are sacrificial in their own way. For example, she offers a balanced assessment of prosperity theology in her chapter on "embrac-ing creation" and reminds readers that an "anthropology of abundance" is appropriate because "we can and should embrace the blessings God bestows."[170] Yet, even here, she notes that genuine enjoyment actually comes from "moderation" rather than profligacy, and that moderation also should encourage sharing of these joys.[171] Hartman's text does not cal-culate consumption ceilings; rather, it offers a Christian imagination for discerning "fitting" consumption. She makes luxury consumption morally problematic by painting it as theologically ugly.

As contemporary examples of Christian theologians working through the prudence of judging economic necessity, Protestant thinkers like Halteman, Sider, Platt, and Hartman are to be commended; unfor-tunately, few Catholic thinkers have dealt with this issue at length in recent times, except perhaps the US Bishops' controversial 1986 letter, *Economic Justice for All*.[172] Recall the topic that opened this chapter: a Catholic sense that the pursuit of higher standards of living might not be right. Recognizing the importance of standard of living is a justice issue: it makes clear what everyone deserves in order to live a life of human dignity. But it is also a luxury issue, warning of the problems involved when the concern is not "just getting by" but rather running far beyond a standard. John Paul II rightly recognized that the picture of the contem-porary world is of "the few who possess much who do not really succeed in 'being' . . . [and] the many who have little or nothing who do not suc-ceed in realizing their basic human vocation because they are deprived of essential goods."[173] Catholics may be countercultural in demanding a living wage, but they also might be countercultural in demanding simpler lifestyle choices from individuals.

Such a simpler lifestyle is not one that must sacrifice quality or even beauty, but it works to define those terms more clearly in the context of justice and charity. In particular, it is alert to the fact that our tendency to adopt necessities that foster luxurious stimulation and independence often come at the price of the sacramental possibilities of these necessities; these possibilities are outlined in Pope Benedict's economy of gift. We still use the image of someone who "will give you the shirt off her back" to exemplify someone who is unfailingly generous. Sharing in both the production and consumption of food, clothing, and shelter can provide plenty of magical connection. The economy depicted in *Caritas in Veritate* is in part a matter of what we do with our excess. But we can also reshape our approach to ordinary necessities, to the systems within which we procure them, and to the tradeoffs we make in seeking them. Seeing the possibilities for communion as present in alternative food economies or in a particular way of thinking about housing choices can inspire our imaginations to use our excess to foster sacramental reciprocity rather than to augment private pleasure and autonomy to infinity.

Notes

1. Thurow, *Zero-Sum Society*, 198.
2. John Paul II, *Sollicitudo Rei Socialis*, no. 28.
3. Michel, "Bourgeois Spirit," 77.
4. Ibid., 80–81.
5. Ibid., 82.
6. Ibid., 83.
7. Ryan, *Church and Socialism*, 191.
8. Ibid., 36.
9. Ibid., 37.
10. Ibid., 183.
11. Ibid., 182–83.
12. See also Day and Maurin's emphasis on "downward mobility."
13. *Catechism*, no. 2402: "The goods of creation are destined for the whole human race. . . . The appropriation of property is legitimate for guaranteeing the freedom and dignity of persons and for helping each of them to meet his basic needs and the needs of those in his charge. It should allow for a natural solidarity to develop between men."
14. Quoted in Horowitz, *Morality of Spending*, 81.
15. Ibid., 81–82.
16. Ibid., 83.
17. Chase, *Tragedy of Waste*, 88, citing economist Paul H. Douglas, "Economic Wastes of Luxury."

18. Ibid., 55.
19. Fallon, *Principles of Social Economy*, 486.
20. Lynds, *Middletown*, 83, 87.
21. Ibid., 87.
22. For more on this key contrast in Middletown between the small town of 1890 and of the 1920s see Fox, "Epitaph for Middletown," esp. 122–26.
23. Lynds, *Middletown*, 73–76.
24. On Taylorism and a Catholic alternative for job design, see Alford and Naughton, *Managing*, 104–6.
25. Barnes, *Wealth of the American People*, 648. Robert Wiebe's well-known history of the period is entitled *The Search for Order*.
26. Fox, "Epitaph," 125.
27. Horowitz, *Morality of Spending*, 36.
28. For example, an amusement park in midtown Minneapolis called Wonderland was completely constructed, used, and torn down in a span of only six years. And it was only open from mid-May to September. See http://en.wikipedia.org/wiki/Wonderland_Amusement_Park_(Minneapolis).
29. Horowitz, *Morality of Spending*, 151.
30. Patten, *Product and Climax*, 43, quoted in ibid., 35. While Patten is sometimes cited as an advocate of the new consumerism (e.g., Lears, "From Salvation"), Horowitz shows effectively that his work moves toward greater suspicion of the new culture and appreciation for self-denial.
31. Horowitz, *Morality of Spending*, 81.
32. Ezekiel, *$2500 a Year*, developed an elaborate plan of national production and distribution that was tied to specific (money) targets of consumption in each area of life.
33. Mitchell, *Backward Art of Spending Money*, 18–19.
34. See chap. 1.
35. Founded in 1936 to be a more stringent version of a "consumer research" group started in 1926, the union was typical of the economics of this period. Its most prominent manifestation is the magazine *Consumer Reports*.
36. *Standards of Living*, 40.
37. Horowitz, *Morality of Spending*, 15.
38. Ibid., 139.
39. Ibid., 174–75.
40. Appleby, "Moderation in the First Era," 150.
41. Horowitz, *Morality of Spending*, 53–56.
42. Rainwater, *What Money Buys*, 112.
43. *Standards of Living*, 26–27.
44. Compare Bernstein et al., *How Much Is Enough?*, 48–49, for some basic-needs budgets from the 1990s, where transportation, even conservatively estimated, takes 10 percent of a budget, and entertainment (if included) can easily push in an additional 5 percent. (Also reference ordinary splits for these.)
45. *Standards of Living*, 46.
46. Rainwater, *What Money Buys*, 124–25.
47. See also 1941 studies in Horowitz, *Anxieties of Affluence*, 23–34.
48. Mitchell, *Backward Art of Spending Money*, 4.

49. Marshall, *Principles of Economics* I, 1.
50. Ibid., 1, 2.
51. For the social and intellectual context for Sidgwick, Marshall, and Pigou, see Robert Skidelsky's chapter on Cambridge economics in *John Maynard Keynes*, 26–50, quoted at 49.
52. Pigou, *Economics of Welfare*, 1, 7.
53. Just as Keynes noted: "We must pretend to ourselves and to every one that fair is foul and foul is fair. . . . Avarice and usury and precaution must be our gods for a little longer still" ("Economic Possibilities for Our Grandchildren," 372). See the lengthier discussion in chap. 5. While not as influenced by Bloomsbury and Moore, Pigou was working in the same context and mentored Keynes, so Keynes's views are explicable as an extension of Marshall and Pigou.
54. Pigou, *Economics of Welfare*, 1, 10.
55. See chap. 3.
56. Indeed, there are ambiguities in Pigou's work about whether economics can provide any real analysis of the "non-economic" or if it can merely do the best it can to promote economic welfare and then hand off the baton to someone else.
57. Horowitz, *Morality of Spending*, 11, 63–64.
58. Skidelsky and Skidelsky, *How Much Is Enough?*, 89.
59. Suzumara, "Social Welfare Function," 418–19.
60. Robbins, *Essay*, 16, 66.
61. Ibid., 112–20.
62. Ibid., 125.
63. Ibid., 16.
64. Ibid., 38.
65. Ibid., 136–40.
66. Ibid., 148–49.
67. Stapleford, *Cost of Living*, 136, 140, 171, 217.
68. Ibid., 153, 363.
69. Rosenberg, "Consuming the American Century," 42–43.
70. Stapleford, *Cost of Living*, 363. Of course, the multiplier no longer fits the present context, but the formula is unlikely to be changed because it would prompt a sudden, massive "increase in poverty."
71. Berry, *Idea of Luxury*, 6.
72. Medaille, *Toward a Truly Free Market*, 96.
73. Skidelsky and Skidelsky, *How Much Is Enough?*, 75.
74. Schwartz, *Paradox of Choice*.
75. Here some economists would again note that the term "intrinsically satisfying" assumes a judgment of wants. Perhaps the maximizers get more utility out of the shopping experience and so this is where they establish their tradeoff. But this retort illustrates my point: Schwartz is using behavioral economics and happiness studies to demonstrate that there is experimental confirmation of the common intuition that shopping is best seen as a functional activity.
76. Layard, *Happiness*, 48.
77. Barron, *Strangest Way*, 63.
78. Danner, *Ethics for the Affluent*, 91–104.
79. See Musgrave, "Merit Goods," and "Public Finance," 452–53, 1055–61.

80. Berry, *Idea of Luxury*, 199.

81. For example, see the complete guide provided by Minnesota: http://www.health .state.mn.us/divs/fh/wic/newwicfoods/ppt/foods/index.html. The listing includes details such as making only unsweetened applesauces eligible.

82. Ryan, *Church and Socialism*, 58, 61. The quote: Leo XIII, *Rerum Novarum*, no. 34.

83. Cronin, *Social Principles*, 223.

84. Mack and Lansley, *Poor Britain*, 52.

85. This paragraph is partly taken from Cloutier, "Problem of Luxury." Another interesting source: surveys in Schor, *Overspent American*, 17. In 1996 only 13 percent of people saw a videocassette recorder as a necessity, only 26 percent a home computer, and only 17 percent basic cable. She compares air conditioning as a necessity over time: in 1973 only 26 percent saw it as necessary in the home, but in 1996 51 percent. For cars, the number rose from 13 percent to 41 percent. Further, somewhat older detail is well-displayed in Rainwater, *What Money Buys*.

86. Berry, *Idea of Luxury*, 6.

87. Hinze, "What Is Enough?," 183–84.

88. Frank, *Falling Behind*, 120.

89. AP, "Pope Expels German 'Luxury Bishop' from Diocese."

90. Gregory, "Apology for Cost of New House."

91. Frank, *Choosing the Right Pond*, 145. Also see Scitovsky, *Joyless Economy*, 107.

92. Skidelsky and Skidelsky, *How Much Is Enough?*, 89.

93. Johnson, Rogers, and Tan, "Century of Family Budgets," 32–33. The quote is from Goldberg and Moye, *First Hundred Years*, 233.

94. Ibid., 34.

95. Ibid., 34.

96. Mishel, *State*, 57–60.

97. Bernstein et al., *How Much Is Enough?*, 47–52. Inflation adjustments were made using the BLS calculator: http://data.bls.gov/cgi-bin/cpicalc.pl.

98. Ibid., 61. Most costs are equivalent in inflation-adjusted terms to current calculators, but the transportation number is markedly lower and the rental cost is considerably lower than what is now estimated for the Baltimore/Washington area. He includes child care in his budget.

99. Ibid., 16, 40–41. More specifically, he omits any cost for going out to eat, to cover credit card debt, to acquire insurance (other than auto), to save, to take vacations, or to acquire any "consumer durables."

100. 2009 CEX.

101. *World Almanac 2013*, 105, taken from US HUD figures.

102. Stiglitz, *Price of Inequality*, 9–10.

103. For examples of average wages by job, see "Selective Hiring Boom Forecast," with data from BLS 2010 Occupational Statistics Report.

104. Bernstein et al., *How Much Is Enough?*, 54–55. For comparison, total expenditures for the second quintile were actually $24,319 (1996 dollars) compared to his "average family budget recommendation" of $28,187. The breakdown of the data suggests that the underspending was accomplished primarily by skimping on child care as well as spending somewhat less than "recommended" on food and transportation.

105. John Paul II, *Centesimus Annus*, no. 36.

106. See Rainwater, *What Money Buys*; and Johnson et al., "Century of Family Budgets."

107. Ingraham, "Living Paycheck-to-Paycheck," cited a Brookings Institution study that states that roughly one-third of American households live "paycheck to paycheck," with two-thirds of these "not actually poor."

108. Morello and Clement, "'Happy Days' No More."

109. Ryan, *Church and Socialism*, 196. Ryan's figure, if using the year 1918, comes out to just over $150,000 in 2013 dollars. See http://www.bls.gov/data/inflation_calcu lator.htm. This would be somewhere between the top 5 and 10 percent of current households. Ryan's number is roughly five times the basic needs level of his day, a multiple that also matches the 1941 surveys cited by Horowitz.

110. *Standards of Living*, 40, 62. The DC number is $30,464.22 in 2013 numbers.

111. Sen, *Standard of Living*, 14–15.

112. Ibid., 16.

113. Sen, "Living Standard," 85.

114. Stapleford, *Cost of Living in America*, 340.

115. USCCB, "Seven Themes of Catholic Social Teaching."

116. Kyrk, *Theory of Consumption*, 172.

117. Ibid., 182.

118. Ibid., 85.

119. Hutcheson, *Thoughts on Laughter*, 69.

120. See Heilbroner, *Worldly Philosophers*, 98.

121. See Bernstein et al., *How Much Is Enough?*, 48–49. In the EU, by comparison, bottom quintile households spend 23 percent of their budgets for food. See *Living Conditions in Europe*, 83.

122. Johnson et al., "Century of Family Budgets," 33, shows 36 percent for food and 24 percent for clothing in 1919, compared to 18.2 percent for food and 4.5 percent for clothing in 1998.

123. "The Great American Divide," 32.

124. For this and other examples see Olmstead and Rhode, "Transformation of Northern Agriculture 1910–1990," 703.

125. Levinson, *Great A&P*.

126. Shell, *Cheap*, 231.

127. See, for example, Laura Hartman's use of it in *Christian Consumer*, 16–18.

128. For the standard and widespread problems with the pricing structure of the conventional dairy market, see Goodman, "The Future of Milk." On justly produced food overall in the Christian life, see Rubio, *Family Ethics*, 146–55.

129. See the following articles, and also note the *New York Times*'s graphic of the wages in various areas: http://www.nytimes.com/2013/04/25/world/asia/bang ladesh-building-collapse.html?pagewanted=all and http://www.nytimes.com /2013/05/17/world/asia/cambodia-factory-ceiling-collapse.htmland(wagesarticle); http://www.nytimes.com/2013/05/16/business/global/after-bangladesh-seeking -new-sources.html?pagewanted=all and PPP wages (incomplete); http://www .bbc.co.uk/news/magazine-17543356.

130. Lichtenstein, *Retail Revolution*, 173.

131. Rivoli, *Travels*, 176–77. She goes on to tell the lively story of the complex market into which all this used clothing goes, with hunts for "snowflakes" amidst massive bundles of "shoddy." This may sound generous, but "while North Carolina has lost its textile industry to low-wage workers from China, the African textile industry has lost to the high-wage workers of America, who live in a land of such plenty that clothing is given away for free" (199).

132. Ibid., 206.

133. The solution, of course, has been to find constantly lower and lower labor costs. See Schneider, "This Is Why."

134. Rivoli, *Travels*, 140–41, shows that while 60 percent of US textile jobs were lost from 1990 to 2004, the output of US plants stayed steady.

135. http://www.nytimes.com/2013/05/19/opinion/sunday/before-you-buy-that-t-shirt.html. Grieder, *One World–Ready or Not*, 388–412, describes in detail how the economic "miracles" in places like Indonesia and Thailand depend on absurdly low wages.

136. Gonzalez, *Shopping*, 16.

137. Ibid., 16.

138. Schor, *Plenitude*, 28–31.

139. Ibid., 30.

140. The *Wall Street Journal* can feature a story for "fashion week," where designers talk about "the $400 dress" as the "sweet spot" between the real high-end and mass-produced goods.

141. See Cloutier, "American Lifestyles."

142. On house size, see Polter, "Attack of the Monster Houses," and the US Energy Information Administration, "2009 Residential Energy Consumption Survey." The fascinating EIA survey reveals that the average size of all types of US dwelling units combined was 1,971 square feet, but the average single-family detached house was 2,483 square feet. Units constructed prior to 1990 averaged between 1,600 and 1,900 square feet, but the average jumped to over 2,200 in the 1990s and then over 2,400 in the 2000s.

143. See Yunghans, "Average Home Sizes." On the differences in housing size and how subsidies for mortgages and home-equity loans drive this problem, see also Garon, *Beyond Our Means*, 338–51.

144. On Levittown, see Jackson, *Crabgrass Frontier*, 234–39.

145. Schor, *Plenitude*, 34–35.

146. Speck, *Walkable City*.

147. Bernstein et al, *How Much Is Enough?*, 52.

148. Even a Prius commands a price premium, as calculated in Sexton and Sexton, "Conspicuous Conservation."

149. I will be exploring the difficulties of this problem in a paper to be presented at the 2015 Society of Christian Ethics conference.

150. "Travel" is particularly difficult to track in the BLS data because the data for various components of "vacation" (food, transportation, events) appear in different categories. For the category breakdown, see the diary used for the survey: http://www.bls.gov/cex/csx801_2013.pdf.

151. See USDA, "Expenditures on Children," 26–30.

152. See Stelter, "Comcast Reports Progress," and Wyatt, "As Services Expand."
153. Halteman, *Clashing Worlds*, 73. He suggests $30,000 in 1995, which is $45,000 in 2013 dollars.
154. Ibid., 84.
155. See chap. 1, and MacDonald, "Christians Shatter Taboos," 17.
156. Ryan, *Church and Socialism*, 71.
157. Hirschfeld, "Standards of Living and Economic Virtue," 73.
158. Crook, "Phantom Menace," 41.
159. See chap. 6.
160. Mankiw, *Principles of Economics*, 552–53. I cannot help but note that the British picture *helps* my case because, relatively speaking, their possessions are not that great compared to those of many upper-middle-class Americans. For example, one notes a minimal amount of relatively small and ugly kitchen appliances and two thirteen-inch tabletop television sets.
161. Harst and McConnell, *Amish Paradox*, 208.
162. Kraybill et. al., *Amish Grace*, 15, 199–200.
163. Harst and McConnell, *Amish Paradox*, 212.
164. Phillips, "Can We Afford to Eat Ethically?." She and her husband describe how they ate on the $248 government-defined minimum food budget for a two-person household.
165. See Hartman, *Christian Consumer*, 46.
166. Platt, *Radical*, 19. The term "bestseller" definitely applies: half a million copies were in print after less than a year: http://awakengeneration.wordpress.com/2011/02/03/radical-by-david-platt-reaches-radical-sales-500000-copies-in-print-after-only-10-months/.
167. Ibid., 87.
168. Ibid., 128. He adds we should not be asking "What can I spare?" but instead, "What will it take?"
169. Hartman, *Christian Consumer*, 5, 21.
170. Ibid., 66.
171. Ibid., 72–73.
172. An exception: Dubay, *Happy Are You Poor*, includes a chapter on "necessities and superfluities." Danner, *Ethics for the Affluent*, and Hinze, "What Is Enough?," begin to sketch proposals. Also Grisez, *Living a Christian Life*, contains an extensive treatment of handling possessions without any concessions to free-market conservatives. His contribution will be explored in chap. 8.
173. John Paul II, *Sollicitudo Rei Socialis*, no. 28.

CHAPTER 8

Luxury and Sacrament

What Is Beyond Enough?

In his encyclical *Sollicitudo Rei Socialis*, Pope John Paul II, following Pope Paul VI, noted the difference between "having more" and "being more." He writes that "[t]o 'have' objects and goods does not in itself perfect the human subject, unless it contributes to the maturing and enriching of that subject's 'being.'" The problem is not "having as such," but rather "the cult of having" that reverses "the hierarchy of values" and involves "possessing without regard for the *quality* and the *ordered hierarchy* of the goods one has" (italic in original). Goods must be subordinated to "man's 'being' and his true vocation."[1] The pope reaffirms the idea of the identification of "higher goods." If naming luxury prudently requires a contrast with some account of basic needs, it also relies on distinctions among different ways of disposing of material super-abundance. There must be a language (as Charles Taylor puts it) of "qualitative contrast" with luxury in the use of surplus goods that is dependent on the ends to which it is directed. If it is reasonable to suggest that a standard of living could be met for a family through the wise spending of $45,000 to $55,000 a year, then categories are needed for discerning what one could do with the rest of it . . . if one were not disposed to luxury.

What does this mean? As a fellow choir member queried, is it just a matter of giving away all the rest to the poor? This chapter suggests a more sophisticated set of distinctions, one that identifies how excess resources can be oriented to the manifestation of the sacramental economy of reciprocity rooted in gift (see chapter 4). While various sorts of charitable giving can be considered sacramental in this way, it is reasonable to imagine that our surplus can be used in additional ways, albeit ways that counter the tendency toward personal and social luxury. Above all, we need a positive moral language to specify our prudent use of excess resources because a language for critiquing luxury via limitation and self-denial is not enough; we must also offer alternatives that inspire a new "yes."

Christopher Berry makes the crucial point that the rise of "the commercially assumed innocence of luxury goods" is linked to an increasing "legitimacy of private desire."[2] Thus, fulfilling private desires becomes the default norm for surplus resources. But categories that are alternatives to the undisputed "legitimacy of private desires" need to be developed. The word "private" comes from the Latin *privatus*, to be lacking something.[3] To call goods private is to suggest they lack a proper ordering to the universal destination of goods at the heart of the Catholic understanding of property. Private desires themselves need to be critiqued in the light of some teleology and in particular their relationship to more "public" questions (work/vocation, investment, social cooperation, the sacrament of the poor).

The point here is not to reject private desire altogether, but rather to question the understanding of "private" that is being implied. Does private mean without social responsibility? Without standards of excellence? In other words, without any teleology beyond personal preferences and gratification? We have seen how questionable it is to imagine that any of our choices are private in this fashion. Rather, they involve underlying trade-offs that mark the idea that our surplus goods can be used well or badly. In this sense private desire is not, strictly speaking, private. Every choice is a moral choice in that it shapes both our character and the world around us.[4] The vice of luxury does not mean that all consumption beyond necessity is morally questionable, but rather that non-necessities must still be judged in relation to the order of reason instead of being understood as automatically legitimate. Put differently, Peter Danner indicates that the tendency of a culture of affluence's enabling of "want-proliferation" and "want-intensification" should instead be "sublimated into want-elevation."[5] Surplus should be devoted to higher ends, not private desires.

But what is that order and what are those ends? I propose a fourfold understanding of the proper ordering of surplus. Choices that are not oriented toward these goals, it seems, are instead oriented toward no end of genuine flourishing, whether a natural or a supernatural one. They in fact serve artificial or illusory ends, the ends of luxury described in prior chapters. Such choices are futile rather than fertile; by contrast, devoting these surplus resources to shared goods, vocational goods, festival goods, and enrichment goods directs our excess wealth toward our true transcendent ends in communion with others. It is important to carefully note how contemporary consumer culture plays upon these genuine desires by offering us luxury goods and services that are supposed to satisfy transcendent ends, but often they merely distort or lead to simulacra of them. Thus, this chapter develops further the ways in which the economy of luxuries is a misleading alternative to the genuine joy of the economy of reciprocity.

Shared Goods

Peter Danner writes: "People must share in order to be truly human."[6] The obvious importance of love and communion leads to a first category of sacramental consumption: "shared goods." At the heart of Catholic thinking on property is the universal destination of goods, whereas the definition of luxury has always entailed a kind of private exclusiveness, as though we can achieve happiness through an enjoyment of something as specifically our own, whether by maintaining exclusive control over it or, as Hume suggested, by sharing it in order to elicit admiration or simply to "lord it over others."[7] Identifying shared goods will help distinguish between the enjoyment derived from contributing to a common resource—one made available to others (especially the poor)—versus procuring goods for private and exclusive enjoyment. Many of our expenditures involve consuming goods that could be understood as private replacements for shared goods. A backyard playset or pool is a replacement for the neighborhood park. Purchase of leisure reading replaces queuing up for bestsellers at the local library. The use of public transportation or the more recent phenomenon of car sharing is rejected in favor of the personal car.[8]

The moral importance of shared goods can be seen in the reasons we might be tempted to forsake them for private goods. First, they are not at our immediate beck and call. Second, they may involve social interaction with strangers. Third, a choice may be limited or constrained and incapable of satisfying our exact desires. Note how preferring private goods manifests the characteristics of luxury and, in so doing, trades off the cooperation and sharing that allows sacramental reciprocity to develop. Moreover, support of these goods often turns out to be economically advantageous to myself and to others: my "share" of my county library's overall budget amounts to less than the cost of two hardcover bestsellers per year. And, as mentioned before, the goods are made available to those who might not otherwise have the opportunity to share the goods in the first place. The library budget not only supports reading materials for the poor; it gives access to job application materials, government information, Internet service, kids' books, and even a warm or cool place of temporary shelter.

Creative sharing of goods can go on in less formal ways as well, and this sharing can cut against tendencies to luxury. For example, I know a neighbor with a fine house who practices constant hospitality to many different people, hosting guests in and out in the way of the Old English manor houses, including some who need it because of their own lack of resources. Another friend shares a cabin in the North Woods with her extended family; family members schedule different weeks for use and they all share weekends when everyone pitches in on maintenance. Consider neighborly sharing with garden equipment and babysitting: why does everyone need to go to the local home improvement warehouse to buy twenty hedge trimmers when one or two could be shared by people on the same block, since they are used only for a couple hours every summer? The list could be multiplied many times over.

A more structural form of community sharing is the pooling of both capital and skills in a cooperative. Catholic social teaching has long highlighted the cooperative business form as particularly worthy of praise.[9] In their 1920 statement on social reconstruction, American bishops insisted on the importance of just wages, unions, and labor laws, but they also maintained that the "full possibilities" of the economy "will not be realized so long as the majority of workers remain mere wage-earners." Rather, they "must somehow become owners." This stage can be reached "gradually through co-operative productive societies and co-partnership arrangements."[10] In *Caritas in Veritate*, Benedict XVI commends "forms of cooperative purchasing like the consumer cooperatives that have been in operation since the nineteenth century, partly through the initiative of Catholics."[11] In a cooperative, both the capital and the profits from an enterprise are shared responsibilities and rewards of those who actually participate in the enterprise. The enterprise is responsible to the community using it, not through some external party (government law), but directly. Cooperatives allow for a wide sharing of real ownership in productive property.

Our willingness to share resources actively not only benefits others but facilitates relationships. Relationships, of course, make us vulnerable. A good friend suggested that one definition of a luxury could be "something where you get angry with a friend if they break it." But, it might be objected, don't good fences make for good neighbors? After all, Aquinas's classic defense of private property indicates that separating possessions is practical because people are more careful with their own goods and there is less occasion for quarreling.[12] This is true enough, especially in the context of a basic medieval agricultural economy. But shared goods also provide occasion for positive interaction, not just fights. One can think of many examples where one is more careful when borrowing someone else's goods. It is worth noting that Aquinas's main concern here is to defend ownership of property in terms of procuring and dispensing rather than in terms of use. Perhaps with expensive or necessary possessions, such as a computer or a car, shared possession makes less sense given the risks and potential problems. And perhaps it is better to avoid a purely communal shed of tools. But in many cases, informal neighborly sharing seems to be a risk worth taking. Our avoidance of it perhaps means we accord too much importance to particular goods and are unwilling to expose them to others' use.

The consumer economy recognizes this desire for goods for the purpose of sharing, making use of this sacramental meaning, but simultaneously redirects it toward conspicuous consumption. Ads contain images of elaborate kitchens and patio sets that echo with strains of hospitality (even as we entertain friends and neighbors in our homes far less than we used to). A long-standing advertising theme is the promise that consuming a particular good will lead us into communion with others. One well-known recent example is the MasterCard advertising campaign that totals up the spending on various outings, like a baseball game, and ends by noting that the time spent with family is "priceless" It concludes with the tag line, "For everything else, there's MasterCard."

These images especially invoke *family* sharing. When faced with the charges for excessive spending, many people defend themselves on the grounds of doing it "for their family." There is truth here, but prudence must carefully consider whether this is in fact more private than we let on. "Individualism" in the American context is often a privatized familialism in which the antisocial aspirations of luxury are simply extended to one's spouse and children. Thomas Masters and Amelia Uelman note this by quoting Alexis de Tocqueville's definition of American individualism as a sentiment "that disposes each citizen to isolate himself from the mass of those like him and to withdraw to one side with his family and friends, so that after having thus created a little society for his own use, he willingly abandons society at large to itself."[13]

Festival Goods

A second category not unrelated to shared goods is festival goods: the occasion of special expenditures and excess in service of communal celebration.

Lest the critique of luxury turn too dour, we should recognize the truth manifested in the classic movie *Babette's Feast*: elaborate goods can be the occasion for sacramental communion—if it truly is a special occasion. The movie, which centers on an elaborate feast that French Catholic servant Babette throws for her puritanical Protestant villagers, leading them to overcome their bitter community conflicts, is often cited as an example of a Catholic notion of sacramentality. The movie beautifully displays the ways in which joyful sharing of material goods can lead to interpersonal and spiritual peace and reconciliation.

Shannon Jung's theological writings on food similarly capture the central importance of the material world for fostering celebration. He writes enthusiastically that "there is a feast laid out for us, and we cheat ourselves and God out of enjoying it" because we are not open to recognizing God in the enjoyment of food.[14] "The forces of the universe sometimes line up in the pecan pie or the pasta. They become not only concrete and tangible; they are also succulent!"[15] Notably Jung's book also emphasizes that good food should be a shared good

Contrasted with luxury, the important point about festival goods is that they are occasional, both in the sense of being infrequent and in the sense of marking some more significant "occasion"; that is, the consuming is not an end in itself. Remember that luxury is a disposition—virtue and vice are about desiring the right things in the right circumstances. It is the regular, habitual desiring of excess—not its occasional celebratory use—that indicates the vice.

The importance of occasions of feasting and celebration is captured in the story of Jesus responding to queries about why his disciples eat and drink, whereas the disciples of John the Baptist fast. Jesus replies, "Can the wedding guests fast while the bridegroom is with them? As long as they have the bridegroom with them they cannot fast. But the days will come when the bridegroom is taken away from them, and then they will fast on that day" (Mk. 2:19–20). The point here is about timing: Jesus is not turning water into fine wine every day, but rather at a particular celebration. Similarly, exemplifications of sacramental understandings of creation can be trivializing and even misleading if there is not a recognition that delighting in material abundance is meant to be occasional. The needed prudence is a determination of timing.

Our feasting also might display a better connection to honoring producers and the poor. An outstanding example is the story of the Welcome Table at St. James Episcopal Church in Black Mountain, North Carolina, which offers "a high-quality meal, using fresh and often local organic ingredients" prepared by a former five-star chef under the slogan, "Whoever will, may come." The poor and homeless are treated like "patrons of the finest restaurant . . . like dignified human beings deserving of the best food available." Fred Bahnson, telling the story, says, "Why feed Jesus the dregs . . . when we could offer him fresh, organic vegetables?" The church collaborates with a local farmer, who runs a farm called The Lord's Acre; he notes that the work "makes social justice beautiful."[16]

These sorts of institutions should give us some sense of what constitutes festival. They mark time effectively and regularly, they are bound up with the actual social pattern of people's lives, they involve a kind of loosening or opening up of ordinary social relationships, and they entail a generosity about who is included in the celebration. Traditional communal festivals are intertwined with work, religion, and intergenerational connections, as in the neighborhood festivals of Italian Catholics highlighted by Robert Orsi.[17]

The category invites us to prudent discernment in our own lives. In today's world we might consider many variations on the neighborhood festival or some community sports celebrations. The event of holiday or vacation can also be a time for this. Certainly the restaurant dinner to mark an anniversary (or the end of the semester) is a kind of festival good, though in a limited way. Evidently the struggle in our culture is to figure out how to prevent these from becoming simply private occasions.

Festival goods can be corrupted in our consumer culture. The multiplication of regular "holidays," each with its own set of "sales," has become a kind of capitalist liturgical calendar. The market for festival goods can be expanded, and thus celebrations can be (a) produced for profit, and (b) marketed simply as a kind of personal entertainment or amusement. Key examples include the excesses of the wedding industry and the Christmas shopping season. Rebecca Mead notes that the sophisticated wedding-retailing business in the United States is now a $40–$50 billion industry, and since the number of weddings a year is pretty much given (one industry association called it "the purest example of an inelastic market"), the most important strategy is to upsell items constantly and push the need to make the wedding "magical" to the point of even using "a bride's anxiety" as an "opening for the self-assured salesperson."[18] Combatting Christmas excess, Bill McKibben writes of the experience of his church campaign for a "hundred dollar holiday," urging people to exchange homemade gifts, services, and the like instead of the "sprawling pile of presents under the tree."[19] Such a strategy is radical because in many lines of business, a significant chunk of sales volume is reliant on keeping up relentless new spending on the hottest (and even not so hot) items. But, as with the commodification of weddings, McKibben notes the most insidious problem of Christmas is that this "cram course in consumption" makes us believe that we need all this in order to celebrate. Commercializing Christmas means "consumption is made literally sacred. Here, under a tree with roots going far back into prehistory, here next to a crèche with a figure of the infant child of God, we press stuff on each other, stuff that becomes powerfully connected in our heads to love, to family, and even to salvation." The commercial Christmas could be seen as the great feast of the false religion of luxury marketing!

How might we prudently discern where the line is here? Consider four aspects of these examples. First, the festival aspect may be overwhelmed by a concern for self and/or status. Weddings become about me—and especially what I am communicating to others about my status—rather than about the festival itself (and, in particular, the actual liturgies). Second, this concern for self may actually mean that hospitality is restricted rather than opened generously. Properly speaking, while it is reasonable to invite people to weddings, it also seems appropriate that those invitations be extended as broadly as possible. A third problem might be characterized in terms of simple excess, which actually undermines the festivity. We have all been at Christmas gatherings where children do not enjoy presents simply because there are too many of them. As McKibben noted of his campaign, its beginnings were driven by "earnest and sober" issues like environmental impact and donations to the poor, but, "as we continued our campaign, we found we weren't really interested in changing Christmas because we wanted fewer batteries. We wanted more joy." Exchanging gifts at Christmas makes sense, but more and fancier gifts don't necessarily enhance the festiveness and may actually distract from it. A final criterion: the celebratory goods ought to bear some identifiable relationship to the occasion. I know of parents who practice giving their children three gifts each Christmas in order to connect the celebration to the gifts brought to Jesus.

Festival goods are robbed of their ability to delight when they creep into routine life. Going to a resort isn't very celebratory if all the rest of the time you live the resort lifestyle that is advertised by many housing complexes—or the actual resort must go even further upscale. Alcohol, a delight on occasion, becomes mind-numbingly dumb to downright deadly when drunken celebration is the highlight of every week . . . or every day. Advertisements may encourage us to put a little "holiday" in every day or "make every day a celebration" by habituating us to a pattern of little luxuries; reliance on such patterns for happiness obscures much more important goals.

Vocational Goods

The third and fourth categories of consumption that go beyond necessary are less directly oriented to other persons. One's vocation and one's spiritual nourishment really *are* about developing your own identity and they do usually require some reasonable material expenditure. But in the larger scheme of the Christian life, one's work and one's spiritual enrichment should be directed not primarily at personal satisfaction but toward building the Kingdom of God through love of others and of God. Vocation and enrichment are personal but should not be private.

One's vocation or work might well be an obvious area where one's expenditures go beyond necessity. A GPS device may be a luxury for an ordinary person following a usual routine, but for a taxi driver or a delivery service it may be invaluable. (A reader pointed out that this reference is out of date since all smartphones have GPS. In that case, one might consider the necessity of the smartphone or its proper use.) Regarding one's vocation, consumption is both functional and relational—it is a matter of things serving to carry out tasks but also to establish relationships. A reasonably sized faculty office, for example, both facilitates work and makes a hospitable space for meeting with students and colleagues.

An analogous premodern distinction about the right use of property has to do with "station." Aquinas's relatively brief treatment of the virtue and vice of clothing illustrates this point well. He maintains that virtue and vice can be evidenced in clothing; quoting Ambrose, he criticizes "costly and dazzling apparel." He advocates "ordinary clothes with "nothing added to increase [the body's] beauty." A lack of temperance can be displayed by excessive attention to comfort, vanity, or simply because too much attention is paid to this matter.[20] However, Aquinas also notes that moderation should be governed by custom, so that one neither exceeds nor falls below what is expected; further, certain apparel is "an indication of man's estate" and is judged based on "the virtue of truthfulness."[21] The notion of "station" is also applied to women's clothing, whereby a woman's "adornment" is acceptable if she seeks to "please her husband" but not if she dresses so as to "incite men to lust" or out of "frivolity or . . . vanity."[22] Setting aside the manifestly problematic sexism here, temperance in dress is to be understood not in terms of absolute simplicity but rather in social terms, and particularly in terms of one's calling in life. Elaboration may not exceed the bounds of temperance if it is appropriate to one's station. Aquinas further makes this clear when he suggests that almsgiving is not obligatory if coming from one's necessities, including "if a man cannot without it live in keeping with his social station, as regards either himself or those of whom he has charge."[23] He does, however, note that such giving may be praised as a "matter of counsel" and becomes obligatory in cases of easy replacement (an interesting point) or of "extreme indigence in an individual, or great need on the part of the common weal."

Transposing this into an egalitarian setting without ranks of nobility is no easy thing. The most obvious transposition of this distinction would have to do with the genuine needs of one's work and family. A larger house might be appropriate for a family; a room devoted to books or files might be appropriate for a person who does a lot of work at home. Germain Grisez's detailed and serious treatment of material goods insists that the "Christian should subordinate possessions to the Kingdom," by which he means that "an individual's personal vocation or a group's proper mission provides the standard for judgments about acquiring, holding, and disposing of things."[24] He goes on: "Therefore, to devote material goods to the service of Jesus' kingdom means acquiring, using, and retaining them precisely insofar as they are necessary for survival or are suitable for fulfilling responsibilities pertaining to one's personal vocation . Desiring or clinging to things which exceed this limit, whether by their quantity or their quality, is inconsistent with the total giving of self which Jesus requires of every one of his disciples."[25] Grisez's treatment of these matters is acutely aware of advertising and the creation of excessive needs, as critiqued repeatedly in the works of Pope John Paul II. Therefore, he rejects the idea that one's station now means "Christians may retain all the wealth they need to maintain their standard of living, no matter how high."[26]

Grisez's articulation is supported by several of my arguments. The moral importance of work (including often-uncompensated domestic labor, especially of women) suggests that the vice of luxury would be manifest when surplus resources are devoted to elaborating leisure pursuits, particularly at the expense of doing the best possible job in one's calling. Also, the importance of recognizing the universal call to holiness as a support for building a sacramental economy suggests the appropriateness of expenditures that "sacramentalize" one's work relationships and that a focus on things irrelevant to vocation is a way laypeople hold back from "total giving of self."

Grisez's account of vocation is strongly shaped in reaction to our cultural context: "Organizing a life is considered a project in which one sets goals, identifies a means of achieving them, and then pursues them. In this scenario, the goals that organize one's life are those that seem to promise maximum personal satisfaction, consistent with one's tastes and abilities."[27] That is to say, one's vocation is mistakenly understood as a matter of pursuing one's preferences. Understood in this way, nearly any material possession could be seen as a vocational good. By contrast, Grisez suggests that life is fundamentally about commitment-making rather than preference-fulfillment. The commitments one makes then must lead increasingly to the other important concept: integration. "Integration" is Grisez's way of saying that one's choices must become more and more coherently shaped by one's overall commitments rather than one's preferences. He is not afraid to go into extraordinary detail in examining our choices. For example, he considers whether a man who enjoys relaxing by going off from his duties and playing golf when time allows might instead consider joining a bowling league if the league is made up of families of co-workers, because the latter would allow him to include his wife and his co-workers in his recreation.[28] On the other hand, he may consider golfing better exercise for his health or for the opportunity it provides to speak of his faith with strangers. The point here is not necessarily which option is chosen but rather that the options are seen in light of vocation and integration instead of simply in terms of personal preference.

Grisez's argument is misunderstood if it is taken to mean something like "all work, no play." Instead, he would agree with Douglas Schuurman's comment that "vocation is not mainly about guiding individual choice of spouse or paid work; it is about interpreting these, and other relational settings, in faith as divinely assigned places to serve God and neighbor."[29] A more theological way of grasping this point is Thomas Merton's claim that "we must be ourselves by being Christ."[30] This is necessarily ascetic, but also necessarily joyful, since we are freed from a preoccupation with self. Merton nicely dispels what he calls the "game of hide-and-seek with divine Providence" view of vocation by reminding us that vocation is a matter of two loves and two freedoms coming together; it is not a mechanical or bureaucratic or impersonal cosmic context of determination.

Capping this understanding, we can turn to Joseph Ratzinger's distinctive Christological claim that Christ manifests his full humanity by completely "becoming" his work. In Christ, person and work are one, which is to say that his identity simply is his mission. Ratzinger seeks to overcome the early twentieth-century temptation to separate "Jesus" from "Christ," emphasizing the fact that the word Christ is not a name that signifies divinity but rather a title (like "Kaiser") that "denoted a function."[31] To proclaim belief in Jesus Christ is to indicate a "fusion of the name with the title," such that "it is not possible to distinguish office and person . . . there is no 'I' separate from the work; the 'I' is the work, and the work is the 'I'."[32] Jesus' work is to be "for us"; He doesn't simply do *something* or give *something*, but rather He "performs *himself* and gives *himself*" (italics in original).[33] His death on the cross is the ultimate manifestation of who He is. Further, it is precisely in "this unity of being and doing" that He reveals both the character of His divine Sonship and what true humanity looks like. In giving all He has and is to His mission, He manifests Himself as "the true man, the man of the future, the coinciding of man and God."[34]

Thus, to be truly human is to devote one's self wholly to one's vocation rather than holding back part of oneself for private satisfaction. As argued earlier, our tendency toward luxury is both an effect and cause of the degradation of work. For the Catholic, work understood as vocation should be central to one's life and expenditures should be devoted to fostering it. The proper spending of excess resources should be understood through serious discernment of vocation. While this vocation may include a specific job, it needs to be understood more broadly than that in recognition of the fact that all things are opportunities to sign and manifest the Kingdom through our work with others.

The proper use of goods for one's vocation can be challenging. Pierre Bourdieu notes that "liberal professionals" (e.g., lawyers or doctors) and teachers share an extensive educational background, similar incomes, and common political leanings. Yet the teachers generally eschew luxury in favor of "the least expensive and most austere leisure activities," while other professionals seek expensive and prestigious cultural goods in order to exhibit the signs of wealth and success that "make and keep up their connections and accumulate the capital of honorability they need in order to carry on their professions." Their "prodigality" becomes "a business necessity."[35] If Bourdieu is right, does a stadium luxury box or a country club membership or a custom-tailored wardrobe become a vocational good for a high-level businessman or lawyer that is justifiable for the sake of good work? Obviously, negotiating this terrain provides ample opportunity for self-deception. Still, it also indicates that some degree of sensitivity to appearances and propriety can be accepted in the same way Aquinas accepted the importance of station. Once again, prudential judgment is required. Perhaps a local parish could convene its doctors and lawyers and businessmen (and professors) to discern with one another what is reasonable and what is excessive.

Enrichment Goods

A final category is enrichment goods. John Paul II acknowledges that goods can lead to the "enrichment" of a person's being.[36] But the category is tricky because it contains elements that have the potential to be so broad as to apply to anything. The prior three categories are reasonably stringent such that they can be prudently applied. But the notion of "enrichment" is more difficult and can dissolve any distinction between luxury and personal "growth." They are especially difficult to uncover because consuming for the purposes of "personal enrichment" or "self-actualization" is a proven marketing tool. Like the luxury marketing strategies noted earlier, products and services are sold by promising not this or that pleasure but "something more"—even Walmart, in a move to broaden its appeal beyond the company's original slogan of "always low prices, always" now promises that its stores will help you "save money" and "live better." As Jackson Lears shows, the marketing potential of connecting a product to "higher" aspirations and not just base pleasures was a key move in the early twentieth-century legitimation of increased consumption: "In the emerging consumer culture, advertisers began speaking to many of the same preoccupations addressed by liberal ministers, psychologists, and other therapeutic ideologues," which in turn "reinforced the spreading culture of consumption."[37] Ministers and psychologists who extolled "full living" and "continuous growth" played into the hands of advertisers, who were selling products in terms of a "quest for self-realization through consumption."[38] Today, sales claims about health or psychological "benefits" mix in with a sense of luxurious indulgence, such as the now-standard half-joke about drinking red wine for its health benefits. Is a crossword puzzle book enriching? Do yoga lessons count? A noise machine to help you sleep? Special high-tech exercise clothes, better suited to changing weather? Specially framed aphorisms on your wall, to encourage you? Indeed, what about hobbies in general—are they a sign of luxury?

To bring some order to this discussion let us turn to some potential distinctions among these sorts of goods and services. Tibor Scitovsky's distinction between defensive and creative goods suggests that defensive goods provide "comfort" and protect against harm, whereas creative goods "stimulate." Scitovsky's book *The Joyless Economy* criticizes Americans of the

1970s for overvaluing comfort and undervaluing pleasures that stimulate (supposedly because of our Puritan heritage).[39] Because of "our acceptance of dull food and drab surrounding, and our tendency to sit at home," we then seek out constant novelty in what he calls "unskilled stimulus enjoyment" activities like TV-watching, shopping, and driving for pleasure.[40] Since these activities are monotonous and boring in themselves, constant novelty must be introduced to keep them interesting. He even criticizes the American tendency toward "carelessness" in dress by noting how we do not dress up when we "go out."[41] Scitovsky recognizes that despite its wealth, the American economy is joyless because its consumption is defensive and dumb, not creative and stimulating. Care in dress, in food, in music: this is "creative consumption" that potentially enriches both the self and the society.

Whether one agrees or not about Scitovsky's analysis of the American way of life, he is getting at some kind of qualitative distinction within personal consumption. This is crucial to a project on luxury. It might be quite easy simply to dismiss all personal leisure goods and services as luxury—but there does seem something peculiarly Spartan and inhuman about this. Even Grisez names recreation as a basic human good. It may be reasonable to suggest that a person can be inordinately focused on leisure goods (relative to some other goods), but some development in this area seems like a legitimate contribution to natural human flourishing.

Consider examples of similar distinctions. In Charles Karelis's study of why poverty persists, he attempts to explain why it is that some poor people seem to spend their scarce money on wasteful goods.[42] Karelis is convinced that it is wrong to imagine the poor as simply profligate. Instead, he notes that studies suggest a distinction between acts of consumption as "relievers" versus "pleasers." For those in poverty, daily life often means an endless stream of discomforts. Moreover, in many cases there is no certain end to these discomforts—rather, life is just this way, day in and day out. Thus, when there is an opportunity to spend, poor people do not think about "saving for a rainy day"; instead, they go for something that will provide some quick relief from the constant discomfort. By contrast, middle-class people don't simply have better self-discipline; what they have is a kind of daily stability and comfort that enables them to shift focus onto "pleasers" like a more creative hobby or more long-lasting and richer leisure options. "Pleasers" could be opportunities for enrichment in ways that "relievers" might not be.

Another distinction is made by Tim Kasser, who argues against consumerism by contrasting it to human needs for skill development and authentic self-expression. Robert Frank's differentiation between positional and nonpositional goods is that the latter are sources of intrinsic pleasure and delight and do not suffer from the crowding and relative deprivation effects of positional goods. Whether it be chess, team sports, playing a musical instrument, or doing theater, these activities both enhance the self and likely create communion with others who share one's passion. Presumably a person who spends hours on woodworking in his garage will be delighted when a neighbor moves in down the block who is also passionate about woodworking. Both one's woodworking skill and one's delight from it will be enhanced, not diminished, by another woodworker . . . unless he or she is a deeply envious person. While these activities can become the source of interpersonal competition even on a consumption level (e.g., runners obsessed with the latest gear), they can also provide noncompetitive enrichment to all participants because they involve the kind of genuine skill development that "humanizes" us.

When using these kinds of distinctions, prudence encounters ample opportunity for both snobbery and self-deception. To some extent one must simply be vigilant about that tendency. One way to distinguish may be to delve further into how such activities involve the contemplation of beauty and the exercise of creativity. There are both philosophical and Christian reasons for suggesting that full human development involves the contemplation of beauty as well as the development of creativity, perhaps especially through skills not typically exercised in one's vocation. If we accept the division of labor, it might be fair to admit that "brain workers" need to do something with their hands while "brawn workers" need to develop skills of contemplation in areas like art and literature.[43] One need make no judgment about particular cultural achievements to recognize that creative music-making in any culture seems to contribute to human development in a way that simple consumption does not.

But might this include skilled consumption? Colin Campbell contrasts the "romantic consumer" with the "hedonistic" one. As in the realm of sexual relationships, hedonists simply want to maximize their pleasure; romantics seek to form "deeper relationships," in this case with brands or hip locations or other identity markers. The category of the romantic consumer comes close to some of Scitovsky's examples of skilled consumption, but it also comes close to the kind of luxury marketing that makes us believe buying and consuming the correct products is important and meaningful. Is the wine connoisseur an example of skilled leisure and therefore of an enrichment good, or is it an example of the romantic consumer heading toward luxury? What about craft beers and exotic coffees and teas?

I certainly know where my own life displays the haziness and difficulty of this distinction: my music collection. On two levels it could be subject to criticism. First, it may simply be too large. There may be a point at which any enrichment good, no matter how much enjoyment it brings, can simply involve an accumulation that may actually lessen the enjoyment of the activity. Sometimes I look at my music collection and instead of picking out a CD I just push shuffle. Second, despite my saying that I "love music," it raises questions about consumption versus actual creativity. As a singer wouldn't I be better off putting more time and effort in the focal practice of singing with others instead of just listening to commercially produced music?

On the other hand, music (at least in my case) is not a matter of passive consumption. As Vince Miller points out, "As illuminating as the narrative of commodification is, one notices anomalies that challenge its portrayal of unremitting decline. A conversation with colleagues about students writing term papers on popular music reveals a striking correlation between an interest in the band U2 and the pursuit of nontraditional, politically committed career paths."[44] Miller's point is that, at least in some cases, popular music and other kinds of consumption are expressive, motivating, and cultivating of an important personal identity and mission. Michel de Certeau similarly argued that consumers were not simply passive recipients of mass production. Rather, they exercised creativity in their uses of what is produced. These "ways of operating," he says, "constitute the innumerable practices by means of which users reappropriate the space organized by techniques of sociocultural production."[45] Such "tactics" (de Certeau's term) mean "there is a gap of varying proportions" that opens up between the intention of the producer and the uses of the consumer.[46] Marketers may try to sell us something (music, art objects), but our use of what they sell us may be creative rather than simply conformist.

Is identifying with the band U2 different from identifying with the tech company Apple or the leather goods company Coach? There may be valid arguments for the difference, but the line is tricky. For prudent Christians, any devotion to enrichment goods must be less central than others more urgently and obviously recommended in the scriptural literature, especially care for the poor. Certainly there is a case to be made that these kinds of pursuits do not require a lot of purchasing but can be done simply and cheaply. Fortunately, many have available to them inexpensive, publicly sponsored resources—concerts, libraries, museums—where beauty can be appreciated. One might also add the beauty of sports (especially baseball!) but this would come with the caveat that these easily fall into patterns of limitless status consumption through collecting and commercialization.

At the core of distinguishing enrichment from luxury consumption may be the issue of emulation. Keynes contrasted the value of "emulation goods" with the enjoyment of aesthetic goods in company with others.[47] For some, attendance at a particular sporting event, consumption of a particular wine, owning a certain kind of running gear, or collecting rare books are pursued as status markers rather than out of a deep appreciation and love for the practice in question. This kind of passionate love and commitment to an activity is likely a sign that it offers intrinsic enrichment rather than merely "showing off" to others. Perhaps a key sign would be that one's pursuit of enrichment goods would end up being quite focused. Rather than mere entertainment or status, the goods represent an expression of the human spirit and a kind of communion in beauty. In short, genuine enrichment goods should be noncompetitive, enhanced by wide participation, and somehow point toward transcendence.

Sacramentality beyond Necessity

We have identified four categories by which we can identify nonluxury goods that exceed a level of general necessity. In many ways these goods overlap—in one's vocation, one often encounters a venue for sharing goods. One may engage enrichment goods when celebrating communally. The point of all these categories is to develop a positive language for the direction of our resources so that, in cases where these labels don't apply, we might also be able to discern the inordinate excess of luxury. This positive language is designed to be applicable in broad terms and without extensive theological specification. Aiming as it does at "higher goods," the taxonomy could be called a "spirituality of possessions" because all of the categories ask us to transcend our focus on ourselves in order to serve larger ends.

For Christians, and Catholic Christians, the categories are particularly specifiable in terms of worship and the poor. Joseph Ratzinger notes that the specific sacramental moments when we are able to see Christ are in the Eucharist and in the poor. He insists these must always be kept together as the twin foci of the Christian life.[48] Thus, sharing at worship and sharing with the outcast—having our vocation flow from the Eucharistic giving of Christ to the works of mercy, celebrating the festivals of the Christian calendar, and even engaging in enrichment oriented to prayer and service—make the most prudential sense when the Christian supernatural goal of charity is in view.

Finding our joys in these categories of goods—rather than in the private pursuit of luxury—is akin to what Peter Danner discusses as the appropriate "spirit of poverty" for Christians living in an affluent society. Going beyond mere detachment, Danner recognizes in our particular context "a brake [on material consumption] is meaningless considered in itself unless we open our attitudes to dimensions beyond ourselves and to meanings deeper than personal want gratification."[49] This true meaning of wealth is not a "Puritan/Jansenist" harsh poverty. Rather, it is "a joyful dependence upon a bountiful God" that involves three particular elements.[50] One must make a fundamental commitment to the divine will. We must honestly recognize the ways in which our anxiety about and concern for material goods constitute a resistance to it. We must recognize the sacramental opportunity of those in need—for example, by planning a celebration, dedicating our resources to serving our students, or pitching in on community projects. Rather than see these as draining away our resources (presumably from personal consumption opportunities) we should see them as the real purpose of excess wealth. And these two recognitions should issue in an "all embracing and creative" freedom for genuine life. Danner's phrase echoes the false promises of real living so prevalent in advertising that attempts to make us think we are really living when we are only consuming. Does that mean we simply give all our excess away? Well, in a sense, yes. But giving it away is not simply a charity dump. It's building and participating in a life that is sacramental through and through and a sign of the Kingdom for which we hope.

Notes

1. John Paul II, *Sollicitudo Rei Socialis*, no. 28.
2. Berry, *Idea of Luxury*, 19.
3. Medaille, *Toward a Truly Free Market*, 158–59.
4. Keenan, *Virtues for Ordinary Christians*, 12.
5. Danner, *Ethics for the Affluent*, 136.
6. Ibid., 150.
7. Ibid., 59–63.
8. On the dynamics of a possible new "sharing economy," where people rent infrequently used goods rather than buying them, see Wolverson, "Rental Nation."
9. For a book-length description of the harmony of Catholicism and the cooperative model, see Schmiedeler, *Cooperation*. Schmiedeler's title is "Lecturer in Cooperation" at the School of Social Science at CUA.
10. National Catholic Welfare Council, "Bishops' Program," 345–46.

11. Benedict XVI, *Caritas in Veritate*, no. 66.
12. ST II–II, 66, 2.
13. De Tocqueville, *Democracy in America*, 482, cited in Masters and Uelman, *Focolare*, 129–30.
14. Jung, *Sharing Food*, 144. I am grateful for Laura Hartman's excellent discussion of Jung's work as exemplifying "embracing creation," in *Christian Consumer*, 54–83.
15. Jung, *Sharing Food*, 6.
16. Bahnson and Wirzba, *Making Peace with the Land*, 103. I cite this story also in Cloutier, *Walking God's Earth*, 80.
17. Orsi, *Madonna of 115th Street*.
18. Mead, "You're Getting Married," 316–17.
19. McKibben, "Christmas."
20. ST II–II, 169, 1.
21. II–II, 169, 1, resp. 3.
22. II–II, 169, 2. He makes a fascinating distinction about makeup ("women painting themselves"), which is normally a sin of "falsification" but can be acceptable "to hide a disfigurement arising from some cause such as sickness."
23. II–II, 32, 6.
24. Grisez, *Living a Christian Life*, 803.
25. Ibid., 804.
26. Ibid., 805.
27. Grisez, *Personal Vocation*, 85.
28. Grisez, *Personal Vocation*, 111.
29. Schuurman, *Vocation*, 117.
30. Merton, *No Man Is an Island*, 134.
31. Ratzinger, *Introduction to Christianity*, 202.
32. Ibid., 203.
33. Ibid., 204.
34. Ibid., 226.
35. Bourdieu, *Distinction*, 286–87.
36. John Paul II, *Sollicitudo Rei Socialis*, no. 28.
37. Lears, "From Salvation to Self-Realization," 4.
38. Ibid., 15, 29.
39. Scitovsky, *Joyless Economy*, 205.
40. Ibid., 203, 232.
41. Ibid., 211.
42. Karelis, *Persistence of Poverty*, 50.
43. See Barron and Barron, *Creativity Cure*.
44. Miller, *Consuming Religion*, 8.
45. De Certeau, *Practice of Everyday Life*, xiv.
46. Ibid., 32.
47. On Keynes's distinctions of better and worse consumption, and their roots in his cultural milieu, see Goodwin, "Art of an Ethical Life," 218–23.
48. Ratzinger, "Face of Christ in Sacred Scripture," 29.
49. Danner, *Ethics for the Affluent*, 137.
50. Ibid., 196–97.

Conclusion

Resisting with Discipline,
Responding with Hope

As this book was nearly completed, Bloomberg News debuted a new section dedicated to "the good life," a phrase used as the section's new Twitter handle. Recent stories featured airlines overhauling their first-class cabins with better wines and bigger televisions, a set of new gadgets designed to keep your home safe when you're away, a rise in the supply of homes available at the Hamptons, and (of course) a review of the latest BMW compact SUV.[1] The name of this new section? "Luxury."[2] We all know that's the good life.

Though we may want to resist this characterization, we need language for that resistance. I began this book by noting how Christian moral reflection about possessions gets stuck between complacency with the status quo and what could be called "the Francis problem," that is, falling into an all-or-nothing trap of radical renunciation versus indifference with a little almsgiving. A similar tone is struck in some analyses of our economic system. The present system is either hero (bringing unprecedented wealth and lifting millions out of poverty) or villain (promoting self-interested behavior and injustice everywhere it appears).

In the day-to-day Christian life, however, encounters with things like Bloomberg's "Luxury" section are inadequately served by such arguments. This book is not so much the search for a middle road as it is a search for an expanded and reworked framing for economic concerns that is focused on the question of how we know when we've gone too far. It calls for sustained reflection on and strong evaluation of the micro-level choices and trends that make up the market system. Most important, it recovers the morally charged and prudentially applied language that shapes both our individual choices and the creation of the system. Keeping a focus on the term "luxury" as a particular vice is a critical task in exposing our situation accurately. Certainly the ancients and the early Christians saw luxury as a significant problem and a major moral issue to address on the road to happiness and to the Kingdom. The term, as with any ancient term, cannot be simply transferred from the past to the present; thus, chapters 2–4 provided a contemporary analysis of the problem of luxury as it conflicts with good work, practices, a sacramental economics, and an adequate economic model of consumption under conditions of affluence.

Two points seem most important to emphasize in conclusion. First, on the human level there is real harm in luxury. The attention we individually and collectively pay to unnecessary consumption goods is massive, and it does not lead to better lives. This work is not anti-market or anti-capitalism, per se. Yet, more and more, what markets deliver to those in affluent economies are the kinds of elaborated goods and services whose marketing depends on spurious appeals to transcendent promises that those goods and services cannot fulfill (see chapter 4). In the meantime, we ignore or accept degraded work, unjust practices, and unsustainable debt and natural resource use as tradeoffs for keeping us moving toward the introduction of the next "revolutionary" gadget.

There is no natural reason why markets need to work this way. Attention to luxury as a problem reminds us that, for all its massive failings, the market system depends in large part on consumer demand. This project urges a view of consumer-side disciplined demand as an important element of a just and sustainable economy. Benedict XVI, in *Caritas in Veritate*, invites us to understand a market system that can be marked by a different kind of ethics. Part of this is manifested in different structures (i.e., mutualist enterprises). But a good deal of the Pope's encyclical asks us to consider how actors within market structures can act with "quotas of gratuitousness" and a different sort of morality. Both structural change and market infusion ultimately depend on agents rethinking the way they go about choosing their daily bread.

Endorsing forms of market organization of the economy does not mean endorsing luxury, any more than endorsing the move to voluntarily selecting one's own spouse means endorsing divorce or promiscuity. The harm of luxury is not merely about its inability to give us psychological good feeling. It is about undermining our dignity, particularly as workers (see chapter 2), and distorting our economic system in fruitless pursuit of positional goods (see chapter 4). Luxury is important because our attachment to it often lies at the heart of intractable disputes over social problems, particularly poverty. If we were less luxurious perhaps we could make grand steps in overcoming the economic scarcity that still afflicts so many. Without restraint, our economic pursuit of more may indeed do some incidental good. But such good is unsustainable, both for what it does to us as agents immersed in "super-development" and for what it requires of others and the earth.

A second point to reemphasize is theological: the acceptance of luxury in contemporary society is an idolatrous satisfaction of spiritual longing for meaning and transcendence through experiences of buying and possessing. We want goods to be more than goods; we want our lives to be meaningful, special, even magical. We want our goods to give us access to communion and beauty. The more we live in a society that lives beyond daily bread, the more accessible that luxury temptation becomes.

This is a particularly important temptation to confront, because Catholics believe the material *does* mediate the spiritual. We do come to communion with God and with others through the goods of God's creation. Luxury is therefore a critical falsification of sacramentality. It is a false holiness, all the more important in light of Vatican II's call for true holiness by the laity. *Lumen Gentium* commissions lay Catholics to engage the task of "work for the sanctification of the world from within, in the manner of leaven" (31) and in sharing a "common dignity" and "the same vocation to perfection" held by radicals who follow the path of Franciscan poverty (32). The laity's special task in perfection is "to illuminate and organize [temporal] affairs in such a way that they may always start out, develop, and persist according to Christ's mind, to the praise of the Creator and the Redeemer" (31). In accord with this mission, the laity are called "by their combined efforts" to "remedy any institutions and conditions of the world which are customarily an inducement to sin" so that they "may favor the practice of virtue rather than hinder it" (36). This is holiness for the laity; it is not a rejection of the world but a relentless, challenging reordering of it.[3]

Writing this book has been a strange exercise; in one sense I feel like I am stating the obvious: most of us consume too much unnecessary stuff, and such consumption is obviously contrary to Christian discipleship. Yet in another sense the message is far from obvious in the sense that it hits home for so many of us in our daily lives and we resist it. The book "runs into" my own daily living constantly. But this is a sign of its importance, not its triviality.

The recent and striking example of Pope Francis's renunciation of excess simply illuminates how far we have departed from the Church

Fathers, who regarded excessive wealth as an obvious danger to the Christian life. It should not surprise us when the pope says, "It hurts me when I see a priest or a nun with the latest model car, you can't do this. A car is necessary to do a lot of work, but please, choose a more humble one. If you like the fancy one, just think about how many children are dying of hunger in the world."[4] Lulled into complacency by social habit and economic sound bites, we have forgotten how fundamentally unseemly it is for the followers of a poor savior to be manifesting lives of economic profligacy. Much of the text of this book was framed before Francis was elected. I have written elsewhere about Francis's words and example cohering with a critique of luxury.[5] While his style and emphasis on being a church of the poor and for the poor is forthright, he has simply continued (or perhaps walked the walk of) the basic themes outlined in the encyclicals of Paul VI, John Paul II, and Benedict XVI. His evocation of these ideas, however, is simple and direct. He frequently speaks of the "throw-away culture" and the "culture of waste";[6] this highlighting of our careless extravagance is likely to be central for his 2015 encyclical on the environment. Carelessness and waste are surely marks of the disposition to luxury.

Some may suggest that developing grand schemes to manifest sacramental relationships in conducting our daily business represents an impossible eschatological hope; I worry more about proposals that suggest that more and more super-development is the way to end poverty! But addressing the problem of luxury as a way toward economic sufficiency and abundance is really little different than other long-term Christian projects that have succeeded, like the abolition of slavery, the practice of lifelong monogamous egalitarian marriage, and even the increasing (though far from complete) pacification of many societies. None of these projects heralded the eschaton in the sense of making humans perfect and unable to fail. Nor were they a matter of immediate and total success. We stumble individually and collectively on the way to freeing ourselves from these vices; surely the same will be true about luxury. Mercy is always needed, and we are blessed to receive its riches from God and each other. Nevertheless, we really have achieved some social progress on these questions of promoting the dignity of the person and the love of neighbor found at the heart of the Gospel.

Yet, somehow, on this particular issue of excess possessions, we have abandoned this sense of hope for the triumph of human dignity and have gotten trapped by a vision of the human person proffered to us largely by Enlightenment philosophes and modern social scientists. This is a vision of the human being as inevitably work-avoiding, self-interested, vain, and preoccupied with continual material progress. We may sigh and criticize but we somehow simply accept that this is just the way most people are. Imagine if Catholic sexual ethics was shaped by a similar understanding of our sexual viciousness instead of being guided by a vision animated by love, mutuality, and self-sacrifice. The same theological anthropology can and should animate Catholic economic ethics, insisting that as humans we can work and produce and trade in ways that involve . . . yes, love, mutuality, and self-sacrifice. We cannot get to that economic vision of sharing, cooperation, and solidarity unless we address our attachment to luxury. Just as Catholic sexual ethics is likely to be meaningless if one is mired in promiscuity, so, too, Catholic economic ethics cannot work if we accept "economic promiscuity"—that is, luxury. Rich visions of spousal love and economic mutuality will remain idle dreams without some basic levels of restraint. In this book, I have tried to display the logic of this restraint and attend to the particular ways our contemporary lives are afflicted by this disposition to excess.

Is luxury what we really want? I think most of us have a vague sense of excessive extravagance. But it is so easy for our imaginations to be captive to the ongoing stream of material aspirations that mark our weeks, years, jobs, and retirements. Right now I am daily reminded of this by a contemporary creepy experience: seeing ads pop up for items you've looked up on websites. A certain internet merchant is working very hard to convince me that I need a vacuum cleaner. Every day, for several weeks now, when searching different websites, the ads pop up—for vacuum cleaners I researched weeks ago. This is saying to me, "Remember that vacuum cleaner you looked at? You know you want it." This phenomenon of ads following us around should make us uneasy, not for privacy reasons but because of the persistence of the salesman. He won't leave us alone (even after we've made a purchase!).

The omnipresent salesman creates a world where we are constantly aware of what we lack. A world of scarcity in the midst of abundance. Economics has always been preoccupied with scarcity, and to some extent scarcity is simply a fact of finitude. A recent book on scarcity used the tools of behavioral economics to outline the problems experienced when we face what the authors call "the feeling of scarcity." They note that scarcity, though it can increase focus and urgency, also imposes a tax on mental "bandwidth" and harms our decision-making abilities. This feeling of scarcity affects not only the poor (for whom money is actually scarce) but also the over-busy, the lonely, and anyone else who is preoccupied with a "scarcity trap." The authors summarize that "scarcity captures our attention, and thus provides a narrow benefit . . . but, more broadly, it costs us: we neglect other concerns and we become less effective in the rest of life."[7]

The salesman is pushing me, but ultimately the disposition to luxury is a key way by which we impose the feeling of scarcity on ourselves, individually and as a culture. Peter Danner notes that, paradoxically, scarcity can become "the essence of affluence" and that "abundance creates scarcity"; this is "the paradox which is at the heart of the affluent psyche" and is "qualitatively different from survival scarcity."[8] As such, we cannot address it by the same means we might address survival scarcity—through markets or a redistributive safety net that we have devised to overcome the problem of basic scarcity. When we do, we simply intensify our conflicts, both inside ourselves and among us as a society. Socrates's essential point was right: luxury introduces an artificial lack, within us and between us, from which stems endless conflict.

Is this conflict over unnecessary goods what we truly desire? Many of us want something else, something more, something deeper, something that still echoes in the words of President Carter, with which the book began. Barry Schwartz notes that pursuing "the freedom of the marketplace in all aspects of our lives" actually leads to the discovery that "many of the things we value most deeply—meaningful, satisfying work; intimate, compassionate friends, family, and community; real education; significant spiritual and ethical commitment; political involvement; and even, ultimately, material well-being—are increasingly difficult to achieve."[9] It seems that most people do in fact value meaningful work, friends and family, education, and religious commitment more than they value the latest gadget or the largest kitchen. But we've lost our ability to name the contradictions between the pursuits driven by luxury and what will provide this meaning.

We must make that reconnection even though it is not the most intuitive connection to us. It's much like beginning an exercise program: we have to do little things right for a while before we see the payoff. When I first started running, I hated it; but I kept doing it, and it took a good three years, but now I look forward to it. Letting go of luxury requires this, both individually and as a society. It won't make us into St. Francis or Mother Teresa; a critique of luxury isn't an all-or-nothing proposition. For the majority of us living in wealth, it's an important invitation to let go of what is less important in favor of what is more important. Perhaps all we need to do is seek out a few opportunities for meaning-giving and relationship-building economic alternatives to our standard spending diet. Thinking of our spending as sacramental is unusual for most of us. I'll admit, I fail at it all the time, but when we are able to see and seek alternatives, we find much more personal delight, much more hope, and much more solidarity. Delight, hope, solidarity: these are the marks of an economy of reciprocity where as consumers we choose in ways that are not ultimately about some private collection or aspiration.

In a certain sense the truism that the market gives us what we want should be accepted. The evidence all around us is that we want luxury. Luxury, as Veblen saw and as the clever marketers continue to demonstrate, is quite profitable. As Adam Smith saw, luxury consumption does contribute to a partial distribution of the wealth of the rich to others. But it is insufficient to blame marketers or praise trickle-down theories. The root issue of luxury is that we still want these things, and we want them *instead* of wanting other things. Let us instead seek first the Kingdom.

Notes

1. All stories from the Bloomberg "The Good Life" Twitter feed for July 24 to 26, 2014.
2. See http://www.bloomberg.com/luxury/.
3. For an elaboration of this call to make creation holy in terms of environmental concerns, see Cloutier, *Walking God's Earth*, 117–25.
4. See http://news.yahoo.com/jesus-drive-pope-tells-priests-buy-humble-cars-18390 3106.html.
5. Cloutier, "Sending the Wrong Signal."
6. Francis, *Evangelii Gaudium*, no. 40, and "General Audience, June 5, 2013."
7. Mullainathan and Shafir, *Scarcity*, 10–15.
8. Danner, *Ethics for the Affluent*, 31–33.
9. Schwartz, *Costs of Living*, 10.

Bibliography

Abbott, Walter, ed. *The Documents of Vatican II*. Piscataway, NJ: New Century, 1966.

Ahuvia, Aaron. "Wealth, Consumption, and Happiness." In *The Cambridge Handbook of Psychology and Economic Behaviour*, edited by Alan Lewis, 199–226. New York: Cambridge University Press, 2008.

Alford, Helen, and Michael Naughton. *Managing As If Faith Mattered*. Notre Dame, IN: University of Notre Dame Press, 2001.

Anderson, Gary. *Charity: The Place of the Poor in the Biblical Tradition*. New Haven, CT: Yale University Press, 2013.

Appleby, Joyce. *Economic Thought and Ideology in Seventeenth-Century England*. Princeton, NJ: Princeton University Press, 1978.

———. "Moderation in the First Era of Popular Consumption." In *Thrift and Thriving in America*, edited by Joshua J. Yates and James Davidson Hunter, 139–59. New York: Oxford University Press, 2011.

———. *The Relentless Revolution: A History of Capitalism*. New York: Norton, 2010.

Aquinas, Thomas. *On Evil*. Translated by Richard Regan. New York: Oxford University Press, 2003.

———. *Summa Theologica*. Translated by the Fathers of the English Dominican Province. New York: Benziger Brothers, 1948.

Arbo, Matthew. *Political Vanity: Adam Ferguson on the Moral Tensions of Early Capitalism*. Minneapolis: Fortress, 2014.

Aristotle. *Eudemian Ethics*. Translated by J. Solomon. In *The Complete Works of Aristotle*, edited by Jonathan Barnes, 1922–85. Princeton, NJ: Princeton University Press, 1984.

———. *Nicomachean Ethics*. Translated by W. D. Ross and J. O. Urmson. In *The Complete Works*, edited by Jonathan Barnes, 1729–1867. Princeton, NJ: Princeton University Press, 1984.

———. *Politics*. Translated by Benjamin Jowett. New York: Modern Library, 1943.

Associated Press. "Pope Expels German 'Luxury Bishop' from Diocese," *New York Times*, October 23, 2013.

Augustine. *City of God*. Translated by Marcus Dodds. New York: Modern Library, 1993.

Ayres, Clarence. "The Coordinates of Institutionalism." *American Economic Review* 41 (1951): 47–55.

Bacevich, Andrew, ed. *The Short American Century: A Postmortem*. Cambridge, MA: Harvard University Press, 2012.

Bahnson, Fred, and Norman Wirzba. *Making Peace with the Land*. Downers Grove, IL: InterVarsity, 2012.

Baier, Annette C. *The Pursuits of Philosophy: An Introduction to the Life and Thought of David Hume*. Cambridge, MA: Harvard University Press, 2011.

Bajaj, Vikas. "Before You Buy That T-Shirt," *New York Times*, May 19, 2013; http://www.nytimes.com/2013/05/19/opinion/sunday/before-you-buy-that-t-shirt.html.

Baker, David L. *Tight Fists or Open Hands?* Grand Rapids, MI: Eerdmans, 2009.

Baldwin, Spencer. "Some Aspects of Luxury." *North American Review* 168 (1899): 154–62.

Bambrick-Santoyo, Paul. *Leverage Leadership*. San Francisco: Jossey-Bass, 2011.

Banner, Stuart. *American Property*. Cambridge, MA: Harvard University Press, 2011.

Barnes, James A. *Wealth of the American People*. New York: Prentice Hall, 1949.

Barron, Carrie, and Alton Barron. *The Creativity Cure*. New York: Scribner's, 2012.

Barron, Robert. *The Strangest Way: Walking the Christian Path*. Maryknoll, NY: Orbis, 2002.

Beadle, Ron. "Why Business Cannot Be a Practice." *Analyse & Kritik* 30 (2008): 229–41.

Beadle, Ron, and Kelvin Knight. "Virtue and Meaningful Work." *Business Ethics Quarterly* 22 (2012): 433–50.

Benedict XVI. "Address to Young People at the Welcoming Celebration of World Youth Day 2008," July 17, 2008, http://www.vatican.va/holy_father/benedict_xvi/speeches/2008/july/documents/hf_ben-xvi_spe_20080717_barangaroo_en.html.

———. *Caritas in Veritate*, 2009.

———. *Deus Caritas Est*, 2005.

Bennett, Jana. *Water Is Thicker Than Blood: An Augustinian Theology of Marriage and Singleness*. New York: Oxford University Press, 2008.

Berman, Morris. *Dark Ages America: The Final Phase of Empire*. New York: Norton, 2006.

Bernanke, Ben. "The Federal Reserve and the Financial Crisis." Lecture Series, March 2012, http://www.federalreserve.gov/newsevents/lectures/about.htm.

Bernstein, Jared, et al. *How Much Is Enough? Basic Family Budgets for Working Families*. Washington, DC: Economic Policy Institute, 2000.

Berry, Christopher J. *The Idea of Luxury: A Conceptual and Historical Investigation*. New York: Cambridge University Press, 1994.

Berry, Wendell. *Sex, Economy, Freedom, and Community*. New York: Pantheon, 1993.

Berthon, P., et al. "Aesthetics and Ephemerality: Observing and Preserving the Luxury Brand." *California Management Review* 52 (2009), 45–66.

Blinder, Alan. "What's the Matter with Economics?" *New York Review of Books*, December 18, 2014, 55–57.

Blomberg, Craig L. *Neither Poverty Nor Riches*. Downers Grove, IL: InterVarsity, 1999.

Bloomfield, Morton. *The Seven Deadly Sins*. East Lansing, MI: Michigan State University Press, 1952; rpt. 1967.

Blosser, Christopher. "Pope Benedict XVI's *Caritas in Veritate*." *First Things*, July 7, 2009, http://www.firstthings.com/blogs/firstthoughts/2009/07/07/pope-benedict-xvis-encyclical-caritas-in-veritate/.

Boersma, Hans. *Nouvelle Theologie and Sacramental Ontology*. New York: Oxford University Press, 2009.

Borgmann, Albert. *Power Failure: Christianity in the Culture of Technology*. Grand Rapids, MI: Brazos, 2003.

Boss, Shira. *Green with Envy: Why Keeping Up with the Joneses Is Keeping Us in Debt*. New York: Warner, 2006.

Bossy, John. "Moral Arithmetic: Seven Sins into Ten Commandments." In *Conscience and Casuistry in Early Modern Europe*, edited by Edmund Leites, 214–34. New York: Cambridge University Press, 1988.

Bourdieu, Pierre. *Distinction: A Social Critique of the Judgment of Taste*. Translated by Richard Nice. Cambridge, MA: Harvard University Press, 1984.

Boyer, George. *An Economic History of the English Poor Law, 1750–1850*. New York: Cambridge University Press, 1990.

Brown, Peter. *The Rise of Western Christendom*. Malden, MA: Blackwell, 1997.

——. *Through the Eye of a Needle: Wealth, the Fall of Rome, and the Making of Christianity in the West, 350–550 AD*. Princeton, NJ: Princeton University Press, 2012.

Bruni, Luigino. "Common Good and Economics: Toward an Agapic Economy." Translated by Michael Brennen. Available at: http://michaelbrennen.com/common-good-and-economics/.

——. *The Wound and the Blessing: Economic Relationships and Happiness*. Translated by N. Michael Brennen. Hyde Park, NY: New City, 2012.

Bunkley, Nick. "Government Will End Clunker Program Early." *New York Times*, August 20, 2009; http://www.nytimes.com/2009/08/21/business/21clunkers.html?_r=0.

Burns, Gene. "Abandoning Suspicion: The Catholic Left and Sexuality." In *What's Left? Liberal American Catholics*, edited by Mary Jo Weaver, 67–87. Bloomington, IN: Indiana University Press, 1999.

Calvin, John. *Institutes of the Christian Religion*, 2 vols. Philadelphia: Westminster, 1960.

Carr, Nicholas. *The Shallows: What the Internet Is Doing to Our Brain*. New York: Norton, 2010.

Carter, Jimmy. "Energy and the National Goals." In *Representative American Speeches, 1979–80*, edited by Waldo W. Braden, 76–87. New York: H. W. Wilson, 1980.

"Carter at the Crossroads." *Time* magazine 114, no. 4 (July 23, 1979): 20–30.

"Carter's Great Purge." *Time* magazine 114, no. 5 (July 20, 1979): 12–13.

Carvalho, Luis Francisco, and Joao Rodrigues. "On Markets and Morality: Revisiting Fred Hirsch." *Review of Social Economy* 64 (2006): 331–48.

Cassidy, John. *How Markets Fail: The Logic of Economic Calamities*. New York: Farrar, Straus, and Giroux, 2009.

Catechism of the Catholic Church. Mahwah, NJ: Paulist Press, 1994.

Cavanaugh, William. *Being Consumed: Economics and Christian Desire*. Grand Rapids, MI: Eerdmans, 2008.

———. "Consumer Culture." In *Gathered for the Journey*, edited by M. Therese Lysaught and David McCarthy, 241–59. Grand Rapids, MI: Eerdmans, 2007.

Cerne, Matej, et al. "What Goes Around Comes Around: Knowledge Hiding, Perceived Motivational Climate, and Creativity." *Academy of Management Journal* 57 (2014): 172–92.

Chadwick, Owen. *The Reformation*. New York: Penguin, 1964.

Chase, Stuart. *The Tragedy of Waste*. New York: Macmillan, 1925.

Cherlin, Andrew. *The Marriage-Go-Round*. New York: Knopf, 2009.

Chevalier, Michel, and Pierre Xiao Lu. *Luxury China: Market Opportunities and Potential*. New York: Wiley, 2010.

Cicero. *The Offices*. Translated by Thomas Cockman. In *Hellenistic Philosophy*, edited by Herman Shapiro and Edwin M. Curley, 449–500. New York: Modern Library, 1965.

———. "Pro Sexto Roscio Amerino." In *The Speeches*, translated by John Henry Freese, Loeb Classical Library, 188–89. Cambridge: Harvard University Press, 1930.

Clark, Charles M. A. "Catholic Economics 101," *US Catholic*, http://www.uscatholic .org/articles/201306/catholic-economics-101-charles-clark-capitalism-government -spending-and-alleviating.

———. "Wealth as Abundance and Scarcity." In *Rediscovering Abundance*, edited by Helen Alford et al., 28–56. Notre Dame, IN: University of Notre Dame Press, 2006.

Clark, Elizabeth A. *Reading Renunciation: Asceticism and Scripture in Early Christianity*. Princeton, NJ: Princeton University Press, 1999.

Clark, J. B. *The Distribution of Wealth*. New York: Macmillan, 1899; rpt. 1927.

Clark, Meghan J. *The Vision of Catholic Social Thought*. Minneapolis, MN: Fortress, 2014.

Cloutier, David. "American Lifestyles and Structures of Sin: The Practical Implications of Pope Benedict XVI's Ecological Vision for the American Church." In *Environmental Justice and Climate Change*, edited by James Schafer and Tobias Winright, 215–35. Lanham, MD: Rowman and Littlefield, 2013.

———. "Heaven Is a Place on Earth? Analyzing the Popularity of Pope John Paul II's Theology of the Body." In *Sexuality and the US Catholic Church: Crisis and Renewal*, edited by Lisa Sowle Cahill, John Garvey, and T. Frank Kennedy, SJ, 18–31. New York: Crossroad, 2006.

———. "Marriage and Sexuality." In *The Oxford Handbook of Catholic Theology*, edited by Lewis Ayres and Medi Anne Volpe. New York: Oxford University Press, in press.

———. "Moral Theology for Real People: Agency, Practical Reason, and the Task of the Moral Theologian." In *New Wine, New Wineskins: A Next Generation Reflects on Catholic Moral Theology*, edited by William Mattison, 119–42. Lanham, MD: Sheed and Ward, 2005.

———. "The Problem of Luxury in the Christian Life." *Journal of the Society of Christian Ethics* 32 (2012): 3–20.

———. "Sending the Wrong Signal: How Luxury Compromises Christian Witness." *Commonweal* 140, no. 20 (December 20, 2013): 12–15.

———. *Walking God's Earth: The Environment and Catholic Faith*. Collegeville, MN: Liturgical Press, 2014.

——. "Working with the Grammar of Creation." *Communio* 37 (2010): 606–33.

Colvin, Geoffrey. "We're a Nation Helpless to Save Ourselves." *Fortune* 151, no. 8 (April 18, 2005): 52.

Congregation for the Doctrine of the Faith, "Instruction on Certain Aspects," http://www.vatican.va/roman_curia/congregations/cfaith/documents/rc_con_cfaith_doc_19840806_theology-liberation_en.html.

Conway, Edmund. *Fifty Economic Ideas You Need to Know*. London: Quercus, 2009.

Copleston, Frederick. *A History of Philosophy*, vol. 5, part 2. Garden City, NY: Image/Doubleday, 1964.

Coyle, Diane. *The Economics of Enough*. Princeton, NJ: Princeton University Press, 2011.

Cronin, John F., SS. *Social Principles and Economic Life*. Milwaukee, WI: Bruce, 1964.

Crook, Clive. "The Height of Inequality." *The Atlantic* online, http://www.theatlantic.com/magazine/archive/2006/09/the-height-of-inequality/305089/2/.

——. "The Phantom Menace." *The Atlantic*, April 2007.

Cross, Gary. *An All-Consuming Century: Why Commercialism Won in Modern America*. New York: Columbia University Press, 2000.

Csikszentmihalyi, Mihaly. *Flow*. New York: Harper & Row, 1990.

Daly, Herman, and John Cobb. *For the Common Good*, 2nd. ed. Boston: Beacon, 1994.

Daly, Herman, and Joshua Farley. *Ecological Economics*. Washington, DC: Island, 2004.

Danner Peter. *An Ethics for the Affluent*. Lanham, MD: University Press of America, 1980.

Dasgupta, Partha. *Economics: A Very Short Introduction*. New York: Oxford University Press, 2007.

Davidson, Adam. "Making It in America." *The Atlantic* online, January-February 2012; http://www.theatlantic.com/magazine/archive/2012/01/making-it-in-america/308844/?single_page=true.

Davidson, Adam, and Alex Blumberg. "Taxpayer Beware: Bank Bailout Will Hurt." NPR Morning Edition, February 27, 2009.

De Certeau, Michel. *The Practice of Everyday Life*. Translated by Steven Rendall. Berkeley, CA: University of California Press, 1984.

de Graaf, John, and David K. Batker. *What's the Economy For, Anyway?* New York: Bloomsbury, 2011.

De Vries, Jan. *Industrious Revolution: Consumer Behavior and the Household Economy, 1650 to the Present*. New York: Cambridge University Press, 2008.

Dietz, Rob, and Dan O'Neill. *Enough Is Enough: Building a Sustainable Economy in a World of Finite Resources*. San Francisco: Berrett-Koehler, 2013.

Douglas, Paul H. "The Economic Wastes of Luxury." *The World Tomorrow* 5, no. 6 (June 1922): 165–66.

Dubay, Thomas, SM. *Happy Are You Poor: The Simple Life and Spiritual Freedom*. San Francisco: Ignatius, 1981; rpt. 2003.

Dyer, Christopher. *Standards of Living in the Later Middle Ages*. New York: Cambridge University Press, 1989.

Eatwell, John, Murray Milgate, and Peter Newman, eds. *The New Palgrave: A Dictionary of Economics*, 4 vols. London: Macmillan, 1987.

Eggemeier, Matthew T. *The Sacramental-Prophetic Imagination*. Collegeville, MN: Liturgical Press, 2014.

Engerman, Stanley, and Robert Gollman, eds. *The Cambridge Economic History of the United States*, 3 vols. New York: Cambridge University Press, 2000.

Ezekiel, Mordecai. *$2500 a Year: From Scarcity to Abundance*. New York: Harcourt Brace, 1936.

Fallon, Valere, SJ. *Principles of Social Economy*, edited by Bert Goss, translated by Rev. John McNulty. New York: Benziger Brothers, 1933.

Farrell, Chris. *The New Frugality: How to Consume Less, Save More, and Live Better*. New York: Bloomsbury, 2010.

Ferguson, Adam. *An Essay on the History of Civil Society*. Kitchener, Ontario: Batoche, n.d.

Fine, Ben. "From Political Economy to Consumption." In *Acknowledging Consumption*, edited by Daniel Miller, 125–62. New York: Routledge, 1995.

Finn, Daniel K. *Christian Economic Ethics: History and Implications*. Minneapolis, MN: Fortress, 2013.

——. *The Moral Ecology of Markets*. New York: Cambridge University Press, 2006.

——. "Reciprocity, Trust, and Social Capital." In *The Moral Dynamics of Economic Life*, edited by Daniel K. Finn, 76–80. New York: Oxford University Press, 2012.

——. "Social Causality and Market Complicity." In *Distant Markets, Distant Harms: Economic Complicity and Christian Ethics*, edited by Daniel K. Finn, 243–59. New York: Oxford University Press, 2014.

"Five Families, Five Fixes," *Money*, January-February 2011, 80–87.

Foley, Duncan. *Adam's Fallacy: A Guide to Economic Theology*. Cambridge: Harvard University Press, 2006.

Fox, Richard Wightman. "Epitaph for Middletown." In *The Culture of Consumption: Critical Essays in American History*, edited by Richard Wightman Fox and T. J. Jackson Lears, 101–41. New York: Pantheon, 1983.

Francis I. *Evangelii Gaudium*, 2013.

——. "General Audience, June 5, 2013," http://w2.vatican.va/content/francesco/en/audiences/2013/documents/papa- francesco_20130605_udienza-generale.html.

Frank, Robert. *Richistan: A Journey through the American Wealth Boom and the Lives of the New Rich*. New York: Crown, 2007.

Frank, Robert H. "Are Concerns about Relative Income Relevant for Public Policy? Positional Externalities Cause Large and Preventable Welfare Losses." *American Economic Review* (May 2005): 137–41.

——. *Choosing the Right Pond*. New York: Oxford University Press, 1985.

——. *Falling Behind: How Rising Inequality Harms the Middle Class*. Berkeley, CA: University of California Press, 2007.

——. *Luxury Fever*. New York: Free Press, 1999.

——. "Why Do Americans Save So Little and Does It Matter?" In *Thrift and Thriving in America*, edited by Joshua J. Yates and James Davidson Hunter, 417–36. New York: Oxford University Press, 2011.

Franks, Christopher. *He Became Poor: The Poverty of Christ and Aquinas's Economic Teachings*. Grand Rapids, MI: Eerdmans, 2009.

Freisen, Steven J. "Injustice or God's Will? Early Christian Explanations of Poverty." In *Wealth and Poverty in Early Church and Society*, edited by Susan Holman, 17–36. Grand Rapids, MI: Baker, 2008.

Frend, W. H. C. *The Early Church*. Philadelphia: Fortress, 1982.

Frey, Bruno, and Alois Stutzer. "What Can Economists Learn from Happiness Research?" *Journal of Economic Literature* 40 (2002): 402–35.

Friedman, Benjamin. "Who Stole the American Dream?" *New York Review of Books* 59, no. 15 (October 11, 2012): 36–38.

Friedman, Thomas. *The World Is Flat: A Brief History of the Twenty-First Century*. New York: Farrar, Straus, and Giroux, 2005.

Friedman, Thomas, and Michael Mandelbaum. *That Used to Be Us*. New York: Farrar, Straus, and Giroux, 2011.

Frontline, "The Merchants of Cool," http://www.pbs.org/wgbh/pages/frontline/shows/cool/etc/hunting.html.

———. "The Persuaders": http://www.pbs.org/wgbh/pages/frontline/shows/persuaders/.

Fukuyama, Francis. *The End of History and the Last Man*. New York: Free Press, 1992.

Galbraith, John Kenneth. *The Affluent Society*. Boston: Houghton Mifflin, 1958.

———. *The New Industrial State*. In *The Affluent Society and Other Writings*, edited by James K. Galbraith, 607–1017. New York: Library of America, 2010.

Garland, David E. *Reading Matthew: A Literary and Theological Commentary*. New York: Crossroad, 1995.

Garon, Sheldon. *Beyond Our Means*. Princeton, NJ: Princeton University Press, 2013.

Garvey, James. *The Ethics of Climate Change*. New York: Continuum, 2008.

George, Cardinal Francis. "Reflections on *Caritas in Veritate*." *Origins* 39 (2009): 210–14.

Goldberg, Joseph P., and William T. Moye. *The First Hundred Years of the Bureau of Labor Statistics*. Washington, DC: Bureau of Labor Statistics, 1985.

Goldberg, Michael. "Business Ethics: Kindred Spirit or Idolatry?" In *Virtues and Practices in the Christian Tradition*, edited by Nancy Murphy et al., 306–23. Harrisburg, PA: Trinity, 1997.

Gonzalez, Justo. *Faith and Wealth*. San Francisco: Harper & Row, 1990.

Gonzalez, Michelle. *Shopping*. Minneapolis: Fortress, 2010.

Goodman, David. "The Future of Milk." *Eating Well*, July–August 2010, http://www.eatingwell.com/food_news_origins/food_news/the_future_of_milk.

Goodman, Percival, and Paul Goodman. *Communitas: Means of Livelihood and Ways of Life*. Chicago: University of Chicago Press, 1947.

Goodwin, Craufurd. "The Art of an Ethical Life." In *The Cambridge Companion to Keynes*, edited by Roger Backhouse and Bradley Bateman, 217–36. New York: Cambridge University Press, 2006.

Gorman, Hugh S. *The Story of N: A Social History of the Nitrogen Cycle and the Challenge of Sustainability*. New Brunswick, NJ: Rutgers University Press, 2013.

Graeber, David. *Debt: The First Five Thousand Years*. New York: Melville House, 2011.

"The Great American Divide." *Time* magazine 178, no. 14 (October 10, 2011): 26–40.

Gregory, Archbishop Wilton. "Apology for Cost of New House." *Origins* 43 (2014): 719–20.

Gregory, Brad. "The History of Christianity in the Reformation Era." The Great Courses series. The Teaching Co., http://www.thegreatcourses.com/courses/his tory-of-christianity-in-the-reformation-era.html.

———. "The Unintended Reformation." Lecture at Lumen Christi Institute at the University of Chicago, May 8, 2012. Video available: http://www.lumenchristi.org /unintended-reformation/.

———. The Unintended Reformation: How a Religious Revolution Secularized Society. Cambridge, MA: Harvard University Press, 2012.

Greider, William. One World—Ready or Not: The Manic Logic of Global Capitalism. New York: Simon & Schuster, 1997.

Grisez, Germain. Living a Christian Life. The Way of the Lord Jesus, vol. 2. Quincy, IL: Franciscan, 1993.

Grisez, Germain, and Russell Shaw. Personal Vocation: God Calls Everyone by Name. Huntington, IN: Our Sunday Visitor, 2003.

Hager, Paul. "Refurbishing MacIntyre's Account of Practice." Journal of the Philosophy of Education 45 (2011): 545–61.

Halteman, James. The Clashing Worlds of Economics and Faith. Scottsdale, PA: Herald, 1995.

Harrington, Michael. The Other America: Poverty in the United States. New York: Macmillan, 1964.

Harrison, Nonna Verna. Introduction to On the Human Condition, Saint Basil the Great. Crestwood, NY: SVS, 2005.

Harst, Charles E., and David McConnell. An Amish Paradox. Baltimore: Johns Hopkins University Press, 2010.

Hartman, Laura. The Christian Consumer: Living Faithfully in a Fragile World. New York: Oxford University Press, 2011.

Hauerwas, Stanley. Working with Words. Eugene, OR: Cascade, 2011.

Hausman, Daniel, and Michael McPherson. Economic Analysis and Moral Philosophy. New York: Cambridge University Press, 1996.

Hayek, Friedrich. "Freedom and the Economic System." In Socialism and War, edited by Bruce Caldwell, 189–212. Chicago: University of Chicago Press, 1939; rpt. 1997.

Hays, Richard. The Moral Vision of the New Testament. San Francisco: HarperCollins, 1996.

Heilbroner, Robert. The Worldly Philosophers, 6th ed. New York: Simon & Schuster, 1986.

Hendel, Charles. Editor's Introduction to Hume's An Inquiry Concerning the Principles of Morals, vii–lix. Indianapolis, IN: Bobbs-Merrill, 1957.

Hengel, Martin. Property and Riches in the Early Church. Philadelphia: Fortress, 1974.

Henwood, Doug. After the New Economy. New York: New Press, 2003.

Herdt, Jennifer. Putting on Virtue: The Legacy of the Splendid Vices. Chicago: University of Chicago Press, 2008.

Hervaeus Natalis. The Poverty of Christ and the Apostles. Translated by John D. Jones. Toronto: PIMS, 1999.

Hillerbrand, Hans. The Division of Christendom. Louisville, KY: WJKP, 2007.

Hinze, Christine Firer. "What Is Enough? Catholic Social Thought, Consumption, and Material Sufficiency." In Having: Property and Possession in Religious and

Social Life, edited by William Schweiker and Charles Mathewes, 162–88. Grand Rapids, MI: Eerdmans, 2004.

Hirsch, Fred. *The Social Limits to Growth*. Cambridge: Harvard University Press, 1976.

Hirschfeld, Mary, "Standards of Living and Economic Virtue." *Journal of the Society of Christian Ethics* 26 (2006): 61–77.

Hirschman, Albert O. *The Passions and the Interests: Political Arguments for Capitalism before Its Triumph*. Princeton, NJ: Princeton University Press, 1977.

Holt, Douglas, and Juliet Schor. "Introduction: Do Americans Consume Too Much?" In *The Consumer Society Reader*, edited by Douglas Holt and Juliet Schor, vii–xxiii. New York: New Press, 2000.

Horowitz, Daniel. *The Anxieties of Affluence: Critiques of American Consumer Culture, 1939–1979*. Amherst, MA: University of Massachusetts Press, 2004.

———. *The Morality of Spending: Attitudes toward Consumer Society in America, 1875–1940*. Baltimore: Johns Hopkins University Press, 1985.

Hume, David. *An Enquiry concerning the Principles of Morals*. In *Hume's Ethical Writings*, ed. Alasdair MacIntyre, 23–156. Notre Dame, IN: University of Notre Dame Press, 1965.

———. "Of Commerce." In *Political Essays*, edited by Charles W. Hendel, 130–41. Indianapolis, IN: Bobbs-Merrill, 1953.

———. "Of Refinement in the Arts." In *Political Essays*, edited by Charles W. Hendel, 123–29. Indianapolis, IN: Bobbs-Merrill, 1953.

———. *Treatise on Human Nature*, edited by L. A. Selby-Bigge. Oxford, UK: Oxford University Press, 1888.

Hutcheson, Francis. *Thoughts on Laughter and Observations on "The Fable of the Bees" in Six Letters*. Bristol, UK: Thoemmes, 1989.

Hyman, Louis. *Borrow: The American Way of Debt*. New York: Vintage, 2012.

Ingraham, Christopher. "Living 'Paycheck-to-Paycheck': It's Not Just for the Poor." *Washington Post*, March 21, 2014.

Irwin, Terence. *The Development of Ethics*. New York: Oxford University Press, 2007.

Jackson, Kenneth. *Crabgrass Frontier: The Suburbanization of the United States*. New York: Oxford University Press, 1985.

James, Laurence. "Activity and the Meaningfulness of Life." *Monist* 93 (2010): 57–75.

John Paul II. *Centesimus Annus*, 1991.

———. *Familiaris Consortio*, 1980.

———. *Laborem Exercens*, 1981.

———. *Sollicitudo Rei Socialis*, 1987.

———. *Veritatis Splendor*, 1993.

John XXIII. *Mater et Magistra*, 1961.

Johnson, David, John Rogers, and Lucilla Tan. "A Century of Family Budgets in the United States." *Monthly Labor Review* (May 2001): 28–45.

Johnson, Luke Timothy. *Sharing Possessions: What Faith Demands*, 2nd ed. Grand Rapids, MI: Eerdmans, 2011.

Jung, L. Shannon. *Sharing Food: Practices for Christian Enjoyment*. Minneapolis: Fortress, 2006.

Kahneman, Daniel. *Thinking Fast and Slow*. New York: Farrar, Straus, and Giroux, 2011.

Kapferer, Jean-Noel, and Vincent Bastien. *The Luxury Strategy: Break the Rules of Marketing to Build Luxury Brands*. London: Kogan Page, 2009.

Karelis, Charles. *The Persistence of Poverty*. New Haven, CT: Yale University Press, 2007.

Kasser, Tim. *The High Cost of Materialism*. Cambridge, MA: MIT Press, 2002.

Keenan, James. *Virtues for Ordinary Christians*. Franklin, WI: Sheed & Ward, 1996.

Kelly, J. N. D. *Golden Mouth: The Story of John Chrysostom—Ascetic, Preacher, Bishop*. Ithaca, NY: Cornell University Press, 1995.

Kennedy, David. *Freedom from Fear: The American People in Depression and War, 1929–1945*. New York: Oxford University Press, 1999.

Kessler, David. *The End of Overeating*. New York: Macmillan, 2009.

Keynes, John Maynard. "Economic Possibilities for Our Grandchildren." In *Essays in Persuasion*, 358–73. New York: Harcourt Brace, 1932.

———. "The End of Laissez-Faire." In *Essays in Persuasion*, 312–22. New York: Harcourt Brace, 1932.

———. *The General Theory of Employment, Interest, and Money*. San Diego: Harcourt, 1936; rpt. 1964.

Killerby, Catherine. *Sumptuary Law in Italy, 1200–1500*. New York: Oxford University Press, 2002.

King, William Casey. *Ambition, a History: From Vice to Virtue*. New Haven, CT: Yale University Press, 2013.

Knight, Frank H. "Economic History." In *Dictionary of the History of Ideas*, edited by Philip P. Wiener, 2:44–61. New York: Scribner's, 1973.

Knight, Kelvin. "Practices: The Aristotelian Concept." *Analyse & Kritik* 30 (2008): 317–29.

Kocieniewski, David. "Home Tax Credit Called Successful, but Costly." *New York Times*, April 26, 2010; http://www.nytimes.com/2010/04/27/business/27home.html.

Kohn, Alfie. *Punished by Rewards*. Boston: Houghlin Mifflin, 1993.

Kraybill, Donald B., et al. *Amish Grace: How Forgiveness Transcended Tragedy*. San Francisco: Jossey-Bass, 2007.

Kroger, Joseph. "Prophetic-Critical and Practical-Strategic Tasks of Theology: Habermas and Liberation Theology." *Theological Studies* 46 (1985): 3–20.

Kuttner, Robert. *The Economic Illusion*. Boston: Houghton Mifflin, 1984.

Kyrk, Hazel. *A Theory of Consumption*. New York: Arno, 1923; rpt. 1976.

Langan, John. "Sins of Malice in the Moral Psychology of Thomas Aquinas." *Annual of the Society of Christian Ethics* 11 (1987): 179–98.

Lasch, Christopher. *The True and Only Heaven: Progress and Its Critics*. New York: Norton, 1991.

Layard, Richard. *Happiness: Lessons from a New Science*. New York: Penguin, 2005.

Leach, William. *Land of Desire: Merchants, Power, and the Rise of a New American Culture*. New York: Pantheon, 1993.

Lears, T. J. Jackson. "From Salvation to Self-Realization." In *The Culture of Consumption: Critical Essays in American History*, edited by Richard Wightman Fox and T. J. Jackson Lears, 1–38. New York: Pantheon, 1983.

Lehrer, Jonah. *How We Decide*. Boston: Houghton Mifflin, 2009.

Leibenstein, H. "Bandwagon, Snob, and Veblen Effects in the Theory of Consumer Demand." *Quarterly Journal of Economics* 64 (1950): 183–207.

Leo XIII. *Rerum Novarum*, 1891.

Levinson, Marc. *The Great A&P and the Struggle for Small Business in America*. New York: Hill and Wang, 2011.

Lewin, Tamar. "If Your Kids Are Awake, They're Probably Online." *New York Times*, January 20, 2010; http://www.nytimes.com/2010/01/20/education/20wired.html.

Lewis, C. S. *The Four Loves*. New York: Harcourt Brace, 1960.

Lewis, Michael. *The New New Thing: A Silicon Valley Story*. New York: Norton, 2000.

Lichtenstein, Nelson. *The Retail Revolution: How Wal-Mart Created a Brave New World of Business*. New York: Henry Holt, 2009.

Liddell, H. G., and Robert H. Scott. *Intermediate Greek-English lexicon*, based on 7th edition. New York: American Book, 1888.

Lind, Michael. *Land of Promise: An Economic History of the United States*. New York: Harper, 2012.

Lindstrom, Martin. *Buy-o-logy*. New York: Doubleday, 2008.

Living Conditions in Europe, Data 2002–2005. Belgium: Eurostat, 2007.

Livingston, James. *Against Thrift: Why Consumer Culture Is Good for the Economy, the Environment, and Your Soul*. New York: Basic, 2011.

———. *Pragmatism and the Political Economy of Cultural Revolution, 1850–1940*. Chapel Hill, NC: University of North Carolina Press, 1997.

Livy. "Book 34." Translated by Evan Sage. In *Livy* vol. 9, books 31–34, Loeb Classical Library. Cambridge, MA: Harvard University Press, 1935.

Lohfink, Gerhard. *Jesus and Community*. Translated by John P. Galvin. Philadelphia: Fortress, 1984.

Lynd, Robert Staughton, and Helen Merrell Lynd. *Middletown: A Study in American Culture*. New York: Harcourt Brace, 1929.

Lyubomirsky, Sonia. *The Myths of Happiness*. New York: Penguin, 2013.

MacDonald, G. Jeffrey. "Christians Shatter Taboos on Talking about Money." *Christian Century*, July 12, 2011, 17.

MacIntyre, Alasdair. *After Virtue*, 2nd ed. Notre Dame, IN: University of Notre Dame Press, 1984.

———. *Dependent Rational Animals: Why Human Beings Need the Virtues*. LaSalle, IL: Open Court, 1999.

———. Editor's Introduction to *Hume's Ethical Writings*. Notre Dame, IN: University of Notre Dame Press, 1965.

———. "Intractable Disputes about the Natural Law." In *Intractable Disputes about the Natural Law: Alasdair MacIntyre and Critics*, edited by Lawrence Cunningham, 1–52. Notre Dame, IN: University of Notre Dame Press, 2009.

———. "A Partial Response to My Critics." In *After MacIntyre*, edited by John Horton and Susan Mendus, 283–304. Notre Dame, IN: University of Notre Dame Press, 1994.

———. "Politics, Philosophy, and the Common Good." In *The MacIntyre Reader*, edited by Kelvin Knight, 235–52. Notre Dame, IN: University of Notre Dame Press, 1998.

———. *A Short History of Ethics*. London: Routledge & Kegan Paul, 1967.

———. "Three Perspectives on Marxism." In *Ethics and Politics: Selected Essays*, vol. 2, edited by Alasdair MacIntyre, 145–58. New York: Oxford University Press, 2006.

———. "The Recovery of Moral Agency?" In *The Best Christian Writing 2000*, edited by John Wilson, 112–36. New York: HarperCollins, 2000.

———. *Whose Justice? Which Rationality?* Notre Dame, IN: University of Notre Dame Press, 1988.

Mack, Joanna, and Stewart Lansley. *Poor Britain*. London: George Allen and Unwin, 1985.

Macpherson, C. B. *The Political Theory of Possessive Individualism: Hobbes to Locke*. New York: Oxford University Press, 1962.

Mandeville, Bernard. *The Fable of the Bees*. Edited by F. B. Kaye. Indianapolis, IN: Liberty Fund, 1988.

Manik, Julfikar Ali, and Jim Yardley. "Building Collapse in Bangladesh Leaves Scores Dead." *New York Times*, April 25, 2013; http://www.nytimes.com/2013/04/25/world/asia/bangladesh-building-collapse.html?pagewanted=all.

Mankiw, N. Gregory. *Principles of Economics*. 5th ed. Mason, OH: Southwestern Cengage, 2008.

Manning, Robert. *Credit Card Nation*. New York: Basic, 2000

Markus, R. A. *The End of Ancient Christianity*. New York: Cambridge University Press, 1990.

Marshall, Alfred. *Principles of Economics*. 9th (variorum) ed. Edited by C. W. Guillebaud. New York: Macmillan, 1920; rpt. 1961.

Martin, James. *The Jesuit Guide to (Almost) Everything*. New York: HarperCollins, 2010.

Masters, Thomas, and Amy Uelman. *Focolare: Living the Spirituality of Unity in the United States*. New York: New City, 2011.

Matthews, Christopher. "Ritzy Retail: Why Shopping Mall Developers are Catering to the Well-Off." *Time* magazine 180, no. 12 (September 17, 2012): 18.

Mattison, William. *Introducing Moral Theology: True Happiness and the Virtues*. Grand Rapids, MI: Brazos, 2008.

Mattison, William C., and David Cloutier. "Bodies Poured Out in Christ: Marriage Beyond Theology of the Body." In *Leaving and Coming Home: New Wineskins for Catholic Sexual Ethics*, edited by David Cloutier, 206–25. Eugene, OR: Cascade, 2010.

McBride, Bill. "April Vehicle Sales Forecast to Be above 15 Million SAAR for Sixth Consecutive Month." In *Calculated Risk: Finance and Economics*, April 24, 2013; http://www.calculatedriskblog.com/2013/04/april-vehicle-sales-forecast-to-be.html.

———. "New Home Sales at 417,000 SAAR in March." In *Calculated Risk: Finance and Economics*, April 23, 2013; http://www.calculatedriskblog.com/2013/04/new-home-sales-at-417000-saar-in-march.html.

McCabe, Herbert. "The Truth about God." In *God Still Matters*. New York: Continuum, 2002.

———. *What Ethics Is All About*. Washington, DC: Corpus, 1968.

McCarthy, David M. "Procreation, the Development of Peoples, and the Final Destiny of Humanity." *Communio* 26 (1999): 698–721.

———. *Sex and Love in the Home: A Theology of the Household*. London: SCM, 2011.

McCloskey, Deidre. "Avarice, Prudence, and the Bourgeois Virtues." In *Having: Property and Possession in Religious and Social Life*, edited by William Schweiker and Charles Mathewes, 312–36. Grand Rapids, MI: Eerdmans, 2004.

McDaniel, Rhonda L. "Pride Goes Before a Fall: Aldheim's Practical Application of Gregorian and Cassianic Conceptions of Superbia and the Eight Principal Vices." In *The Seven Deadly Sins: From Communities to Individuals*, edited by Richard Newhauser, 95–110. Leiden, Netherlands: Brill, 2007.

McKibben, Bill. "The Christmas." *Mother Jones*, November-December 1997; http://www.motherjones.com/politics/1997/11/christmas.

——. *Deep Economy: The Wealth of Communities and the Durable Future*. New York: Times, 2007.

McRorie, Christina. "Adam Smith, Ethicist: A Case for Reading Political Economy as Moral Anthropology." *Journal of Religious Ethics* 43, no. 4 (December 2015), in press.

Mead, Rebecca. "You're Getting Married: The Wal-Martization of the Bridal Business." In *Perspectives on Marriage*, 3rd ed., edited by Kieran Scott and Michael Warren, 314–25. New York: Oxford University Press, 2007.

Medaille, John. "Equity and Equilibrium." In *The Crisis of Global Capitalism: Pope Benedict XVI's Social Encyclical and the Future of Political Economy*, edited by Adrian Pabst, 255–68. Eugene, OR: Cascade, 2011.

——. *Toward a Truly Free Market: A Distributist Perspective on the Role of Government, Taxes, Health Care, Deficits, and More*. Wilmington, DE: ISI, 2010.

——. *The Vocation of Business*. New York: Continuum, 2006.

Medema, Steven. *The Hesitant Hand: Taming Self-Interest in the History of Economic Ideas*. Princeton, NJ: Princeton University Press, 2009.

Merton, Thomas. *No Man Is an Island*. New York: Harcourt, 1956.

Michel, Virgil. "The Bourgeois Spirit and the Christian Renewal." In *The Social Question: Essays on Capitalism and Christianity*, edited by Robert Spaeth, 76–87. Collegeville, MN: St. John's, 1987.

Michman, Ronald D., and Edward M. Magee. *The Affluent Consumer: Marketing and Selling the Luxury Lifestyle*. Westport, CT: Praeger, 2006.

Milbank, John. *Being Reconciled: Ontology and Pardon*. New York: Routledge, 2003.

——. *Theology and Social Theory*. Malden, MA: Blackwell, 1990.

Miller, Vincent J. *Consuming Religion: Christian Faith and Practice in a Consumer Culture*. New York: Continuum, 2004.

Minsky, Hyman. *Keynes*. New York: Columbia University Press, 1975.

Mishel, Laurence R., et al. *State of Working America*. Ithaca, NY: ILR, 2012.

Mitchell, Wesley Clair. *The Backward Art of Spending Money and Other Essays*. New York: McGraw-Hill, 1937.

Morello, Carol, and Scott Clement. "'Happy Days' No More: Middle-Class Families Squeezed as Expenses Soar, Wages Stall," *The Washington Post*, April 26, 2014; http://www.washingtonpost.com/local/happy-days-no-more-middle-class-families -squeezed-as-expenses-soar-wages-stall/2014/04/26/f4a857f0–7a47–11e3-b1c5 –739e63e9c9a7_story.html?hpid=z2.

Morgan, Mary. *The World in the Model: How Economists Work and Think*. New York: Cambridge University Press, 2012.

Mullainathan, Sendhil, and Eldar Shafir. *Scarcity: Why Having Too Little Means So Much*. New York: Times, 2013.

Muller, Jerry. *The Mind and the Market*. New York: Knopf, 2002.

Musgrave, Richard. "Merit Goods." In *The New Palgrave*, edited by John Eatwell, Murray Milgate, and Peter Newman, 3:452–53. London: Macmillan, 1987.

——. "Public Finance." In *The New Palgrave*, edited by John Eatwell, Murray Milgate, and Peter Newman, 3:452–53. London: Macmillan, 1987.

Myrdal, Gunnar. *Challenge to Affluence*. New York: Pantheon, 1962.

Nash, James. "Toward the Revival and Reform of the Subversive Virtue: Frugality." *Annual of the SCE* 15 (1995): 137–60.

National Bureau of Economic Research. *Income in the United States*, vol. 1. New York: Harcourt Brace, 1921.

National Catholic Welfare Council. "The Bishops' Program of Social Reconstruction." In *American Catholic Thought on Social Questions*, edited by Aaron I. Abell, 325–48. Indianapolis, IN: Bobbs-Merrill, 1968.

Nettle, Daniel. *Happiness: The Science behind Your Smile*. New York: Oxford University Press, 2006.

Nixon, Mark G. "Satisfaction for Whom? Freedom for What? Theology and the Economic Theory of the Consumer." *Journal of Business Ethics* 70 (2007): 39–60.

Novatian, "On the Jewish Meats." in *The Ante-Nicene Fathers*, vol. 5, edited by Philip Schaff, chap. 6; www.ccel.org/print/schaff/anf05/vi.iv.vi.

O'Boyle, Edward J., ed. *Looking Beyond the Individualism and Homo Economicus of Neoclassical Economics*. Milwaukee, WI: Marquette University Press, 2010.

Offer, Avner. *The Challenge of Affluence: Self-Control and Well-Being in the United States and Britain Since 1950*. New York: Oxford University Press, 2006.

Olmstead, Alan L. and Paul W. Rhode. "The Transformation of Northern Agriculture 1910–1990." In *Cambridge Economic History of the United States*, 3 vols., edited by Stanley Engerman and Robert Gollman, 3: 693–742. New York: Cambridge University Press, 2000.

Orsi, Robert. *The Madonna of 115th Street: Faith and Community in Italian Harlem, 1880–1950*. New Haven, CT: Yale University Press, 1985.

O'Toole, Patricia. *Money and Morals in America*. New York: Clarkson Potter, 1998.

Pabst, Adrian, ed. *The Crisis of Global Capitalism: Pope Benedict XVI's Social Encyclical and the Future of Political Economy*. Eugene, OR: Cascade, 2011.

Patten, Simon. *Product and Climax*. New York: B. W. Huebsch, 1909.

Paul VI. *Populorum Progressio*, 1967.

Peppard, Christiana. *Just Water: Theology, Ethics, and the Global Water Crisis*. Maryknoll, NY: Orbis, 2014.

Pesch, Heinrich. *Ethics and the National Economy*. Translated and with an Introduction by Rupert Ederer. Norfolk, VA: IHS, 2004.

Pettis, Michael. *The Great Rebalancing*. Princeton, NJ: Princeton University Press, 2013.

Phan, Peter C. *Social Thought: Messages of the Fathers of the Church*. Wilmington, DE: Michael Glazier, 1984.

Phillips, Kevin. *Bad Debt: Reckless Finance, Failed Politics, and the Global Crisis of American Capitalism*. New York: Viking, 2008.

Phillips, Siobhan. "Can We Afford to Eat Ethically?" Salon.com, April 25, 2009, http://www.salon.com/2009/04/25/pinched_ethically/.

Pieper, Josef. *Guide to Thomas Aquinas*. New York: Pantheon, 1962.

Pigou, A. C. *The Economics of Welfare*. Library of Economics and Liberty; http://www.econlib.org/library/NPDBooks/Pigou/pgEW.html.

Piketty, Thomas. *Capital in the Twenty-First Century*. Cambridge, MA: Harvard University Press, 2014.

Pincoffs, Edmund. *Quandaries and Virtues: Against Reductivism in Ethics*. Lawrence, KS: University of Kansas Press, 1986.

Pius XI. *Quadragesimo Anno*, 1931.

Plato. *The Republic*. Translated by Richard Sterling and William Scott. New York: Norton, 1985.

Platt, David. *Radical: Taking Back Your Faith from the American Dream*. Sisters, OR: Multnomah, 2010.

Plotnick, Robert D., et al. "The Twentieth-Century Record of Inequality and Poverty in the United States." In *The Cambridge Economic History of the United States*, 3 vols., edited by Stanley Engerman and Robert Gollman, 3:249–300. New York: Cambridge University Press, 2000.

Pocock, J. G. A. *The Machiavellian Moment*. Princeton, NJ: Princeton University Press, 1975.

Polanyi, Karl. *The Great Transformation*. Boston: Beacon, 2001.

Polter, Julie. "Attack of the Monster Houses." *Sojourners* 36, no. 3 (2007): 38–42.

Pope, Clayne. "Inequality in the Nineteenth Century." In *The Cambridge Economic History of the United States*, 3 vols., edited by Stanley Engerman and Robert Gollman, 2:109–42. New York: Cambridge University Press, 2000.

Posner, Richard. "Working 9 to 12," review of *How Much Is Enough?*, *New York Times*, August 17, 2012; http://www.nytimes.com/2012/08/19/books/review/how-much-is-enough-by-robert-skidelsky-and-edward-skidelsky.html?pagewanted=all.

Powers, William. *Twelve by Twelve: A One-Room Cabin off the Grid and beyond the American Dream*. Novato, CA: New World, 2010.

Prudentius. "Psychomachia." In *Prudentius I* (Loeb Classical Library). Translated by H. J. Thomson. Cambridge, MA: Harvard University Press, 1949.

Rainwater, Lee. *What Money Buys: Inequality and the Social Meanings of Income*. New York: Basic, 1974.

Ramsey, Dave. *The Total Money Makeover: A Proven Plan for Financial Fitness*. Nashville, TN: Thomas Nelson, 2003.

Rasmussen, Dennis. *The Problems and Promise of Commercial Society*. Philadelphia: University of Pennsylvania Press, 2006.

Ratzinger, Joseph Cardinal. *Church, Ecumenism, and Politics: New Endeavors in Ecclesiology*. Translated by Michael J. Miller et al. San Francisco: Ignatius, 1987; rpt. 2008.

——. "The Face of Christ in Sacred Scripture." In *On the Way to Jesus Christ*, translated by Michael J. Miller, 13–31. San Francisco: Ignatius, 2004.

——. *Introduction to Christianity*, with a new preface. Translated by J. R. Foster. San Francisco: Ignatius, 1968; rpt. 2004.

——. "Liberation Theology." In *The Essential Pope Benedict XVI: His Central Writings and Speeches*, edited by John Thornton and Susan Varenne, 217–26. New York: HarperOne, 2007.

——. "Review of the Postconciliar Era—Failures, Tasks, Hopes." In *Principles of Catholic Theology: Building Stones for a Fundamental Theology*, translated by Sr. Mary Frances McCarthy, 367–93. San Francisco: Ignatius, 1982; rpt. 1987.

——. *The Yes of Jesus Christ: Exercises in Faith, Hope, and Love*. New York: Crossroad, 2005.

Rhee, Helen. *Loving the Poor, Saving the Rich: Wealth, Poverty, and Early Christian Formation*. Grand Rapids, MI: Baker, 2012.

——. "Wealth, Poverty, and Eschatology." In *Reading Patristic Texts on Social Ethics*, edited by Johan Leemans, Brian Matz, and Johan Verstraeten, 64–84. Washington, DC: Catholic University of America Press, 2011.

Riesman, David. *Selected Essays from Individualism Reconsidered*. Garden City, NY: Doubleday, 1955.

Rivoli, Pietra. *The Travels of a T-Shirt in the Global Economy*. Hoboken, NJ: Wiley, 2005.

Robbins, Lionel. *An Essay on the Nature and Significance of Economic Science.* New York: New York University Press, 1981.

——. "Interpersonal Comparisons of Utility: A Comment." *The Economic Journal* 48 (1938): 635–41.

Rogoff, Kenneth. "Europe's Debt Wish." Project Syndicate, https://www.project-syndicate.org/commentary/kenneth-rogoff-is-convinced-that-economic-recovery-will-require-some-form-of-debt-restructuring-or-rescheduling.

Rosenberg, Emily. "Consuming the American Century." In *The Short American Century: A Postmortem,* edited by Andrew Bacevich, 38–58. Cambridge, MA: Harvard University Press, 2012.

Roubini, Nouriel, and Stephen Mihm. *Crisis Economics.* New York: Penguin, 2010.

Rubin, Gretchen Craft. *The Happiness Project: Or, Why I Spent a Year Trying to Sing in the Morning, Clean My Closets, Fight Right, Read Aristotle, and Generally Have More Fun.* New York: HarperCollins, 2009.

Rubio, Julie Hanlon. *Family Ethics: Practices for Christians.* Washington, DC: Georgetown University Press, 2010.

Ryan, John A. *A Better Economic Order.* New York: Harper, 1935.

——. *The Church and Socialism and Other Essays.* Washington, DC: The University Press, 1919.

Sachs, Jeffrey. *The End of Poverty: Economic Possibilities for Our Time.* New York: Penguin, 2005.

Salatin, Joel. *Everything I Want to Do Is Illegal: Stories from the Local Food Front.* Swoope, VA: Polyface, 2007.

Samuelson, Paul, and William Nordhaus. *Economics.* 13th ed. New York: McGraw-Hill, 1989.

Sandbrook, Dominic. *Mad as Hell: The Crisis of the 1970s and the Rise of the Populist Right.* New York: Knopf, 2011.

Sandel, Michael. *What Money Can't Buy: The Moral Limits of Markets.* New York: FSG, 2012.

Saporito, Bill. "What's in a Name? Adidas Jumps to Make NBA Star Derrick Rose a Brand." *Time* magazine 180, no. 19 (November 5, 2012): 54–55.

Schlefer, Jonathan. *The Assumptions Economists Make.* Cambridge, MA: Harvard University Press, 2012.

Schmiedeler, Edgar, OSB. *Cooperation: A Christian Mode of Industry.* Ozone Park, NY: Catholic Literary Guild, 1941.

Schneider, Howard. "This Is Why the Textile Industry Is Relocating to Places Like Bangladesh." *Washington Post,* July 12, 2013; http://www.washingtonpost.com/blogs/wonkblog/wp/2013/07/12/this-is-why-the-textile-industry-is-relocating-to-places-like-bangladesh/?wprss=rss_policy&tid=pp_widget.

Schor, Juliet. *The Overspent American: Upscaling, Downshifting, and the New Consumer.* New York: Basic, 1998.

——. *Plenitude: The New Economics of True Wealth.* New York: Penguin, 2010.

Schuurman, Douglas. *Vocation: Discerning Our Callings in Life.* Grand Rapids, MI: Eerdmans, 2004.

Schwartz, Barry. *The Costs of Living.* New York: Norton, 1994.

——. *The Paradox of Choice: Why More Is Less.* New York: Ecco, 2004.

Scitovsky, Tibor. *The Joyless Economy.* New York: Oxford University Press, 1976.

Sekora, John. *Luxury: The Concept in Western Thought, Eden to Smollett*. Baltimore: Johns Hopkins University Press, 1977.

Selby-Bigge, L. A., ed. *British Moralists: Being Selections from Writers Principally of the Eighteenth Century*. New York: Dover, 1897; rpt. 1965.

"Selective Hiring Boom Forecast." *Chicago Tribune*, December 26, 2011, 2: 1–2.

Sen, Amartya. "The Living Standard." *Oxford Economic Papers*. New Series, vol. 36: Supplement: Economic Theory and Hicksian Themes (November 1984): 74–90.

———. *The Standard of Living*. New York: Cambridge University Press, 1987.

Sen, Amartya, and Bernard Williams, eds. Utilitarianism and Beyond. New York: Cambridge University Press, 1982.

Seneca. "On Providence." In *Hellenistic Philosophy*, edited by Herman Shapiro and Edwin M. Curley, 79–96. New York: Modern Library, 1965.

Sexton, Steven E., and Alison L. Sexton. "Conspicuous Conservation: The Prius Halo and Willingness to Pay for Environmental Bona Fides," http://www.ncsu.edu/cenrep/workshops/TREE/documents/ConspicuousConservation-TREE.pdf.

Shachar, Ron, et al. "Brands: The Opiate of the Non-Religious Masses?" *Marketing Science* 30 (J-F 2011): 92–110.

Shell, Ellen Ruppert. *Cheap: The High Cost of Discount Culture*. New York: Penguin, 2009.

Shipler, David. *The Working Poor: Invisible in America*. New York: Knopf, 2004.

Shovlin, John. *The Political Economy of Virtue: Luxury, Patriotism, and the Origins of the French Revolution*. Ithaca, NY: Cornell University Press, 2006.

Sidgwick, Henry. "Luxury." *International Journal of Ethics* 5, no. 1 (October 1894): 1–16.

———. *The Theory of Political Economy*. London: Macmillan, 1901.

Silverstein, Michael, Neil Fiske, and John Butman. *Trading Up: The New American Luxury*. New York: Penguin, 2003.

Sinn, Hans-Werner. *Can Germany Be Saved?* Cambridge, MA: MIT Press, 2007.

Skidelsky, Robert "Gloomy about Globalization," http://www.nybooks.com/articles/archives/2008/apr/17/gloomy-about-globalization/.

———. "Inventing the World's Currency," http://www.nybooks.com/articles/archives/2014/jan/09/inventing-worlds-money/?page=2.

———. *John Maynard Keynes: Hopes Betrayed, 1883–1920*. New York: Viking Penguin, 1986.

Skidelsky, Robert, and Edward Skidelsky. *How Much Is Enough? Money and the Good Life*. New York: Other, 2012.

———. "In Praise of Leisure." *Chronicle of Higher Education*, June 18, 2012, http://chronicle.com/article/In-Praise-of-Leisure/132251/.

Skinner, Quentin. *The Foundations of Modern Political Thought*. New York: Cambridge University Press, 1978.

Smith, Adam. *The Theory of Moral Sentiments*. Oxford, UK: Clarendon, 1976.

———. *The Wealth of Nations*. New York: Modern Library, 1937.

Smith, James K. A. *Imagining the Kingdom*. Grand Rapids, MI: Baker, 2013.

Snell, K. D. M. *Annals of the Laboring Poor: Social Change and Agrarian England, 1660–1900*. New York: Cambridge University Press, 1985.

Speck, Jeff. *Walkable City*. New York: Farrar, Straus, and Giroux, 2012.

Spiegel, Henry William. *The Growth of Economic Thought*, 3rd ed. Durham, NC: Duke University Press, 1991.

Standards of Living: A Compilation of Budget Studies. Washington, DC: Bureau of Applied Economics, 1920.

Stapleford, Thomas. *The Cost of Living in America: A Political History of Economic Statistics, 1880–2000.* New York: Cambridge University Press, 2009.

Stassen, Glen, and David Gushee. *Kingdom Ethics: Following Jesus in Contemporary Context.* Downers Grove, IL: InterVarsity, 2003.

Stelter, Brian. "Comcast Reports Progress at NBC, but Declines in Cable Subscriptions." *New York Times,* May 2, 2012; http://mediadecoder.blogs.nytimes.com/2012/05/02/comcast-reports-progress-at-nbc-but-declines-in-cable-subscriptions/?_r=0.

Stiglitz, Joseph, Amartya Sen, and Jean-Paul Fitoussi. *Mismeasuring Our Lives: Why GDP Doesn't Add Up.* New York: New Press, 2010.

———. *The Price of Inequality.* New York: Norton, 2012.

Sullivan, Paul. "Seeing a Supersize Yacht as a Job Engine, Not a Self-Indulgence." *New York Times,* July 26, 2014; http://www.nytimes.com/2014/07/26/your-money/seeing-a-supersize-yacht-as-a-job-engine-not-a-self-indulgence.html?ref=business.

Suzumara, Kotaro. "Social Welfare Function." In *The New Palgrave: A Dictionary of Economics,* 4 vols., edited by John Eatwell, Murray Milgate, and Peter Newman, 4: 418. London: Macmillan, 1987.

Tawney, R. H. *The Acquisitive Society.* New York: Harcourt Brace, 1920.

Taylor, Charles. "The Diversity of Goods." In *Utilitarianism and Beyond,* edited by Amartya Sen and Bernard Williams, 129–44. New York: Cambridge University Press, 1982.

———. *Modern Social Imaginaries.* Durham, NC: Duke University Press, 2004.

———. "Reason, Faith, and Meaning." *Faith and Philosophy* 28 (2011): 5–18.

———. *A Secular Age.* Cambridge, MA: Harvard University Press, 2007.

———. "What Is Human Agency?" In *Philosophical Papers I: Human Agency and Language,* 15–44. New York: Cambridge University Press, 1985.

Thaler, Richard, and Cass Sunstein. *Nudge: Improving Decisions about Health, Wealth, and Happiness.* New Haven, CT: Yale University Press, 2008.

Thomas, Dana. *Deluxe: How Luxury Lost Its Luster.* New York: Penguin, 2007.

Thorngate, Steve. "Defining the Middle: The Rhetoric and Reality of Class." *Christian Century* 129, no. 22 (October 31, 2012): 30–32.

Thornton, John, and Susan Varenne, eds. *The Essential Pope Benedict XVI: His Central Writings and Speeches.* New York: HarperOne, 2007.

Thurow, Lester. *The Future of Capitalism: How Today's Economic Forces Shape Tomorrow's World.* New York: Morrow, 1996.

———. *The Zero-Sum Society: Distribution and the Possibilities for Economic Change.* New York: Basic, 1980.

Tocqueville, Alexis de. *Democracy in America.* Edited by Harvey Mansfield and Delba Winthrop. Chicago: University of Chicago Press, 2000.

Tungate, Mark. *Luxury World: The Past, Present, and Future of Luxury Brands.* London: Kogan Page, 2009.

Turkle, Sherry. *Alone Together: Why We Expect More from Technology and Less from Each Other.* New York: Basic, 2012.

Twitchell, James. *Living It Up: Our Love Affair with Luxury.* New York: Columbia University Press, 2002.

Tyler, Tom. *Why People Cooperate: The Role of Social Motivations*. Princeton, NJ: Princeton University Press, 2011.

Uchitelle, Louis. *The Disposable American*. New York: Knopf, 2006.

US Conference of Catholic Bishops. "Seven Themes of Catholic Social Teaching." http://www.usccb.org/beliefs-and-teachings/what-we-believe/catholic-social-teaching/seven-themes-of-catholic-social-teaching.cfm.

US Department of Agriculture. "Expenditures on Children by Families, 2013." http://www.cnpp.usda.gov/sites/default/files/expenditures_on_children_by_families/crc2013.pdf .

US Energy Information Administration. "2009 Residential Energy Consumption Survey." http://www.eia.gov/consumption/residential/data/2009/#undefined.

Veblen, Thorstein. *Engineers and the Price System*. New York: Viking, 1921.

——. *The Instinct of Workmanship*. New York: Viking, 1914.

——. "Instinct of Workmanship and the Irksomeness of Labor." in *Essays in Our Changing Order*, edited by Leon Ardzrooni, 78–96. New York: Viking, 1945.

——. *The Theory of the Leisure Class*. In *The Portable Veblen*, edited by Max Lerner, 53–214. New York: Viking, 1948.

Viner, Jacob. "Mercantilist Thought." In *Essays on the Intellectual History of Economics*, edited by Douglas Irwin, 262–76. Princeton, NJ: Princeton University Press, 1991.

Volcker, Paul. "The Time We Have Is Growing Short." *New York Review of Books*, June 24, 2010, 12–14.

Wadell, Paul J. *Friendship and the Moral Life*. Notre Dame, IN: University of Notre Dame Press, 1989.

Wallace-Hadrill, Andrew. *Rome's Cultural Revolution*. New York: Cambridge University Press, 2008.

Walsh, Bryan. "The Future of Oil." *Time* magazine 179, no. 14 (April 9, 2012): 28–35.

Warren, Elizabeth, and Amelia Warren Tyagi. *The Two-Income Trap*. New York: Basic, 2003.

Westberg, Daniel. *Right Practical Reason: Aristotle, Action, and Prudence in Aquinas*. New York: Oxford University Press, 1994.

Wheelan, Charles. *Naked Economics: Understanding the Dismal Science*. New York: Norton, 2002.

Wheeler, Sondra Ely. *Wealth as Peril and Obligation*. Grand Rapids, MI: Eerdmans, 1995.

"Whoops—'Cash for Clunkers' Actually Hurts the Environment." Yahoo News, http://news.yahoo.com/why-cash-clunkers-hurt-environment-more-helped-024848694.html, January 3, 2013.

Wiebe, Robert. *The Search for Order*. New York: Hill & Wang, 1967.

Wirzba, Norman. *Food and Faith: A Theology of Eating*. New York: Cambridge University Press, 2011.

Wogaman, J. Philip. *Christian Ethics: A Historical Introduction*. Louisville, KY: WJKP, 1993.

——. *Economics and Ethics*. Philadelphia: Fortress, 1986.

Wolf, Martin. *Fixing Global Finance*. Baltimore: Johns Hopkins University Press, 2010.

Wolverson, Roya. "Rental Nation." *Time* magazine 180, no. 13 (September 24, 2012), 44–54.

Wood, Diana. *Medieval Economic Thought*. New York: Cambridge University Press, 2002.

Wyatt, Edward, "As Services Expand, Cable Bills Keep Rising." *New York Times*, February 15, 2014; http://www.nytimes.com/2014/02/15/business/media/as-services-expand-cable-bills-keep-rising.html.

Yates, Joshua J., and James Davison Hunter, eds. *Thrift and Thriving in America: Capitalism and Moral Order from the Puritans to the Present*. New York: Oxford University Press, 2011.

Yergin, Daniel. *The Quest: Energy, Security, and the Remaking of the Modern World*. New York: Penguin, 2011.

Yunghans, Regina. "Average Home Sizes around the World." *Apartment Therapy*, http://www.apartmenttherapy.com/average-home-sizes-around-the-151738, accessed July 20, 2014.

Zamagni, Stefano. "Fraternity, Gift, and Reciprocity in *Caritas in Veritate*." In *Crisis of Global Capitalism: Pope Benedict XVI's Social Encyclical and the Future of Political Economy*, edited by Adrian Pabst, 155–72. Eugene, OR: Cascade, 2011.

Zamagni, Stefano, Luigino Bruni, and Antonella Ferrucci, eds. *Handbook on the Economics of Reciprocity and Social Enterprise*. Northampton, MA: Edward Elgar, 2013.

Zarroli, Jim. "Urban Poor Cope with Help from Informal Economy." NPR, March 15, 2007; http://www.npr.org/templates/story/story.php?storyId=8928346.

Index

A&P, 235

acquisition without limits, 3, 56, 202–3, 209–10, 242. *See also* insatiability

acquisitive ceiling, 3, 12, 159, 204n8, 210–11, 245. *See also* moderation in consumption

Adidas, 134

affluent society, 2, 77, 230, 254, 270, 274

agape, 118, 123, 131–32, 143n135

alcohol consumption, 218, 260

Alford, Helen, 93, 143n135

altruism, 69. *See also* charity

ambivalence toward luxury, 73, 96, 118

Ambrose, Saint, 113–14, 116, 140n48, 261

American Dream, 3, 238

American Institutionalists, 170n26, 172n78, 210, 213, 219

American Time Use Survey, 187n22

Amish practice, 243

Amos, 29

ancient philosophers: on luxury, 26–31; on sentiments, 75. *See also* criticism of luxury; historical survey of luxury; *luxuria*

antecedent desires, 86

anthropology: of abundance, 245; normative anthropology, 217; theological anthropology, 277

Appleby, Joyce, 149

Apple marketing strategy, 112

Aquinas, 36, 101n118, 181, 185, 188n26, 256–57, 261, 264; *De Malo*, 181

Arbo, Matthew, 180

Aristotle, 32, 34, 36, 60, 64, 104n172; *Eudemian Ethics*, 28; *Nicomachean Ethics*, 27–28, 32

artificiality, 36

asceticism, 71, 87, 113, 132, 140n48, 143n137, 263

asotia (licentiousness), 36

Augustine, 29, 65, 113–14, 116–17, 121, 141n64, 189; *The City of God*, 189

authenticity, 66, 77, 100n56

autonomy, 55, 60–61, 64, 96, 98n28, 154

avarice. *See* greed

Babette's Feast (movie), 258

Bahnson, Fred, 259

Bambrick-Santoyo, Paul, 104n172

Barnes, James, 212

Basil, Saint, 113–15, 116, 140n48

behavioral economics, 248n75

Benedict, 113

About the Author

David Cloutier holds the Knott Professorship in Catholic Theology at Mount St. Mary's University, Emmitsburg, Maryland, where he teaches courses in fundamental moral theology, sexual ethics, and social ethics, and directs a year-long faculty seminar on the Catholic Intellectual Tradition. He is the author of *Walking God's Earth: The Environmental and Catholic Faith* (Liturgical) and *Love, Reason, and God's Story: An Introduction to Catholic Sexual Ethics* (Anselm). He has commented on Catholic life for many publications, including *Commonweal*, the *Washington Post*, the *New Republic*, and NPR, and is editor of the group blog, catholicmoraltheology.com.